CLASSIC FOOD OF CHINA

Yan-kit So is Britain's leading authority on Chinese food.
She was born in Zhongshan, China, but grew up and was educated
in Hong Kong and later in England, where she obtained a Ph.D.
in history from London University. She has also lived in
India and the USA.

Yan-kit's first book, *The Classic Chinese Cookbook*,
has over 125,000 copies in print and won the Glenfiddich
best book of the year award 1984, the first time a Chinese cookbook
had ever won a major food award; she also won, in the same year,
the prestigious André Simon Award.

Yan-kit So

CLASSIC
FOOD
OF
CHINA

M

MACMILLAN
LONDON

IN MEMORY OF MY FATHER, YIN-MO SO, WHOSE OWN
INTEREST IN FOOD GAVE ME MY FIRST PERCEPTION OF
TASTE AND FLAVOUR

First published 1992 by Macmillan London Limited

This edition published 1994 by Macmillan London Limited
a division of Pan Macmillan Publishers Limited
Cavaye Place London SW10 9PG
and Basingstoke

Associated companies throughout the world

ISBN 0-333-56907-5

1 3 5 7 9 8 6 4 2

A CIP catalogue record for this book is available from
the British Library

Photoset by Parker Typesetting Service, Leicester
Printed by Butler & Tanner Ltd, Frome and London

CONTENTS

ACKNOWLEDGEMENTS

I wish to extend my heartfelt thanks to my friends and family for their contributions to this book. The names of those connected with a particular recipe are already credited in the introduction of the recipe itself, and so will not be repeated.

My grateful thanks to Grace Wu Bruce for suggesting as well as supplying the woodcut illustrations on pages 76 and 77, and to John Naylor for letting me use a royal menu in his possession. The successful deciphering of some of the Chinese characters in the menu is due to the unstinting efforts of Dorcas Hu, who enlisted the help of a Peking chef in Hong Kong. I am also most grateful to Harold Wong for letting me reproduce the portrait of Yuan Mei in his private collection.

Professor Richard Hosking, Thomas Flögel, Hung-wai Tang, Gregory Fu, Pearl Kong Chen and my brother, Yan-kin So, provided me with some very valuable research material and Dr Lily Cheung enlightened me on the medicinal properties of some Chinese ingredients. Hin-cheung Lovell was very helpful on the question of choosing the Pinyin system of spelling for the book, and Kathleen Fu gave very generously of her time in combing through the works of Su Dongpo for me.

When I was 'cooking my book' for the photographs, I had invaluable help when preparing at home the day before from friends, Marina Chan, Bianca Fu, Cynthia Ma Flieger and Betty Yao and from my sister, Yan-lap So. They know they lightened my task considerably. Grateful thanks are also due to Veronica Berning and Tilla Yip for lending their precious china for use in the photographic sessions.

Dr William Fong has written all the Chinese characters, which not only add an artistic dimension to the book but also provide identification of the recipes and the Chinese ingredients for reader/users, both Chinese and non-Chinese. I am indebted to him for his time and effort, given so generously and freely.

Last but not least, an enormous thank you to my editor, Judith Hannam, without whose gentle and caring encouragement, not to mention consummate skill in polishing my English, writing this book would not have been such an enjoyable experience for me.

Every effort has been made to trace all copyright holders but if any has been overlooked, the author and publishers will be pleased to make the necessary arrangement at the first opportunity.

A NOTE ON THE SPELLING OF CHINESE WORDS

The Mandarin spelling of Chinese names in this book is based on the Pinyin system, which was devised by the Chinese and is now used internationally. On the whole, Pinyin names are pronounced as written in English with, however, the following main exceptions:

c = ts   q = ch   x = hs   z = dz   zh = j

The spelling of the very familiar places such as Peking, Canton and Shanghai remains the same, and when a Cantonese name is the more universally accepted norm, such as wok and dimsum, Cantonese rather than Pinyin spelling is used.

A NOTE ON THE TRANSLATIONS

Unless otherwise credited, all the Chinese quotations, be they in prose or in verse, have been translated into English by me. I therefore have only myself to blame for any mistakes.

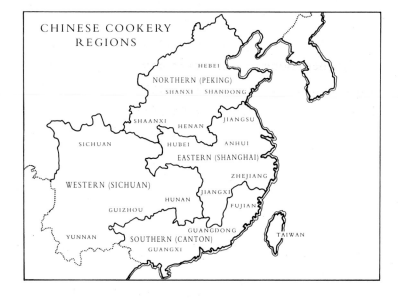

CHINESE COOKERY REGIONS

HEBEI
NORTHERN (PEKING)
SHANXI   SHANDONG
SHAANXI   JIANGSU
HENAN
SICHUAN   HUBEI   ANHUI
EASTERN (SHANGHAI)
ZHEJIANG
WESTERN (SICHUAN)
JIANGXI
HUNAN   FUJIAN
GUIZHOU
YUNNAN   GUANGDONG   TAIWAN
SOUTHERN (CANTON)
GUANGXI

MAIN CHINESE DYNASTIES

XIA	approx. 21st–16th century BC
SHANG	approx. 16th–11th century BC
ZHOU	11th century–221 BC
Chunqiu (Spring and Autumn)	770–476 BC
Zhanguo (Warring States)	475–221 BC
QIN	221–206 BC
HAN	206 BC–AD 220
Western Han	206 BC–AD 25
Eastern Han	25–220
THREE KINGDOMS	220–265
JIN	265–420
SIX DYNASTIES	420–589
SUI	581–618
TANG	618–907
FIVE DYNASTIES	907–960
SONG	960–1279
Northern Song	960–1127
Southern Song	1127–1279
YUAN	1271–1368
MING	1368–1644
QING	1644–1911

PREFACE

TO my great delight, my first book, *Yan-kit's Classic Chinese Cookbook*, won both the Glenfiddich and the André Simon awards for 1984, as well as the following accolade from Derek Cooper, 'At last a Chinese cookbook that works'. Even so, I have always been aware of its singlemindedly practical nature and, despite its continued success, have felt that there was also room for a book that explored related aspects of Chinese cookery. I know all too well that, beyond workable recipes, there is the broader scope which covers the whys and wherefores of the culture of Chinese food. It has always been my ambition to write a book that dealt with this aspect and *The Classic Food of China* is the result.

Why do Chinese people love to eat, to the extent of becoming obsessive about food? Who were the people who initiated this most rich of culinary traditions, with its ever-increasing influence throughout the world? Who wrote down the recipes and spread the word as to how particular dishes were created? What have been and still are the special foods the Chinese eat when they celebrate their festivals? Given the immense size of the country, and the diverse geographical regions, can one speak of a single Chinese cuisine? What are the regional differences, and how does one trace their origins? Have the Chinese always cooked exclusively with their own ingredients or have they merely incorporated foreign ones and made them taste Chinese? As a student of history, I have always been fascinated by these questions, and they are the ones I have tried to answer here.

In my first book, I presented a balanced spread of notable regional dishes. You may well wonder, therefore, whether in this book I have simply repeated myself. The answer is an emphatic no because, thanks to the enormous number of well-known Chinese dishes, and the nature of the Chinese cuisine itself – which is at once traditional and innovative, classic and fluid – there is endless material and an inexhaustible range of dishes upon which to draw. Even if I wrote another half a dozen or more books, I would still not run the risk of duplicating myself. I have, nevertheless, put in again those dishes that are so synonymous with Chinese food – such as Peking Duck, Cantonese *char siu* and *Lohan zhai* – that they demand inclusion. Otherwise, the recipes in the book are all new.

Each of the recipes has been tried, tested and tasted by myself, more than once, in my own kitchen, which is equipped with domestic, rather than restaurant stoves, and then painstakingly interpreted for you in print. As well as simple, basic dishes, I have also included complex recipes which I have adapted so that they can be made by the ordinary cook. Ever since 1985, when the idea of writing this book was no more than a dream, I have continued to travel and eat in different parts of mainland China, as well as in Taiwan, Singapore and also Hong Kong, where I grew up. Besides family, I have entertained Chinese and non-Chinese friends, cooked with enthusiasts, taught classes, given demonstrations and learned from and 'held the wok' with famous Chinese chefs, in China, Hong Kong and London. Unbridled by commercial restraints, I have not had to resort to formula food, nor to gimmicks or fads which, frankly, I loathe. My recipes, if I take pride in them at all, are a synthesis of the best Chinese restaurant food and home cooking, and represent at once the sophisticated and the simple, the rustic and the refined, the elegant and the easy. Above all, I am for real food.

In selecting my recipes, I have made sure that the ingredients derive either from local produce or, if they come from the East, are available in Chinese or Oriental supermarkets. Fortunately, since the middle of the 1980s, there have been two encouraging developments. Firstly, more and more Chinese products, which used to be thought of as exotic and inaccessible, are now available here in Chinese stores, either in their fresh or dried form. Secondly, and even more importantly, Chinese vegetables, especially of the brassica family, which are responsible for making the Chinese cuisine one of the healthiest in the world, are now grown in farms in Essex and Kent in England, in Holland and Spain, not to mention in New Jersey and California in the States. As a result, not only have I been able to include many more alluring recipes, but I have also been able to write one chapter specially for vegetarians and another featuring bean curd, the healthy Chinese alternative to dairy products.

I believe my audience to be both Chinese and non-Chinese, the one common bond between them being their enthusiasm for food, especially Chinese food. I originally began to cook for Westerners more than thirty years ago, first as a foreign student trying to connect with fellow students, exploiting to the full my limited repertoire of two recipes – *Char siu* and stir-fried vegetables. Later, as the wife of an American academic, I entertained my husband's colleagues and students in Syracuse, upstate New York, as well as his family in Philadelphia and Waterford, Connecticut, and it always filled my heart with pride and joy to see everybody having seconds and thirds of such things as braised ox tongue, steamed sea bass or blue fish and stir-fried chicken with cashewnuts.

During the past ten years, I have also come to realize how much my own compatriots living in different continents value my efforts to communicate to them through my books a knowledge of Chinese food. Having learned to cook after I came abroad myself, I know all too well the problems facing Chinese people when they go to live in other countries. Many second and third generations of overseas Chinese are quite at sea as to what Chinese food is, let alone the culture behind it. I know that these people, whom native Chinese, not always kindly, refer to as 'bamboo poles' because, like a section of a bamboo pole, they are blocked at both ends and are hence neither Chinese nor Western, would dearly love to know more about Chinese culture. Then, there are the Eurasians who, like my own son, Hugo Martin, can benefit from both worlds. I hope, therefore, for all my audience, that this book will connect them with Chinese food, and hence with other aspects of Chinese culture.

INTRODUCTION

WHEN the Chinese eat together, whether at home or in a restaurant, sharing communally a number of dishes and rice, the favourite topic of discussion is, inevitably, food. As they eat, they criticise or praise each dish, its ingredients, flavours and fragrance, and comment on the alternative methods of preparing it. They note the number of dishes they are eating, and also the numerous other dishes they haven't been able to include. This instantly provokes a discussion about what dishes they ought to have at their next meal, how they should be prepared, and what their flavours and fragrances should be. By the end of the meal, they will have talked about hardly anything else but their favourite topic – food.

The Chinese preoccupation with food has a long tradition, and has been embraced with particular enthusiasm by men of letters. It is the stories of their extreme fondness of food, to the point of obsessiveness, that has nurtured this continued trait. The 17th-century playwright and gourmet, Li Yu, for example, wrote a eulogy about the taste of crab that has been a source of inspiration not only for all lovers of crab, but also for anyone who has an addiction to a particular kind of food.

'As regards the excellence of food and drink,' he began, 'there is not one single thing whose exquisiteness I am unable to describe. Nor is there anything that can exhaust my imagination as regards revealing its innermost quality. And yet when it comes to crabs, while I take them to my heart, while my mouth enjoys their delectable taste, and in my whole life there has not been one day when I have forgotten them, I can't even begin to describe, nor can I make clear, why I love them, why my appetite feels replete with them and why I can never forget them.

'I have loved crabs all my life,' he continued, 'so much so that every year prior to their being in season, I have saved up money in anticipation. Because my family have teased me for regarding crabs as my life, I decided I may as well dub these savings my "ransom money". From the first day crabs come into season, until the last day they are sold in the market, I never waste my time or miss even one single evening without

Su Dongpo

eating them. All my friends know about my obsessive love of crabs, and they entertain me and fête me with them during the season. I therefore call the ninth and the tenth months "crab autumn" . . . Some time ago we had a house-maid who spared no effort in the preparation of crabs, and I changed her name to "Crab-slave". Alas, she is no more. Dear crab, dear crab, you and I, are we going to be life-long companions?'

If Li Yu has inspired a love of crab amongst the Chinese people, the 11th-century

Song poet, Su Dongpo, has inspired an overall love for food, especially for pork. It was not for nothing that Su called himself 'the old gourmand' for, among all the poets in the Tang and Song dynasties, when poetry reached its zenith, he was the most unabashed and unrestrained when writing about food and wine. Despite his spiritual awareness and his leaning towards Buddhism and Daoism (Taoism), he remained an omnivore for most of his life, only becoming a vegetarian in old age when his health began to fail.

Although born in Meishan, Sichuan province, Su's turbulent career took him from the northeastern corner of Shandong province down to the southernmost Hainan Island off Guangdong province. His enforced mobility was not welcomed by either Su or his family, but did provide a wonderful opportunity for him to sample different regional cuisines and produce. He took advantage of this opportunity to the full. In fact, with his irresistible zest for life and his ability to laugh at himself, Su found that his enjoyment of local food went a long way towards compensating for missing out on achieving high office.

In 1080 he was exiled to Huangzhou, a rather small, poor town near Hankou in Hubei province. There, even though living in penury, he spent four blissful years with his family, enjoying the local produce to the hilt. To make ends meet, he started tilling a piece of land where he grew his own vegetables and herbs and, unlike other scholar-officials of his status, he actually cooked himself, delighting his wife and favourite concubine, Zhaoyun, with the results. In particular, he enjoyed the local oranges and persimmons, venison and mutton, as well as the fish he bought or netted with his friends. But, above all, he indulged in the local pork, and posterity has much to thank him for for this predilection.

He became an expert in the different ways of cooking pork and, eager to share his enjoyment with others, waxed lyrical over his ideal way of slowly braising it in the poem, 'In Praise of Pork':

> *Wash the pot clean*
> *Add a little water*
> *Firewood smouldering, the fire dimly gleams*
> *Hurry it not, let it slowly simmer*
> *When cooked long enough it will be beautiful*

It has been said that until the Song dynasty, lamb was the most highly rated meat amongst the Chinese in the north. It is a moot point, however, for pork was also highly regarded there (*see* introduction to Pork, p. 305). Nevertheless, Su Dongpo's passion for pork did more than anything else to raise its status and, since his time, it has become the most popular meat for the whole of China. In the same poem, he goes on to say:

> *There is good pork in Huangzhou*
> *Its price as cheap as dirt*
> *The rich will not eat it*
> *The poor know not how to cook it*
> *Rising early in the morning I down two bowls*
> *Never you mind, I'm full and content*

The pork that Su savoured daily has been immortalised in the famous Hangzhou dish Dongpo Pork (*see* recipe p. 313).

During another period of his life, when he was posted to a small county in Jiangsu province, he became addicted to the delectable Yangzi porpoise or globe-fish (fugu in Japanese), even though he was fully aware that it could be fatally poisonous – the poison lodging in the liver, the roe and the reproductive glands. Every year when it was in season during late spring, Su could be counted on to eat the fish and enthuse about its ineffably sensuous taste. One day, he was holding forth about it again in Mr Li's house when the latter pressed him, 'Come now, what is its actual taste?' Su shot out the answer. 'It is worth dying for.'

Not all Chinese attitudes to food are as obsessive and passionate; those credited to Confucius carry a decidedly different tone. Confucius, who was born of noble ancestry in either 552 or 551 BC and died in 479 BC in modern Shandong province, was China's foremost sage. His moral philosophy has had the most immense influence on Chinese thinking and behaviour for more than two thousand years. Although not a religion, his importance to the Chinese can be likened to that of Jesus to the Christian world. His philosophy centres on the relationship between mankind; each man must first of all build up his own moral character, pursuing morality for its own sake. His teachings, which take the form of conversations between Confucius, the Master, and his disciples, can be found in *The Analects*. From these evolve on the one hand the concept of the ideal moral man, the 'gentleman', who aspires to benevolence, virtue, intelligence, courage and learning, and on the other the 'small

Confucius

man' or ordinary person. Confucius made a pronouncement on every aspect of life, however mundane or lofty, for both the gentleman and the small man.

Although Confucius regarded food as very important for the contentment of the people if they were to keep their trust in their government, he was ambivalent, at times contradictory, when it came to the enjoyment of food. He spoke disparagingly of the pleasure to be had in feasting, as this kind of enjoyment could not be beneficial to the building of one's moral character. For himself, 'with coarse rice to eat, with water to drink, and my bended arm for a pillow, I have still joy in the midst of these things' (trans. J. Legge, 1893, p. 85). In a similar tone, he praised the virtue of one of his disciples, Hui, who, despite being impoverished, led a joyful life. 'The Master said, "How admirable Hui is! Living in a mean dwelling on a bowlful of rice and a ladleful of water is a hardship most men would find intolerable, but Hui does not allow this to affect his joy. How admirable Hui is!" ' (trans. D.C. Lau, 1979, p. 82).

Even though these two quotations have been debated endlessly by Confucian scholars who seek their inner philosophical meaning, they have also been taken at face value by those who look to Confucius for practical guidance. The words have provided much moral courage for poor people who have had to subsist on coarse food, and endure famine. For those who are not food lovers, they also feel they have an ally.

But when Confucius talks at length about food and drink, he comes across as a gourmet, being both particular and demanding as to how food should be prepared and served.

'He did not eat his fill of polished rice, nor did he eat his fill of finely minced meat.

'He did not eat rice that had gone sour or fish and meat that had spoiled. He did not eat food that had gone off colour or food that had a bad smell. He did not eat food that was not properly prepared nor did he eat except at the proper times. He did not eat food that had not been properly cut up, nor did he eat unless the proper sauce was available.

'Even when there was plenty of meat, he avoided eating more meat than rice' (trans. D.C. Lau, 1979, p. 103).

These words have formed the basis of a culinary tradition coursing through the dynasties. Even in the China of today, which went through a vehement anti-Confucius era, especially during the ten years of the Cultural Revolution from 1966 to 1976, the tradition is being referred to again. In the kitchen, those who prepare food must do it properly, irrespective of the labour and time they may have to spend over it. Cutting up food correctly is of primary importance: ingredients are cut into small cubes, slices or shreds before they are marinated in sauces and condiments. At the table, parents readily quote Confucius when they teach their children to eat a lot of rice but to take only a small measure of the accompanying dishes. In family budget planning, the same guideline is followed: more rice than meat. Hygienists praise Confucius for having been concerned about food hygiene so far back in time, and for having provided his example of not eating spoiled food to set a high standard of cleanliness.

Rightly or wrongly, another aspect of social behaviour at the table that is laid at the door of Confucius concerns conversation. 'He did not converse at meals; nor did he talk in bed' (trans. D.C. Lau, 1973, p. 103). With these words in mind, parents have for generations taught their children not to engage in stimulating dialogue while they are eating. Perhaps this is why there is no tradition of interesting conversation at the table on topics other than food.

There is also a tradition that 'gentlemen' should not soil their hands in the kitchen, which is based on the following saying of Mencius, 'That is why the gentleman keeps his distance from the kitchen' (trans. D. C. Lau, 1970, p. 55). Biographical facts about Mencius, who is considered second only to Confucius, are scanty, save that he lived during the 4th century BC, and was a devout disciple and expounder of Confucius' teachings. His own teachings, in discourses between himself and kings who sought his advice, as well as contemporary philosophers, are enshrined in the book *Mencius*. The story that led to the saying (quoted above) concerns a discussion on benevolence between the King of Qi and Mencius.

The King of Qi was sitting in a hall when he saw an ox, shaking all over with fright, being led away. Upon enquiry, he was told that the blood of the ox was required for the consecration of a new bell. So moved by the sight of the ox's fear, which conjured up in his mind the picture of an innocent man being led to the gallows, the king ordered that the ox be spared. Not that the ritual of the consecration of the bell should be abandoned, he insisted, but that a lamb should be used instead. This incident led his people to question the real motive behind his action. They queried whether the king was, in substituting a lamb for an ox, merely being miserly, for an ox would cost more. There ensued a dialogue between the king and Mencius, who also tried to probe the real motive behind the king's action. The king reassured Mencius that it was truly his pity for the ox that made him spare it, even though he could understand why his people should think he was being miserly in using a lamb instead. If there was pity for the ox, why not pity for the lamb as well, Mencius asked. To this the king had no ready answer. Thereupon Mencius reassured him that what he had done was truly worthy of a benevolent man, concluding:

'You saw the ox but not the lamb. The attitude of a gentleman towards animals is this: once having seen them alive, he cannot bear to see them die, and once having

Mencius

heard their cry, he cannot bear to eat their flesh. That is why the gentleman keeps his distance from the kitchen' (trans. D. C. Lau, 1970, p. 55).

For the last two thousand years, Chinese men in general, and Chinese husbands in particular, have effectively hijacked the last sentence to excuse themselves from entering the kitchen and participating in cookery chores, assigning all such duties to women. This saying was also responsible for the lowly status of cooks, as it put them in the category of the small man, the opposite of the gentleman. In Mencius' defence, it may be said that it was taken out of context from a longer quotation, which should have served as an inspiration for vegetarians.

Another culinary tradition that can also be traced to Mencius is, however, universally welcomed by the Chinese – both men and women. It endorses, if indeed endorsement is needed, the very relaxed attitude the Chinese have towards the necessity of food, and enjoying it to the full. Hanging on every lip is this saying, even though not every one knows of its origin: 'Appetite for food and sex is nature' (trans. D. C. Lau, 1970, p. 161).

Mencius and Gaozi, a contemporary philosopher, were having a discussion on human nature, a subject in which they had a mutual interest but held diverse views. While Mencius was trying to make Gaozi concede that human nature was naturally good, Gaozi came out with the statement, 'appetite for food and sex is nature'. Unfortunately, there did not ensue a direct discussion on this, so that it has always remained at once profound, enigmatic, undeniable and debatable. Scholars have pointed out that nowhere in Mencius is there any evidence that Mencius denies the validity of Gaozi's statement. But Mencius makes it clear that, unlike the nature of animals, the appetite for food and sex is only a part of human nature. There is also, he avers, something else to human nature and that is morality, which distinguishes a man from an animal. The inherent moral issue of this saying is conveniently put aside, however, at least as far as food is concerned. What has endured as a strong tradition is the licence to satisfy a man's appetite for food – it being human nature.

CULINARY TRADITIONS

IN China today, cooks enjoy a professional status. After being trained in cookery schools, then in restaurants, they are graded, and the talented ones rise above the grading to become special chefs. Even though their social status does not match the kind of stardom European, especially French, chefs enjoy, they are recognised as artists in the great Chinese gastronomic tradition, with much to contribute to the other food cultures of the world. This 20th-century phenomenon, however, is in stark contrast to the pattern set up during the previous two thousand years, when cooks were looked down upon as 'lowly people'. Little wonder then that not much is known about individual Chinese cooks, and written descriptions of their art are few. And yet, paradoxically, in ancient times Chinese cooks seem not only to have enjoyed high social standing, but also to have wielded great political power. Two cooks became ministers at the royal court, one of whom left indelible gastronomic theories upon which the many facets of Chinese cookery are based.

Yi Yin, who lived in the 16th century BC, is regarded as China's first master of gastronomy. His role as cook and later prime minister to King Tang, founder of the Shang dynasty (16th–11th century BC), is mentioned in official history, but it is through the writing of Lu Buwei, of the 3rd century BC, that Yi Yin's gastronomic tenets have come down to posterity.

A wealthy merchant, shrewd manipulator of politics and altogether a colourful figure of his time, Lu wrote an essay entitled 'Benwei Pian' or 'The Root of Tastes'. It tells the story of Yi Yin's legendary birth and his discourse with King Tang, which, although political in intent, is entirely gastronomical in content. As literature, it is seen as China's first short story; in the realm of gastronomy, it is the oldest extant treatise on the subject.

Yi Yin's mother, who lived near the Yi River (in modern Henan province), found herself with child. In a dream, God said to her, 'If you see water shooting out of the stone mortar, start running eastwards as fast as you can. Do not turn your head and do not look back.' The following day she saw water coming out of the stone mortar and, as soon as she had alerted her neighbours, she started to run towards the east, never stopping until she had run for ten miles. Then she turned her head and looked back towards the village from where she had come; all she could see was water. After this she stayed in a mulberry forest and, in due course, gave birth to a son, whom she named Yi Yin, remembering the Yi River.

Not long afterwards, however, she died. A young maiden of the Youshen House was picking mulberry leaves in the forest and saw the baby. She picked him up and presented him to the king, Youshen, who asked a cook to raise him.

When Yi Yin grew up, he became a man of many talents, the art of cookery not the least of them. As his name became known, King Tang of the House of Shang wanted to recruit him, but when the king sent for him, Youshen refused to let him go, even though he himself desired to go to the court of King Tang. Thereupon King Tang asked for the hand of Youshen's daughter. Youshen was delighted with the marriage proposal, and sent Yi Yin as a part of the marriage entourage accompanying his daughter to the House of Shang.

As soon as Yi Yin arrived, carrying on his shoulder a 'ding' (a meat cauldron usually with three feet and two ear-shaped handles) and in his hands a chopping board and kitchen knife, King Tang received him in the temple (a mark of respect). He then consulted him not on matters of gastronomy, but on the art of ruling the country. Yi Yin's answer, which took the form of a long allegorical discourse on the art of cookery, teems with wisdom that Chinese cooks have adhered to, consciously or subconsciously, throughout the ages.

To begin, Yi Yin described the characteristics of fish and meat, the main ingredients:

'As for the three groups of creature, those which dwell in water are rank and fishy, those which prey on others are rancid, and those which graze on grass are frowzy. Stinking and foul as they are, yet they can be excellent in taste, as everything can be put to its best use.'

The Chinese have always insisted on ingredients being fresh, so much so that there is a special word, 'xian', meaning fresh flavour, which describes that sensational yet elusive taste only truly fresh ingredients can impart. Yet, paradoxically, they have regarded their natural odours, be they derived from sea or land, as undesirable. 'Xing', for instance, is a special word to described rank fishiness, and there is also the notion, especially among southern Chinese, that lamb and mutton, and to a certain extent beef, have a frowzy smell. Herbs and spices are used primarily to counter the odour, even though they enhance the taste at the same time. Thus ginger, either sliced, shredded or squeezed into juice, is associated with steamed fish, first of all to rid it of the xing rankness, but also to bring out its xian or fresh flavour. Likewise, ginger is used with wine and bean curd 'cheese' in a sauce for braised lamb, and this sauce has the effect of transforming the foul smell into a deliciously palatable flavour.

Stretching the principle that everything can be put to its best use, Chinese cooks have turned what are, by Western standards, the most lowly and unlikely ingredients into delectable dishes. Fish heads, chicken's feet, duck's tongues and duck's webs, not to mention offal, beef tendons, pig's trotters, jellyfish and sea slugs are cooked in different ways to realise their excellent taste and texture. They are by no means poor man's food; on the contrary, they grace many a Chinese banquet table.

From ingredients Yi Yin moved on to the technique of cooking: 'At the root of all tastes, water is fundamental. Among the five tastes and three materials, the nine boilings and nine transformations, fire is the modulator. At times fierce and at times gentle, it eliminates fishiness, removes rancidness and erases frowziness. Thus the control of fire is pivotal to successfully retaining the inherent qualities of all ingredients.'

What truer words could have been said about boiling and braising? They are also the cornerstone on which the special Chinese cookery techniques – steaming and stir-frying – were built. Even though Yi Yin did not speak about steaming *per se*, bronze steamers were in use during the late Shang dynasty. Stir-frying was yet to come, but Yi Yin's advice on how to control the fire, 'at times fierce and at times gentle', describes the quintessence of stir-frying itself. Every time a Chinese cook wields a wok over a flame, at one instant engulfing yet at another gentle and slow, he causes a small miracle inside the wok: not only is the foul odour of the ingredients eliminated, but as their natural juices are sealed over a high heat, their inherent qualities are preserved, and the exclusive 'wok fragrance' is produced.

Coming to the end of his quest for the root of all tastes, Yi Yin averred:

'As for the matter of harmonious blending, one must make use of the sweet, sour, bitter, pungent and salty. But which tastes one adds first or later, and how much or

how little, the balance is very subtle, for each produces its own effect. The trans-
formation which occurs in the ding is wonderful and delicate. The mouth cannot
express it in words, nor can the mind illuminate its meaning. It is like the subtlety of
archery and horsemanship, the difference between yin and yang and the changes of
the four seasons. Thus the dishes last for a long time yet are not spoiled; they are
cooked yet not ragged, sweet yet not cloying, sour yet not acid, salty yet not severely
so, peppery-hot yet not burning, mild yet not insipid and rich yet not greasy.'

These words, at once poetic, profound and mysterious, also speak for themselves
as a most down-to-earth description of the characteristics of Chinese cooking as it has
developed to the present time. The tenet of the five tastes – salty, bitter, sour,
pungent and sweet – which correspond to the five elements – water, fire, wood,
metal and earth – was already rooted in Chinese beliefs by the 3rd century BC, when
Lu was writing, and has remained the nub of truth for the Chinese tastebud ever
since, even though in other gastronomic cultures peppery-hotness may not be
regarded as a taste. In the kitchen, a cook's first lesson is to learn the harmonious
blending of tastes, and he is a successful cook only if he can master the techniques.
With every dish he prepares, he is mindful of Yi Yin's guidelines. Likewise, he must
know the intrinsic property of every ingredient, so that when he plans a menu, he can
achieve a perfect balance. Again, by Lu's time, the belief that the Chinese universe
was regulated by the balance of two forces, Yin and Yang, or moon and sun, female
and male, darkness and brightness, was formulated, and this concept, being all
embracing, was applied to food as well.

Unlike Yi Yin, Yi Ya, who was also promoted from the kitchen to become a
minister at court, was anything but a virtuous man. Yet he has come down in
Chinese history as one of the great chefs, excelling in the art of the blending of
flavours, and as such has been referred to by many writers, including Yuan Mei, the
most famed gastronome and food writer of the 18th century. By the same token, his
name was used in the title of a Ming dynasty cookbook to invoke taste itself.
Nothing, however, is known of the delectable dishes he was supposed to have
cooked. Nor has he left any legacy of profound statements. In fact, all that is known
of him for certain is the following unedifying story. He lived in the second half of the
7th century BC. It was a period of political chaos when the country, then being ruled
by the Zhou dynasty (11th century–221 BC), was broken up and four dukes were
contesting for power. Yi Ya began his career in the kitchen of the Duke of Qi and,

being a clever cook, came to the duke's notice when he served dishes late one night as a means of relieving the duke from boredom and insomnia. As the duke found the flavours of the dishes sensational, he got into the habit of sending for them whenever he could not sleep. In this way Yi Ya became closer and closer to the duke, who in time made him a minister in his court. But the duke was a wicked man and, one evening, he summoned Yi Ya and told him he desired to taste the flesh of an infant, as it was the only taste that had eluded his palate. Yi Ya, in complying with the duke's bestial desire, steamed his own son and served him to the duke. Delighted with his feast, the duke granted Yi Ya even more power, turning a deaf ear to his prime minister, who advised him against trusting a man who could commit such an unnatural act.

Enough of this horrid tale. We shall be better served to turn to the tale of Cook Ding, written by the Daoist philosopher, Zhuangzi, who lived about the 4th century BC and whose philosophy of intuitive and spontaneous action in life, the antithesis of Confucius' moralistic code of behaviour, is the embodiment of Daoism. Whereas Yi Yin entered straightaway into an allegorical discourse with King Tang, Cook Ding first impressed Lord Wenhui with the seemingly effortless perfection of his work before he explained the Way. The story is told in Zhuangzi's own words:

'Cook Ting [Ding] was carving an ox for Lord Wen-hui. As his hand slapped, shoulder lunged, foot stamped, knee crooked, with a hiss! with a thud! the brandished blade as it sliced never missed the rhythm, now in time with the Mulberry Forest dance, now with an orchestra playing the Ching-shou.

' "Oh, excellent!" said Lord Wen-hui. "That skill should attain such heights!"

' "What your servant cares about is the Way, I have left skill behind me. When I first began to carve oxen, I saw nothing but oxen wherever I looked. Three years more and I never saw an ox as a whole. Nowadays, I am in touch through the daemonic in me, and do not look with the eye. With the senses I know where to stop, the daemonic I desire to run its course." '

Cook Ding went on to describe how he carved through the cavities of the ox with his chopper, which he had had for nineteen years and kept very sharp. In conclusion, he said: ' "However, whenever I come to something intricate, I see where it will be hard to handle and cautiously prepare myself, my gaze settles on it, action slows down for it, you scarcely see the flick of the chopper – and at one stroke the tangle has been unravelled, as a clod crumbles to the ground. I stand chopper in hand, look proudly round at everyone, dawdle to enjoy the triumph until I'm quite satisfied, then clean the chopper and put it away."

' "Excellent!" said Lord Wen-hui. "Listening to the words of Cook Ting, I have learned from them how to nurture life" ' (trans. A. C. Graham, 1981, pp. 63–4).

Whatever profound philosophical insight is to be read into the Cook Ding story, what also springs to mind is the similarity with the noodle master making northern, hand-drawn 'dancing' noodles. Transcribe the action of carving the ox to the gentler but equally, if not more, skilled manoeuvre of making noodles, and Zhuangzi himself may have liked to witness the scene which is at once vivid and spectacular, but also intuitive and spontaneous.

The noodle master who knows the Way follows five distinct procedures. First, he adds cold water to strong flour, makes it into a smooth dough and leaves it for several hours or overnight. Second, he throws the dough on a hard work-top many times in order to strengthen the gluten before he rolls it out into a tubular dough. Third, with each hand holding one end of the dough, he picks it up as high as his own shoulder level and starts to stretch and elongate it horizontally, yet without letting it break in the centre. He puts it down, folds it back to more or less the original length, then takes it up again to repeat the rhythmic 'dancing' of the dough. This he repeats many times until he knows it is strong and elastic enough for him to proceed to the next step. Fourth, away from the work-top, he stretches the dough even longer, so long that it falls to form a semi-circle. Just as the onlooker holds his breath lest the dough fall to the floor, the noodle master, with one hand and great dexterity, swiftly passes one end of the dough to the other hand and, in the course of doing so, causes the semi-circle to twist into a rope hanging in mid-air. With both hands, he stretches out the rope again and repeats the rope-twisting several times until he feels that the dough is at last inherently strong and outwardly smooth enough for the splitting, the ultimate step that turns the dough into strands of noodles. Fifth, he places the rope back on the work-top and begins the splitting procedure. Magically, holding the ends in a special way and folding them back and forth, he splits the dough, doubling the strands every time. From 1 to 2, then 4, 8, 16, 32, 64, 128, 256; in eight splittings, he has a very impressive spread of individual noodle strands which he hangs across a thin bamboo pole, to the thunderous applause of his audience. The action from dancing the dough to splitting it into noodle strands takes a consummate master about fifteen minutes, but it takes him about two years before he succeeds in harnessing the spontaneous energy to perform it.

Fortunately for us laymen, even though we may not be able to learn the Way of the 'dancing noodles', we can easily comprehend the Way of stir-frying, steaming, mixing of flavours and the other techniques of Chinese cookery.

Traditionally, women have always been the cooks in Chinese families. At many archaeological sites, kitchen murals show women in the process of preparing food, sometimes bending down to knead noodle dough, at other times in front of the brightly-lit stove ready to cook meat and fish. A bride's culinary duties would start three days after her marriage, as charmingly described in verse by a Tang dynasty poet, Wang Jian:

> *Three days after the wedding she enters the kitchen*
> *Hands rinsed she makes stews and soups*
> *Not sure what delights mother-in-law's palate*
> *Maiden sister-in-law she sends for to taste*

Women's cookery duties at home were taken for granted, and their skills were passed from generation to generation through word of mouth, within the family walls. Few women became cooks of public standing, even fewer have earned a place in history. In spite of this, there were some whose food was so distinctive that contemporary writers wrote about them.

One such woman cook was a Buddhist nun, Fan Zheng, whose story was told by Tao Gu, himself a Song writer, who had eyes and ears for recording strange and marvellous matters. Fan, who lived in the first half of the 10th century AD, may be hailed as the originator of sculpted dishes and vegetable carving, an art especially popular with Peking chefs today. The technique calls for elaborate carving of food morsels with special knives and implements so that they resemble mosaics on a serving platter, often in the image of birds or animals in an artistic setting, carrying a symbolic message as well. One popular image is a phoenix, which brings happiness and luck. Another familiar one is the panda, the rare and exotic Chinese bear treasured by the whole world. Yet another is the crane amidst pine trees, carrying the message of longevity. Ambitious young cooks sometimes go overboard, and they end up with neither appetising food nor artistic creation. Among chefs themselves, there is debate about the merit of sculpted dishes, but none can deny the long tradition behind them.

Fan Zheng's own inspiration derived from a highly artistic source. The 8th-century poet–painter, Wang Wei, so well versed in both poetry and painting that he was dubbed 'a poet in his paintings' and 'a painter in his poetry', lived in the idyllic Wangchuan Villa during the twilight years of his life. He painted a series of twenty-one scenes of the villa and wrote twenty-one poems describing the gardens and tranquil ambience. Fan Zheng recreated these scenes as cold dishes on platters. Using all the ingredients at her disposal, which ranged from vegetables, gourds, meat and fermented fish, finely shredded and cubed, pickled and stewed, she would sculpt each of the twenty-one scenes. She would then invite twenty guests for dinner, and present a scene to each one of them. Her guests, enthralled and mesmerised, could hardly bear to demolish such works of art; they would gaze at their plates for a long time before they could be persuaded to eat.

No woman cook ever attained high office at court, though one did come close to usurping the title of Imperial Chef, a role reserved for men. During the reign of the first emperor of Southern Song, Gaozong (1127–63), there was a female *sous-chef*, Liu, in the Imperial kitchen. She had cooked for Gaozong when he was the crown prince and after he had ascended to the throne she continued to please him with her dishes. She was especially skilful in shredding vegetables and meat, in using condiments and seasonings and in controlling the fire so as to produce perfect results. By court rule, only a man could be in charge of the Imperial table, but Liu excelled so much over all the other male cooks that she was put into *de facto* charge. Gradually, one and all conceded she was the best and addressed her, albeit unofficially, as 'Madame Imperial Chef Liu'.

Two women cooks are still household names, each with an eponymous dish to their credit. The 12th-century Mrs Song used to work in the kitchen of a noble house in Kaifeng, the capital of Northern Song. One of her specialities was a chunky fish soup, made with carp from the Yellow River. When the Song emperor, facing defeat from the Jin forces, moved his court southward to Hangzhou in 1127, Mrs Song and her husband joined the emigrating marches, and eventually settled in the outskirts of Hangzhou. Like their fellow refugees, they missed the taste of food from their erstwhile country. They also faced the hardship of having to look for a new livelihood. To assuage their homesickness, Mrs Song tried to reproduce her fish soup, using the local carp, and, to her delight, she found these fish even more succulent. Her neighbours were soon attracted by the fragrant smell and started to buy the thick and tasty soup by the bowlful. Having stumbled on this new livelihood, the Songs set up a stall in the market place to sell nothing but this fish soup, which became the talk of the town. The Emperor Gaozong heard about it and sent a eunuch to ask Mrs Song to cook a huge pot for the palace. Once the emperor had tasted it and given his royal patronage, the fame of Mrs Song was guaranteed.

The Southern Song writer, Wu Zimu, whose book *Mengliang Lu* or *Dreaming of the Capital* contains reminiscences about the picturesque and urbane social and commercial life in Hangzhou in the 13th century, and is an important source of information for that period, mentions Mrs Song's fish soup by name, but without divulging any details of the recipe. This dish has, nevertheless, become famous in Hangzhou menus, and many a restaurant there creates its own version of the soup in honour of Mrs Song's memory.

The other cook with an eponymous dish was the 19th-century Mrs Chen, mockingly dubbed 'Mapo', or the pock-marked woman. She and her husband, also a cook, lived in Chengdu, capital of Sichuan, where they ran a small tavern together. But it was her bean curd dish, with its spicy meat sauce, that has enshrined her scarred face in the Sichuanese menu. Mapo Doufu is one of the most renowned Chinese dishes in the world (*see* recipe p. 218).

Incredible as it may seem, Wang Xiaoyu is the only chef who has had a biography written about him, albeit brief and published posthumously. For ten years until his death, Wang was in the employ of Yuan Mei, the most renowned 18th-century gourmet and cookery writer. Wang's impact went beyond his master's kitchen and dining table and is reflected in Yuan's cookbook, *The Cookery Lists of Suiyuan* (*see* p. 38), which echoes many of Wang's philosophical and practical approaches towards cookery. After Wang died, Yuan missed his cooking so much that he would mourn him 'whenever he ate', ruminating in his own mind his chef's words. Yuan had written many short biographies and each was about a person of special merit, either a literary figure, an official, a member of the aristocracy or one of his female pupils from noble families. That he included in his series Wang, whom he identified as but 'a lowly person', reflects the great admiration he had for his cook. Seen from the perspective of a time when the work of a cook was taken for granted by his master, the tribute is all the more remarkable.

Even before Wang joined Yuan's household, he had a reputation as an excellent cook. Whenever Wang cooked, the aroma of his dishes would waft through the air and people in the neighbourhood, mouths watering, would follow the smell to his house, hoping for a tasting. It was because of this that Yuan decided to ask him to come for an interview. Fearing that he was only used to cooking expensive *haute cuisine* for noble houses, Yuan decided to lay his cards on the table.

'I am the son of a poor family,' Yuan said, 'and our budget for each meal measures only in copper coins.'

With a broad smile, Wang nodded and retired into the kitchen to make his trial meal. A short time later, he presented Yuan with a simple dish, which nevertheless was so delicious that Yuan wanted to have more – alas, Yuan has not enlightened us as to what the dish was. It was thus because of their shared penchant for simple food, that Wang was hired as the cook for the Yuan household.

Thereafter, for ten years, Yuan and Wang developed an unusual relationship, so close that it transcended the norm between a master and a servant. The bond between them was Wang's true understanding of Yuan's taste, something Yuan thought was more difficult to realise than to have a friend understand him as a person.

With Wang presiding in the kitchen, Yuan entertained extensively at home. His guests were enamoured of Wang's cooking and they never seemed to be able to have enough of it. Wang had a strict code of never preparing more than six or seven dishes at a dinner, and Yuan took this as a model principle for other cooks to follow. So enthusiastic were his guests about the dishes that they would jump up and down, clamouring to eat the actual plates as well! His friends also borrowed Wang as guest cook at their own houses; with pride, he complied with their wishes.

Wang did his own shopping at the market, for he liked to choose the ingredients himself. 'Every ingredient has its natural property,' he said. 'If its property is fine, I will use it.' When he cooked, in spite of the numerous helping hands he had in the kitchen, he would lean against the stove and never turned his eye from the pots. So concentrated was he on his work that he would not hear if other people were calling him. He was also so adept with seasonings of salt, soy sauce, wine and sauces that nobody ever saw him stick his finger inside the pot in order to test for flavour.

Wood was the fuel used in his time, and he knew that control of the fire was of paramount importance to the success or failure of his dishes. He therefore maintained a near tyrannical rein over his kitchen in respect of this. He would suddenly shout,

'Fierce flame', and his assistants in charge of the fire would instantly effect a red hot flame; after a while, he would order, 'Gentle flame', and his underlings would immediately withdraw some of the wood to reduce the flame. When he ordered, 'Stop the fire', his men would bring the fire to a stop. When the time came for serving, he would call out, 'Serve the dishes', and immediately the assistants would bring forward the plates. If there was any delay, Wang would be so angry that he would start shouting, believing that any slackening of speed would cause the dishes to spoil.

Once dinner was over, he would wash his hands, sit down for a while, then start cleaning and washing his special utensils and grinding his knives. He had more than thirty of them, which he stored in a special box.

Yuan noticed that other cooks tried to emulate Wang but could not reach his heights of perfection. Like others, Yuan asked for his philosophy and the secret of his success. In his answer, Wang likened his skill to that of a doctor, in that he treated all the ingredients with care. Asked in what order one should serve dishes, his answer was that the rich dishes should come first, followed by plainer ones, and the main dishes should precede the more exotic. He would not judge an ingredient solely on its monetary value: vegetables to him could be as delicious as poultry and meat. In sum, he treasured every ingredient as if it had a soul, so that when it was cooked, it would not die a worthless death in the pot.

Much of Wang's thought and practice Yuan reiterated in his cookbook, since Yuan was proud to feel that Wang, instead of seeking employment with aristocratic families with 'lacquer doors', preferred to remain in his kitchen until he died.

IMPORTANT COOKERY BOOKS

EVEN though Chinese historical and literary records on food go back to the Zhou dynasty (11th century–221 BC), many of the books written on cookery before the 6th century AD have been lost to posterity, and it is not clear why or how they disappeared. We only know of their existence through references in other books or fragments of what is left of them. The most poignant example is *Shi Jing* or *The Book of Food*, written by Cui Hao, who was prime minister at the beginning of the Northern Wei dynasty (AD 386–534), but was executed for treason in AD 450. All of his book, save for the preface, has been lost. In what remains we learn of how, as a child, he used to watch his mother, as well as his father's concubines and other aunts and women, all cooking together. Even though the family was a large, wealthy household in Hebei province in the north of China, his mother, assisted by other women, would herself cook on all the important family occasions – such as ancestor-worship, birthdays and annual festivals – rather than assign the work to servants and maids. Later, however, for more than ten years, as the country was going through political turmoil, both festive and formal entertaining in the house came to a complete halt. His mother was worried lest her cookery art and the family recipes be lost to the generations to come. She therefore sat her son down to take dictation from her while she recounted every recipe, from day-to-day fare to banquet dishes, together with the cookery methods. What Cui wrote down, he attested, amounted to nine chapters which he compiled into a book. Alas, not even one recipe from it has survived.

Fortunately, *Qimin Yaoshu* or *Essential Skills for the Daily Life of the People*, a very important work on agriculture by Jia Sixie, written most probably between AD 533 and 544, is intact. Not a great deal is known about Jia, except that he was well born, from an aristocratic family, and served as the Prefect of Gaoyang in Shandong province. As a government official he was devoted to agriculture and wrote this encyclopaedic work on the subject. In volumes 8 and 9 he wrote about food and these two volumes may be said to be the first extant Chinese cookery books, since they were the first to discuss food processing, give methods and quantities for recipes and cover a wide variety of ingredients. They also contain numerous references to earlier books, and this indicates that Jia was only putting down in writing what had already been achieved by this time. Unfortunately, when Jia quoted an earlier work, he was not in the habit of naming its author as well. For example, *Shi Jing* or *The Book of Food*, a favourite title used by different authors, is referred to many times without identifying the author, and this has caused scholars today to continue debating whether or not it was Cui Hao's *Shi Jing* he was quoting. This notwithstanding, Jia's book reveals how advanced the Chinese were with food processing and how Chinese cookery was evolving.

The volumes on food discuss in detail the refining of salt and the milling of flour, and also the fermentation techniques used to make alcohol, vinegar, pickled vegetables and 'jiang' (a word that has no English equivalent, but which is usually translated as relish or sauce). It is the fermentation of jiang, the genesis of soy sauce, that interests us most.

Soy sauce, more than any other Chinese seasoning, has been assimilated into other cuisines all over the world, including those of Japan, Korea and Southeast Asia, Europe and America. The precise date it was invented is not certain, but many Chinese food scholars believe that soy sauce had become a commercial product by Han times, and that it was then being sold in shops along with vinegar and salt. Certainly, by the time Jia wrote in the 6th century, he was able to give a detailed description of the hydrolysis of soy beans. Jia used the Han terminology 'jiang qing' (clear sauce) to describe the end product. More conservative scholars, however, have noted that in his book Jia does not use the term 'jiangyou' (soy sauce), as we know it today. They have pointed out that jiangyou (soy sauce) was first referred to by the Song writer, Lin Hong (*see* p. 27), who recommended it as a dipping sauce for bamboo shoots and chives, among other things.

Whatever the definitive answer, the method given in *Qimin Yaoshu* gives the basic principles of making soy sauce by fermentation. Put simply, it required first of all selecting the best soy beans, soaking them for a long time, then steaming them. It then required a mixture of 30 parts steamed soy beans to 10 parts ground wine starter, 10 parts yellow mould and 5 parts table salt to be put in a large basin, which was well stirred and then covered with a lid to allow fermentation to take place. When the fermented mixture ripened into a 'stock', salt was added and the mixture stirred until it became a syrupy mass. This mass was then baked in the hot sun for one hundred days until it became the flavoursome jiang, or soy-hydrolysate.

From the inscriptions discovered in 1972 on bamboo slips in what is known as 'Han Tomb No. 1 at Mawangdui' in Hunan province, we know that salted black beans ('chi'), the condiment so widely used in Chinese dishes today, were already in use in Han times. Black beans are also made from cooked soy beans which, halfway through their hydrolytic decomposition, are dried at a very high temperature and become darkened as a result of oxidation. Jia was the first person to describe, in *Qimin Yaoshu*, how to make them.

As a whole, *Qimin Yaoshu* reflects what people cooked and ate in northeastern China and along the Yellow River from the Han dynasty until the 6th century. A wide range of animal meat, seemingly of equal importance, was eaten: beef, lamb, roebuck, deer, horse, donkey, bear, pig, rabbit and dog. Poultry included chicken, duck and wild duck, goose and wild goose, pigeon and quail. A popular food at the time was 'zha', or raw fish or meat fermented with cooked rice in an urn until it matured. Zha remained popular in northern China until about the 12th century, after which time, for reasons still unclear, it disappeared. Among the core of recipes, some are both timeless and relevant to present-day cuisine.

One that has excited a lot of discussion is a recipe for duck, which can be said to be the first stir-fried dish. According to the recipe, after a duck has been cleaned, the meat is to be minced as if for making stuffing. Then, with shredded white spring onions, salt and black bean sauce, the meat is to be 'stir-fried' until very well done. The focus of interest is in the word 'stir-fried' used by Jia, since what he describes is taken to be the forerunner of the technique of stir-frying as we know it now. Certainly, by the 6th century, cast-iron pots were already in use and it is these, with their fast transmission of heat, that made stir-frying possible.

One of the most sought-after dishes in the Chinese repertoire is whole suckling pig, and there is a recipe in *Qimin Yaoshu* that is reminiscent of what the Chinese savour today. The piglet used must be still suckling and plump, though it can be either male or female. The skin is washed well with boiling water, and the hair scraped and shaved off. A small hole is inserted in the belly from which the entrails are removed. The cavity is then stuffed with herbs and the piglet, supported by a firm wooden pole, is slowly roasted, being turned constantly for even roasting. Wine is brushed all over the skin in order for it to take on colour until it becomes golden. Pure lard or sesame oil is also smeared on the skin. 'When roasted,' Jia enthuses, 'the colour of the suckling pig resembles amber and is shiny like gold. When you put it in your mouth, it melts like ice. Exuding juices and oil, it is very different from ordinary meat.'

Nowadays, roasting suckling pig may call for use of sauces and condiments not mentioned by Jia, but the effect to aim at, in terms of colour and crispness of the skin, is the same.

Some cookery terms coined by Jia are still popular with both professional and home cooks today, even though they may not be aware of their origin. To differenti-ate the gentle simmering of liquid that causes only tiny ripples on the surface from the fierce boiling that results in large bubbles, Jia graphically uses two terms, 'crab eyes simmering' for the former and 'fish eyes boiling' for the latter. These terms have come down by word of mouth as well as in writing for fourteen centuries.

From the Sui and Tang dynasties, two works have survived, but they provide only limited interest. The one written around 600 AD by Xie Feng with the lofty title of *Shi Jing* or *The Book of Food* consists of no more than the titles of fifty-three dishes, many of which are very esoteric. As people in succeeding centuries have tried to guess what some of these dishes were, it has a curiosity value. The prime example is a dish called Whole Lamb Mohu, which seemingly originates from the Huns. As interpreted by gourmets in the 10th century, it is prepared this way. First count the number of diners and allow one goose per person. Pluck the feathers and remove the viscera. Stuff into the cavity of each goose cooked rice already seasoned with herbs and spices, then sew it up. Place the geese into the cavity of a lamb, shorn of its wool and cleaned of its guts, then sew it up again. Now roast the whole lamb until it is thoroughly cooked. Cut open the lamb and remove the geese. Serve only the geese to the diners.

The novelty is in using the lamb as an insulating device for the geese, which must be succulent and tasty. It is not a recipe that is used now, if only because of its wastefulness, but as a legendary recipe it is still talked about.

The other work reveals the menu of a grand feast, most probably for a Tang emperor. During the first part of the 8th century it was customary for a Tang official, upon attaining high office, to present a grand feast, dubbed 'shaowei' or 'tail-burned' feast, in order to show his gratitude to the emperor. When Wei Juyuan became Grand Secretary, he held such a feast and recorded fifty-eight dishes of the menu in his *Shi Pu* or *Book of Recipes*. Underneath some of the exotic titles he describes what they are and gives instructions, albeit scanty, as to how they should be prepared.

The implication of the name shaowei or tail-burned feast has stirred inconclusive discussions among scholars. The most likely explanation centres around the folklore of the mythical metamorphosis of the common carp into a dragon. There is a gorge between the two neighbouring provinces, Shaanxi and Shanxi, which is so dangerous and precipitous that it is named the Dragon Gate. Every year during springtime carp swim against the currents in the Yellow River towards the Dragon Gate. Most of them never get through it, but are hurled back by the rolling waves. The carp that jumps through the Gate, however, will cause a scorching flame to descend from the heavens, which burns off its tail and transforms it into a dragon. This story was always used as an analogy to show how, in the Imperial Chinese meritocratic system, a commoner could, once he passed the palace examination, be instantly elevated to the ruling class to hold high office.

Whatever the meaning of shaowei, the menu of the feast reflects what the rich people ate in the capital of Chang'an (near modern Xi'an) during the Tang dynasty. Lamb is mentioned in six recipes, confirming it as the meat served most frequently. The others feature beef, pork, venison, rabbit, bear, raccoon, chicken, duck, goose and quail. Not surprisingly, cakes and noodles made of wheat flour are mentioned, for they were being sought after by people who could afford them. But the most significant dish is for twenty-four kinds of 'huntun' of different patterns and stuffings. This is probably the first time the term huntun, with its ancient astronomic connotation of the sky wrapping around us, was used to describe a kind of food. Huntun, which is now known as 'jiaozi' to northern Chinese and 'wonton' to southern Chinese (and ravioli to the Italians), is made with thin wheat flour skins or wrappers. Jiaozi is usually stuffed with meat and vegetables, whereas wonton calls for shrimp in the stuffing. Archaeological remains confirm that jiaozi date from the Tang period. Today, some restaurants in Xi'an, where tourists go to view the wondrous Terracotta Army of the First Emperor of the Qin dynasty (221–06 BC), offer an exclusive jiaozi banquet, serving nothing but dumplings of different shapes, sizes and stuffings throughout the meal, and they boast one hundred different kinds of them.

It is not until the Song dynasty (AD 960–1279) that we find cookery books of broad scope again. Two in particular warrant our attention. The first, *Zhonggui Lu* or *Records of Home Cooking*, was written by a Mrs Wu, who may be called the first Chinese woman cookery writer. Not even her first name is known, let alone other biographical details, save that she lived in Pujiang in Zhejiang province. About 6,500 words in length and containing seventy-six recipes with instructions and quantities of ingredients, her book reflects the evolving Shanghai or Eastern regional cuisine. More than thirty are vegetable recipes, six fish, three crab, two prawn, one razor clam, six pork, one chicken, one yellow bird and two on fermenting soy beans. Among the fifteen sweet recipes, most are on noodles and cakes. The one sweet 'zong' recipe (the dumpling made to celebrate the Double Fifth Festival, *see* p. 56) calls for a rich stuffing consisting of dates, chestnuts, dried persimmon, almonds and red beans, which is not dissimilar to those made today.

Other traits characteristic of Eastern regional cooking can be traced to her recipes, notably, the Shanghaiese penchant for drunken crabs and for using 'zao' or wine sediments, together with wine, to enrich the main ingredients, which can be meat, poultry, aquatic foods and vegetables. In her recipe to intoxicate crabs, she recommends using either one bowl each of zao, vinegar, wine and soy sauce and a lot of salt or seven bowls of wine, three of vinegar and two of salt. In three vegetable recipes, she uses zao to preserve aubergine, radish and ginger. To steam a shad (the seasonal summer fish of the Yangzi basin) with a subtle texture and taste, she firmly advises against removing the scales. This is still the set rule, for it is vital not to take away the natural fish fat embedded underneath the shad's delicate skin, lest the flesh becomes dry and wooden when cooked. Nowadays, the most scrumptious way to steam a shad is to wrap it in pig's caul, so that the melting fat percolates through the scale to enrich the flesh.

Mrs Wu's one and only chicken recipe is noted for its complex method and indicates the sophisticated style of Yangzhou cooking. First of all she poaches a chicken until it is 80 per cent cooked before cutting it up into small pieces and frying them in oil in a saucepan. She then adds an equal portion of wine and vinegar, plus a little salt and continues to cook the chicken until the liquid is absorbed. This last procedure is repeated several times until, she assures us, the chicken pieces are fragrant and well done.

Zha food, which Jia Sixie recorded in his book (*see* p. 21) was still popular, and

Mrs Wu has a recipe for razor clam zha. Razor clams, marinated in salt and weighted down with stones, are mixed with seasonings and cooked rice and put into an urn, which is sealed by mud, for ten days until the clams are mature enough to eat. While pork is featured six times, lamb is mentioned only once in passing, an indication that, unlike in northern China, pork was already popular in the east by Song time. She seems very keen on vegetables, as their recipes outnumber meat and fish. She specialises in pickling and preserving them, using salt and vinegar, and her repertoire extends to gourds, mustard greens, aubergines, radishes, ginger, bamboo shoots, etc. One recipe deals with making mustard powder from two-year-old mustard seeds, one of the first of its kind to be written.

The impression Mrs Wu's work made on writers in succeeding dynasties was considerable, so much so that one Ming writer, Gao Lien, who had two cookery books under his belt, transcribed the whole of *Zhonggui Lu* into one of his books. A Qing woman writer in the 19th century, Zeng Yi, who was as well versed in medicine and poetry as in cookery, also chose the same title for her small cookery book of twenty recipes, although her recipes were her own.

The other book of interest is *Shanjia Gongqing* or *The Simple Offerings of a Mountain Hermit* by Lin Hong, a hermit who lived in Zhejiang province towards the end of the Song in the 13th century. Not a pure vegetarian, Lin nevertheless preferred vegetables to meat, and this is reflected in his book. Of the hundred or so dishes, most use only vegetables, fruit, flowers, fungi and bean curd. He was particularly fond of using regional vegetables, such as watershield, Chinese clover, bamboo shoots, and chrysanthemums. Whereas other people liked to use a small amount of meat to season bamboo shoots, Lin loathed this, insisting that bamboo shoots were fresh and sweet on their own and should never 'be friends' with meat. An enthusiastic proponent of medicinal herbs, he also aimed, with his recipes, to provide cures for illnesses.

Besides being acknowledged as the first person who used the modern term jiangyou for soy sauce, Lin Hong is also credited with being the first to write about a dish reminiscent of the now celebrated Peking Lamb Hot Pot, sometimes called Rinsed Lamb. In his recipe, he tells the story of making good by ingenuity a chance encounter. He was touring the Wuyi mountain with its numerous twists and turns in north Fujian province, *en route* to visit a friend, when it began to snow. In the storm that ensued, he caught a rabbit, which he took to his friend Shi, with a view to having it for dinner. As there wasn't a cook around to prepare it properly, Shi averred: 'In the mountain we usually cut the meat into very thin slivers, and we marinate them with wine, soy sauce and huajiao (fagara). We place a stove on the table, on top of which we place a saucepan with some water, which we wait to come to a fierce boil. At this point we give everybody a pair of chopsticks and let them pick up their own slices to submerge in the water to cook until they are done. Suiting their own taste, they will dip the morsels into different sauces. This, in sum, is what we do, which is not only easy and simple, but enhances the atmosphere of eating together.'

Five or six years later, Lin was visiting the capital Hangzhou and encountered a similar dish in a banquet given by an unpretentious scholar. Remembering his own experience in the mountain, he was impressed that his cultured host ate in such a similar, simple manner. Pork and lamb, he discovered, could be done in the same way, and he recommended the use of both of them in his recipe. What we use now, in what we consider a very sophisticated dish, is lamb, sliced very thin and cooked in a broth by ourselves around a table (see recipe p. 335).

Lin may have used the term 'simple offerings' in the title of his book, but many of his dishes are anything but simple, both in their preparation and their conception. Lin was fond of using his ingredients to project artistic and sensual images, and he liked to write poems or borrow classical allusions to enhance their significance. Two of his most outstanding recipes are fine examples of this. In Lotus Stuffed with Mandarin Fish, the tender lotus stems are cut off from the lotus flowers, and into the seed-cases are stuffed minced Mandarin fish fillets seasoned with wine, soy sauce and herbs. These are then steamed and the stuffing, enhanced with the subtle lotus fragrance, is savoured. Lin recounts in the recipe how, having been served such an exotic treat at a banquet given by his friend Li, he was inspired on the spot to write a poem which he presented to Li who, in return, was so delighted with the praise of the dish that he gave him an ink-slab and five ink-sticks as a gift. In the other recipe, Oranges Stuffed with Crabmeat, the 'image' of chrysanthemums and oranges is fused with the aroma of new wine, and the *Yijing* or *The Book of Changes* is alluded to in praise of the movement of crabs. Since the 1980s, the revival of Song dishes has become a vogue in Hangzhou, the capital of Southern Song (AD 1127–1279), and one particular restaurant, Bagualou, specialises in recreating dishes described by various Song writers. These two dishes of Lin's are part of its menu.

In 1279 Kublai Khan, grandson of Genghis Khan who a century previously had established the Mongols as the greatest power of Central Asia, put an end to the Southern Song and began the Yuan, the first foreign dynasty, which ruled China until 1368. The Mongols did not care about the myriad refined Chinese dishes developed in Hangzhou; instead, they persisted with their diet from the steppes. They ate boiled whole mutton, carved into pieces by the daggers they carried around their waists, washed down with either mare's milk or 'koumiss', an alcoholic drink made with fermented mare's milk.

Nevertheless, one food book written towards the end of the short dynasty is remarkable for both its content and influence. *Yinshan Zhengyao* or *The Principles of Correct Diet* was written in Chinese by Hoshoi (or Hu Sihui in Chinese) who was the Imperial physician and dietician from 1314 to 1321. There is next to nothing known of Hu's life, not even his nationality – some say that he was a Mongol, others that he was a Uighur, and still others that he was a Naiman. His book, which is based on ancient Chinese theories on medicine and herbs, is about food cure and nutrition, and refers to the Yin and Yang principles related to the cooling and heating elements in the viscera. Besides admonitions and advice for those who wish to nourish their lives, such as pregnant women and nursing mothers, he prescribes remedies which use every known ingredient from land and water. As such, his book is indispensable to anyone who wishes to research the specialised field of Chinese food cures. The general reader will find the woodcut illustrations both fascinating and humorous (see illustrations, pp. 30–3).

Rather surprisingly, one of the four leading landscape painters of the Yuan dynasty (AD 1279–1368), Ni Zan, has left a cookbook of considerable influence. As a painter, Ni's minimalist style, unique in its purity and spareness of brush strokes, has never been surpassed, despite the fact that many have tried to emulate him. Much has been written about his artistic *œuvre*, but few seem to wish to recognise the gourmet side of his nature, which is manifested in his book *Yunlin Tang Yinshi Zhidu Ji* or *The Food System of the Yunlin House*, Yunlin being the other name by which he was known.

Ni Zan (1301–74) was the heir of a wealthy landed family from Wuxi, a charming small town a stone's throw from Suzhou, the canal city of romantic rock gardens known to the West as the Venice of China. During his youth he led a life of leisure and luxury, growing up in the family estate where he became steeped in culture from the family library, which contained several thousand books, collections of ancient bronzes, scrolls of painting and calligraphy. Later, as a successful businessman, he multiplied the family fortune. But towards the end of the Yuan dynasty, he sold his properties and gave away his wealth. This was considered a most extraordinary thing to do, and it earned him derision rather than admiration from other people; but, undeterred, he took his family with him and lived as a near-hermit on a boat on the local lake, the Taihu, where he continued to paint the misty landscape of the lake and the hills until he died.

In the epilogue of his *Food System*, Ni declared, in line with the thinking of many

The beneficial and ill effects of food

philosophers of ancient time, that he regarded the desire for food and sex to be inherent in the nature of man, so that food must not be wanting in one's life. His book reflects the food of Wuxi and Suzhou, whose local fare, inclined to be rather sweet, is a force to be reckoned with in mainstream Shanghai regional cuisine. Since there are only fifty-odd recipes in his book, arranged haphazardly in terms of categories of main ingredients, one can safely surmise that these represent Ni's own favourite dishes, and those of the well-to-do people of the Yangzi delta. Like so many Chinese since the Song time, Ni had a predilection for pork but no stomach for lamb,

The various kinds of soup

so there are no recipes for the latter at all. Like the gourmand poet Su Dongpo, he was fond of using wine to braise pork slowly – very much a characteristic of Shanghai braised dishes today. But being an omnivore to boot, he questioned the wisdom of Su becoming a vegetarian near the end of his life, for Ni recalled that the ancient sages never prescribed vegetarianism as a way to nurture old age.

As aquatic food abounds in the area, it is not surprising to find fifteen recipes for it in Ni's book. What is remarkable was Ni's understanding of how each should be treated in the kitchen, which should be eaten raw and which cooked. The recipe for raw clams, which Ni lauds as excellent, could well be one served today by the Japanese or the Americans. Basically, after the clams in the shell have been washed

Food cures for various ailments

and opened, the juices inside are reserved. The clams, again cleansed of any impurities by warm water, are put into a bowl and a sauce, made from the reserved juices seasoned with shredded spring onions, peppercorns and wine, is poured over them. Ni also recommends serving scallops raw, which are first cut up into strips then seasoned with ground peppercorns, vinegar and a little salt and sugar. But to serve them warm, he advises rinsing them with wine, shredding and then cooking them in very hot wine. The method for cooking conch is very different. First you break the shell of the conch, take out the flesh but discard the juices inside. Just like peeling a pear, you then use a small knife to peel the conch into rounds, or simply cut it up into thin slices. These are then served after being very briefly cooked in chicken stock. He

Collecting exotic and rare delicacies

has two ways of serving snails, though both involve first marinating them for about an hour in lots of sugar, which is then rinsed off. One way is to cut them up into slices, marinate them in spring onions, ground peppercorns and wine for a short time, then poach them briefly in clear chicken stock. The other way is to eat them uncooked, having first marinated them in salt, wine and fennel for three to five days. He warns, however, that they mustn't be eaten raw in the summer.

As with pork, Ni liked to braise carp and other fish in equal portions of water and wine. Likewise, in one recipe he uses just wine to braise crabs, seasoning them with his favourite triumvirate of spring onions, pepper and salt. Freshwater crabs are the speciality of the region, and in the autumn they are studded with yellow roes which have such a distinguishing flavour that these days, in addition to the Chinese, people from other countries such as Japan, Taiwan and Korea flock to the Shanghai area just to eat the crabs. They are known as Shanghai crabs, and are prepared simply steamed or boiled. The method of cooking them as well as the ritual of eating them was laid down in one of Ni's recipes written more than six hundred years ago:

'Boil the crabs with fresh ginger, 'zisu' or purple perilla [*Perilla frutescens var crispa*], cassia bark and salt together. As soon as the water comes to a rolling boil, turn the crabs over, and when it returns to a fierce boil again, the crabs are ready to eat.

'For preparing crabs, the best way is to eat them as soon as they are done. Take one person as an example, cook only two at a time; when they are eaten, then cook some more. Serve them with a dipping sauce of orange peel and vinegar.'

By and large, the same procedures are followed when Chinese people sit around the table to eat hairy crabs every autumn, and they treasure the yellow roes as the Italians do white truffles. Some have been known to gorge half a dozen at a sitting.

One of Ni's sweet recipes, Stuffed Warm Lotus Roots, is the precursor of a famous Shanghai dish of a similar name today, even though it is hardly heard of outside of China. In Ni's recipe, a mixture of flour, honey and musk is poured from the thick end into the holes of a lotus root which, wrapped in greased paper, is boiled until cooked, then served in slices. In Shanghai restaurants today, glutinous rice mixed with a scattering of red dates is used as stuffing, filling the holes of the lotus root which, when steamed, is cut up into slices and served with a sugary syrup. Quite an unusual dish, but scrumptious.

Ni's greatest contribution, however, lies in his influence on Yuan Mei, the consummate 18th-century gourmet who has left an indelible mark on Chinese gastronomy. Yuan, who used to dismiss other fellow gourmets as not possessing discerning enough palates, was a fan of Ni Zan and his *Food System*, so much so in fact that he included Ni's one and only goose recipe in his own cookery book (*see* p. 287). Although it was entitled Yunlin's Goose, Yuan remarked that the same method could be used for a duck. Since Western ducks are similar to Chinese geese in size and texture, I have adapted Ni's recipe using a duck, and I can vouch that it is worth the considerable bother when you taste the end result (*see* recipe p. 287).

Born in 1716 in Hangzhou, to a rather poor but genteel family, Yuan Mei began his formal education at the age of six, and he immediately got into the habit of making notes of everything he learned. This was to stand him in good stead for the rest of his life. From the age of eleven he began to climb the ladder of examinations and eventually reached the top in 1739, when he passed the Palace Examination in Peking, becoming a Hanlin scholar. In the winter of the same year, he went back to Hangzhou and was married to a Miss Wang, to whom he had been betrothed since childhood. His official career, begun in 1743 as Prefect in a district near Nanjing (Nanking) and later in Nanjing, lasted for only five years before he sought sick leave, a customary prelude to retirement. As soon as he gave up his official residence, he bought a piece of land for three hundred ounces of silver. There he built his dream residence, Sui Yuan or Garden of Contentment which, when completed, consisted of some twenty-four pavilions joined by picturesque courtyards, and beautiful gardens with romantic bridges and cascading waterways.

In this idyllic setting he lived and worked for the rest of his life, writing poems and essays which, by his own admission, earned him much money. He tutored many pupils and, adopting what was considered a very avant-garde attitude, had many female pupils as well.

His other passion in life was food, which he regarded as being as sensual as it was poetic. As befitting a Mandarin of his station, he did not do any cooking himself, but instead kept a tight rein on the kitchen, telling his cooks what dishes he wanted to eat and how they should taste. His meticulousness was partially due to a sensitive stomach, the result of illness as a young man, but largely due to his conviction that he knew best. He controlled his kitchen on a strict but fair punishment-and-reward system, which he highly recommended to all those who were serious about enjoying good food at home. He was adamant in not putting up with any dishes that had not been well prepared even for one day, lest the standard spiralled downward the

Yuan Mei
(courtesy of Harold Wong)

following day. The right thing to do, he advised, would be not only to praise the cook at once for the fine dishes he had done, pointing out why they were delicious, but also to rebuke him for any sub-standard dishes, again pointing out the pitfalls so that he could improve on them. 'When the cook slackens and the consumer does not care enough,' he said, 'gastronomy will suffer greatly.' To him, searching for taste was just like searching for knowledge; both needed a curious mind, humility in learning and judicious judgment.

In his search for taste, he was frequently invited to the aristocratic and wealthy houses of his day, which vied with each other in showing off their cooks' talents. Applying his note-taking habit, cultivated as a fledgling student, he would jot down the dishes he liked, how they looked, how they tasted and how he surmised they were prepared. When he got home, he would regale his cook with the details and ask him to reproduce them. As double insurance, he would ask his friends to let his cook go to their houses and, 'observing the formality of being a disciple', be taught by their cooks the secrets of the respective dishes. The secrets his cook received and subsequently translated into delectable dishes Yuan again wrote down.

Some of these houses had in their employ women cooks who held their own. As Yuan did not disdain female pupils, he seemed more than happy to learn from female cooks. One who worked for a Ming house was an expert in making mooncakes decorated with floral pleats. From time to time, Yuan would send a sedan chair to bring her to his house and he would watch her make mooncakes. As she kneaded the larded dough one hundred times before adding the date stuffing and making the floral pleats with her fingers, he sat spellbound. Later, when he tasted the cake which melted in his mouth, he noted that the secret was all in the kneading.

At monasteries he learned many vegetarian dishes from the monks, some of whom were superb cooks. But his other main source of culinary information came from his own cooks, especially the talented Wang Xiaoyu (see also p. 18), who was in his employ for more than ten years until Wang died. He observed Wang closely in the kitchen and discussed every aspect of cookery with him, from ingredients to techniques and from food philosophy to practical details. After Wang's death, Yuan missed him so much that he even wrote a biographical essay about him, an unprecedented act of respect by a Mandarin for his cook.

Thus, in the course of some forty-five years, Yuan accumulated a repertoire of more than three hundred dishes. These, prefaced by his opinions and advice to cooks in two lists labelled 'the list of essential knowledge' and 'the list of taboos', he compiled into a cookery book called *Suiyuan Shidan* or *The Cookery Lists of Suiyuan*. It was published in 1792, five years before his death.

Unique in his approach and seriousness, in *Suiyuan Shidan* Yuan assumed the role of a culinary master, an arbiter of taste and a teacher giving a comprehensive cookery course, the like of which was unprecedented. No one before had mustered so much passion in writing about the activity of cooking, eating and entertaining. Likewise, no one before had been as didactic and opinionated, or as honest and direct in his criticism, or as open about his penchants and prejudices. His *Shidan* has remained the most influential Chinese cookbook and is regarded with great respect by both professional and home cooks, and not least by restaurants. It is also well known in Japan and in the West.

Yuan's advice to cooks, which covers the basics, as well as theories, techniques and ingredients, is still valid and continues to be quoted as rules either to be followed or, when considered out of date, used for reference. On cleanliness, Yuan says a cook must wash his hands and change his tea towel often, mustn't use the same knife to slice spring onions and bamboo shoots, and must take care not to let cigarette ash, sweat from the forehead and flies hovering over the stove fall on the dishes and contaminate them.

A successful cook, Yuan avers, must be aware of the natural inherent qualities of the ingredients, be they meat, fish or poultry. 'For an excellent banquet,' Yuan says, 'sixty per cent of the credit goes to the chef, and forty per cent to the buyer of ingredients.' Likewise, to harmonise the flavours of these ingredients, the quality of herbs and condiments used, including basics of salt, sugar, vinegar, sesame oil and wine, which are like fine garments and jewellery even a beautiful woman can hardly do without, must be of a superior quality.

Yuan is also particular about matching ingredients of similar likeness; thus the plain ones, the rich ones, the subtle ones and the robust ones must be paired together. Ingredients with strong and rich flavours, such as turtle, crab, shad fish, beef and lamb must be served on their own, well seasoned with the full range of condiments in order to bring out their best and mask their flaws. 'People in Nanjing love to mix sea cucumber and turtle, and match shark's fin with crab roe. I always frown upon this practice. For me, the flavours of turtle and crab roe, once imparted to sea cucumber and shark's fin, become too insipid, and yet the rank odour of the latter two are sufficiently strong to spoil the turtle and crab roe,' Yuan wrote.

With a respectful nod to the ancient theory of the five flavours (salty, sour, bitter, pungent and sweet), Yuan also sees an ordered sequence in serving dishes in a banquet. The salty dishes should precede the blander ones, the subtler ones should follow the rich ones, and the dishes without stock should be served before the dishes with stock. Since there are five flavours and saltiness cannot monopolise the realm of taste, when the guests are feeling full, revive their appetite with pungent and spicy dishes, and when they have drunk too much wine, serve sweet and sour dishes to revive their flagging desire for food.

If this is a moot point, his advice on never disdaining inexpensive ingredients is exemplary. He himself finds bean curd, by any account cheap, far more agreeable in taste than bird's nest. Nor does he think one should be impressed by the sheer number of dishes served at a banquet. To drive home this lesson, he tells the story of being invited to dinner by a *nouveau riche* merchant. There were no less than sixteen different sorts of dimsum and about thirty other dishes, and the host was smugly proud of the spread he had displayed. But Yuan, not finding the quality of the food up to his standard, went home hungry, and resorted to eating rice congee to fill his still empty stomach.

Unlike the Song gourmand and poet Su Dongpo (*see* p. 3), Yuan was not one who indulged in the cup. On the contrary, for, in Yuan's opinion, in as much as judging between true and false facts relies on a clear head, so does discerning between fine and foul tastes. A noisy and rowdy drinker, tipsy with alcohol, would find no difference in savouring fine dishes and in eating 'wood chips'. 'If you must drink,' he coaxes, 'it would be best if you tasted the dishes first at the banquet, after which you can show off your drinking prowess. That way, perhaps you can get the benefit of both.'

On the technique of cooking, what he observed from his cook Wang he wrote down for others to practise. The control of heat is paramount, he says. For stir-frying and sautéing, 'warrior-fierce' heat is required, lest the ingredients wither; for braising and simmering, gentle heat is necessary, lest the ingredients dry up; and for reducing liquid, fierce heat should be followed by gentle heat. If, for lack of patience, fierce heat is applied throughout, food can be burned outside but remain uncooked inside.

Since different ingredients require different degrees of heat in cooking them, Yuan, the purist, hated fire pots which these days bring so much fun and enjoyment to people at a do-it-yourself dinner when one and all dip the cut-up ingredients, be they meat, fish, seafood or vegetables, into a boiling pot of stock and cook them instantly.

Again, learning from the experience of Wang, he concluded that even a master cook can only produce but four or five dishes of top quality in one day. He, for one, believed in quality rather than quantity. When he had festivities at home, such as a wedding or a birthday feast, he used to bring in caterers, but would first train them so that they came up to his standards.

The recipes themselves are divided into chapters, or lists, which include the whole spectrum of ingredients; aquatic food, fish and shellfish, meat, poultry, vegetables, bean curd, noodles and cakes, rice and congee, to name but the main groups. Not that all the recipes are complete with quantities and methods; many of them consist of only one or two lines which, nevertheless, identify the ingredients and Yuan's interest in them. Perhaps the most unique feature of the book is that the sources of no less than one hundred recipes are named and traced to the houses or monasteries where he ate them or where he found them to be the most outstanding. Among the dozen or so recipes on bean curd, a food he was most fond of and found agreeable to his delicate stomach, nine are credited, and likewise nine recipes on duck out of eleven. In some of them, more than one source is given and Yuan delights in comparing the quality of the same dish served in two different houses. Restaurants and taverns, on the other hand, are conspicuously absent as a source of gastronomic inspiration. Yuan and his friends did not go to restaurants, which did not begin to sprout and blossom until the 19th century. As each of them had a kitchen manned by a super cook and his team, they took turns to entertain at home and got their cooks to learn from each other. Yuan was, however, a patron of delicatessens, for he gave credit to those which excelled in their products. Chez Xu's roast duck, for example, was so special that Yuan did not think it could be reproduced at home, and Chez Wang in Hangzhou, which prepared a Jinhua ham in honey and wine, also won his admiration.

If Yuan was quick to give credit where credit was due, neither did he mince words about the houses where the dishes served were, according to his own palate, below par. Not surprisingly, when credit was given, the dishes were named after the masters of the houses, while their cooks, with just one or two exceptions, are hardly mentioned. Even Yuan's own cook, Wang, whose talent and devotion won him a biographical essay from his master, never had a dish named after him. Such, however, was the prevailing ethos of the time, and it would be unfair for us to take Yuan to task and judge him from the perspective of today when chefs, quite rightly, get full credit for the food they create or cook.

The recipes reflect a broad geographical palate far beyond the Yangzi delta. Yuan speaks about tasting meat dumplings as well as a flavoured duck in Guangdong province, recommends the white fermented bean curd 'cheese' in Guangxi and Chinese celery cabbage (Chinese leaves) from the north as the best, and talks about a vegetable from as far away as Hubei. But the majority of the ingredients in the recipes are native to eastern China, and what Yuan has covered is remarkably comprehensive. They represent what the people, both the middle and upper classes, but not so much the peasants, ate in the 18th century, and they seem to be eating more or less the same things today.

As Yuan was an omnivore, his recipes include animal meat: beef, ox tongue, lamb, lamb's head, tail and tripe, deer, including the tendon and tail, roebuck, civet cat, pork and ham and other parts of the pig such as the head, stomach, lungs, kidney, trotter and tendon. There is no mention of dog's meat whatsoever. Poultry and fowl include chicken, duck, goose, pigeon, sparrow and quail and their eggs. Seafood consists of bird's nest, shark's fin, sea cucumber, abalone, mussel, scallop, oyster, snail, jelly fish and ink fish roe, although not ink fish itself. Freshwater fish are numerous, such as shad and bream and the silver fish from Tai Lake. Other aquatic ingredients are the eel, water turtle, prawn and shrimp, crab, clam and razor clam.

But Yuan was just as interested in vegetables and vegetarian food, as his recipes call for numerous vegetables, some of which are native only to eastern China. The common ones are Chinese celery cabbage, Shanghai cabbage, spinach, aubergine, winter melon, broad bean, water chestnut, kidney bean, bamboo shoots, bean sprouts, taro, radish and different fungi such as wood ears and mushroom. Some of the local ones are red-in-snow or a winter mustard which sprouts through the spring snow, 'lablab' beans, oil seed rape, water bamboo, lotus seeds and bracken.

Yuan's *Shidan* is not the genesis of what is now referred to as Shanghai or Eastern regional cuisine (*see also* p. 88), but in it Yuan has put on record what refined Eastern regional cooking, as represented by cities and towns such as Hangzhou, Nanjing, Zhenjiang, Suzhou, Yangzhou, was already like by the end of the 18th century. Being the purist and fastidious critic that he was, he set a high standard culled from the offerings of the best tables in the region. Even though he did not frequent restaurants, many of his recipes, taken up and adapted by restaurants established in the 19th and 20th centuries, have since gained wider fame through them. In one guise or another, prepared at home or eaten in restaurants, many of his recipes have endured.

In Iced Bean Curd (*see* recipe p. 222), Yuan instructs freezing bean curd cakes overnight, and mentions the resulting 'beehives' inside which change the texture of the bean curds. During his time, people had to put bean curd on a tiled roof in order to achieve this, but for us living in our freezer-convenient age, putting it in the freezer is the easiest thing. In another recipe, where he quotes the Hangzhou description of bean curd and spinach as 'white jade inlaid with gold' (*see* recipe p. 216), the romantic image has caught on in the menus of many restaurants. One easy way to serve aubergines is cold, seasoned with sesame oil and rice vinegar (*see* recipe p. 132). In Drunken Prawns, Yuan describes setting aflame prawns first inebriated in wine and then marinated in light soy sauce and rice vinegar. The novelty of this method, practised in restaurants in Hangzhou for some time, has become all the rage since the 1980s in up-market restaurants in Canton and Hong Kong. Yuan's Steamed Duck calls for a deboned duck stuffed with glutinous rice, ham, preserved vegetable, mushroom, spring onion and bamboo shoots and seasoned with wine, soy sauce and sesame oil. The modern dish, sometimes known as Eight-treasure Stuffed Duck and stuffed with similar ingredients, is an off-shoot of Yuan's Steamed Duck. Another famous Shanghai or eastern chicken dish is Deep-fried Eight Pieces, a title directly borrowed from Yuan. In Yuan's recipe, a chicken, cut into eight pieces, deep-fried in hot oil and well drained of grease, is then braised until just done in a cup of thin or light soy sauce and 'half a catty' (about 300 ml/10 fl oz/1¼ cups) of wine. No water is to be added while fierce heat is used, he adds. Although Yuan did not refer to it, this recipe could have been inspired by Mrs Wu's chicken (see p. 26).

Another equally famous dish, Pork Steamed in Lotus Leaves (*see* recipe p. 317), is based on Yuan's steamed pork, which he identifies as a well-known dish from Jiangxi province. His roast suckling pig matches the Cantonese suckling pig of today to a 'T', in the way it is roasted and what its ideal result should be. The suckling pig (3.5–4 kilos or 8–9 lb) is roasted on a large metal fork over charcoal, and the skin is brushed periodically with oil. Yuan affirms that the superior result is if the skin melts in the mouth, the next best is if it is crisp, but if the skin is tough, it is without doubt inferior. His honeyed ham, in which chunks of the best ham are cooked in honey and wine until very tender, is prepared today as a savoury dish with a considerable amount of crystal or rock sugar, sliced very thin and served with sweetened lotus seeds. Another rather novel Hangzhou dish, Stir-fried Chicken with Pear (*see* recipe p. 291) can be traced to Yuan's dish of the same name.

CHINESE FESTIVALS

IN 1912, the Republic of China officially adopted the Gregorian calendar used in the West, but the old lunar calendar, calculated more than four thousand years ago, has persisted, and it is according to this system that all the traditional Chinese festivals are celebrated to this day.

By the Chinese lunar calendar, there are twelve months to every year, some months having twenty-nine days and some thirty days. Every two or three years, there is an 'intercalary month', or the same month repeated successively. The last month and the first month, however, are never duplicated. Each month is numbered and is thus called 'the first moon', 'the second moon', etc. When a 'thirteenth' month occurs, it is called, for example, 'intercalary fifth moon', or 'intercalary ninth moon'. This system came about after Chinese astronomers established the relationship between the sun, the moon and the stars, and their effect on the change of seasons. They noticed that the cycle from new moon to new moon took about twenty-nine and a half days, and that twelve moon cycles made 354 days. But a true solar year, they were aware, took 365¼ days. They resolved the problem this caused most ingeniously by adding seven intercalary months every nineteen years, and in such a way that the winter solstice would always fall in the eleventh month, the summer solstice in the fifth, the spring equinox in the second, and the autumn equinox in the eighth.

Whereas the Gregorian calendar dates from the birth of Jesus, the Chinese date their lunar calendar from the time of the legendary 'Yellow Emperor'. In 2637 BC, the Emperor was supposed to have ordered his minister to start grouping the years together into cycles, each to span sixty years. Each year of this cycle was to be given a name regulated by the same combination of ten 'celestial stems' and twelve 'earthly branches'. From the start, twelve animals, all real except the mythical dragon, were assigned to correspond with the twelve earthly branches, in the following sequence: rat, ox, tiger, hare, dragon, snake, horse, sheep, monkey, rooster, dog, pig. Why these particular animals were chosen is not clear; what is important is that the animals mark the twelve signs of the Chinese Solar Zodiac, or the twelve constellations by which the position of the sun is fixed each month.

The study of the Chinese horoscope has become fashionable in recent years, and everyone is curious to know which animal year he or she was born in. The animal signs correspond to the Western calendar in this century as follows:

Animal signs		*Western calendar*
RAT	鼠	1900, 1912, 1924, 1936, 1948, 1960, 1972, 1984, 1996
OX	牛	1901, 1913, 1925, 1937, 1949, 1961, 1973, 1985, 1997
TIGER	虎	1902, 1914, 1926, 1938, 1950, 1962, 1974, 1986, 1998
HARE	兔	1903, 1915, 1927, 1939, 1951, 1963, 1975, 1987, 1999
DRAGON	龍	1904, 1916, 1928, 1940, 1952, 1964, 1976, 1988, 2000
SNAKE	蛇	1905, 1917, 1929, 1941, 1953, 1965, 1977, 1989, 2001
HORSE	馬	1906, 1918, 1930, 1942, 1954, 1966, 1978, 1990, 2002
SHEEP	羊	1907, 1919, 1931, 1943, 1955, 1967, 1979, 1991, 2003
MONKEY	猴	1908, 1920, 1932, 1944, 1956, 1968, 1980, 1992, 2004
ROOSTER	鷄	1909, 1921, 1933, 1945, 1957, 1969, 1981, 1993, 2005
DOG	犬	1910, 1922, 1934, 1946, 1958, 1970, 1982, 1994, 2006
PIG	豬	1911, 1923, 1935, 1947, 1959, 1971, 1983, 1995, 2007

Whichever animal year it may be, the annual festival celebrated throughout the country, albeit with regional diversity related to social customs and food, are the same. There are three major festivals celebrated for the living, and each has special foods to go with it. They are the Chinese New Year, the Double Fifth Festival and the Mid-Autumn Festival which, by custom, are also the three days in the year on which debts must be settled.

CHINESE
NEW YEAR

CHINESE NEW YEAR is celebrated on the first day of the first moon. Just as Christmas was not always celebrated on 25 December, in ancient times the date of the Chinese New Year varied, for every emperor regarded it as his royal prerogative to change the calendar upon accession to the throne. By royal command, astronomers were invited to make a new calculation which, nevertheless, had to correlate with the sowing of seeds and subsequent planting of crops by the farmers. The royal proclamation that followed was a major event, for on this new calendar depended the success of agriculture, and hence the well-being of the people which, in turn, would ensure that the emperor continued to have the mandate of heaven to rule the country. Ever since the reform of the lunar calendar in 104 BC, however, the Chinese New Year always occurs between 21 January and 19 February.

The New Year, officially called the Spring Festival in Communist China, is of primary importance to all Chinese, for it means the renewal of life, new beginning, new hope and new determination. For those who are Buddhist or Daoist, or who adhere to the ritual of ancestor-worship, the celebration begins with the sacrifice on the 23rd (in north China) or the 24th day (in south China) of the twelfth month of the year to Zao Wang, or the Kitchen God. Worshipped since the Han dynasty as the inventor of fire, and hence the giver of cooked food, he has also come to be regarded as the watchdog of family behaviour. His paper shrine in the kitchen often shows him either on his throne, with his wife beside him, or with his horse. Only sweet things,

The Kitchen God

such as sweetmeats and candied fruits, are placed as offerings in front of his image on that day, later to be eaten by the family. At the appointed hour, the head of the family, by custom a man, for women are considered unclean to perform this ceremony, first smears honey on his lips, then prays to Zao Wang to send a good report about the family to the Jade Emperor in Heaven. His image is then set on fire, accompanied by the setting off of fire-crackers. Just after the New Year, or even before, he will be given a new paper shrine, having been welcomed back to reign in the kitchen again.

For two weeks the Chinese New Year is celebrated everywhere, though different social and regional customs – most symbolising good luck, prosperity and longevity – add colour and variety to the festivities. None more so than the preparation and sharing of the special Chinese New Year foods, which are rich in symbolism of a very practical nature. The favourite symbolic food hinges on puns. The Chinese language is rich with words that have the same sound but convey totally different meanings, so that it has always been a national game to use puns to represent one's real desires. Chinese New Year pudding, served all over the country, is called 'nian gao' in Mandarin and 'nin go' in Cantonese: gao or go means pudding, but it also means high, tall, and growth. The pudding is thus eaten by children to express their desire to grow taller next year, and by adults to climb higher up the ladder of promotion and success, or to realise further growth in their business. Made with glutinous rice flour, it is sweetened with brown sugar and steamed for a long time until sticky and chewy (see recipe p. 342). In Shanghai, there is also a savoury kind of nian gao, made with sticks of processed rice flour. These are stir-fried and eaten as a noodle dish (see recipe p. 230).

In the south, another favourite punning dish is Braised Dried Oysters and Hair Moss, for the sound of the title, 'hosi fatchoi', can also echo 'robust market and riches galore' – surely every merchant's desire. The same sentiment hangs on everybody's lips in the Chinese New Year greeting, 'gunghei fatchai' (may you have riches galore). Among the fruits displayed in the south, a must is the Mandarin orange, or tangerine, again for the punning sound of 'gum', meaning both the fruit and gold! Pomegranate is another favourite fruit for both the north and the south, for the many seeds in the fruit represent the children in the family, already born or to be born.

Cookery activities gradually gather momentum during the latter half of the last month of the year, culminating in the Rounding the Year Off dinner on Chinese New Year's Eve. All the family members, including the elderly and young children, gather to have dinner together. Even for very well-to-do families, for whom going out to eat is a frequent occurrence, a restaurant is not the venue for this occasion; rather, the home is the place where everyone rounds off the year together, sharing the dishes and raising cups of tea or wine to look back on the year's achievements and to look forward to those to come. While there is no set formula for either the kind or number of dishes, pork and chicken will be among them. Wind-dried meat, such as sausage, belly pork or duck, dried by the bitter wind during the previous month (the twelfth month, known in China as the Bitter Moon), are also favoured, as are fish and seafood. In the north, a sweet dish, called Eight-treasure Rice, made with glutinous rice and a stuffing of such symbolic ingredients as lotus seeds, red dates and red bean paste, is eaten to signify family union.

After dinner, not even the young go to bed, but one and all stay up to welcome in the New Year. Those who are inspired by the muse may follow the example of the Tang poets, Du Fu and Bai Juyi, and write poems about the evening; others may hang on the door spring couplets written on red paper to invoke good fortune and prosperity for the family. Others may have gone earlier to the flower market, set up specially during that week, to purchase a branch or two of fortune-bearing peach blossoms, narcissus or peonies, or even a kumquat plant, betting on the wishful pun of 'kum' for gold. Often the womenfolk spend the evening in a last-minute rush preparing the food for New Year's Day, for there are many who hold to the superstitious belief that if they use a kitchen knife or chopper on New Year's Day, their luck will be cut off. Before long, the sound of fire-crackers, let off to drive away evil spirits and to welcome the dawn of the New Year, breaks the vigil and a new start has begun.

In the north, New Year's Day food is 'jiaozi', or dumplings made with wheat flour, stuffed with mostly vegetables, such as cabbage or chives with a small amount of pork, then boiled or, less frequently, steamed (*see* recipe p. 246). The underlying motivation for this tradition is family union and togetherness, for the execution of the dish involves much chopping and preparation of the stuffing beforehand, which is often done during the previous days, by the old and the young alike. As Chinese New Year food is never without symbolism, these dumplings are sometimes made into the shape of 'yuan bao', or the old silver ingots. Small silver coins are included in the stuffing, so that there is great excitement to see who will find one and thus enjoy wealth and prosperity in the coming year.

In the south, many families eat vegetarian food during the first day of the New Year, a custom rooted in Buddhism but one which has gained popularity throughout China, since many people would just as soon have a break from meat before the rounds of 'spring banquets' begin. Otherwise, a favourite New Year dish is 'chaji gaai' or deep-fried spring chicken, the skin of which is prepared in such a way that when deep-fried, it will turn brick red, beckoning luck throughout the year.

All over China, the New Year period is a time for visits, for paying respect to one's elders and renewing relationships. When visitors arrive, they will first be offered tea with an assortment of symbolic seedlings, such as watermelon seeds dyed red, crystallised lotus seeds and peanuts. They will then be treated to a sample of what the family have been preparing for the New Year, very often the sweet Chinese New Year pudding discussed earlier, in sautéed slices (*see* recipe p. 343). In south China, two other kinds of savoury 'go' often supplement the sweet one, as if to increase people's chances of prosperity, and they are the Taro Pudding and the White Radish Pudding, both of which are served sautéed (*see* recipes p. 153 and p. 151). When visiting, people may take similar foodstuffs as token gifts or, in keeping with the old custom, may send live poultry, such as a couple of cackling chickens! Behind the giving or offering of food lies the deep-rooted sense of respect the Chinese hold for their elders, and the belief that one should share good fortune with friends (though at times it can also involve a certain amount of showing off). Another universal custom, observed by married couples, is that of putting a small amount of money into red packets and handing them out to children. The giving will rebound on the givers, bringing them prosperity.

The seventh day of the New Year is the birthday of mankind. Although in the

north it is customary to eat red beans on that day, purportedly for health reasons, elsewhere people just have a few good dishes, which usually include a chicken.

Traditionally, the New Year draws to a close with the Lantern Festival on the fifteenth day, or the first full moon of the year. Starting from the evening of the thirteenth day and continuing until the evening of the eighteenth day, every family hangs out a decorative lantern on its door, together with some evergreen branches to reflect the illumination of the moon and to invite prosperity and longevity. Originally a religious festival dating back to the Han dynasty, it has long since lost all its religious significance, becoming instead, since

A pacing-horse lantern

Song times, the occasion when lovers used to have their secret trysts. The early Song poet, Ouyang Xiu, immortalised this in his poem:

Last year at the Lantern Festival
Lanterns in the flower market were lit like daylight
The moon climbed above the tip of the willow tree
Two lovers kept a tryst after twilight

This year at the Lantern Festival
The moon and the lantern lit as before
I did not see my beloved of last year
The sleeves of my spring robe were moistened by my tears

The food associated with this festival is a dumpling which used to be called 'Yuan-xiao', or Lantern Festival dumpling, but which is now commonly known as 'tang-yuan', or round dumpling (*see* recipe p. 346). Made with glutinous rice flour with a filling of sweet sesame seed paste or red bean paste or just sugar, the stickiness, the sweetness and the roundness of the food are symbolic of togetherness. Easy to make, the dumplings are eaten whenever they take people's fancy, as well as during the festival.

Besides the special home-made Chinese New Year foods and dishes, there are the spring banquets which usually take place in a restaurant. This custom, still very much in favour amongst the business community, both in China and abroad, became popular during the last century. With the rapid development of trade between China and the West, and also within China itself, it became customary for any 'hong' or trading company that had made a profit during the previous year to hold a banquet in a restaurant during the first month of the New Year, usually after the seventh day, if only because many restaurants themselves were closed before then and the hong itself was also on holiday. The bigger the profit a hong had made, the more sumptuous the banquet would be. I remember with nostalgia those banquets given year after year by my father, at which braised shark's fin, bird's nest soup and braised dried abalone, all considered essential, were paired with suckling pig and turtle soup. Dried oyster and hair moss – to attract vigorous trading and prosperity for his hong during the coming year – were also always served. With the current escalating prices of what the Chinese collectively call 'the dried flavours of the sea', bird's nest soup and dried abalone have, for most banquets, become dishes of the past. Instead, abalone from a tin is used, and shark's fin comes in a soup rather than braised. Also, banquets now include ingredients that have become available due to modern means of transport, such as lobster and soft-shell crabs.

Whatever the changes to the menu, however, the symbolic number of eight dishes remains sacred. For more than two millennia, eight has been a number of paramount importance to the Chinese, its significance rooted in philosophical and religious beliefs. The 'bagua' or Eight Diagrams in the ancient Yijing (*I Ching*) or *Book of Changes*, used for divination and fortune-telling, is eight-sided, containing eight groups of continuous and broken lines, the former emblematic of the yang or

The Taiji (Tai Chi)

The Eight Immortals crossing the sea

male principle and the latter of the yin or female principle, which together constitute the Taiji (Tai Chi) or The Ultimate. For Chinese Buddhists, there are the Eight Symbols and Eight Treasures, and for the Daoists, the Eight Immortals. Many people, especially the southern Chinese, even if they are unaware of the broader significance, have nevertheless latched on to the fact that the sound 'baat' (eight) is very similar to 'faat' (prosperous), and hence have eight dishes for a banquet. Still, the number can be juggled around and interpreted according to the size of one's wallet. In north China, and along the eastern coastal provinces where a range of small cold dishes precede the main dishes, only the eight main dishes, also called 'eight large bowls', count. In south China, they include in the total the couple of 'small hots', usually stir-fried dishes, that are served as starters. As long as the number eight can somehow be worked into the banquet, it will bring luck and prosperity, not to mention the immediate sensual pleasure to the palate, to all present.

In both the north and the south, the sequence of the main dishes traditionally ends with a fish. As it comes to the table, a simultaneous murmur can be heard in cadence: 'You yu' in Mandarin or 'yau yue' in Cantonese. The sound, not surprisingly, carries the double meaning of 'to have fish' and 'to have more or surplus'. In the pun, the fish becomes the agent signalling the holding of another banquet in due course.

A friend of mine, John Naylor, has very kindly given me a copy of the menu of a banquet given by Pu Yi, the last Emperor of the Chinese dynasty, the Qing, in 1927 in honour of his former tutor, R. F. Johnstone, who had returned to China for a visit. Among the honoured guests were John's father, the Reverend Arthur T. A. Naylor, who was chaplain to the British Army at the time. The Reverend Naylor not only kept the menu but, as a memento, also asked the Emperor's three Chinese guests, prominent men of letters as well as influential political figures at that time, to sign their names, which appear at the extreme left of the menu.

The dinner itself was very much a spring banquet, for it took place on the evening of Saturday, 12 February which, by the Chinese lunar calendar, was the eleventh day of the first moon just after the New Year. Although prepared by the Imperial cook, the banquet was held in a Manchu restaurant in Tianjin (Tientsin), and the menu in Chinese (see illustration), which should be read vertically from right to left, vividly reflects what I have discussed before. For your interest, I have translated it into English:

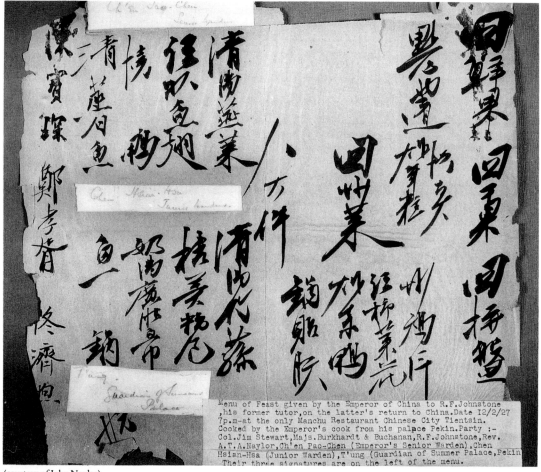

Menu of Feast given by the Emperor of China to R.F.Johnstone
,his former tutor,on the latter's return to China.Date 12/2/27
7p.m-at the only Manchu Restaurant Chinese City Tientsin.
Cooked by the Emperor's cook from his palace Pekin.Party :-
Col.Jim Stewart,Majs.Burkhardt & Buchanan,R.F.Johnstone,Rev.
A.T.A.Naylor,Ch'en Pao-Chen (Emperor's Senior Warden),Chen
Hsian-Hsa (Junior Warden),T'ung (Guardian of Summer Palace,Pekin
Their three signatures are on the left of the menu.

(courtesy of John Naylor)

FOUR FRESH FRUITS, FOUR DRIED FRUITS, FOUR MIXED APPETISERS

TWO DIMSUM:

Siumai

Stir-fried niangao (Chinese New Year pudding)

FOUR STIR-FRIED DISHES:

Stir-fried chicken slivers

Tomato and cai hua (oil seed rape)

Stir-fried vegetarian duck

Guotie kidney

EIGHT LARGE DISHES:

Clear soup with bird's nest

Red-braised shark's fin
Roast duck
Clear-steamed white fish
Clear soup with bamboo fungus
Steamed buns with mandarin orange stuffing
Fish maw in milk stock
Fish fire-pot

Not only is the magic number eight featured in the main dishes, but the pre-liminary dishes also add up to two sets of eight. The four fresh seasonal fruits and four dried fruits would already have been adorning the table when the guests arrived, as would probably the four cold appetisers, which comprised such things as shredded edible jelly fish, shrimps and fragrant mushrooms. The seasonal fruits would be taken away, however, to be served at the end of the banquet.

Serious eating would have begun with the two dimsum, one of which, not surprisingly, was stir-fried Chinese New Year pudding. This would have been followed by four, rather than two, small hot dishes, the customary number for a banquet of this calibre. As for the main eight dishes, bird's nest and shark's fin would have been *de rigueur*, the roast duck was most likely Peking duck (*see* p. 279), the white fish a fish which comes from the largest river traversing the northeastern region of China, the Songhua (Songari) River. The exotic bamboo fungus and fish maw would have been in tune with the other ingredients and the fish fire-pot fulfilled the symbolic pun of having surplus and signalling more for the future. But one may well wonder why out of the eight dishes, at least three, if not four – including the fish fire-pot – were soups or of a soupy nature. The answer is that there is a tradition that the more elaborate and expensive a banquet, the more exotic soups will be included, because soup often takes on the role of being a tonic as well. If the sweet dish, the steamed buns, seems out of place amidst the other savoury courses, it only confirms that it is not traditional for a Chinese banquet to end with a dessert. In this instance, it was another symbolic dish, for mandarin oranges, with their golden colour, beckon luck and riches.

Underneath the Chinese characters of the last dish, the fish fire-pot, the price of the banquet is noted as twenty dollars, by no means a trifling sum. If translated into today's value, given the current exorbitant price of bird's nest and shark's fin, this feast could easily have cost the Emperor more than one thousand pounds sterling or one thousand eight hundred dollars.

THE DOUBLE FIFTH FESTIVAL
(DUANWU JIE)

THE DOUBLE FIFTH FESTIVAL, also known as the Dragon Boat Festival, falls on the fifth day of the fifth month. It is the next major festival observed throughout the country and is celebrated with a special food made from glutinous rice, called 'Zongzi' in Mandarin or 'chung' in Cantonese, which people both eat themselves and send as presents to relatives and friends. A chung is basically a rice parcel made with white glutinous rice wrapped in bamboo leaves (or lotus leaves) into a triangular shape and then tied together. What accompanies the rice depends on the region and can be anything from roast or seasoned pork, beans and chestnuts, to preserved duck egg yolks, etc.

The origin of this festival is lost in a web of myth, but it is strongly connected

Dragon boats racing

with agriculture. It occurs during the summer solstice, which from time immemorial has been celebrated all over the world. For the Chinese, the growth of the crops has reached a turning point, and heavy rain, due from the last week of the fifth month, is needed to ensure that they ripen. In order to placate the Dragon (the controller of waterways and dispenser of rain) and to induce him to bring heavy rain, an offering of rice is made to him. From this has originated the racing of 'dragon boats', a custom still very much alive in southern China where rivers abound. A 19th-century Sinologist, De Groot, ventured a romantic theory that the boat races represent fighting

Dragon gods

dragons in the heavens: the fierce fighting is bound to be followed by heavy down-pours. In the 20th century, the boat race in Hong Kong is always a remarkable scene, with one boat proudly dubbed 'fan kuei' or foreign devils (a term which, in the 19th century, caused diplomatic uproar between the Chinese and the West). This boat is rowed by Europeans racing against another rowed by Chinese. The ensuing race, fought with fervour yet good humour, may or may not bring downpours, but it engenders a rapport and understanding between the two peoples that is greater, perhaps, even than food, which is usually the best ambassador.

Chinese folk tradition, however, traces the origin of the festival to the Warring States period (475–221 BC) and claims that it commemorates the death by suicide in 277 BC of the poet Qu Yuan, who is revered for his exemplary loyalty and stirring poetry. His king, the Duke of Chu, repeatedly failed to heed his counsel and was lured into enemy land where he eventually died in exile. The heir who succeeded was also too weak to save the country from further decay, or to use Qu Yuan's services judiciously. In utter despair, Qu Yuan roamed the country for twenty years, then jumped into the Miluo River, which flows into the Dongting Lake in modern Hunan province, but not before he had written his farewell poem, 'Li Su', to vent his anxieties. The people mourned his death greatly. As they could not recover his body, they came up with an idea of how they could preserve it. Thus, they wrapped rice with leaves into triangular parcels (zongzi or chung) which they cooked and took on to their boats. As they rowed on the river, they dropped the chung into the water so that the fish, in chasing after the parcels, would leave Qu Yuan's body intact.

Others pooh-pooh this belief, and quote the literary reference in *Qimin Yaoshu* (*see also* p. 21) written by the agricultural writer, Jia Sixie, in the 6th century AD. Without any reference to Qu Yuan, Jia mentions the custom of eating chung on the fifth day of the fifth month and on the day of the summer solstice. The wrapping of rice with artemisia leaves, he avers, reflects the fact that both the yin and the yang element are still enveloped together, without being dispersed. When yin and yang are in harmony, it can only augur well.

MID-AUTUMN FESTIVAL
(ZHONGQIU JIE)

SECOND ONLY in importance to the Chinese New Year, this festival is celebrated annually on the fifteenth day of the eighth month. It is the time when all the harvests, both in the south where there are two crops of rice annually, and in the north where wheat, millet and 'gaoliang' or sorgham are grown, are all in, and everyone can rejoice and relax. It is also the time when the moon is at her fullest and most brilliant, and, as the Chinese say, perfectly round.

According to the Chinese yin-yang principle of the dual forces which regulate the universe, yang is male, and personified by the sun, the source of heat, light and energy; yin is female, submissive, dark and cold, and is personified by the moon, the source of ocean tides, rain and cloud. As the sun's consort, she is the feminine deity by night, to be honoured and worshipped.

Other peoples in the world besides the Chinese have their myths about the animal inhabitants on the moon. The Chinese version of the three-legged toad and the jade hare who inhabit the moon is derived from Indian Buddhism. The story that has emerged is the tale of the Lady of the Moon, Heng O (sometimes called Chang O) and her husband, Hou Yi, who ultimately represent yin and yang.

Heng O, a lady of peerless beauty, and her husband, a skilled archer, lived during the time of the legendary virtuous Emperor Yao, about 2000 BC. Hou Yi, having built a multi-coloured jade palace for the Goddess of the Western Heaven who lived with immortals, was rewarded by her with a pill of immortality. As there were strict dietary instructions before he could take the pill, Hou Yi hid it under a rafter in his thatched roof before going off to perform some urgent military duties. At home, Heng O was surprised to see a beaming white light from the roof, which was accompanied by a perfumed smell wafting through the air. She discovered the pill and swallowed it. Immediately, she felt as light as a feather and her body began to levitate. Just then, Hou Yi returned and, realising the treachery committed by his wife, pursued her at once, bow in hand, ready to shoot her down. But Heng O broke through the window and flew skyward towards the moon. Undaunted, her husband chased her across the sky – his skill obviously went far beyond archery! Alas, his

Heng O flies to the moon

pursuit was thwarted by the forces of the wind, and she was getting further and further from the danger of his arrows. As soon as Heng O reached the moon, she coughed, being breathless, and the outer coating of the pill was spat out, which was immediately transformed into a hare. She herself also underwent a metamorphosis, becoming a three-legged toad. Ever since then she has lived on the moon while her husband, having built himself a palace in the sun, lives there. After their reconciliation, he comes to visit her once a month, on the fifteenth when the moon is full and the Moon Lady shines dazzlingly. Together, they rule nature as yin and yang.

The Goddess of Western Heaven (Xi Wang Mu)

As the moon is the female deity, it is fitting that she is worshipped by women at the Mid-Autumn Festival. An old Chinese proverb, in fact, forbids men to bow to the moon, enjoining: 'Men do not worship the moon; women do not sacrifice to the Kitchen God.' The only exception to this rule is the emperor himself who, as the celestial brother of the moon, can do as he pleases. As women make their bows, they also pray to the moon to arrange a good marriage for them, for the moon is also regarded as the marriage broker.

More poetically, the festival is highlighted by the viewing of the moon. Indeed, way back about 100 BC, Emperor Wudi of the Han dynasty built elaborate terraces where musicians and maiden dancers enhanced the festivities while he and his officials toasted the moon with wine. With this ancient example to follow, the celebration can span three evenings, beginning with the fourteenth, to 'welcome the moon', continuing on the fifteenth, to 'view the moon', and ending on the sixteenth, to 'bid farewell to the moon'. The venue can be the idyllic garden, the courtyard, or just the verandah in a modern high-rise building.

Whether it is for worshipping, viewing, or using the moon as the muse for writing poetry, the special fruits set on the table must be round, such as peaches, apples and melons. Families and friends get together for a dinner of whatever dishes take their fancy, but the special food for the festival is mooncake. A pyramid of thirteen mooncakes piled up on a plate, for thirteen moons represent the complete year with the intercalary month, bestows full happiness.

To symbolise the roundness of the moon, a mooncake is round. It is made with a golden-brown casing of wheat flour and a filling sweetened with sugar and enriched with lard. In the north, the filling is often made with just a brown date paste or a red bean paste. But along the Yangzi River, and in the south, the filling is essentially of lotus seed paste, embedded in which are preserved duck egg yolks, which represent the moon itself. Sometimes this is augmented by ham, watermelon seeds and other sweetmeats, so it is little wonder the mooncake can be cloyingly rich, and often not to the liking of a Westerner's palate. But if you stick to the lotus-paste-and-egg-yolk kind and are prepared for the intriguing flavour which results from the amalgam of the mildly savoury egg yolk and the sweet lotus paste you are in for a treat. It is the more scrumptious, I find, if the Fujianese Tieguanyin (Tit Koon Yam) or Iron Goddess of Mercy tea, made very strong, is sipped with it.

Mooncakes are no longer made at home; they are purchased at bakers and in restaurants. But when the Chinese send each other boxes of mooncakes, usually four packaged in one box, the popular tale of mooncake patriotism is never far from their minds, told and retold, especially by women.

In the 14th century, when mooncakes were still made at home, they turned out to be a secret weapon used cunningly by women to start a revolution against their hated foreign rulers, the Mongols. In order to police the Chinese population, there was one Mongol stationed at every Chinese household, interfering with family life and the general movements of the men. The women were especially resentful, finding the policy oppressive. But there was little they could do until they hit upon the brilliant idea of hiding paper strips with secret messages inside mooncakes as a means of organising revolts. This they did, year after year, during the Mid-Autumn Festival, when sending mooncakes to neighbours, friends and families was so traditional and universal a custom that even the security-minded Mongols never suspected what was really going on on the kneading board. The fact that the Mongols never took to the taste of mooncakes only made the task easier for the women. Eventually, the time was ripe for the all-out revolt, designated to be at midnight, when the illumination of the harvest moon reached its zenith, and this message was passed on in the usual way inside the mooncakes. The popular revolt that ensued ushered in the dawn of the Ming dynasty in 1368.

This account may not accord with the official history of the Ming, but mooncake patriotism, attributed to Chinese women rather than men, has never lost its mystique. The tale will always be a part of folk tradition in China.

TEA

CHINESE tea from Fujian was first shipped to Europe in the early 17th century by the Dutch East India Company, which used Amoy as the shipping port. By the 18th century, it had become an important beverage in the West. Most European words for tea derive from the Chinese; in the Amoy dialect, tea is pronounced 'tay'. From 'tay' has derived the English word 'tea', the French 'thé', the German 'tee', the Spanish 'te', and the Swedish 'te'. Similarly, tea in Hindi as well as in Russian is 'chai', while in Portugese it is 'cha', all of which derive from the Mandarin pronunciation of 'cha'.

It comes as no surprise, therefore, to learn that it is generally accepted that the Chinese were the first people to discover tea trees, and the fact that their leaves could be used to make an infusion. The discovery is attributed to the legendary Shen Nong, or Emperor of Agriculture, who lived during the 27th century BC. Having experimented with the tasting of hundreds of herbs (and been poisoned by some), he allegedly came across one which, though slightly bitter, possessed a medicinal property that cured his upset stomach. If this is myth, certainly by the 1st century BC (Han dynasty), people in Sichuan province were already infusing tea leaves in hot water to make a drink for themselves, and they were writing contracts of sale for them. The Chinese character for tea, cha, also dates from that time.

From Sichuan, tea drinking gradually spread to the neighbouring provinces of Yunnan, Gansu and Hunan, then to the eastern provinces and to the north. By the 7th century AD, or the Tang dynasty, tea drinking had become a cult at court, and in monasteries, where monks found that it kept their minds alert and uplifted their spirit. But the person who made it nationally popular was Lu Yu and, as a result, his name has, ever since, been synonymous with Chinese tea. He is honoured as 'the ancestor of tea', 'the sage of tea', and worshipped by people in the tea trade.

Lu Yu lived in the 8th century AD, although his exact date of birth is unknown, as is his parentage. It is thought that a Zen Buddhist monk, Zhi Ji, found him abandoned as an infant near a lake and rescued him. As it was out of the question for a monk to bring up a new baby in the monastery, he asked a patron of his, a Mr Li, whose wife had recently given birth to a daughter, to give a home to this child, whom he named Lu Yu. And so it came to pass that Lu Yu grew up with Miss Li until, aged eight or nine, he was returned to Zhi Ji when Mr Li left the area to take up a government post elsewhere. As Lu was now old enough to become Zhi Ji's acolyte, the monk taught him how to chant sutras and how to brew tea for his master, thereby unwittingly planting the seed for what became a lifelong passion. Later, Lu became very interested in writing and reciting poetry, much more so than chanting sutras. The neglect of his religious duties incurred the wrath of Zhi Ji who, in meting out punishment, assigned him menial tasks. Eventually, at the age of thirteen, Lu ran away and joined a theatrical troupe. A year later, fortune smiled on him, for he re-met Mr Li, who by then had returned as Prefect of the area. Li became his patron, and Lu was put under the tutelage of a famous scholar, with whom he studied for seven years. Thereafter, encouraged by the Prefect, he travelled widely in the provinces of Zhejiang, Jiangsu and Jiangxi, where tea trees abounded, and he learned much about their growth and the processing of tea leaves.

Miss Li, who had become a petite and elegant lady, well versed in playing the lute and in writing poetry, was, unusually for her times, still unmarried. Lu, with the blessing of Li, planned to marry her, but the An Lushan rebellion, which lasted for two years from 755 to 757, intervened, and the two sweethearts became separated. From 760 Lu lived as a near recluse in a county in Zhejiang and concentrated on writing. *Cha Jing* or *The Treatise on Tea* is his masterpiece. He never married and died in 804.

Only eight thousand words in length, Lu Yu's *Cha Jing* is the earliest book, not just in China but in the world, on the subject of tea. During the succeeding dynasties of Song and Ming, many other works on tea were written, some much longer and more detailed, but none ever surpassed it.

Lu Yu divides *Cha Jing* into ten sections. The first eight deal with the origin of tea, the tools used for picking it, how tea leaves are processed, the utensils and techniques for brewing, the different customs of drinking tea, the regions where tea is grown, and where tea appears in ancient historical records. Section nine discusses which utensils can be omitted. The last section, in which Lu Yu reveals his sense of self-importance, advises tea enthusiasts to copy out his treatise on four to six silk scrolls and then to hang them up for quick and ready reference at all times.

'For making tea,' he writes, 'mountain spring water is superior, river water is middling, but well water is inferior.' He would not have thought much of the chlorine-filled water from the tap that we city dwellers have to put up with when making tea today! On the temperature of the water, he is fastidious: 'When the water comes to the boil with fish-eye ripples and emits a light, murmuring sound, it is the first boiling. When the water surges up like round beats along the sides of the pot, it becomes the second boiling. When the water rolls up like waves, it is the third boiling. After this, if the water continues to boil, it is over the hill and no longer fit for making tea.'

Lu Yu's everlasting contribution lies in the fact that he made tea drinking into a cult in China – natural, informal and accessible to everyone. By the time of the Song dynasty, in the middle of the 10th century, the cult had taken root and was evolving at two levels. At the spiritual level, it was espoused by monasteries, where monks practised the art of making tea, regarding it as the outflowing of nature. Poets and writers drank it as an alternative source of inspiration to wine and as a means of communication through which they spouted poetry and fine prose. On the practical level, tea was being made at home as a daily beverage, and the custom of serving it to guests started at that time. In fact, tea had become so popular that there were tea caterers who would sell tea from door to door and, if booked ahead of time for festivals or private parties of either a celebratory or mournful nature, they would come to the house and serve it.

The tea plant (*Camellia sinensis*) is a small evergreen tree, usually no more than one and one-third metres (four feet) tall, with toothed shiny leaves and white flowers. It abounds in China, growing in no less than eighteen of the twenty-six provinces, but the most famous producing regions are in Fujian, Anhui, Zhejiang and Yunnan. The tea plants are the same, but it is the plucking and then processing of the leaves after they are plucked that differentiates one type of tea from another. When plucking tea leaves by hand, the best are considered to be the tender sprouts with one leaf, or at most two leaves, one on each side. For Dragon Well green tea, what are known as 'the sparrows' tongues' or the sprouts with no leaf are the *crème de la crème* that fetch the top price. After plucking, the processing consists of rolling, drying and firing, a very complex art which produces Chinese teas with scores of different names.

Yet there are only three kinds of Chinese tea: the unfermented, the fermented and the semi-fermented. More commonly referred to by colour, the unfermented is called green tea and the fermented red (black in English) tea. Green tea is made from tea leaves which, after they have been picked, are steamed and then dried by firing. True to its name, green tea looks greenish in the cup and carries a pure and refreshing aroma. The most aristocratic green tea, as well as the most expensive, is Longjing or Dragon Well, which is produced in small quantities near Hangzhou in Zhejiang. Among the different grades of Longjing, the best is labelled with the prefix 'before the rain', meaning that the leaves were plucked before the rains in the spring. Connoisseurs drink it for breakfast, loving it both for its delicate aroma, which rises ever so gently to the nostrils, and the pure and subtle taste which puts the mind in an alert yet tranquil state. Red tea is made from tea leaves which are left to ferment first before they are rolled and dried by firing. The tea looks amber red in the cup and tastes robust. The most popular red tea in the West, especially among the English, keenest of European tea drinkers, is Qimen from Anhui province, which is better known by its anglicised name Keemun.

Among the Chinese, however, Pu'er tea from Yunnan province with its dark russet colour, strong earthy taste and, above all, its medicinal properties to help indigestion, upset stomachs and lung congestion, is both the most valued and the most popular. It is regarded as a very good beverage to drink with dimsum, and is drunk after lunch and dinner. Pu'er tea is often pressed into a brick form, although it is also sold as loose tea leaves. Unlike other teas, the longer Pu'er tea is kept, the smoother the cup of tea it makes. My father used to deal in tea in his hong or trading company, and he left his children some Pu'er tea bricks which are at least a hundred years old. The tea made from these leaves is so silkenly smooth and soothing that whenever I serve it to family and friends, we can't help but roll it around our tongues before swallowing it.

The semi-fermented tea, not referred to by colour but known as Oolong, exudes a subtle fragrance. It is produced mostly in Fujian province and Taiwan, and is treasured by Chinese devotees. In Taiwan, Dongding Oolong from the mountain of the same name is the most sought after and Baozhong or Paper Wrapped, so called because formerly the tea was packed in odourless paper before firing, comes second. In Fujian, numerous types of Oolong teas come from the Wuyi mountain range, and topping the list is Tieguanyin or Iron Goddess of Mercy tea, especially that from Anxi county, which the Chinese consider on a par with the Dragon Well tea from

Hangzhou. The tea leaves, which are blackish green and edged with a brownish tinge, require longer steeping in water to bring out their full aroma. The Fujianese and people from Chaozhou are mad about Iron Goddess tea and they love to have it so strong that the tea appears jet black in the cup and tastes utterly bitter to the uninitiated. The tea is poured from a small clay teapot into tiny cups, and one picks up the cup and sips it slowly, savouring the initial shock of the bitter tannin that rolls down the throat, only to be replaced by the lingering and sweet aftertaste that is ineffably satisfying. This is the ideal of tea, as described by Lu Yu in his book.

Other Oolong teas have similarly poetic names, such as Shuixian or Narcissus, Da Hongpao or Great Red Robe, Xiao Hongpao or Small Red Robe, Shoumei or Old Man's Eyebrows and Baijiquan or White Cockscomb, to name but a few. Each of them has its own distinctive, albeit subtle, fragrance, which only an experienced tea connoisseur can readily identify. As teenagers, we used to giggle whenever Father laid on one of his tea-tasting sessions. The lidded tea cups containing different tea leaves were lined up, boiling water poured into them, then, after the appropriate minutes of brewing, Father would first of all sniff the bouquet, then imbibe a mouthful of tea from each cup, roll it noisily round his tongue before spitting it out into the awaiting spittoon. When I attended my first wine tasting some years ago, the scenes flashed back in my mind.

Lapsang Souchong from Wuyi mountain, much better known by its anglicised name than the Chinese Lishan Xiaozhong or Small Leaf from Li Hill, is a tea smoked slowly over wood. It is a great favourite of Westerners, but is seldom, if ever, drunk by the Chinese themselves. There are also scented teas, or teas of both the green and the red or black types scented with a variety of flowers, such as roses, cassia, jasmine and lotus. Jasmine tea, green tea scented with jasmine petals, is a favourite of the Shanghaiese and is ubiquitous in Chinese restaurants outside China. Litchi tea, a red tea scented with the fragrance of the fruit, is quite popular with the Chinese. Flowers on their own are not used to make tea, or more precisely, an infusion for drinking, save for a sweet variety of white chrysanthemums from Hangzhou, which are dried for the express purpose of infusing them in boiling water to make tea in the normal way. When Chrysanthemum tea is poured into cups, sugar may be added to individual taste, and it is drunk for its cooling effect to dispel the summer heat or to neutralise the internal yang or heating element caused by rich food. A trend which has emerged during the last decade or so is to infuse the dried chrysanthemums with the dark Pu'er; the resultant tea, which needs no sugar, is a pleasant drink believed to have a beneficial effect on one's health.

Indeed, tea is much appreciated by the Chinese for the medicinal qualities attributed to it. Drunk early in the morning, it stimulates the mind, clears the throat, brings up harmful phlegm, facilitates the flow of urine and helps to cleanse the bowels. Drunk after a meal, it assists digestion and prevents indigestion caused by grease or overeating. Drunk after excess imbibing of alcohol, it makes one alert again and nullifies the harmful effects of alcohol. Drunk in the summer heat, it revives the languorous spirit; drunk when the winter wind is blowing, it warms the viscera. It is also good for the circulation of the blood, keeps one's complexion fresh, eases aches and pains in the joints and counteracts tiredness. In other words, tea is considered a general panacea for all ills except insomnia. And, above all, it is thirst-quenching.

And so the Chinese drink tea all day long, in the morning, after every meal and on every social occasion. Serving tea when guests arrive, which originated in Song times, has become a time-honoured custom throughout China. When a guest comes to the house, regardless of the time of the day, he or she is offered a cup of tea straight away. Often, the tea is not freshly brewed, but comes out of a teapot kept warmed inside a padded tea cosy. If the tea has become too strong in the pot, hot water may be added to it. In any event, tea is drunk straight, with no sugar, or milk, added to it. The only exception to this way of drinking tea is the brewing of gongfu tea, an art which can possibly be traced back to the monks of the Song monasteries, but which is now upheld by the Fujianese and the Taiwanese. Two years ago, when visiting Taiwan, a painter made gongfu tea for us, and I gained some insight into how it should be done. Strictly speaking, it requires a special tea set and water heating stove, as well as special fuel, but the emphasis is nevertheless on how to make the best infusion rather than on the ritual, unlike the Japanese tea ceremony.

The two written characters may be the same, but gongfu tea has no connection with martial arts; rather, the characters convey the meaning of requiring skill and demanding labour and patience to brew this tea. Put very simply, after your guests have arrived, you first of all empty the ceramic teapot (the best are made of clay from Yixing in Jiangsu province) in which tea from the previous infusion remains on purpose, because the more tea the clay pot absorbs, the better the quality of the freshly made tea. You then heat the water and, remembering Lu Yu's words, when it hisses with fish-eye ripples on the surface and before it boils over roaringly, it is ready. Pour a little water into the teapot to rinse it, warming it at the same time. Then put in the tea leaves, the ones from Wuyi mountain being the best, pour in some more of the water and add the lid for a few moments. You should then pour out and discard this initial lot of water, for it is only meant to wash the tea leaves, and, at the same time, to open them up somewhat. Next pour in boiling water, add the lid and continue to pour water over the pot so as to increase the temperature inside it. Let the tea leaves steep for more than five minutes, during which time you may pour hot water over the pot again. Now have the cups ready on the table, ideally no more than four, and when you pour the tea, do it in a rotary fashion rather than finish pouring into one cup before pouring into the next. The idea is to ensure an even quality of tea in each cup. The guests themselves must lift the tea cups and 'sniff the fragrance' first before sipping the tea, slowly savouring the taste and aftertaste rather than gulping it down. After finishing the first infusion, make a second infusion. This is considered just as good, but the third infusion is hardly worth talking about.

There is also the long tradition of the public teahouse, which began as early as the Tang dynasty as a place for relaxation and leisure. By the time of the Song, when life was lived to the hilt, teahouses in Hangzhou were favourite haunts for men who, more often than not, went there for more than just the refreshing tea. Even modest teahouses would be decorated with seasonal flowers and hanging scrolls by famous painters, with the view to adding visual delight to the pleasure of sipping tea. Many different varieties of tea, including cooling medicinal teas for the summer, were served, as were exotic soups and even wine, such as black bean soup for the winter and foaming iced plum blossom wine to counter the summer heat. Some teahouses catered specially for cultivated young men from wealthy families, and served as venues where they could learn instruments or vocal music and share their enthusiasms with kindred spirits. Though the distinction between them was sometimes unclear, these were different from the 'floral teahouses', where prostitutes were stationed on the upper floor and were thus places of ill-repute, not suitable for gentlemen. A select few were where the literati and people in high office met and, over a cup of tea, entered into political and philosophical discussions. But not all teahouses catered for the upper classes; some were places where labourers, craftsmen, theatrical troupes and the like could seek rest and rejuvenation after a day's work or tiring journey.

This tradition continued throughout the Ming and Qing dynasties until the 20th century, and, with the passing of time, public teahouses became places where people met, not just to share refreshing tea, but for all sorts of other activities. In Peking, operatic singing, drum playing and various theatrical performances used to take place in teahouses, and people thronged to them, paying a few pence for the entertainment. In Suzhou, the city famed for its maze of canals and picturesque gardens, story-telling became a special feature of the teahouses. Men and women, young and old, went to them in the evenings to listen to the classic romances, some of which they already knew by heart. By all accounts, it was a mesmerising experience. After the Communists took over China in 1949, however, the teahouse culture went into decline and many simply disappeared. But since the 1980s, there have been some signs of a revival. To my regret, when I went to Suzhou in 1988, I missed going to the teahouse for a story-telling session. But, when I was in Shanghai in 1985 and 1989, I went to the teahouse in the famous Yu Gardens. There, after paying a few pence each for our tickets, we joined the many old men, and a sprinkling of young people of both sexes, sitting on wooden or bamboo stools. We were brought a pot of jasmine tea and tea cups. The men on their own read the newspaper, coughed intermittently and sipped tea after every coughing. Those in twos either played Chinese chess or just talked. A waiter carrying a huge kettle with a long spout came by from time to time and filled the pots which had had their lids replaced (an indication that they were empty). It is customary for the refilling of hot water to continue for as long as a person chooses to while away his time there, even though the infusion gets weaker and weaker with each refilling.

In the south, notably in Canton and Hong Kong, teahouse culture developed in a different way. With the rise of both places as bustling trading ports in the 19th century, teahouses became emporium-type restaurants where dimsum or savoury hot titbits, some steamed, some deep-fried and some sautéed, were served with tea from early morning to lunchtime, but never in the evening, when the menu changed over to rice and main dishes. Men went there at the crack of dawn and, over 'a pot of tea and two dimsum', as the saying goes, would discuss business right then and there. So as not to interrupt the flow of discussion, one man would lightly tap the table with two bended fingers, the index and the middle, to indicate politely to the person sitting opposite him that he wished to have more tea. This gesture, known colloquially as 'kowtow' or knocking of the head on the floor, has survived in restaurants where you can see men, and sometimes even women, tapping their fingers away. Dimsum have now become all the rage and increasingly appear in many restaurants abroad as well.

While business discussion over tea is mundane, a serious contractual relationship between two families in the form of marriage was signified by the offering and accepting of tea. When plans for marriage were mooted and close to agreement, the man's parents would send over to the maiden's parents a present of tea, and if the maiden's parents accepted the tea, it was a clear sign that they had consented to the union and would not change their minds. This old custom, known as 'the rite of offering and accepting tea', continues to be observed throughout China today, if only nominally, and gave rise to the saying 'a maiden does not accept tea from two families'. The rationale behind the custom is explained by the Ming writer, Xu Cishu. 'In growing tea trees,' he wrote, 'they cannot be grafted. Rather, they must be planted by seedling. In ancient times, it was a marriage custom to give tea as a present, thereby symbolising the growth by seedling without transplanting.'

At the level of the relationship between mother-in-law and daughter-in-law, the offering of tea is also steeped in symbolism. In many parts of China, especially in the south, it is customary for a bride to offer to her mother-in-law, with both hands, a cup of tea sweetened with a couple of crystallised lotus seeds and honey as a gesture of affection and obedience, if not also a wish – implied by the symbolic lotus seeds – to bear her grandsons. As the old lady sips the tea, she will return her affection in kind, more often than not in the form of sparkling jewellery!

Besides being a daily beverage, tea is also occasionally used in Chinese cooking. Tea Eggs, a Shanghai dish, uses tea and soy sauce to colour and flavour eggs through the cracked shells. Sichuan Smoked Duck (see recipe p. 286) originally called for camphor wood as a smoking agent, but because camphor wood is not now so easily available, a very satisfactory substitute is tea leaves. The most exotic dish using tea, however, has to be the Hangzhou one called Stir-fried Shrimps with Dragon Well Tea. The subtle tannin from these green leaves impart a special flavour to the fresh-water shrimps, so that it is a dish best appreciated in springtime in Hangzhou.

REGIONAL DIVERSITIES

ASK any non-Chinese what the term 'Chinese cuisine' conjures up in their minds and the answer will often be some combination of the following: rice, noodles, spring rolls, pork, prawns, unusual vegetables, well-seasoned bits and pieces that aren't always readily identifiable, all of which are eaten with chopsticks. Most people will also mention stir-frying, the wok, and perhaps steaming. Oversimplified as this answer may be, it does reflect the fact that geographically vast as China is, spanning several regions of diverse climates and produce, many common factors course through them to give a unity to what is known as Chinese cuisine.

All over China, the basic concept of a meal is the same. It consists of grain food – ideally boiled or steamed rice, which is called 'fan' in both Mandarin and Cantonese – accompanied by a few dishes made up of different ingredients, called generically 'cai' in Mandarin and 'sung' in Cantonese. Rice is served individually in bowls, whereas other dishes are placed on the table, to be shared communally. The number of dishes often reflects the financial standing of the family, or whether it is a special occasion. For an everyday meal, four dishes and a soup are the norm for a family of six to eight people. Elders, when teaching good manners to young children, have traditionally urged them to eat a lot of rice, but not to take too much from the dishes. A good host, on the other hand, will always serve guests the choicest bits from the dishes and a greater amount than they take for themselves. When it is a special dinner or a banquet, however, rice will not be served until the very end, after everything else, served in sequence rather than all together, has been enjoyed.

For the Chinese, knives belong only to the kitchen, and chopsticks are used both to pick up the morsels of cai or sung from the dishes on the table and to shovel rice into the mouth. Like the wok, chopsticks have, in recent years, become part and parcel of many Western kitchens. Although the Western adoption of them is recent, their origin dates possibly as far back as the end of the Shang dynasty and the beginning of the Zhou, or some three thousand years ago. It is generally agreed among Chinese historians that by the Han dynasty (206 BC–AD 220), chopsticks were in popular use all over China. Some early chopsticks were made of bronze, for the use of the rich and noble, but bamboo and wooden chopsticks were commonly used among ordinary people. The Chinese name for chopsticks, 'kuaizi', however, is more recent, and only dates from the Ming dynasty (1368–1644). Written with a slight difference, but pronounced the same way, kuaizi can also mean 'to bear a son very soon'. It is therefore customary for a bride and groom to be given two pairs of chopsticks, tied together with lucky red threads.

Chopsticks are generally about 20–25 cm (8–10 inches) long and have a square top end which tapers to the round end used for picking up food. Nowadays most are made of bamboo or wood. Many used to be made of ivory, but these, especially in restaurants, have long since been replaced by plastic ones. Silver chopsticks were used at the Imperial table as a means of safeguarding against poison being put into the food, as it was believed that silver would turn black if it came into contact with arsenic. But as they are heavy and slippery, and hence not conducive to picking up small morsels, they are seldom, if ever, made now. Lacquer chopsticks on the other hand, which first became fashionable in Han times, together with other lacquerware such as bowls and trays, are often used at home.

Compared to a Western table setting, the Chinese setting is much simpler, consisting of no more than one pair of chopsticks and a three-piece porcelain set: a spoon for soup, a bowl for rice and a base saucer for spitting out fish bones and the like. Chinese table manners are also very relaxed and informal, as the emphasis is on the enjoyment of the food itself rather than on the ritual of eating. For an everyday meal at home or in a restaurant, diners pick from different dishes whatever morsels take their fancy at a given moment, without having to conform to a set pattern of finishing one dish before embarking on another. The fun is in the random picking, and in alternating from one dish to another throughout the meal. Everybody picks with ease at the same time, either from the same dish or from a different dish, and because of their consideration for one another, the likelihood of chopsticks clashing with each other is minimal. While it is considered polite to pick some choice bits from a dish for those sitting near you, it is not customary to pick up the whole dish and offer it to them. Each picking of cai, however, should be accompanied by one shovelful of rice into the mouth. From childhood, Chinese are taught to pick up the bowl with the left hand, put its rim between their lips and shovel the rice with chopsticks held in the right hand, into the mouth. The rationale behind this is that rice, which is symbolic of blessings in life, must be received in abundance. It is therefore bad manners to eat rice by picking up a few grains at a time.

Chinese usually eat together at a round table, which is most conducive to the sharing of dishes placed in the centre of the table. The concept of a round table is rather modern, however, with less than two hundred years of history. Back in the Han times, as depicted on wall murals in archaeological sites, men used to sit on the floor, and they were served by women who brought in the food. Dining on stools and tables, albeit ones as low as modern Western coffee tables, began during the Tang dynasty, from the 7th to the end of the 9th century. By the time of the Northern Song, second half of the 10th to the early part of the 12th century, the format had graduated to dining on chairs around square or rectangular tables, which were about the same height as today's tables. This continued throughout the Yuan and Ming dynasties, when men sometimes sat alone at different tables at dinner parties (see woodcut illustration, p. 77). The transition to round tables seems to have come about only in the 19th century. These tables were small, however, seating between four and six. The large tables we see today in restaurants are often misleading. The so-called round table seating ten to twelve people is, in fact, a large board on top of a smaller table. As for the 'lazy Susan' on top, it was originally American rather than Chinese. This brilliant revolving gadget is ideal for Chinese meals since it allows access to all the dishes on the table. Little wonder the Chinese have adopted it as their own.

The main cookery methods used are by and large the same throughout the different regions in China. Put succinctly, they consist of blanching, simmering, boiling, roasting in the oven, pot-roasting, braising, assembling, flavour-potting, smoking, sautéing, deep-frying, steaming and stir-frying. The last two techniques, which are uniquely Chinese, have, in recent decades, exerted unprecedented influence on the world's other major cuisines.

The steamer is one of the oldest Chinese cookery utensils and its origin can be traced back to the New Stone Age when it was made of pottery. Called a 'xian', it consisted of a base with three breast-shaped hollow legs called 'li', and a vessel on top with a slotted flat bottom called a 'zeng'. Sat over a fire, water was boiled or rice cooked in the li, and the steam that rose up through the perforated bottom of the zeng cooked the food resting in there. By the time of the Shang dynasty (16–11th century BC), bronze cookery utensils of all sorts, including the steamer, were being used in the kitchens of the rich and the noble. The celebrated bronze steamer of the second half of the Shang dynasty, called Lady Hao's Three Joint Xian because it was part of her burial artifacts, was excavated in 1976 and is now in a museum in Peking. This sophisticated xian was constructed in such a way that three zeng were joined together on a long zeng stand. Once invented, this ingenious method of harnessing the energy

Illustration from the novel
The Tale of the Pair of Fishes
(Shuang Yu Ji)

from steam to cook food in the steamer has been in constant use ever since. The modern steamer, consisting of a base container for boiling water and one or more slotted bamboo baskets or perforated metal containers on top, is fundamentally the same as the ancient xian with its li and zeng. The Chinese idea that food cooked by steaming retains a more succulent texture has caught on, and many European chefs are steaming away, using bamboo baskets. (*See also* p. 355 for application of the technique.)

Illustration from the drama
A Thousand Ounces of Gold
(Qian Jin Ji)

The wok, made of cast iron or carbon iron, is the indispensable cookery utensil used in every corner of China. Compared to the steamer, it has a rather recent history. Cast iron pots, called 'fu', and also cast iron pans, called 'guo' (the Mandarin pronunciation of wok), which had oval bottoms and an open and wide rim with two handles, were first made during the Han dynasty (206 BC–AD 220). The thinness of the metal allowed for fast transmission of heat, and the curvy shape facilitated quick turning and tossing of ingredients. But it was also its capability to withstand more intense heat than bronze that made the iron wok the logical utensil in the development of stir-frying, or 'chao' in Chinese. Although no one knows exactly when this cookery method started to take root in China, the first stir-fry recipe is attributed to the agriculturist writer, Jia Sixie, who lived during the 6th century AD (*see* p. 21). By the Song dynasty (AD 960–1279), stir-fried dishes were mentioned by contemporary writers who depicted the food scene in the capital, Hangzhou, while the mending of the guo or wok as a service rendered by some shops was also noted. When Yuan Mei wrote his *Cookery Lists* in the 18th century, stir-fried dishes had obviously become very popular for, out of Yuan's three hundred plus recipes, more than fifty are stir-fried dishes.

Due to the rapid growth of Chinese restaurants abroad from the second half of the 19th century, word gradually spread outside China about the efficacy of stir-frying. Vegetables stir-fried speedily and briefly in a wok remain crisp and crunchy (and retain their vitamins); meat and fish are tender and juicy, while a special 'wok fragrance' permeates all the cut-up morsels, making one's mouth water. In recent decades, the art has invaded both Western homes and restaurants, and chefs and laymen alike have learned to wield a wok and stir-fry dishes as the Chinese do.

This intensified interest in Chinese food has also brought an awareness that not all Chinese food from different areas of China is the same in terms of taste, appearance and ingredients. Indeed, although they share many characteristics, there are marked differences between one regional cuisine and another. The main reasons for this are the differences in climate and soil with their resultant agricultural produce, the proximity or distance from the sea and their effect on the yield of aquatic foods, differing historical developments and, last but not least, the customs and lores of a region.

Be that as it may, there have never been any hard and fast rules about the way to classify the regional cuisines. Some Chinese like to talk in the broadest terms of a northern cuisine and southern cuisine, using the Yangzi River or Chang Jiang as the dividing line. This thinking is not without historical support: for several hundred years the saying 'south of the river' has meant the country south of the Yangzi River, where it is 'a land of fish and rice', the copiousness of which is envied by the north. Others refer to eight distinctive regional cuisines, which not only correspond to the eight provinces, but also reflect the Chinese belief in the magical nature of the figure of eight. These eight cuisines are Shandong, Sichuan, Guangdong, Fujian, Jiangsu, Zhejiang, Hunan and Anhui. Still others prefer to carve up China geographically into four gastronomic areas – northern, southern, eastern and western – corresponding to the pivotal urban centres of Peking, Canton, and Shanghai and the province of Sichuan. This more recent classification, which is the one I shall use, does not, in fact, conflict with the eight-cuisine school of thought, for Shandong represents Peking cuisine; Jiangsu and Zhejiang – and to a lesser degree Anhui – are part of Shanghai cuisine; Guangdong and Fujian together make up Cantonese cuisine; and Sichuan and Hunan are natural allies, if only because of their indulgence in the use of chilli peppers.

PEKING
OR NORTHERN CUISINE

NORTHERN CUISINE, better known as Peking cuisine, embraces the distinctive styles of cooking in the provinces of Shandong, Shanxi, Henan, Hebei and Inner Mongolia. Culturally and racially it includes Mongolian, Muslim, Manchurian and Chinese influences. Peking first became important as a capital as far back as the Warring States period (475–221 BC) and it later returned to prominence in the 13th century when Kublai Khan made it the capital of the Yuan dynasty. It remained the capital during the Ming dynasty (AD 1368–1644) and the following Qing dynasty, when China was under the rule of the Manchus. The Republic of China briefly made Nanjing the capital in 1911, but the People's Republic of China reinstated Peking (Beijing) when they formed the government in 1949. With such a long history as the capital of China, it is no surprise that it mirrors the kaleidoscopic richness of several cuisines, whether in the street, at home or in the restaurant.

Rice is considered the ideal staple but remains a treat for many people. Millet, soy bean, corn and gaoliang (sorghum) are all grown in the north, and feature in the diet, along with sweet potato and potato. The main staple, however, is wheat, and wheat flour products make up many forms of food, the most common being 'mantou' or steamed bread (*see* recipe p. 239) and noodles. For many people, the everyday dishes that go with the grain food are, compared with the other main regional cuisines, coarse and robust and on the salty side.

Peking street food stalls and hawkers supply substantial snacks, such as steamed buns, plain or stuffed with meat, baked sesame cakes, Oily Spring Onion Cakes (*see* recipe p. 250), deep-fried bean curd triangles or squares, and roasted sweet potatoes, which are more popular in the winter. For breakfast, they serve the freshly made, warm soybean milk, which is naturally sweet, to go with 'youtiao', the deep-fried, twin-strip dough that is mildly savoury, and not unlike an elongated doughnut, only more crispy to the bite and soft inside. Unless you are an early riser, you run the risk of them having been sold out before you get to the street corners where they are sold.

Youtiao are arguably the most sought after and adored breakfast street food sold in China, though it is only in the north that they are twinned with soybean milk. In the south they are eaten with thin rice congee and are called oil-fried devils, after the hated Qin Hui who engineered the death of a national hero, Yue Fei, during the Southern Song dynasty (AD 1127–1279). Yue Fei, Emperor Gaozong's loyal and prescient military general, was leading an army against the encroaching forces of the Jin in the northeast of China. But the prime minister, Qin Hui, who advocated appeasement of the enemy, won the royal approval to dispatch in one day no less than twelve Imperial edicts written on golden tablets to recall Yue Fei, just at the time when the tide had turned against the Jin. Yue Fei had no choice but to obey and return to the capital. As soon as he reached Hangzhou, Qin Hui had him clapped in gaol where, after being tortured and maltreated, he died, only thirty-nine years old. The people were outraged, even though they dared not openly vent their indignation against the prime minister. Instead, they came up with the idea of selling a street food which they contemptuously dubbed 'oil-fried devils'. Each consisted of two well-kneaded dough strips joined in the centre, representing Qin Hui and his wife, and was deep-fried in a big wok before being torn apart and gobbled up by the people. As youngsters in Hong Kong, the story made us eager to take even bigger bites of the delicious strips. Oh, how I hanker after them as I write.

For home cooking, the most celebrated northern food has to be jiaozi, or dumplings (*see* recipe p. 246). Made of wheat flour dough skin or wrappers, they are stuffed most commonly with vegetables and minced pork, then boiled or steamed. They are a meal on their own, and are always eaten during Chinese New Year, when the whole family gather together both to make and eat them, while at the same time reinforcing family reunion and social contact. It has often been said that they are the best peacemakers for, in the rolling of the skins followed by the stuffing of them and then the cooking, the ice is bound to be broken and peace made between feuding parties in the family. But because they are so delicious, they are also prepared whenever an excuse can be found to make them. As they are not very large, men often boast of being able to eat dozens of them, simply dipped in the famous Shanxi vinegar from the neighbouring province of the same name and soy sauce, spiced with hot oil to taste.

When people cook their daily fare, especially when they are in a hurry, they quickly stir-fry meat or vegetables and then splash some soy sauce and a measure of Shanxi vinegar into the wok before scooping everything on to a serving dish. This has given rise to the impression that all Peking food is flavoured with soy sauce and vinegar, even such simple things as poached eggs. More refined Peking dishes, however, call for some more specific techniques.

One is the use of lightly beaten egg white mixed with a small amount of cornflour to envelope, ever so lightly, the chopped ingredients, especially pork, chicken or fish, with the result that when stir-fried, they look pleasingly whitish (*see* recipe p. 316).

Another is a technique involving both sautéing and braising, called 'guotie'. Fairly large pieces of ingredients – by Chinese standards at least – such as bean curd or prawns are covered with a thin layer of flour, then dipped into beaten egg before being fried in oil. The fried pieces are then braised in a well-seasoned stock until the sauce is absorbed (*see* recipe p. 220).

The most famous restaurant dish, however, is, without a shadow of a doubt, Peking Duck (*see* recipe p. 279), made with ducks raised in the farms surrounding Peking. These beautiful ducks, with snow-white feathers, have rounded breasts and thin skin, underneath which is a layer of fat that keeps the flesh tender and succulent when being roasted. A description of a fat duck being roasted on a stand appeared during the Ming dynasty (AD 1368–1644), penned by the writer Song Xu, who lived with his family in Peking and whose mother was an excellent cook. It was during the Ming dynasty that duck farming near Peking became a fledgling business. Each year Ming emperors had tons and tons of rice shipped to Peking from the south through the Grand Canal, and a certain amount of it fell into the water and became the fodder for ducks. The ducks that fed on rice seemed to gain weight easily, and had fattened and rounded breasts. Having noticed this phenomenon, duck farmers worked to improve the quality of their ducks. Finally, with force-feeding, they succeeded in producing the fattened ducks that are most suitable for roasting.

The famous Peking duck has a more recent origin, however. It dates from the 19th century, when a Mr Yang came from the country to Peking and set up a small stall in Qianmen selling chickens and fattened ducks. After working there for more than twenty years, he was able, in 1864, to buy a small shop. Having consulted a guru on 'fengshui' or geomancy, which is a Chinese belief maintaining that the configurations of a house (or a tomb) influence the prospects of the people who live in it, he decided to make the shop into a small restaurant, which he called Quanjude (the amalgam of virtues). He employed Shandong cooks who, by tradition, had always been known for their cookery skills. It is believed that they learned the secret of roasting ducks from the chefs in the Imperial kitchen, many of whom were natives of Shandong, and they applied this method of roasting to Mr Yang's fattened ducks. The ducks that came out of the specially constructed oven had crisp russet red skins which, when carved into small pieces and wrapped in pancakes, dissolved in the mouth. Gradually, word of this astonishingly delicious, succulent duck spread to Western diplomats at the foreign embassies in Peking. So impressed were the Americans with this dish that, in the 1870s, they actually shipped duck eggs to the States in order to breed the same strand. Ever since then, the reputation of Peking duck has been assured.

Besides duck, there are numerous other local products that are special to northern China. In the mountainous Yanshan district east of Peking, chestnuts have grown in profusion for two thousand years. Often known as Liangxiang chestnuts, because of the place from where they are distributed to the rest of China, their high sugar content and glutinous texture distinguish them from other chestnuts. In the autumn, when they are harvested, street stalls and hawkers sell piping hot chestnuts to passers-by, and not only in Peking but all the way down to the south of China, in

Canton and Hong Kong, and across to Japan and Korea. Known as sugared, sand-fried chestnuts, they are actually fried in sand mixed with sugar and fruit in a huge wok over a stove until they are thoroughly cooked.

Even more copiously grown near Peking and in northern China is the white Chinese cabbage (*Brassica rapa var pekinensis*). Increasingly popular in the West and now grown outside of China, in Israel and in the Napa Valley in California, for instance, it is also known by such names as Chinese leaves or Chinese celery cabbage. It is the mainstay vegetable for northern Chinese throughout the winter and, as refrigeration is not universal, it is often seen piled up in little mountains along the pavements in Peking. It can be stir-fried, put in soups and braised. Braising chestnuts and white cabbage together is a dish combining the two famous products (*see* recipe p. 202).

Sometimes the white cabbage is cut up and preserved in salt, garlic and spices, then packed in earthen jars and sold as Tianjin preserved vegetables. They add flavour to other ingredients, and are used throughout the country.

It has often been said that Peking cuisine is a misnomer, that it is in fact rooted in Shandong cuisine. Shandong province has been associated with gastronomy since the time of Confucius (551–479 BC), who was a native of Qufu county. I have explained how his eating habits – 'He did not eat food that had not been properly cut up, nor did he eat unless the proper sauce was available' – formed the basis of Chinese culinary tradition (*see* p. 5). I have also described how Jia Sixie in his work *Qimin Yaoshu* reflected the high level of Shandong cuisine as long ago as the 6th century AD (*see* p. 21). As the cuisine blossomed throughout the Ming and Qing dynasties, chefs were recruited from Shandong to man the Imperial kitchens and restaurants, leaving an indelible impact on Peking cuisine as a whole. In Peking today, more than half of the restaurants are Shandong restaurants.

As the east of Shandong is a peninsula surrounded by Bohai (Gulf of Chihli) to the north and the Yellow Sea to the south, seafood features to a large extent in the cuisine there. In the spring, large prawns, swimming in pairs, come up from the Yellow Sea toward the Bohai, and these become the famous twin prawns of Shandong which, with the benefit of refrigeration and freezing, are sold both in the south of China and abroad (*see* recipe p. 144). Fresh scallops are dried to become the famed and expensive ingredient, dried scallops, used all over China, and fresh abalones are steamed on a half shell. But more novel are sea cucumbers. For local taste, the best are the finger-sized, dried sea cucumbers which, after being reconstituted and braised, are assembled with prawn roes and leeks. Even more novel is a soup made of the roes of ink fish. After the membranes of the roes have been removed, the thin coin-like pieces inside are elaborately separated, soaked in salt water to remove the rank odour, then cooked in the best chicken stock. Both of these are considered to be very tempting dishes in Shandong restaurants in Peking. A few years ago, I had the good fortune of meeting Mr Wang Yijun, the head chef of one of the classic Shandong restaurants, Fengze Yuan, in Peking and he cooked for me these two delicacies. Every time I recall the flavours, I wish I could take the next plane to Peking.

The capital of Shandong, Jinan, in the western interior, is renowned for its soup dishes, which use either clear stock or a special creamy 'milk' stock (*see* recipe p. 362) as the soup base. Clear stock was talked about by Jia in *Qimin Yaoshu* and is also used elsewhere in China, but creamy stock is special to the north. If shark's fin soup with creamy stock is too elaborate and too expensive to make, Silver Ear Fungus with 'Milk' Stock is easily within reach (*see* recipe p. 160).

Offal is another great favourite, not just as peasant food, but as a very sophisticated restaurant dish. Pig's stomach, liver and intestines and duck gizzard are regular fare. Lowly as these ingredients may seem to be, Shandong chefs spare no effort when cooking them, using herbs and spices to make them into tasty dishes. One of the most famous is called Nine-turned Large Pig's Intestine. Another, using a certain part of pig's tripe and duck gizzards, both cut into floral patterns, is a particular northern Chinese favourite, though not so valued by other people.

Of more universal appeal are Shandong noodles, known as knife-scraped noodles. Every tavern or restaurant makes its own noodle sheets, which are scraped into coarse strips using a knife, hence their name. In addition to the regular long shape, they also come in shapes with graphic names such as cat's ears or floating fish.

Dried cellophane or glass noodles, vermicelli, made from mung beans and hence rich in protein, have found their way into every regional cuisine, not to mention Thai and other Southeast Asian cuisines as well. Wiry and snow-white in colour, they come in bunches neatly tied with red ribbons. Because they are distributed from the town of Longkou, they have earned the name Longkou fensi. When soaked in water, they will become pliable again with a slippery texture.

Shandong also produces a beer, called Tsingtao, which was the first Chinese beer and remains the only one with a worldwide reputation. It owes its origin to the

Clockwise from top right: Fried Shrimps (p. 125), Spicy Cucumber (p. 135),
Dry-braised Fragrant Mushrooms (p. 134), Spicy Peanuts (p. 133),
Drunken Chicken Breasts (p. 126).

PLATE I

Top: Stir-fried Scallops with Mange-tout (p. 148).
Bottom: Sautéed Jumbo Prawns (p. 144).

PLATE 2

Germans who, in 1898, were granted by the Qing court a lease of the bay in the southern peninsula of Shandong. There they built a modern port, Qingdao (Tsingtao), where, in 1903, a German company, taking advantage of the excellent water from the streams of the Lao Shan mountain to the north, started producing an eponymous beer. Since the 1950s, it has been exported not only to Hong Kong and Southeast Asia but also to Europe and America. Pale amber in colour, Tsingtao beer is flavourful without being bitter and has, in recent years, gained international recognition, ranking with other top beers. It goes especially well with sautéed and deep-fried dimsum, and pleasant, fiery, spicy Sichuan dishes.

The other mainstream northern or Peking cuisine is Muslim cooking, enjoyed by Chinese Muslims who, since the 13th century, have lived in Shandong, Shanxi, Shaanxi, Henan and Hebei. For both the Chinese Muslims, and the Mongolians in Inner Mongolia, lamb is the predominant meat, followed by beef. For both peoples, camel, horse, bear, rabbit, goose, duck and chicken are part of their occasional diet. The Mongols also have some pork dishes to their credit. The Muslims, however, regard pork as unclean.

The Muslim–Mongolian dish that rivals Peking Duck is Lamb Hot Pot, also known as Rinsed Lamb (*see* recipe p. 335). The most tender, raw lamb is sliced paper thin and placed on dishes. Diners then pick the slices up with wooden chopsticks and cook or 'rinse' them – hence the name – in a simmering soup held in a specially constructed round chafing dish, called a fire pot. This has a funnel in the centre to hold the fuel – charcoal – which heats the soup. The cooked slices are then dipped in different sauces and eaten with sesame cakes. This method of cooking, believed to have been introduced by the nomadic Mongolians to the Ming Chinese more than four hundred years ago, was officially recorded in a Qing palace feast in 1796. The feast, given in honour of elders and senior citizens, called for the use of 1,550 fire pots. But its popularity as an accessible restaurant treat for ordinary people only goes back to the beginning of the 20th century. In Peking, the oldest and most prestigious Muslim restaurant is Donglaishun, first opened in 1905. Since 1914, it has specialised not only in rinsed lamb hot pot but the whole spectrum of Muslim–Mongolian lamb and beef dishes. It is of interest to note, however, that some Chinese historians claim that Lamb Hot Pot traces its origin to the Song writer, Lin Hong (*see* p. 27).

In recent years, Peking Duck and Lamb Hot Pot have become synonymous with Peking food, and no tourist can go to Peking without sampling them. This has posed a dilemma for tour organisers who can only fit in one banquet in a restaurant. The result is the appearance of strange menus in some restaurants which serve both Peking Duck and Lamb Hot Pot at the same meal. Hitherto, the two dishes were not even served in the same restaurants let alone at the same meals. Many Pekinese regard this as a serious encroachment upon their jealously guarded food tradition, and I have heard some exclaim with great indignation, 'How can you mix up duck grease with lamb grease in your stomach!'

Mongolian Barbecued Lamb is another famous Peking dish served in restaurants. Lamb is cut up into strips and marinated in a sauce consisting of ginger juice, soy sauce, wine, sugar and sesame oil. The strips are then placed on the large round iron grill of a specially constructed barbecue, which uses particular wood, such as pine or willow, in order to enhance the fragrance of the meat. Diners, who are mostly men, hold bamboo chopsticks as long as 60 cm (2 feet) to turn the lamb strips as they are grilled with spring onion. But instead of sitting on the benches around the table, these men put one foot on them, while resting the other on the floor, pick up the meat to eat with the chopsticks and hold a cup of wine with the other hand. This scene creates an ambience which makes the barbecued lamb all the more novel. For this dish, beef can also be used instead of lamb.

A lamb roasted whole is a Mongolian dish reserved for dignitaries. The flesh from a camel hump stir-fried with bamboo shoots and coriander leaves or with mushrooms, and camel paws braised in wine are also valued dishes.

Under the umbrella of northern or Peking cuisine are two more styles of cooking which should be mentioned. The first is Confucius or Kong style, Kong being the Chinese family name for Confucius. The descendants of Confucius, totalling seventy-seven generations over two thousand five hundred years, have continued to live on their native estate of Qufu in Shandong. Their close connection with reigning monarchs, as well as their obligation to entertain dignitaries, led to the setting up of two kitchens, one devoted to entertaining guests and the other for cooking for the large clan. Two kinds of cooking resulted – very expensive and sophisticated banquet dishes and everyday family dishes. The former includes shark's fin, bird's nest, sea cucumber, deer tendon, monkey head fungus and jelly fish among its exotic ingredients, not to mention chicken and duck, carp, Mandarin fish and bean curd. Family dishes make use of pork in many ways, from pig's ear, kidney, heart and tail to spareribs, loin and fillet. Chicken, duck, fish and bean curd are also favourites. It is not so much the ingredients, however, but the thoughtful way in which they are prepared that has made Kong dishes distinctive (*see* recipes pp. 201, 301).

The second is the Qing Imperial palace style which, being a vast subject, can be dealt with here only briefly. Carrying on a tradition established as long ago as the Zhou dynasty (11th century–221 BC), which had an elaborate Imperial kitchen with a staff totalling as many as two thousand, the Qing monarchs ran their kitchens on a grand scale, modelling them after those of the Ming emperors. When the dynasty came to an end in 1911, some of the Imperial kitchen staff were retained to serve the last emperor Pu Yi, who was allowed to continue to live in the Imperial palaces in the Forbidden City of Peking. Most of them, however, had to foray for a living working in restaurants or with rich families. In 1925, Mr Zhao Renzhai, having invited several erstwhile Imperial chefs to join him in the enterprise, opened a restaurant in Beihai Park with the name Fang Shan, which carries the meaning 'fashioned after the Imperial palace cuisine'. The restaurant went through its share of ups and downs with the political turmoil in China but, since 1956, with government endorsement, it has reopened as a very exclusive restaurant with a repertoire designed to revive the Qing palace cuisine.

Not unexpectedly, this style of cooking is both complicated and elaborate, and very time-consuming. Artistically sculpted food, such as abalones stuffed with minced chicken, decorated with hair moss and peas to resemble the heads of toads, is an important element. The use of expensive or rare ingredients, such as bear's paws, camel paws and monkey head mushrooms, not to mention shark's fin and bird's nest, is yet another. A third is the penchant for aphrodisiac dishes, such as the obvious stewed deer penis and the more subtle deep-fried beavers. This is not to say that ordinary ingredients are not used, or prepared quite simply. But, understandably, people who frequent the restaurant prefer to taste some of the more exotic dishes.

Before we leave the northern table, mention should also be made of the very strong Fen Jiu made in Shanxi, the province to the west of Shandong. 'Jiu' is the only Chinese word for alcoholic beverages, which comprise both what the Chinese classify as yellow wines and white wines, the latter being distilled spirits. Fen wine, which dates back to the 6th century AD, is a distilled spirit made using the local grain, gaoliang or sorghum. It is about 60 per cent proof and rivals the celebrated and potent Maotai (*see* p. 108).

SHANGHAI
OR EASTERN CUISINE

THIS COMPRISES the two fertile coastal provinces Jiangsu and Zhejiang, collectively known as Suzhe. As I have mentioned before, it is referred to as 'the land of fish and rice', where lakes, canals and rivers traverse the landscape, yielding freshwater shrimps, crabs, eels and fish to enrich the table. Add to these all the agricultural products of an area growing both rice and wheat, corn, peanuts and tea, and there is all the potential for a rich cuisine.

The Qingming Shanghe Tu (Spring Festival on the River) scroll

Inevitably, it is the cities and towns in this area, with their famous restaurants and dishes, that represent the cuisine: Shanghai, the largest and most cosmopolitan city in China; Hangzhou, the old Song capital with the celebrated West Lake; Suzhou, the Venice of China with the myriad canals and idyllic gardens; Wuxi, by the Taihu Lake; Yangzhou, the ancient commercial centre for salt; Nanjing (Nanching), the capital during the era of the Republic of China; Ningbo, the trading port; Jinhua of the Jinhua ham fame; and Shaoxing, where Shaoxing rice wine is made, to name but the obvious ones. The area has a long history of gastronomic tradition, dating back to the Song dynasty (AD 960–1279), the dawn of modern Chinese cuisine and restaurants. That the capital of Northern Song (AD 960–1127), Kaifeng, was very food-oriented is reflected in Zhang Zeduan's painting, the long scroll Qingming Shanghe Tu or

Spring Festival on the River. Not only did people throng the streets where food hawkers and food stalls abounded, they also frequented restaurants, where, on the second floor, they sipped tea and wine. The threat of the Jin warriors from the north may have forced the Song emperor to move his capital south to Hangzhou in 1127, but culinary activities continued to flourish there, as noted by Chinese and European writers.

Wu Zimu, who wrote a nostalgic tome about Hangzhou during its heyday in the 13th century, *Mengliang Lu* or *Dreaming of the Old Capital*, described in vivid detail the food scenes in the markets, taverns and restaurants, the last of which appear quite similar to present-day establishments. They consisted of different pavilions with more than one storey, separated by gardens, which were decorated with green and red curtains and lit by red gauze lanterns. The menus were long and elaborate, sometimes running to more than two hundred dishes. This heralded the format of menus in Chinese restaurants, which became many-paged booklets containing three, if not four hundred dishes under different ingredient categories.

What Wu and other Song writers wrote was corroborated by Marco Polo, the Venetian traveller who stayed in Hangzhou (or Kinsai as he called it) sometime between 1276 and 1292, towards the end of the Song and the beginning of the Mongol dynasty, the Yuan. In his *Travels*, he described Hangzhou as: 'the city of heaven', 'without doubt the finest and most splendid city in the world'. There were ten principal market-places, he noted, each about half a mile square. Three times a week, people would bring to the markets everything necessary to sustain life: wild game such as roebuck stags, harts, hares and rabbits; fowl such as partridges, pheasants, quails, hens, ducks and geese; livestock such as calves, oxen and lamb; fruits such as pears and peaches; fish such as the 'plump and tasty' ones from the West Lake, not to mention myriad vegetables.

Marco Polo's description of Hangzhou's restaurants is even more amazing:

'Furthermore, in the middle of the lake there are two islands, in each of which is a marvellous and magnificent palace, with so many rooms and apartments as to pass belief, and so sumptuously constructed and adorned that it seems like the palace of an emperor. When anyone wishes to celebrate a wedding or have a party, he goes to this palace. Here their wedding-parties and feasts are held, and here they find all that is needful for such an occasion in the way of crockery, napery, and plate, and everything else, all kept in stock in the palaces for this purpose for the use of the citizenry;

for it was they who had made it all. On occasion the need may arise to cater for a hundred clients at once, some ordering banquets, others wedding-feasts; and yet they will all be accommodated in different rooms and pavilions so efficiently that one does not get in the way of another' (trans. Ronald Latham, 1958, p. 218).

It is generally agreed that the European restaurant tradition started in the 18th century after the French Revolution. It is obvious from the Kaifeng and Hangzhou scenes, however, that China had a much earlier restaurant tradition than Europe. Even though it lapsed, its revival in the 19th century led to the myriad Chinese restaurants found today in every major city.

Ever since the Song dynasty, this Suzhe area has produced more gastronomes who have made a lasting impact with their writing than any other area in China. As discussed earlier, Mrs Wu, Lin Hong and Li Yu came from Zhejiang, Ni Zan was from Wuxi and Yuan Mei was from Hangzhou, while his beloved Sui Garden was in Nanjing. Each of them has left an invaluable book on cookery.

And yet, despite this rich inheritance, among the four main cuisines, Shanghai Suzhe cuisine is the least well known abroad. On the whole, the cuisine is richer, heavier and sweeter than Cantonese cuisine, on account of the amount of oil and fat, sugar and wine used in the cooking. Hongshao or red-braised dishes, cooked slowly in thick or dark soy sauce and Shaoxing wine, are its forte (*see* recipe p. 308). Another type of dish is called 'shaguo', or sandpot, because the ingredients, which can comprise meat, fish and seafood and vegetables, are cooked (and served) in an earthenware pot called a sandpot, made of sandy clay. No doubt due to the availability of Shaoxing wine, alcoholic dishes, such as Drunken Chicken (*see* recipe p. 126) or drunken prawns or crabs, also feature strongly.

Shaoxing wine from the town of the same name in Zhejiang is the leading wine among Chinese yellow wines, and one of the oldest. As far back as the Spring and Autumn period (770–476 BC), wine was already being produced in Huiji, the ancient name of Shaoxing. Made with fermented glutinous rice and the water from the nearby Jian Lake, it looks amber in colour, has a rather sweet taste reminiscent of sherry, and is between fifteen and twenty per cent proof.

It is drunk not just locally but throughout China, and it is warmed in the bottle before being served, always with food. Under the generic name of Shaoxing wine there are different brand names such as Yuanhong, so called because the bottles containing the wine are red (hong), and Jiafen, which means that more glutinous rice than the normal amount has been added in the making of this wine. But the best-quality Shaoxing wines are Huadiao or Florally Sculpted and Nu'erhong or Crimson Maiden. Huadiao wine derives its name from the birds and flowers either painted or sculpted on the wine bottles or jars, which are then stored away for eight to ten years to allow the bouquet of the wine to reach its full potential. Nu'erhong wine, on the other hand, marks the birth of a daughter. As soon as a baby is born, wine is put into an urn which, sealed air-tight with mud, is laid down in the cellar for about fifteen years until the daughter is grown up. At her wedding this wine, which by then has an 'aroma wafting beyond a thousand miles', will be used for entertaining relatives and guests.

Another kind of Shaoxing wine is further processed and scented with flower petals such as cassia, leaves such as bamboo, or fruits such as apple. The most famous is Zhuyeqing or Bamboo Green wine which looks clear but has a faintly greenish tinge. Experts advise that this wine, which goes especially well with fish and seafood, should be drunk cold.

If the greasy and sweet characteristics are partially responsible for the unpopularity of Shanghai food abroad, its reliance on special local ingredients is probably more to blame. Substitutes don't always work, even though at times we have to resort to them if we are to simulate a taste of the cuisine.

Suzhe people are very fond of eel, which is cooked in a number of different ways. The most famous dish has to be Stir-fried Eel (*see* recipe p. 267). It makes no apology for being greasy and, at the end of the cooking procedure, a small ladle of oil – preferably lard! – is poured over the dish to sizzle the puréed garlic in the centre and to enrich the flavour of the eel. The eels used for this dish are the yellow eels which thrive in the silt of local rivers but are not available in the West. In spite of the outcries of purists who rightly declare that white eels lack the firm texture and inherent sweetness of yellow eels, they have to be used if we are to make this dish.

River shrimps and prawns abound in Jiangsu and Zhejiang, and are used as main or complementary ingredients in many dishes. The most distinctive dish is Shrimps with Dragon Well Tea, which uses the aristocratic green tea leaves of Hangzhou, as much for decoration as to add the subtlest aroma of the tea to the shrimps. This dish is best eaten in Hangzhou just after the tea is picked and processed; it would be sacrilegious to use any other tea.

Drunken Prawns is another Hangzhou speciality. Live prawns are inebriated in

Shaoxing wine and are eaten raw – much as oysters are in the West. Yuan Mei, as I have described, has a recipe of Drunken Prawns set aflame (*see* p. 42). This method has been borrowed by restaurants in Hong Kong which have adapted it to produce their own versions. Medium-sized live prawns are marinated in Shaoxing wine, which is then flamed to cook the prawns. Another version involves adding the marinated prawns to a simmering herbal broth, which is served after the prawns have been eaten.

Another delicious dish uses shad fish, which are in season in early summer when, having produced plenty of oil and protein between their scales and skin, they swim from the sea into rivers for spawning. They are cooked using the time-honoured method of steaming and it is necessary to leave the scales on so that the oil keeps the flesh moist and succulent. One well-known story about the cooking of shad involves the Mei family of Hangzhou, who were renowned for their expertise in cooking this particular fish. Soon after their third daughter-in-law, a girl from a small town, joined the family, the mother-in-law, anxious to find out if the new member would fit in well with the family, asked her to cook a shad. Without any hesitation, the young woman calmly held the shad and started to take off the scales one by one, oblivious to the sniggering of her sisters-in-law who, having watched for a little while, rushed to tell Madame Mei what she was doing. Together, the old lady and her two elder daughters-in-law shook their heads, regretting that the new Mrs Mei did not come from a family which, like theirs, knew how to cook this fine fish. When the shad was finally served for dinner, however, one and all were amazed to find that not only was the flesh succulent, but that they had been spared the bother of having to cope with getting rid of the scales. Savouring every mouthful with nods of approval, Madame Mei asked her new daughter-in-law how she could have achieved this miracle, having removed the scales. Thereupon the new Mrs Mei fetched from the kitchen the bamboo lid of the steamer and held it up to show her doubting relations. What they saw was the scales attached to the inside of the lid, which puzzled them even more. Thereupon they asked her to reveal her secret. Smiling gently, the young Mrs Mei explained that her father loved to eat shad and her mother cooked them for him every day when they were in season, so that what she had done was no more than use the method her mother had taught her. This consisted of removing the scales from the fish, stringing them together and then fixing them with dexterity on the inside of the bamboo lid, so that when the shad was being steamed with the lid covering it, the oil from the scales would drip, drop by drop, on the fish, to moisten and enrich it, thereby making the flesh as succulent as if the scales were still attached to the fish. Needless to say, she won the everlasting affection of her mother-in-law, not to mention the respect of her sisters-in-law. For those of us who are less dextrous and less patient, we'd better stick to the simpler method of keeping the scales on the shad!

Many other fish recipes use carp, which generally find favour with the Chinese. One red-braised dish uses the tail of a large carp. Applying the same method when cooking the tail of salmon can be quite successful. But the well-known Hangzhou dish, West Lake Fish with a Sweet and Sour Sauce, is again best tasted there. To make this dish, a grass carp from the West Lake is left in a fish tank with an empty stomach until it has spat out any muddy impurity that could mar its pure taste. The fish is then halved sideways, with the bones still stuck to one side. After poaching it very lightly in water, a sweet and sour sauce is poured over it. Hangzhou restaurants are very particular about the presentation of the fish: the two halves with their bulging eyes need to be linked by the skin. But the success of the dish depends very much on the grass carp coming from the West Lake itself.

Perhaps the ultimate Suzhe dish consists of freshwater crabs, especially those from the lakes in Jiangsu, such as Hongze Hu in the north and Tai Hu and Yangcheng Hu near Suzhou. I have described how Li Yu's example stimulated people's obsessive enjoyment of them (*see* p. 1). The female crabs are at their best during the ninth month (October) and male crabs during the tenth month (November) or, as the Chinese ditty goes, 'ninth month for the rounded and tenth month for the pointed'. Another saying, 'holding a crab and looking at chrysanthemums' describes the height of enjoyment of the season, and many poets in the past were inspired to write fine verses afterwards.

Sometimes called hairy crabs because of the hairy appearance of the claws, their most delectable quality is in the roe, which has an aftertaste like caviar. They are served steamed, accompanied by very basic dippings of vinegar and soy sauce, and one eats them using nature's chopsticks – fingers – aided by other implements, such as specially made pointed picks to remove the meat from the claws. Afterwards, a customary sweet and peppery ginger 'tea', made with lots of ginger juice and sugar, is drunk to counter what is believed to be the cooling, yin effect of the crabs. Besides the roe, the crabmeat is also valued, even though that from the claws is often considered 'too rough' for the palate by local people. Together, the roe and crabmeat are used as a seasoning or ancillary ingredient, giving rise to a whole range of dishes, such as crabmeat and crab roe with pea sprouts or other vegetables, with small steamed buns and with meat balls. They are truly indescribably delicious.

For at least several hundred years, Suzhe people have also indulged in eating drunken crabs. Live crabs are put in an urn, salted and immobilised by a heavy weight being placed upon them. A sauce is then made from wine of a high alcohol content, such as gaoliang or Fen wine, seasoned with salt, soy sauce, sugar, Sichuan peppercorns, ginger and spring onion, and is left to cool completely. It is then poured over the crabs, covering them. After three days of immersion, the weight is removed and the crabs are ready to be served cold.

Sea cucumber is another Shanghai favourite. Large ones, rather than the small, spiky ones served in Shandong, are used and the result is the sweetly savoury red-braised sea cucumber. Another equally famous sweetly savoury dish is Wuxi Spareribs, with a caramelised sauce enriching the meaty spareribs (*see* recipe p. 308). While somewhat heavy in their use of dark soy sauce and wine, Suzhe people use garlic sparingly, if at all. A precedent was set by Li Yu, who was very disparaging about the odour garlic gave to one's breath, so much so that he never allowed it in his food.

CANTONESE
OR SOUTHERN CUISINE

GEOGRAPHICALLY, the coastal provinces of Fujian and Guangdong, Hainan Island, as well as Taiwan, fall into the perimeter of Cantonese or southern cuisine; in fact, Guangdong itself can boast of three sub-regional cuisines, while Fujian has a style of its own.

Guangdong has a tropical or sub-tropical climate, with heavy rainfall between May and September, which enables there to be two crops of rice per year. Three rivers, the Xi Jiang or West River, the Bei Jiang or North River and the Dong Jiang or East River, flowing from different directions, converge in the alluvial Zhu Chiang or

Pearl River delta before emptying into the South China Sea. Livestock is reared in the vast delta plain, vegetables are grown in abundance everywhere, and fish are reared in ponds. The long coastal line also yields plenty of fish and seafood.

Canton, the capital, is, of course, the pivotal centre representing mainstream Guangdong, or Cantonese cuisine, but Hong Kong, since the 1950s, has become the mecca of Cantonese food, vying with Canton itself. 'Eat in Canton' is the hackneyed folk-saying which nevertheless rings with such conviction for Chinese all over China that they flock to Canton and Hong Kong to enjoy eating experiences hitherto unknown to them. Since the 19th century, when the emigration of Cantonese and Fujianese to Southeast Asia, Australia, Canada and the United States gathered momentum, Cantonese cooking has spread to the four corners of the world. One unfortunate consequence was the invention of the notorious dish, chop suey, which for a long time gave Chinese food an undeserved reputation.

The story of the origin of chop suey, with its many inflated versions, must have been told a thousand times. Whatever the truth, the story goes that towards the end of the last century or the beginning of this, a couple of drunken sailors sat down in a dingy Chinatown restaurant in San Francisco and asked for food. As it was very late and the restaurant was about to close, there was hardly anything left, yet not daring to turn away these two hulking fellows, the Chinese just chopped up bits and pieces of meat and vegetables that were to hand, stir-fried them together, seasoned them with a little soy sauce, and then served them up on a plate. Having wolfed down the dish with gusto, the sailors asked for the name of the dish. Still hesitating, the cook burst out with the phrase 'chop suey' which, unbeknownst to the sailors, means 'bits and pieces chopped up', if not also 'left-overs chopped up'. The following evening, the sailors, now sober, came back to the same restaurant and asked for chop suey, and in due course they went away feeling contentedly replete. And so they came back again and again, bringing with them their families and friends, and ate chop suey to their heart's content.

Chop suey apart, Cantonese was the first regional cuisine to make an impact outside of China; even now, it is still better known than the other regional cuisines. In retaliation, northern Chinese have coined a phrase teasing the undiscriminating Cantonese palate. 'The Cantonese will eat anything that flies,' they opine, 'except the aeroplane, anything that swims, except the submarine, and anything that has legs, except the table.'

Indeed Cantonese cuisine does include rather exotic ingredients, among which two are especially sought after every season. From ancient times, as far back as the Han dynasty, the Cantonese have eaten snakes, believing them to have aphrodisiacal and other medicinal properties, such as the ability to cure rheumatism and prevent sweating at night. When the autumn wind blows and the snakes become fattened, it is time for restaurants to serve the celebrated snake dish which takes the form of a 'geng' or thick soup. The most sophisticated, called Taishi Snake Geng, was devised around the turn of the 20th century, by the reigning gastronome in Canton, the wealthy Kong Taishi or Supreme Scholar Kong, who liked to serve snake banquets for his guests. To make the stock for the dish, chicken and ham, sugar-cane, ginger, matured tangerine peels, dried longans and dates are all added to counter the rank odour of the snake. Dried black mushrooms, wood-ear fungus and winter bamboo shoots, shredded very finely, are then added in order to give texture, while shredded chicken and fish maw complement the taste of snake meat. Just before serving, diners add strands of silkenly shredded lemon leaves, a few petals of chrysanthemum flowers and some mini-sized chips made of egg and flour. There was a special kitchen in the Kong mansion in Canton, where the snakes were killed. But as Kong grew older, he grew weary of the scene of snake blood splashing on the cement floor, and one day he gave an instruction to stop the killing of them completely. With that came the end of the era of snake banquets in his house, even though his chefs, who either found jobs in restaurants or in due course opened their own, kept the secret of making the dish alive.

Those who are not aware of Kong Taishi and his eponymous dish may have heard the snake soup referred to as the dragon, the tiger and the phoenix. The dragon is represented by three kinds of poisonous snakes, the cobra (*Naja naja*), the Asiatic rat snake (*Ptyas korros*) and the banded krait (*Bungarus fasciatus*); the tiger is in fact civet cat and the phoenix is chicken. If diners are not told about the ingredients, and hence are free from preconceived prejudice, chances are that they will find this soup scrumptious, the meat therein succulent.

At the beginning of autumn, just after the harvest, the tiny yellow-breasted buntings (*Emberiza aureola*), migrating southward from northeast China and Inner Mongolia, reach the rice fields in Guangdong, where they rest and feed *en masse*. Cantonese farmers net these rice paddy birds and sell them to Canton, Hong Kong and Macau, where they eventually turn up at the table as a gourmet dish. Even

though they are tiny, and weigh less than 50 g (2 oz) after being cleaned, the Cantonese go to a lot of trouble to prepare them. They are marinated for a short time in a
sauce made of ginger juice, wine, sugar and thin soy sauce. A cube of wind-dried
duck sausage is then placed in the cavity of each bird, which, in turn, is wrapped in a
large piece of pig's caul and pot-roasted until the caul has turned golden-brown and
the birds inside are cooked. To serve them, the caul is discarded and the birds are
devoured in their entirety – head, bones, flesh *et al*. As the season is short, lasting only
three to four weeks, the craze of eating them spreads like wildfire so that there never
seems to be a surplus in Hong Kong or Canton. Thus, even with the benefit of
freezing, the chances of savouring these rice birds abroad are pretty much nil.

Another exotic Cantonese ingredient are the rice worms which are flooded by
tidal waves into the paddy fields of the Pearl River delta in May and September. As
they cause damage to the crops, farmers net them as the tides wax and wane. Some
time in the past, it was discovered that these worms, when steamed, were delicately
sweet. Gradually, they became a favourite present which farmers would bring,
wriggling in a bowl, to their urban relatives and friends in Canton and Hong Kong.
Even though I have not tasted them, I have the memory of my grandmother
receiving such a present and then having the worms steamed and put under the grill
to enhance the aroma.

Day-to-day Cantonese food is not, however, as exotic as this. What then are the
characteristics of mainstream Cantonese cuisine? Compared to the other three main
regional cuisines, it is the most versatile and the most varied, because it can command
the widest range of ingredients, from fish to fowl, from vegetables to meat. It is also
the lightest: not as much grease or sugar are used as in Shanghai cuisine, nor as much
salt and vinegar as in Peking food, nor as much garlic, chilli and other spices as in
Sichuan cooking. In mixing flavours, it is the most mindful of achieving a harmonious blending rather than having any one flavour outstrip the others. This
approach works very well when fresh ingredients, especially fish, crustaceans and
fowl, are used, for the condiments do no more than bring out the best, and the
subtlest, of the flavours. Unfortunately, more often than not, this freshness cannot be
achieved in the West, with the result that Cantonese food tastes bland, if not
downright insipid, to many Western palates.

Again, if the emphasis placed on texture is more apparent in Chinese than in other
national foods, then nowhere among the four main regions is texture more stressed

than in Cantonese food. Crispness is of the utmost importance, but the crispness of vegetables is different from that of other fried and deep-fried foods, and there are different words in the Chinese language to describe the precise kind of crispness required (*see* recipes pp. 181 and 297). The anecdote about how the crisp texture of the dish White Cloud Pig's Trotter is achieved is instructive. A young Buddhist monk, going against his religious teaching, was stealthily cooking some pig's trotters at the foot of the White Cloud mountain when he heard the footsteps of his superior approaching. In a panic he fled, abandoning the trotters in a shallow running stream. The following day he went back to the scene of the crime and, to his utter delight, found the trotters were still there, being washed by the constant stream. When he tasted them, he discovered that the texture of the trotter, especially the fatty part and the rind, had changed from being sticky and dense to being bouncily crisp and light. After that, he would use this long rinsing in running water to achieve the same texture. This technique is not just applicable for cooking pig's trotters, but is equally effective when preparing Hainan Chicken Rice (*see* recipe p. 295).

To be smooth and velvety is another textural quality of Cantonese cuisine. More than others, the Cantonese look for slipperiness in many forms of food. Thus chuk or congee must be smooth to the point of having rice and water totally amalgamated, scrambled egg must be creamily flaky and meat slippery enough to be swallowed. To achieve this in meat, for instance, a very small amount – ½–1 teaspoon – of tapioca or potato flour is stirred into the sliced meat during the marinating stage, and another equally small amount is added to the instant sauce at the end (*see* recipe for Stir-Fried Beef with Bitter Melon, p. 329). Some takeaways, in going overboard with their use of flour, have produced the adverse effect of making the food inedibly gluey and gelatinous rather than subtly smooth and velvety.

Although stir-frying is a national Chinese cookery technique used in all regional cuisines, it is the forte of Cantonese cuisine, unmatched by the others. Done with lightning speed by Cantonese chefs tossing their red-hot woks, the food therein, cut up into morsels and lightly seasoned, is quickly cooked by the semi-engulfing flame. At home, the same technique is used, but, understandably, at toned-down speed and with less fierce heat. When fresh ingredients, be they fish, crustaceans, poultry or vegetables, are readily available in south China, it seems most logical for people to stir-fry food, thereby achieving wok fragrance and taste whilst at the same time retaining the goodness, and the vitamins, of the food.

Again, because of the freshness of the food, a very straightforward Cantonese technique of cooking has evolved, called 'white boiling'. Fresh vegetables, such as 'choi sum' of the brassica family, or medium-sized live prawns, are simply immersed in boiling water for a short time until they are just cooked. These are then eaten with a light dipping sauce made with soy sauce or oyster sauce, the special Cantonese sauce made from oyster extract. Similar to 'white boiling' is 'clear steaming': fresh fish are steamed until just done to bring out their sweetness.

No description of mainstream Cantonese cuisine is complete without the mention of dimsum. Literally translated as 'so close to the heart', they are, in reality, a large range of hors d'oeuvres Cantonese people traditionally enjoy in restaurants (previously teahouses, *see* p. 71) for breakfast and for lunch, but never for dinner, washed down with tea. 'Let's go yumcha (to drink tea)', is understood among the Cantonese to mean going to a restaurant for dimsum; such is the twin linkage between the food and the beverage. The familiar yumcha scene at a Cantonese restuarant, which is often on several floors, is one of young girls pushing trolleys replete with goodies in bamboo baskets piled high or small dishes set next to each other. As they mill around the dining tables, they call out the names of their wares and place the baskets or dishes on to the tables when diners signal their wishes.

The range of dimsum in a restaurant easily numbers several dozen and they come under these main varieties: the steamed, the fried and the deep-fried. Among the steamed variety, which are served in small bamboo baskets, 'char siu bao' – buns made with flour stuffed with 'charsiu' or roast pork – are the most basic. Next come 'hargow' – crescent-shaped transparent skin dumplings made with glutenless flour stuffed with shrimp; 'siumai' – open-top minced pork dumplings wrapped with wonton skin made with wheat flour; and 'fanguo' – flat dumplings made with glutenless flour stuffed with chopped mushroom, bamboo shoots and pork. Three kinds of 'tsuenfun' – steamed rice flour dough sheets stuffed with either charsiu, shrimp or minced beef – are sought after for their silken, slippery texture. Among the deep-fried variety the favourites are spring rolls, 'wugok' or taro croquettes, which have an almost honeycomb appearance, and 'harmshuigok' – round dumplings made with glutinous rice flour tasting slightly sweet-savoury. 'Law Baak Go' and 'Wu Tow Go' – savoury puddings made with white radish and taro – are often served shallow-fried (*see* recipes pp. 149, 153).

Besides dumplings, a range of steamed dishes served in bamboo baskets is also popular. Pork spareribs chopped into small cubes and seasoned with black beans or a plum sauce, duck's webs deep-fried then steamed in a spicy sauce, and steamed beef balls seasoned with tangerine peel are but the obvious examples. Beef tripe or 'gnauchaap' and chicken feet, the latter enjoyed perhaps more for their texture than flavour, are, for many Europeans, an acquired taste. But most people adore the dishes of suckling pig, roast pork and cold chicken found on the trolleys of those restaurants which have kitchens specialising in them.

The East River or Hakka food is a sub-regional Cantonese cuisine. Hakka means guests, and it is believed that the people who have settled there trace their antecedents to Song refugees who, in the 12th century, moved southward when Northern Song moved its capital from Kaifeng to Hangzhou to escape the Jin invaders from the north. The specialities the Hakka people have developed are very sophisticated peasant food.

First and foremost is Salt-baked Chicken. After a chicken has been cleaned and wrapped in paper made of flax, it is buried in red-hot coarse salt in either a large wok or a sandpot for about an hour or until it is cooked. The taste from the salt is transferred by heat and absorbed by the chicken, giving it an aroma all of its own. The origin of this dish has a lot to do with the salt fields along the East River. Apparently, about three hundred years ago, people used to bury a whole boiled or steamed chicken, wrapped in paper, in the salt fields, using the salt as a preservative. Gradually, one ingenious person hit on the method of heating up the salt to cook the chicken. This simple method belies, however, the laboriousness and difficulties involved, for heating 2–4 kilos (5–6 lb) of salt by constant stirring alone will take more than an hour, not to mention having to continue to heat the salt, once the chicken is buried in it. The act of burying the chicken in the salt is another hurdle, fraught with the hazard of getting one's fingers burned. Thus, while one and all romanticise the salt-baked chicken, it is prepared, both in restaurants and at home, by an alternative method: cooked in a spiced and salted liquid (*see* recipe p. 297).

Several more sophisticated peasant dishes are synonymous with Hakka cuisine: 'Muichoi' Moulded Pork, East River stuffed bean curd and East River beef meatballs. They are all rather labour-intensive dishes, not the quick stir-fries that Cantonese mainstream cuisine excels in. The pork dish is distinguished not only by the use of preserved muichoi, a vegetable related to the mustard plant and grown in Huizhou county, but also by the multiprocessed method of cooking it (*see* recipe p. 311). It is so delicious however, that it is used for weddings and festivals. The bean curd dish involves making hollows in pieces of bean curd, filling them with a paste laboriously achieved by mincing and mixing together pork and fish, then shallow-frying the stuffed bean curd pieces and finally braising them in a sandpot or casserole. As for the meatballs, the secret is to beat the minced beef until a bouncy, gelatinous texture is achieved. They are often bought or eaten in Hakka restaurants rather than made at home.

The truly peasant Hakka dishes concentrate on tripe of one sort or another, such as East River Deep-fried Intestines or Assembled Mixed Tripe, both of which are labour-intensive and an acquired taste.

Chaozhou cuisine is the other sub-regional Cantonese cuisine, centred around the Han Jiang or Han River delta near Fujian province and bordering on the South China Sea. It is a rich agricultural area producing rice, sugar-cane and sugar, and many citrus fruits, among which the tangerines are especially large, juicy and sweet. The commercial centre, Shantou, more popularly known as Swatow, is the market outlet for embroidery works. With seafood and fish and other agricultural products in abundance, and with money from trade, Chaozhou people have developed their own cuisine, which encompasses both rich dishes that would befit a well-to-do merchant's table and more homely, rustic dishes.

Lard is used in many dishes, and in such a way as to give them their distinctive Chaozhou character. For instance, just before serving braised shark's fins, a lot of pure lard is added, and a slow, circular stirring movement is called for to amalgamate the lard with the sauce, so that the end result is a very delicious, but extremely rich and gelatinous dish. Sweet-fried noodles also require plenty of lard and although it may seem an unlikely application, this technique of adding lard is extended to puddings, as in Taro Mud with Ginkgo Nuts (*see* recipe p. 350).

Many dishes, whether elaborate or simple, are served accompanied by a separate dipping sauce, sometimes sweetish, sometimes vinegary. Take the renowned dish of Chaozhou Braised Goose (*see* recipe p. 284), despite having its own sauce derived from the braising, a dipping sauce made of vinegar and puréed garlic is served on the side.

Yet other dishes are prepared in the simplest way, so as to preserve the inherent goodness of the ingredients which do need, however, to be very fresh indeed to begin with. One such dish is Steamed Lobster. A live lobster, halved, is steamed plainly and simply until just done and then a sweetish dipping sauce accompanies it. A more homely dish along these lines is Steamed Grey Mullet, a fish Chaozhou people are very fond of, served cold and accompanied by a sweet bean sauce (*see* recipe p. 261).

In the Chaozhou area, a special kind of mustard greens, which have large heads with stems curving outwards and are pungent in flavour, abound. The resultant braised mustard greens with ham is distinguished, however, not by the crispness of the vegetables as may be expected, but by their tenderness, having been cooked for a relatively long time.

Chaozhou is very close to Fujian, the coastal province north of Guangdong with its own style of cuisine. Since the 17th century, large numbers of Fujianese have settled in Taiwan and, as emigration to Southeast Asia intensified during the 19th century, many have also settled in Singapore and Malaysia. Fuzhou, the provincial capital, and Xiamen or Amoy, are the two trading seaports where Fujianese cuisine is represented. Because of its long coastline, seafood dishes feature strongly, and include the endearingly named 'Monk Jumps Over the Wall' – so dubbed because a Buddhist monk, lured by the fragrant aroma, jumped over the temple wall to join in the feasting, breaking his vegetarian vow. This dish consists of a casserole into which the most expensive dried seafood products – fresh ones not being so valuable since they lack depth of flavour – including shark's fins, shark's lips, sea cucumbers, abalones and scallops are cooked for a long time in a pot flavoured by ham, pig's stomach and trotters, duck and chicken with their gizzards. Fresh oysters, mussels, conches, prawns and shrimps, not to mention fish, all also find their way to the table.

The Fujianese are very fond of soups, so much so that they may serve more than one soup at the same meal. Even when a dish is dry, as in fried rice, they prefer to add a soupy quality to it (*see* recipe p. 241). Very thin rice sticks and very fine vermicelli noodles made of flour are associated with Amoy. Soupy rice sticks are very popular family fare, but even when it comes to fried rice sticks, a ladle of stock will be added at the end to make them moist and slightly soupy. This same principle is also applied to fried vermicelli noodles (*see* recipe p. 245).

What most distinguishes Fujianese cuisine from the rest of southern Chinese cuisine, however, is the use of 'hongzao' (red sediment). Cooked glutinous rice is fermented with red yeast and rice wine to produce a red paste, hongzao (*see* recipe p. 358) which, when added to other ingredients, imparts to the dish an aromatic and alcoholic sweetness all of its own. Fujian people are especially fond of using it with pork, fish, duck and chicken (*see* recipe p. 292) and sometimes make soups with it as well.

Both the Fujianese and the Cantonese are blessed with an abundance of fruits, as a result of their sub-tropical climate. The serving of fruits after dinner has a tradition going as far back as Han times, and the southern Chinese have always been proud of their large variety. Sweet oranges, star fruits, kumquats, pineapples, gum or tangerines, pomelo from Guangxi province, custard apples, bananas and sugar-cane replenish the fruit bowl from season to season, but litchi (spelled also lizhi, lichi or lichee) and 'longan', are considered the best and their abundance here makes the Cantonese the envy of the rest of China, especially for people in the north.

Litchi, with their crimson, spiky shells and sensually juicy flesh, have long enjoyed the reputation of being a tributary fruit sent by 'pony express' to court since the Han dynasty. The crowning romantic tale, however, concerns the Tang emperor who had his horses ride in relays, at a gallop, in order to bring fresh litchi from Canton to the capital Chang'an. He did this purely because of the seductive smile of his favourite concubine, Yang Guifei, who loved eating them. The Song poet and gourmand, Su Dongpo, when exiled to the south, became so enamoured of the fruit that he was able to console himself that if he could eat as many as three hundred litchi every day, he wouldn't mind being a southerner. And the Bohemian Qing writer from Suzhou, Shen Fu, who, having spent four months in Canton, wrote in his autobiography: 'One of the keenest pleasures of my whole life was tasting the fresh fruit of the lichee in Canton; an experience I shall never forget' (trans. S. M. Black, 1960, p. 52).

From about late April to the middle of July, the litchi trees along the coastal area of Guangdong and Fujian are laden with crimson fruits. There are different kinds of litchi corresponding to respective litchi trees. At the beginning of the season are the Third-Moon Crimson which, even though refreshing, are sharp and lacking in sweetness. As the season progresses, two kinds, the 'gnormaichi' and the 'kueimei', are the most sought after. Both of them are sweet and juicy and are distinguished by their small stones. The former, whose name is borrowed from a sweet pudding made with glutinous rice flour, is round and substantial, and has white, luscious flesh which oozes syrupy juices to the bite. The latter, whose name suggests the fragrance of the cassia flower, is more pointed in shape and has translucent flesh that is crisp in texture, with the flavour of the flower. It is therefore understandable that people flock to the litchi farms and eat 'themselves to extinction'!

Since the 1960s, litchi grown in other parts of the world have appeared in supermarkets in the West. Whilst they are refreshing, they lack the depth, lusciousness and sensuality that the experience of eating Cantonese litchi gives.

When the litchi season nears its end, the longan season, which is even shorter, lasting for only four to five weeks, begins. Longan means dragon's eyes, the image the beige-skinned, round fruits evoke. Pure and sweet, longan is delicious and has a crisp texture all of its own, though it is not as luscious and sensual as the litchi – but then no fruit is quite like the best litchi.

Both litchi and longan are also sold dried, the former still in its shell but the latter always with it removed. When making a stock or a soup, dried longan is often added to the other ingredients in order to enhance the flavour, but a little goes a long way, and if too much is added the end product can become too sweet. The Chinese also use it as a tonic, believing in its medicinal properties.

SICHUAN
OR WESTERN CUISINE

Sichuan province, in the western interior of China, has the largest population in China, but this is balanced, fortunately, by the huge amount of rice and other agricultural products it grows. It is the natural breeding ground of the rare and exotic panda, whose presence in zoos all over the world gives so much joy to visitors. It is also a land of rugged, mountainous terrain, made more impassable by the spectacular Yangzi gorges. Last but by no means least, it has a unique cuisine quite different from the other three regional cuisines. This cuisine represents both Sichuan and its neighbouring province, Hunan, and has its centre in the capital, Chengdu. Since the 1970s, it has become particularly popular in the West. People associate it with Hot and Sour Soup and Fragrant Crispy Duck; many prefer it to other regional cuisines because of its more marked, spicy flavours.

The Chinese themselves sum up Sichuanese cuisine in two words: 'ma' and 'la', or numbing and spicy-hot. These two strong and sensational assaults on one's tastebuds are the result of the use of two condiments: the tiny, russet berries called 'huajiao' (fagara) or Sichuan peppercorns, which give a numbing rather than heating sensation to the tongue; and red chillies, whose pungent effect is well known. Whereas Sichuan peppercorns have grown in Sichuan for more than a thousand years, red chillies first found their way to Sichuan from South America in the late 17th century. Since then, they have been grown extensively and after they are dried, they are exported in large quantities to other countries. After drying, red chillies acquire more potency than in their fresh state, and it is in this form that they are used in Sichuanese dishes. Why do Sichuanese people like the combination of these two condiments? A definitive answer is perhaps not possible, but as the climate in Sichuan is hot and humid, people seem to have found great relief, as well as pleasure, in having the ma and la sensation on their tongues.

That the cuisine is ma and la is just the beginning of the story. After the initial numbing and spicy-hot sensation, one's palate begins to discern the multiple flavours of the food: salty, sweet and vinegary, made all the more intriguing by their simultaneous presence which, nevertheless, doesn't mar the inherent taste of the main ingredient. As with a good wine, one is aware of the tastes and aftertastes of the dishes. Intensity, therefore, is another key element of the cuisine, and in addition to the presence of salt, soy sauce, vinegar and sugar, one is also aware of lots of garlic and ginger. The Sichuan pressed vegetable, 'zhacai', a special kind of mustard green pickled and preserved in brine, very fine chilli powder and other spices, imparts a fragrant saltiness, besides the spicy-hotness, when added to other ingredients (*see* recipe p. 258). The spicy-hot bean paste, made with broad beans or soy beans, when used in conjunction with other condiments, adds another dimension to the already intense flavours (*see* recipe p. 275).

Besides ma and la, another impact the cuisine makes on the palate is 'yuxiang', or the fish-fragrant flavour. Sichuan, being a landlocked province with no access to the sea, is not blessed with sea fish or other seafood. The people, hankering after them, have invented a flavour made of condiments which they would have liked to use to cook fish. It imparts a subtle sweet and sour accent to spicy food, and is used for a string of dishes, the most notable of which is Shredded Pork (*see* recipe p. 320).

Not all Sichuanese food is spicy-hot, even though everyday fare, including noodles (*see* recipe p. 244), tends to be on the fiery side. Many banquet-style dishes are anything but spicy-hot. One fine example is a soup made of puréed chicken breast, which is more reminiscent of the sophisticated Yangzhou food than Sichuan (*see* recipe p. 162). More so than in other regional cuisines, preparing these dishes involves a series of different cookery methods, executed one after the other. Nowhere is this more true than in preparing the celebrated duck smoked in camphor wood or tea. The duck, having been marinated in saltpetre, is smoked, then steamed and finally deep-fried. The result is absolutely scrumptious, even when camphor wood is not used, so long as there is no stinting in the multiplicity of methods (*see* recipe p. 286).

To season their dishes, Sichuan people use their own salt from Zigong, a town situated in the basin between the capital Chengdu and Chongqing (Chungking), the capital of China during the Second World War. For about two thousand years, salt from deep wells has been produced there and distributed to the neighbouring provinces of Yunnan and Guizhou. Many Sichuanese chefs think so highly of the taste of their well salt that they do not shun the trouble of bringing it with them when they go elsewhere to cook, even as far away as Europe and America.

Besides salt, when they make their fermented pickled vegetables, they top them with a measure of the Sichuanese white wine, Wuliang Yi. Made from 'wuliang' or five grains, consisting of gaoliang or sorghum, glutinous rice, ordinary rice, corn and wheat, it is one of China's famous distilled alcohols, even if it is not internationally well known. Connoisseurs enthuse that although 60 per cent proof, it is very smooth and is not liable to cause ill-effects afterwards, such as headaches.

South of Sichuan is Yunnan province, which borders on Burma. It produces two things of national renown: Pu'er tea, the black tea sometimes moulded into a cake, which the Chinese regard as the most health-giving among all Chinese teas as it helps digestion (*see* p. 67); and Yunnan ham, the only other ham that can match Jinhua ham. Whereas Yunnan ham is difficult to come by outside of Yunnan, except sometimes in a tin, Pu'er tea is quite easily available outside China, and is sold in Chinese supermarkets and served in restaurants to those who appreciate it.

Yunnan also produces more varieties of edible fungi than any other province in China – more than two hundred and fifty kinds, apparently. They range from the black or fragrant mushroom (*Lentinus edodes*), wood ear (*Auricularia auricula*), silver ear (*Tremella fucifomis*) to sheep's stomach (*Morchella esculenta*), golden ear (*Tremella mesenterica*) and monkey head (*Hericium erinaceus*), to name but a few. The most special, however, are chicken fungus (*Collybia albuminosa*), delicious ox liver (*Boletus edulis*) and 'songrong' (Tricholoma matsutake) which fetch exorbitant prices in China, Hong Kong and Japan.

The food in Yunnan is not spicy-hot, nor is it held in such high repute as Sichuanese food. One soup, made with chicken, Yunnan ham, Chinese black mushrooms and ginger put into a specially constructed pottery casserole called the Yunnan steam-pot, is very famous. The pot is about 20 cm (8 in) in diameter and 10 cm (4 in) high with a cone-shaped chimney moulded in the centre of the bowl and a separate tight-fitting lid. When this pot is placed on top of boiling water, the steam rises through the chimney and circulates inside the pot, thus cooking the ingredients, with the result that the chicken is succulent and tender and the soup pure and flavourful. There is, regrettably, no substitute for this pot.

The other equally famous dish is called 'Rice Sticks Crossing the Bridge'. Ready-cooked rice sticks are placed in a bowl. Dishes of very finely sliced chicken, fish, pork, pig's liver, pig's kidney and pig's stomach are then placed on the table, together with one or two leafy green vegetables, such as spinach, and herbs, such as coriander leaves and shredded ginger. Each diner is brought a bowl of boiling stock with a layer of chicken fat on top, so fiercely hot that it can cook the thin ingredients a diner picks from the table and puts into the bowl. When they are cooked, the diner adds a few leaves of vegetables, herbs and condiments and some rice sticks before enjoying the whole bowlful of goodies. The essence of this dish is what the Chinese call the 'xian' or fresh flavours of the ingredients, at the risk of not having them cooked long enough. When we ate this dish in a famous hotel restaurant in Kunming, the capital of Yunnan, several years ago, both my fellow-travellers and myself were slightly concerned by the safety aspect of the pork ingredients, even though the delicious result made us throw caution to the wind.

To the eastern borders of Sichuan and Yunnan is Guizhou which, even though a rather poor province, produces the celebrated Maotai wine. By Chinese classification, it is a white wine, but is in fact the most potent Chinese distilled spirit. Fermented from gaoliang or sorghum and a small amount of wheat, it derives its name from Maotai, a small town which would have remained unknown but for its eponymous wine, first made there in 1704. Since President Nixon's historic visit to China in 1972, its fame has escalated by leaps and bounds and it has become the wine with which the Chinese toast their dignitaries at official and business banquets, accompanied by the friendly and traditional greeting of 'ganbei' or 'bottoms up', meaning 'drink up to the last drop'. But as soon as the Maotai glass – fortunately small like a liqueur glass – is empty the hospitable Chinese will fill it again so that it will be ready for the next round of ganbei, a ritual most conducive to enhancing ambience. In drinking Maotai the Chinese find its overwhelming 'jiang' fragrance (reminiscent of Chinese fermented sauces) attractive, and they love the burning sensation it gives rolling down the throat, gradually to be replaced by the ineffably delicate aftertaste.

Having talked about the characteristics of different regional cuisines, it would be as well to point out how thin the line is, sometimes, between them. Take, for example, Hot and Sour Soup. Whilst it is regarded by and large as a Sichuanese dish, Shanghai people claim it as part of their cuisine, maintaining, however, that they would not add duck's blood to the soup as do their Sichuan compatriots. Take dimsum as another example. If dimsum are synonymous with Cantonese cuisine, it is only because they have had more exposure to the outside world than those of other regions. The dimsum in Yangzhou in Jiangsu province are, in fact, just as renowned within China, but with Shanghai and Suzhou competing for tourist attention, Yangzhou dimsum will remain the true regional treat awaiting the few who are lucky enough to get there.

How well the characteristics of a given regional cuisine can be preserved in migration is a moot point, which is often heatedly debated. In posing the question itself, one is already conceding that when a regional cuisine goes out of its natural habitat, it is bound to lose some of its inherent qualities and have to adapt to new conditions. The many Sichuanese restaurants that mushroomed in Hong Kong in the 1950s and 1960s, for instance, soon found themselves in trouble, for the Cantonese were simply not used to taking their food as ma (numbing) and as la (peppery-spicy) as the Sichuan people. In the end, they reluctantly toned down the ma and la intensity and have held their own ever since.

FOREIGN INFLUENCES

FOREIGN foods were introduced to China before the dawn of the Christian era. They arrived as a result of the efforts of the Han emperor, Wudi, to contain his enemies, the Xiongnu (later the Huns in Europe), from harassing China's western border. He sent the very daring explorer, Zhang Qian, on two expeditions, in 138 BC and later in 115 BC, into the unknown territories west of China. The route Zhang Qian and his men traversed gave birth to what is now known as the Silk Road, which starts in present-day Xi'an (famed for its terracotta army) and travels westward through Dunhuang (famed for its Buddhist cave frescoes), to the Taklamakan desert, and on through Turfan, Kashgar, Samarkand, Bokhara, Iran and Iraq, finally ending in Rome. Chinese historical and literary works have credited this 'Great Traveller', the title bestowed on him by his emperor, with bringing back exotic foodstuffs from the West, many of which to this day bear the prefix 'hu' or 'foreign' to their names. These included pomegranates, grapes, sesame seeds, caraway seeds, walnuts, coriander, alfalfa, spinach, peas, broad beans, onion, watermelon and cucumber. It is doubtful, however, that Zhang Qian and his followers alone brought back all these products, even though they were introduced and grown in China around his time or soon after. The traders who courageously followed in his footsteps, braving the treacherous route to take Chinese silk and other precious things to the Middle East, probably deserve just as much credit for the influx of new ingredients.

One thing is certain, however, and that is that these foodstuffs expanded the repertoire of Chinese dishes at a time when Chinese culinary art, which was to blossom during the Song dynasty (AD 960–1279) was still in its infancy. What the Chinese called hu cakes, made with sesame seeds, had the most enduring impact, for the Han emperor, Mingdi, who succeeded Wudi, loved them so much that they became the rage at Imperial dinners. They have retained their popularity today and in north China they are sold in street stalls and served in restaurants.

In the manufacture of sugar, China also owes a debt to other cultures. Ever since the Zhou dynasty (11th century–221 BC), honey had been the common sweetener, supplemented by malt-sugar made from grain. The growth of sugar-cane had begun during the Warring States period (475–221 BC) and its value as a sweetener had been recognised. Around the 1st century BC, in south China, in what is now Guangdong and Guangxi provinces, juice was already being extracted from the cane, boiled, and then dried in the sun until it solidified into cakes, which were known as 'stone honey'. So valuable were they that they were sent as tribute to the Imperial court. Another kind of stone honey, made from the juices of sugar-cane and cow's milk, came from Persia.

In 648 AD, the second Tang emperor, Taizong, sent an envoy to Bactria, in India, for the express purpose of learning the technique of processing sugar from sugar-cane. Soon after, in compliance with the emperor's edict, Yangzhou, the port where the Grand Canal joins the Yangzi River, became the centre for refining cane sugar into a sandy form, though not yet one as refined as the granulated sugar we use today. The colours seemed to range in descending order of superiority from purplish brown to dark amber then to light brown. But official records note with a sense of smug satisfaction that the processing technique, once mastered, was yielding sugar superior both in colour and taste to that from Bactria. Indeed, by the 10th century, white granulated sugar was being manufactured in the eastern coastal provinces, as well as in Sichuan, and, by the 11th century, writers were calling for its use in their recipes. It was around this time, during the Song dynasty, that the method of producing crystal (also called rock) sugar was devised.

The next wave of foreign influence came during the Ming dynasty (AD 1368–1644). Emperor Yongle, who moved the capital from Nanjing to Peking and whose reign lasted for twenty-two years from 1403, had ambitions to expand the country southward, both for territorial gain and for trade with Southeast Asia, India and beyond. To this end, he dispatched, in 1405, an enterprising eunuch, Zheng He, to lead naval expeditions to the Indian Ocean. During the ensuing twenty-eight years, Zheng He's fleet ventured forth no less than seven times, reaching some thirty-eight countries, including Java, Sumatra, Thailand, Ceylon, India, as well as going further west to Arabia and Aden in Africa. Several of those who accompanied

Zheng He on his voyages kept diaries and notes, which were subsequently published. Perhaps the one with the most curious mind and observant eye was Ma Huan, who not only recorded the court rules and social and sexual customs of different countries but also their fauna and flora, listing their staple cereals, fruit plants, vegetables and livestock, which he compared with those extant in China. Besides being enthusiastic about tropical fruit such as watermelon, sugar-cane and coconuts, he and his companions were also fascinated by the jack-fruits they found in Campa (modern Vietnam). True to their adventurous and inventive spirit, they made them into a Chinese dish.

'The jack-fruits look like winter gourds, the outer skin resembling Sichuanese litchi. Inside the skin are large segments of flesh, yellow in colour like eggs, and tasting like honey. Within the flesh are seeds similar to cock's testicles and these, when stir-fried, taste just like chestnuts.'

Similarly, on another expedition, when they reached Sumatra, Ma Huan became intrigued by the Malaysian durian or 'stinking fruit', which he said, 'when ripe, would split into five to six pieces, stinking like rotten beef'. This notwithstanding, he enthused, 'inside there are some fourteen to fifteen segments of creamy white flesh, very sweet and delicious. Inside the segments are seeds which, if stir-fried to eat, taste just like chestnuts.'

Among the poultry in Sumatra, his favourite was chicken. The large cocks there weighed as much as seven catties (almost 4 kilos or 9 lb), he noted, and yet after only a short cooking time, they became tender and 'the flavour is superb, far superior to that in other countries'. But, 'there are no capons, for foreigners know not how to castrate chickens', he observed.

He also noted that many countries bordering the South China Sea, Indian Ocean and Arabian Sea, sent the Chinese Imperial court periodic tribute, which consisted of various local precious stones, pearls and corals, and that, in return, they received their favourite Chinese products, notably silks and colourful brocades, blue and white porcelain, copper coins and camphor. He also noted, without further comment, that one small country where rhinoceros abounded, sent them to China. No doubt the Chinese emperors, with their 'harems of three thousand beauties', especially appreciated the powder ground from the horns, known for its legendary aphrodisiac effect.

These expeditions had a long-lasting impact, for, from the 15th century onwards, trade between China and the Southeast Asian countries gathered momentum, and

Canton, Macao and Fuzhou became important ports through which the trade routes meandered to other Chinese provinces. One of the most celebrated, and exotic, ingredients in the Chinese cuisine, bird's nest, is in fact indigenous to Java, Malaysia and the Philippines, and has been imported along the trade routes since Ming times. Even though it is not clear who discovered its edible quality and used it to gratify the Chinese palate, thereby depriving the swifts of their nests, it was first mentioned as an expensive food by Ming writers in the 16th century, who were quite puzzled as to what it actually was.

It is, literally, what its name suggests. The nests belong to a species of swifts, of the genus *Collocalia*, who hide them in precipitous cliffs. These birds consume seaweed on the beaches and then spit out a predigested gelatinous substance to make their nests. Not only is the process of sorting out the edible spitting – bird's nest – from the feathers and faeces long and laborious, but the job of collecting them is extremely hazardous. Be that as it may, Bird's Nest Soup, prepared either as a savoury dish with shredded or minced chicken and the best stock or as a sweet dish laced with coconut or almond cream, has always been regarded by the Chinese as one of the ultimate gourmet dishes, made the more delectable by its subtly bouncy texture. That it is regarded as a tonic, with a harmonious property veering neither to yin nor yang extremes, has further enhanced its value, especially for women, who believe it improves their complexion. Until two or three decades ago, before bird's nest rocketed in price, Bird's Nest Soup was a must for a smart banquet, but, alas, it is now so expensive that it is out of reach for most people.

For the vast majority of the Chinese population, much more important than rhinoceros horn and bird's nest was the import of foods from the New World. There are different versions of how sweet potatoes, native to America, were introduced to China, but the most credible one relates to the Fujianese merchant, Chen Zhenlong, who traded in the Philippines. When he was in Manila, he saw sweet potatoes being grown and realised their worth as food, but their export was strictly prohibited by the authorities. In 1593, however, on his way home, he surreptitiously smuggled them back to Fuzhou, his home town, by tying the climbing plants to the sailing ropes of his boat. Once home, he immediately experimented with growing them; to his utter delight, he was successful. This proved providential for, during the famine that occurred the following year, sweet potatoes became the food that sustained many lives. It did not take long for the southern Chinese to realise that not only were sweet potatoes nutritious as well as delicious, but that their leaves were the best fodder for pigs, the source of their favourite meat. When it was found that they prospered in very poor soil where other grain plants would not grow, it soon became official policy to encourage their growth in both Fujian and Guangdong, and the Chinese called them 'foreign-' or 'golden-tubers'. At the beginning of the 17th century, an official who was interested in agriculture took them to Shanghai, where he was being posted; there, he advocated their growth in the Yangzi delta, whence they spread to the northern provinces in the 18th century.

Another import from America was Indian corn or maize (*Zea mays*), which is said to have been brought into China during the middle of the 16th century by Muslims making their pilgrimages to Mecca via Gansu province, where Chinese converts lived. At first, corn was regarded as a precious and expensive food, served only at banquets and to special guests. But as time went by it was found that the growth of maize, being suited to the northern climate in China, was easy and hence prolific; consequently, corn became an important famine food. In the 20th-century Chinese kitchen, cornflour (corn starch in the States) is an important thickening agent for sauces and soups and, as a coating agent for meat, poultry and fish, is second only to potato and tapioca flour. In Peking, the centre of northern regional cuisine, corn, known in Chinese as 'pearl rice', is ground roughly then made either into buns or 'zhou' (congee), an alternative staple for the people when they are not eating wheat flour 'mantou' (steamed buns) or rice zhou. In Chinese restaurants in the West, Sweetcorn Soup, made with egg and minced chicken, was arguably the most popular soup for non-Chinese diners until they discovered the Sichuanese Hot and Sour Soup.

Other imports from the continent of America were pumpkins, guavas, papayas, tomatoes, chilli peppers and peanuts, the last two of which have exerted a major influence on Chinese cuisine. The hot chilli peppers (*Capsicum frutescens*) were first brought into Asia by the Portuguese in the 16th century, but once they found their way into China in the 17th century, their growth spread like wildfire in the mountainous southwestern provinces of Hunan and Sichuan, where the population took to their fiery spiciness in their food as God's gift to counter the oppressingly humid climate.

Peanuts or groundnuts from South America were also introduced by the Portuguese during the 16th century, but it took more than two centuries before their use as a new source of cooking oil took hold. Lard was (and still is in China) the major source of animal fat, and rape-seed oil was the vegetable oil used in cooking. Since the 19th century, however, when the growth of groundnuts took off rapidly, peanut oil has become the most important cooking oil. Its importance to Chinese food is like olive oil to Italian cooking. In more recent years, peanut oil has encountered strong competition from corn oil, even though the rich and nutty flavour the former imparts to stir-fried dishes cannot, in my opinion, be matched.

White potatoes, which became an important staple food in Europe from the 18th century, were not introduced to China until the late 18th century, when they were brought by French Catholic missionaries. Called in Chinese 'beans of the earth' (rather than *pommes de terre*), they are part of the staple diet in north China, though not to the same extent as noodles and steamed buns (which are made from wheat flour). In south China, where rice is the daily staple, potatoes are prepared in such a way as to be an occasional dish to go with rice. A popular one is a home-made dish of sautéed potato cake. Potatoes are boiled, mashed, mixed with seasoned minced beef and chopped onion and then sautéed in peanut or vegetable oil until a semi-crispy crust is formed.

Tomatoes have, in the 20th century, become such an integral part of Chinese cuisine that few Chinese would stop to think of their foreign origin, despite the fact that their Chinese name, as with those for guava, papaya, sweet potato and pumpkin, bears the prefix of 'fan' (like 'hu'), meaning foreign. Indeed, the 20th century has seen foreign condiments being adopted by the Chinese as their own, some with enriching results while others have made a more dubious contribution. Tomato ketchup, ubiquitous in a Chinese kitchen both at home and in restaurants, is almost indispensable when making sweet and sour sauce. Sautéed jumbo prawns laced with tomato ketchup is a standard Cantonese dish, which was especially in vogue during the post-war era of the 1950s and 1960s. The problem is that some Chinese restaurants and takeaways, in abusing its use, have given Chinese dishes a uniform pinkish-red look, which is garish and unappetising.

In many Cantonese kitchens Lea & Perrins Worcestershire sauce stands as a twin to the soy sauce bottle, and is used most popularly as a dipping sauce for deep-fried food such as spring rolls and prawn balls. For many years I used to regard the sauce as Chinese as soy sauce until one day, suddenly noticing its English label staring me in the eye, I read it closely and became aware of its foreign origin. I could, therefore, appreciate the rather amusing story told by an English friend of mine. He and an

English journalist were having a scrumptious dinner in a Chinese restaurant in Hong Kong where they found the dipping sauce for deep-fried oysters especially sensational. So impressed were they with it that they asked the waiter what it was. Having disappeared into the kitchen, he returned quoting the chef's reassurance that it was a Chinese sauce. Not quite satisfied with the answer, they wished to know how it was made, and would the chef show them. Thereupon they were taken into the kitchen to meet the chef. Beaming with a broad smile and holding high a huge bottle of Worcestershire sauce in front of them, the chef said, 'Yeh, yeh, it Chinese sauce.'

MSG (monosodium glutamate), the crystalline sodium salt of glutamic acid, is a flavour enhancer originally invented by the Japanese, and it has had the most controversial effect on 20th-century Chinese cuisine. In 1908, Professor Kikunae Ikeda of the University of Tokyo demonstrated that the main ingredient of 'kombu', a kelp traditionally used to make soup stock, was glutamic acid. The following year, he took out a patent for the method of extracting this from wheat gluten. The Suzuki Trading Company advertised it using a geisha as a model, who wore a cook's apron sporting the characters 'Aji no moto'. The commercial product of MSG had been launched with its trademark. MSG 'is now produced mostly through a fermentation process which uses molasses derived from sugar cane and sugar beets. In Southeast Asia, the starch from sago and tapioca is generally used', says the blurb of the producer, Ajinomoto.

Chinese chefs, who were already working as apprentices, tell me how they first became aware of the product in the 1940s, just after the end of the Second World War. All of a sudden, this 'wonder' powder, capable of adding a meaty sweetness to food in general, hitherto provided only by stock which had to be simmered for hours, was passed around from cook to cook and restaurant to restaurant, and one and all marvelled at the result. But, since it was very expensive, it was used sparingly. Before long, however, it was being mass-produced, not only by the Japanese, but also by the Chinese. As MSG became inexpensive and affordable, Chinese restaurants readily adopted it as a substitute for stock, pouring indiscriminate amounts into dishes, and especially into soups.

In the 1960s, the phrase 'Chinese restaurant syndrome' was coined in the United States to describe the symptoms suffered by some people after eating Chinese food, especially in Chinese restaurants. Whilst eating, they would have a heating sensation in their temples, which would be followed later by an extreme thirst and then a

Top of oval platter: Shanghai Spring Rolls (p. 137);
middle: Shredded Chicken with Edible Jellyfish (p. 143);
bottom: Bean Curd Skin Rolls (p. 140).

PLATE 3

Top left: Fried Amoy Vermicelli (p. 245).
Right: Yunnan Laifen (p. 236).
Bottom left: Shanghai Oily Noodles (p. 249).

PLATE 4

headache. Some would even feel chest pains and heart palpitations. But these symptoms would subside after several hours or overnight. Much debate has since been engendered, in the United Nations, in China and among health-conscious people. But for all the complaints of the sufferers, there is no conclusive proof to show that MSG causes permanent harm to the body and to the nervous system.

In mainland China as well as in Taiwan, a stance seems to have been taken. In all the cookbooks published in Chinese, MSG, which is called 'weijing' in Chinese, or gourmet powder, is used in the recipes as a condiment in conjunction with salt and soy sauce. It is used in restaurants, in cookery schools and at home as an efficacious flavour-enhancing seasoning, the liberator from time-consuming stock-making. Among the 400,000 tons of MSG now produced annually in some twenty countries around the world, China, is, apparently, the biggest producer.

My personal attitude, shared by many other Chinese, is this. As frequent and keen restaurant-goers – a Chinese characteristic – we have to put up with dishes containing MSG in any case, so that when we cook at home, why bother with the stuff which at best tends to give the same taste to food? If, during the past two millennia, our ancestors have perfected the cuisine without MSG, I am content to continue this tradition, following their example to make real stock. I was brought up with good and MSG-free food at home, and I have never used it in my own kitchen.

RECIPES

COLD STARTERS

IN PEKING or northern cuisine and in Shanghai or eastern cuisine, it is traditional to serve cold dishes prior to serving something hot. While no one knows the exact origin of this custom, most agree that it can be traced back to the Spring and Autumn era (770–476 BC), when feudal lords were carving up the disintegrating Zhou dynasty and fighting among themselves for supremacy. The Duke Wen of Jin had, among his numerous advisers, Jie Zhitui, who accompanied and supported him as his comrade-in-arms for nineteen years. When, at last, the duke consolidated his power and set up his feudal state in Shanxi province, he rewarded many of his advisers but he neglected Jie. Without a word, Jie left the court and retired to live on a mountain. Jie's followers, feeling aggrieved on his behalf, posted a petition at the palace setting out what they considered to be the injustice done to their master. When the duke read the petition he felt so ashamed that he immediately sent an envoy to invite Jie back to court. But Jie declined the offer. To demonstrate his sincerity, the duke himself went to the mountain only to find that Jie had hidden out of sight. The duke thought that if he set fire to the mountain, Jie was bound to come out of hiding, and he could then convince his erstwhile supporter to rejoin him at court. And so he ordered his men to set fire to the trees. But instead of escaping, Jie stubbornly held on to a tree and was thus burned to death. Full of remorse, the duke grieved with his people for the tragic loss of Jie. As a memorial to him, the duke forbade the lighting of fires on the anniversary of his death, and instead enjoined his people to eat cold food with him. It fell on the day before the Clear and Bright Festival (which occurs around Easter and is the time when Chinese go to sweep the graves as a sign of respect to the deceased), and became known as 'hanshi jie' or the cold food festival.

The cold dishes that are served now range from small things, such as peanuts and pickled vegetables, to elaborate cold platters, such as 'a phoenix resting amidst pine trees' or a colourful 'peacock preening itself', which are normally only served in restaurants. They also include the dishes set out in this chapter, which are both delicious and within the scope of anyone interested in cooking. To accompany this food, the Chinese often drink yellow wines, such as Shaoxing wine, which is served warm.

In southern China where it is hot and humid, the custom of serving cold starters, contrary to expectation, has made little impact. The reason for this seems to be a matter of hygiene. Since refrigeration was unavailable, and typhoid and cholera were diseases particularly feared in the south, it was considered safer to stick to the hot stir-fries. As a result, it became customary at banquets to serve a couple of small hot dishes before the main ones. This is not to say that cold dishes are not served at all in the south, especially now that refrigeration is becoming more and more widespread. What is served cold as an appetiser, for example, are preserved duck eggs with their creamy green yolks and, brownish, jellied whites. These, endearingly dubbed 'thousand-year eggs' by Westerners – though in fact only preserved for about six weeks – are shelled and served immediately with pickled ginger. An acquired taste they may be, but they are addictive.

Edible Jellyfish
and White Radish

TRADITIONALLY a Shanghai–Peking dish, but nowadays loved by the Cantonese as well. Jellyfish poses no problem for the Chinese, for its Chinese name, unlike the English, is of a poetic nature. For non-Chinese, if you can ignore the name, chances are that you will be so won over by its bouncy texture that you won't be able to have enough of it!

SERVES 6

450 g (1 lb) dried jellyfish
350 g (12 oz) long white radish (moolie)
7.5 ml (1½ tsp) salt

FOR THE DRESSING:
45–60 ml (3–4 tbsp) peanut or vegetable oil
2 cloves garlic, peeled and crushed
2 shallots, peeled and sliced
4 thin ginger slices, peeled
5 ml (1 tsp) hot made-up mustard
1.5 ml (¼ tsp) salt
22.5 ml (1½ tbsp) thin or light soy sauce
45 ml (3 tbsp) Chinese rice vinegar
5 ml (1 tsp) caster sugar
30 ml (2 tbsp) sesame oil

1 Prepare the jellyfish. If the jellyfish comes in sheets, shake, then rinse off with cold water the large grains of salt used to preserve them. Soak the jellyfish in plenty of cold water. Change the water 10–12 times at 30–60-minute intervals, each time squeezing the jellyfish with your hands to get rid of the saltiness and the sea odour. If you are not in a hurry, the soaking can be spread over 2–3 days.

   Drain, then cut the sheets into thin strips, 6 mm (¼ in) wide and put into a large bowl. Pour plenty of hot, but not boiling, water over the strips, which will curl up instantly. Pour into a colander and rinse thoroughly with cold water. Repeat the soaking and rinsing 2–3 more times. Test by tasting: if the jellyfish is totally bland, it is ready. Drain well, squeeze out excess moisture, then pat dry.

2 Peel the white radish and shred lengthways into long, thin julienne strips. Put into a clean bowl, sprinkle over the salt and mix.

   Leave for 1–2 hours, drain, then squeeze hard to get rid of excess fluid.

3 Prepare the dressing. Heat a wok over a high heat until smoke rises. Add the oil and swirl it around. Add the garlic and stir, then the shallots and stir, then the ginger and fry until they are brown and the oil aromatic. Strain the oil into a small bowl and let it cool; discard the seasoning condiments.

   In another small bowl combine the mustard, salt, soy sauce, vinegar and sugar and stir to mix until smooth. Stir in the cooled oil and the sesame oil.

4 Mix the jellyfish and radish in a serving dish. Keep in the refrigerator if not served straightaway. Just before serving, add the dressing and mix well.

Duck
Tongues

SERVES 8–10

675 g (1½ lb) frozen duck
  tongues, defrosted

FOR THE SPICED LIQUID:
575 ml (1 pint/2½ cups) water
2 whole star anise (16 segments)
5 ml (1 tsp) Sichuan peppercorns
5 ml (1 tsp) black peppercorns
4 cm (1½ in) cinnamon stick
2 pieces liquorice
1 piece (⅓ of whole) dried
  tangerine peel

FOR THE SAUCE:
4 ml (¾ tsp) salt
2.5–5 ml (½–1 tsp) sugar
30 ml (2 tbsp) thin or light soy
  sauce
30 ml (2 tbsp) hot made-up
  mustard
30 ml (2 tbsp) Chinese rice
  vinegar
45 ml (3 tbsp) sesame oil
100–150 ml (4–5 fl oz/½–⅔ cup)
  spiced liquid

DUCK TONGUES have a gelatinous yet slightly crunchy texture, and are most attractive to the Chinese palate. These tiny things, which do not feature in other cuisines, grace many a regional table in China. In Shanghai, they are red-cooked in dark soy sauce and wine; in Hunan and Sichuan, they are stir-fried with duck's webs; and in Canton, they are sometimes steamed with black bean sauce and served in a saucer as a dimsum. This mustard-vinaigrette sauce I have devised makes for a very appetising first course.

Duck tongues come from China, and they are sold frozen in Chinese supermarkets.

1 Half fill a large saucepan, preferably with a heavy bottom, with water and bring to the boil. Add the defrosted tongues, return to the boil and blanch over a high heat for about 3 minutes. Pour into a colander and rinse off any remaining scum on the tongues with cold running water. Wash the saucepan.
2 Add the ingredients to make the spiced liquid: water, star anise, Sichuan peppercorns, black peppercorns, cinnamon stick, liquorice and tangerine peel. Bring to the boil, then cover the saucepan and reduce the heat to maintain a gentle simmer for 30 minutes so as to fully release the aroma of the spices. Add the tongues and continue to simmer for another 30 minutes. Remove with a perforated spoon, discarding any spices. For those who have the patience and do not shun the labour, debone the tongues by removing the flat bone on the bottom side of the tongue. They can otherwise be left intact.
3 Strain the spiced liquid and discard the solids.
4 Prepare the sauce. In a bowl mix together the salt, sugar, soy sauce, mustard and vinegar. Gently beat in the sesame oil until emulsified. Stir in the spiced liquid.
5 Add the tongues to the sauce and turn to coat well. Leave in the refrigerator for at least 6 hours, but better still overnight, so that the sauce can penetrate the tongues.
6 Mix thoroughly before serving. Serve cold.

Fried
Shrimps

THE SHANGHAIESE call these 'oil-exploded shrimps', which refers to the fact that they are deep-fried, but ever so quickly, in their shells. They can be prepared ahead of time.

SERVES 4

450 g (1 lb) raw shrimps in the shell, without heads (40–60 shrimps)
300 ml (10 fl oz/1¼ cups) vegetable oil
5–10 ml (1–2 tsp) sesame oil

FOR THE SAUCE:
22.5–30 ml (1½–2 tbsp) thin or light soy sauce
5 ml (1 tsp) sugar
2.5 ml (½ tsp) ginger juice (*see* p. 357)
15 ml (1 tbsp) Shaoxing wine or medium dry sherry
15 ml (1 tbsp) peanut or vegetable oil

1 Thoroughly rinse the shells of the shrimps, rubbing with your fingers. Pat dry with kitchen paper.
2 Prepare the sauce. Put the soy sauce, sugar, ginger juice, wine or sherry and the oil into a small bowl. Stir to mix.
3 Heat the vegetable oil in a wok over a high heat until it reaches 180°C (350°F) in temperature. Add all the shrimps and fry, stirring them gently for about 30 seconds or until they curl up and change to a pinkish colour. At this point, the shrimps are just done. Remove with a perforated disc and put on to a dish (no need to drain on kitchen paper). Discard the oil, but it is not necessary to wash the wok.
4 Pour the sauce into the wok and bring to the boil. Let it bubble for a few seconds to release the fragrance of the wine or sherry. Return the shrimps to the wok and stir for absorption. Remove to a serving dish and let the shrimps soak in the sauce for about 1 hour or longer.
5 Just before serving, sprinkle on the sesame oil and mix. Serve at room temperature. To eat, use your fingers to peel the shell unless, like the Chinese, you are used to sucking the juice embedded in the shell, then peeling the shell with your teeth before spitting it out, thereby savouring everything.

Illustrated on Plate 1.

Bean Curd
Salad

SERVES 8

6 cakes bean curd, refreshed (*see* p. 354)
25 g (1 oz) dried shrimps, rinsed
30 ml (2 tbsp) thick or dark soy sauce
2.5 ml (½ tsp) sugar
10 ml (2 tsp) ginger juice (*see* p. 357) or grated ginger
30–45 ml (2–3 tbsp) peanut or vegetable oil
15–22.5 ml (1–1½ tbsp) sesame oil
10 ml (2 tsp) chilli hot oil (*see* p. 357) (optional)
4 large spring onions, trimmed and cut into tiny rounds
2–3 fresh green or red chillies, deseeded and cut into small rounds (optional)

WHEN WE buy bean curd, it is already cooked, even though we must ensure that it is fresh. This easy recipe makes a very palatable bean curd salad, a change from the more common warm bean curd dishes.

1 Dice the bean curd cakes into 1 cm (½ in) cubes. Put on to kitchen paper to absorb excess moisture.
2 Soak the dried shrimps in just sufficient water to cover, about 30–45 ml (2–3 tbsp), for 30 minutes. Drain, reserving the soaking liquid, if any. Chop up fairly finely, leaving just sufficient texture in the bite.
3 Place the chopped dried shrimps and juice in a large serving bowl. Add also the soy sauce, sugar, ginger juice or grated ginger, peanut or vegetable oil, sesame oil and hot oil, if you prefer the dish to be spicy, and stir to mix. Add the bean curd cubes, thoroughly dried, and toss to mix well. Sprinkle with the spring onions and mix again. Leave to stand for about 30 minutes, tossing and mixing once or twice more. Just before serving, add the chillies, if used. Serve at room temperature.

Drunken
Chicken Breasts

SERVES 8–10

675–900 g (1½–2 lb) boned but not skinned chicken breasts, about 4–6 pieces
7.5–10 ml (1½–2 tsp) fine sea salt
1.5–2.5 ml (¼–½ tsp) sugar
15–22.5 ml (1–1½ tbsp) ginger juice or purée (*see* p. 357)

Illustrated on Plate 1.

THIS IS my own adaptation of the well-known Shanghai dish, Drunken Chicken, which is usually made using a whole chicken. When drunken, the chicken, including the skin and bones, is chopped up into small pieces and served cold. Whilst Chinese people love to chew the meat around the bones, most non-Chinese find it an awkward way to enjoy chicken. Following the identical method, but using only the breasts, works just as well and the result is a welcoming, robust drunken flavour.

1 Place the chicken breasts in a heatproof dish with raised edges suitable for steaming. Sprinkle half the salt on one side, turn the pieces over and sprinkle on the remaining salt. Sprinkle on the sugar, then dribble over the ginger juice or purée and place the spring onions on top.

2 Transfer the dish with the chicken to a steamer (see p. 355) and steam over a high heat for about 15 minutes or until cooked. Test by piercing the meat with a fork or a chopstick; if it goes through easily, the chicken is cooked. Remove the dish from the steamer.

3 While still hot, put half of the chicken breasts into an earthenware or glass pot so they fit snugly and pour over them half of the wine or sherry. Place the remaining chicken breasts on top and pour in the rest of the wine or sherry. Pour in all the juices accumulated from steaming from the heatproof dish, discarding the spring onions. The juices, together with the wine or sherry, should ideally just cover the chicken. Cover the pot with the lid.

4 Leave in a cool place for 4–6 hours. If the juices have not covered the chicken, shift the order of the pieces on top of each other and then put into the refrigerator, covered. The liquid will turn into thin jelly or jellylike sauce. The chicken becomes quite drunkenly delicious overnight and is ready to be served cold, but it will become even more inebriated if left for 1–2 more days – or longer.

5 To serve, simply put the chicken breasts on a dish and carve crossways at 4 mm (⅛ in) intervals. Scoop some sauce and put on top or on the side. This sauce is also delicious with noodles.

2–3 spring onions, trimmed and halved crossways
175–250 ml (6–8 fl oz/¾–1 cup) Shaoxing wine or medium dry sherry

Cold
Grey Mullet

SERVES 6

1 very fresh grey mullet, about
   1 kilo (2¼ lb), scaled, gutted and
   cleaned
22.5–30 ml (1½–2 tbsp) salt

DIPPING SAUCES:
Chaozhou bean sauce (if available)
East-meets-West sauce:
   30 ml (2 tbsp) HP, OK, A1 or
      Worcestershire sauce
   10 ml (2 tsp) thick or dark soy
      sauce
   2.5–5 ml (½–1 tsp) chilli sauce

GREY MULLET, which abounds in the Chaozhou area not too far from Canton, is a favourite with the local people, who serve it hot, steamed with pickled lime, or cold as in this very simple recipe. Do not be put off by the seemingly large amount of salt being used. In fact, the salt, used as a preservative against the hot climate as well as to dissipate any rank fishy odour, hardly penetrates the skin, which is in any case removed and discarded before the fish is served. There is a special Chaozhou bean sauce to go with the fish, called Puning Bean Sauce, which is produced commercially in a bottle. As it is not available in the West, some of my Chaozhou friends, Ellie Alleyne and her family, make up their own East-meets-West concoction which, surprisingly, is highly successful. I agree with them when they say they prefer it to the salty Chaozhou bean sauce.

1 Scrape off the black membrane that lines the cavity of the grey mullet, as it has a slightly bitter taste. Rinse and pat dry.
2 Rub the salt all over the skin of the fish and some into the cavity. Leave to stand for 2–3 hours in a heatproof dish at room temperature. If the fish is too long, halve it crossways.
3 Place the dish in a steamer and steam (see p. 355) for 15 minutes until the fish is well done. Remove the dish from the steamer. Lift the fish from the dish and place on a wire rack to let any liquid drip off and to cool, as it is always served cold. Discard the salty juices in the dish. Put into the refrigerator, covered, if it is to be served several hours later or the following day.
4 Prepare the East-meets-West sauce: mix the HP, OK, A1 or Worcestershire sauce with the soy sauce and chilli sauce in a dish and place on the dining table for people to help themselves.
5 Just before serving, tear off and discard the skin from the fish.

Lu
Flavours

SERVES 10–12

IN EVERY province and region of China, there is a universal method of slowly simmering meat and offal, poultry and eggs and even some seafood, such as ink fish and octopus, in a pot of liquid known as 'lu' stock. Lu stock (flavour-potted stock) is always seasoned with salt, soy sauces, sugar, wine and a variety of spices consisting generally of star anise, Sichuan peppercorns, cassia bark or cinnamon sticks, cloves, fennel, liquorice and others. When a family wish to start a master lu stock, one person will go to a Chinese pharmacy and ask for lu stock ingredients. Depending on the price, the pharmacist may include very esoteric things such as dried lizard and sea horse, which are valued for their tonic properties. But the packets of mixed spices found in Chinese supermarkets definitely do not contain any such exotic ingredients! The master lu stock, once prepared, can go on for a long, long time, for you can add more seasoning ingredients; and the ingredients flavoured in the stock will themselves add to its richness and flavour. Initially, you should cook a strong meat such as beef in the first spread of this recipe, for it can take the full impact of the spices in the stock. Thereafter, chicken wings and drumsticks, gizzards and livers are very popular items to be flavour-potted. Alternatively, poussins or Cornish hens, quails and quail eggs (which nowadays are easily available and inexpensive) make a delicately delectable second spread. For the third spread, try ink fish or even octopus.

1 Tie strings, about 3 rounds, across the shin of beef and 1 round lengthways round the centre. Put into a large, deep stockpot and add the water, ensuring the beef is well covered. Add the bag of mixed spices, tying a string between it and one handle of the stockpot for easy removal of the bag. Add also the ginger and tangerine peel and bring to a rolling boil. The scum will foam to the surface. Spoon off the scum until the liquid is relatively clear.

2 Add the salt, soy sauces, sugar and wine or sherry and return to a simmer. The stock should be quite salty and

1st spread:

1.35 kilos (3 lb) shin of beef in one piece

3½ litres (6 pints/14 cups) cold water

about 50 g (2 oz/¼ cup) mixed Chinese spices in a muslin bag, tied:

  5 whole star anise (each 8 segments)

  10 g (⅓ oz) cassia bark or cinnamon stick pieces

  1 caoguo (*Amomum tsao-ko*)

  2.5 ml (½ tsp) cloves

  15 ml (1 tbsp) fennel seeds

  15 ml (1 tbsp) Sichuan peppercorns

  2.5 ml (½ tsp) black peppercorns

  3 pieces liquorice

  4 pieces dried ginger

50 g (2 oz) ginger, rinsed but unpeeled and bruised

3 large pieces dried tangerine peel

22.5 g (1½ tbsp) sea salt

250 ml (8 fl oz/1 cup) thick or dark soy sauce

50 ml (2 fl oz/¼ cup) thin or light soy sauce

115 g (4 oz/½ cup) candy or crystal sugar

100 ml (4 fl oz/½ cup) Shaoxing wine or medium dry sherry

12 eggs

30 ml (2 tbsp) Mei Kuei Lu wine or gin

15–30 ml (1–2 tbsp) sesame oil, or to taste

5–10 ml (1–2 tsp) roasted ground Sichuan peppercorns (*see* p. 359)

5–10 ml (1–2 tsp) chilli powder or to taste

rich. Put on the lid, reduce the heat to maintain a gentle simmer for 1½–1¾ hours or until the shin of beef is tender but still firm in texture. To test, pierce through the meat with one chopstick; if it goes through easily, the meat is sufficiently tender.

3 Meanwhile, hard-boil the eggs in a pot of water for about 8 minutes. Pour into a colander and rinse under cold running water. Peel the eggs. About 10–15 minutes before the beef is ready, add the eggs to the stockpot to simmer with the beef.

4 Remove the pot from the heat. Add the Mei Kuei Lu wine or gin. Leave the beef and eggs as well as the bag of spices and other seasoning solids in the lu stock in a cool place for 6 hours or overnight. The lu stock has now become the master stock which can be used again and again to flavour other ingredients.

5 Remove and discard any congealed fat on the surface of the lu sauce. Remove the beef and refrigerate for 2–3 hours to firm up the texture, and hence facilitate slicing. Remove also the eggs.

6 To serve, untie the strings round the beef. Halve lengthways into 2 pieces. Put 1 piece back into the refrigerator for another meal. Carve 1 piece crossways into very thin slices and arrange on a serving plate. Sprinkle on the sesame oil to taste. Cut 4 eggs into slices and add to the plate. Keep the rest of the eggs for another meal with the beef or serve on their own.

7 To serve the beef Sichuanese style, in addition to the sesame oil, sprinkle on the roasted ground Sichuan peppercorns and chilli powder.

2nd spread:
12–48 quail eggs
12 well-plucked quails
the master stock with the bag of
  mixed spices and other
  seasoning solids

1 Put all the quail eggs in a saucepan and cover with plenty of cold water. Gradually bring to the boil, lower the heat and simmer, covered, for 1–2 minutes until they are cooked. Pour into a colander, refresh them under a cold tap, then soak them in plenty of cold water for 20 minutes or longer. This facilitates the peeling of the eggs later.

2 Drain the eggs, then, one by one, roll them on a worktop to crack the shells so that the stock can seep through to season the eggs.

3 Clean the quails. With your fingers, remove the innards from the cavity of each quail, then rinse well. Drain.

4 Bring the master stock to the boil, with the bag of spices

and other seasoning solids in it. Add all the quails and quail eggs and gradually bring to the boil again. The stock should more or less cover the ingredients; if necessary, add a little water. Reduce the heat to maintain a simmer and continue to cook, covered, for about 6 minutes. Remove the stockpot from the heat without even once replacing the lid to peep. Let the quails continue to poach, covered, in the liquid for at least 45 minutes until they are just done. If this spread is prepared in the morning they, and the eggs, can be left in the stock until ready to be served at lunch or dinner.

5 Serve them at room temperature. Peel the eggs before serving them. The quails can be served whole or cut in two. Put some lu stock in a bowl as a dipping sauce.

3rd spread:
1 cleaned octopus, 1.1–1.35 kilos (2½–3 lb)
the master stock with the bag of mixed spices and other seasoning solids
5 ml (1 tsp) salt (optional)
50 ml (2 fl oz/¼ cup) thick or dark soy sauce (optional)
25 ml (1 fl oz/⅛ cup) thin or light soy sauce (optional)
30–45 ml (2–3 tbsp) sesame oil
chilli sauce as dipping sauce

1 Heat a large pot of water until only fairly hot. Add the octopus and continue to heat, uncovered, for about 1 minute. Pour into a colander and rinse with cold water. Pull off as much as possible the membrane which covers the body and the tentacles. Using cocktail sticks, remove and discard the chalky eyes in the suckers on the tentacles. Rinse clean and drain.

2 Bring the master stock to a simmer over a moderate heat, with the bag of mixed spices and the seasoning solids in it. Taste the stock before adding the salt and the soy sauces. Add the octopus and continue to simmer gently, covered, for about 1 hour until it is tender. Care must be taken not to boil the octopus fiercely, lest its texture becomes rubbery and tough.

3 Remove from the heat but leave the octopus in the stockpot for 6 hours or overnight for it to absorb the lu flavours. Remove the octopus from the stock and if it is to be served later keep in the refrigerator.

4 Serve either at room temperature or cold. Cut the body pouch and the tentacles into pieces. Brush with the sesame oil and serve with chilli sauce on the table as an optional dipping sauce.

NOTE: Keep the master stock (with or without the bag of mixed spices and the other seasoning solids) either in the cold larder or the refrigerator. Bring it to the boil again once a week, lest moulds develop on the surface and spoil the stock. To make the next 2–3 spreads, discard all the old spices and solids. Add a fresh bag to the stock of 25 g (1 oz) mixed spices, 25 g (1 oz) ginger, 2 large pieces dried tangerine peel, about 10 ml (2 tsp) salt, 50 ml (2 fl oz/¼ cup) each thick or dark and thin or light soy sauce, 25–50 g (1–2 oz) candy or crystal sugar and 50 ml (2 fl oz/¼ cup) Shaoxing wine. Use your own judgment after you have tasted the stock. Replenish also with water and top up with Mei Kuei Lu wine or gin from time to time.

Aubergine Salad

SERVES 6

3–4 aubergines, about 900 g (2 lb), rinsed and stalks removed
5 ml (1 tsp) roasted sesame seeds (*see* p. 359), or to taste
small bunch of coriander leaves, trimmed and torn into pieces

FOR THE DRESSING:
2.5 ml (½ tsp) salt
5 ml (1 tsp) caster sugar
15 ml (1 tbsp) Chinese rice vinegar (or about 10 ml/2 tsp white wine vinegar)
30 ml (2 tbsp) thin or light soy sauce
30 ml (2 tbsp) sesame oil

THE FAMOUS 18th-century gastronome, Yuan Mei, in his *Cookery Lists* (*see* p. 38) opines that, in the summer, aubergines are delicious cooked this way: 'Steam them until limp then break them up. Dress them with sesame oil and rice vinegar.' Inspired by his words, I have made up the following recipe, which I find not only suitable as a summer salad but also delicious as a winter starter before hot dishes are served. When entertaining, it is ideal, as you can prepare it ahead of time.

1 Put the aubergines straight into a bamboo steaming basket or a metal steamer container. Steam (*see* p. 355) over a high heat for 30–35 minutes or until they are limp and the skin wrinkled.

2 Remove and peel with a small knife when they are cool enough to be handled; the skin should come off very easily. Break up each aubergine lengthways into unbroken strips with a knife or a pair of chopsticks. If you wish, remove some of the seeds inside. During this process, water will ooze out of the aubergines. Drain off as much water as possible.

3 Carefully pick up the strips and line them in a spiral fashion on a serving dish, making sure you get rid of any dripping water. Put into the refrigerator for at least 30 minutes until cold, or longer. Cover the dish if left for a long period.

4 In the meantime, make the dressing. Place the salt, sugar, vinegar, soy sauce and sesame oil in a small bowl and stir to mix well. Keep nearby.

5 Just before serving, give the dressing a thorough stir, then pour over the aubergine. There is no need to mix,

thereby disturbing the spiral pattern and making the strips mushy. Sprinkle with the sesame seeds and scatter on the coriander leaves as garnish. Serve cold.

Spicy
Peanuts

PEANUTS, also called groundnuts, have a universal appeal as a titbit to go with drinks, not least in China, where they are cheap and plentiful. While they are roasted in other countries, the Chinese excel in deep-frying them, and the flavours differ from region to region. These spicy ones, Sichuanese in flavour, are made the more crunchy by the outer skin and flour coating. As they are so irresistible, you may as well make two batches in one go; put the second batch in an air-tight jar or tin and they will stay crisp for at least two weeks. On the other hand, once you start eating them, finish them within the day, lest they go soggy.

脆
辣
花
生

SERVES 10–20

FOR EACH BATCH:
170 g (6 oz/1¼ cups) cornflour
150 ml (5 fl oz/⅔ cup) cold water
450 g (1 lb) red-skinned peanuts
115 g (4 oz/¾ cup) plain flour
vegetable oil for deep-frying
5–10 ml (1–2 tsp) spiced salt (*see* p. 360)
5–10 ml (1–2 tsp) chilli hot oil (*see* p. 357)

Illustrated on Plate 1.

1 Put the cornflour in a large bowl and slowly add the water to make a gluey batter, stirring all the time with a fork or wooden spoon to prevent lumps from forming. Add all the peanuts to the bowl and stir to coat evenly with the batter. Tip the peanuts into a sieve to allow excess batter to drip off.

2 Pour the flour into a large bowl and add the peanuts. Press the flour over them until they have a snow-capped appearance. Transfer the floured nuts to a large wide-meshed sieve set over a basin and lightly shake off any excess flour, taking care not to shake off the snowy coating.

3 Fill a wok just under half full with vegetable oil, other-wise the oil may spill over when the peanuts are added. Heat the oil over a high heat to a temperature of 180°C (350°F). Carefully tip in the peanuts; the oil will foam momentarily. Moving the peanuts around from time to time with a pair of long chopsticks or a wooden spoon, deep-fry for about 7–8 minutes or until the coating of flour has become a pale golden colour and the nuts crunchy. Remove the nuts from the wok with a large

hand strainer or perforated spoon, and spread them out on kitchen paper to drain off excess oil. Leave to cool for about 15–30 minutes, then transfer to a bowl and sprinkle with the spiced salt and hot oil. Serve cold.

4 If you intend to deep-fry another batch at this stage, allow the loose flour in the oil to settle for about 20 minutes or longer, during which time you can prepare another batch of peanuts by repeating steps 1 and 2. Carefully pour the oil into another container, leaving the sediment in the bottom of the wok.

5 Discard the sediment, wash and dry the wok. Return the oil to the wok (add more if necessary) and repeat step 3 to deep-fry the second batch.

Dry-braised Fragrant Mushrooms

SERVES 6

24, or about 40–45 g (1½ oz) medium dried Chinese black mushrooms, reconstituted in 300–350 ml (10–12 fl oz/1¼–1½ cups) water (see p. 353)
30 ml (2 tbsp) peanut or vegetable oil
10 ml (2 tsp) Shaoxing wine or medium dry sherry
10 ml (2 tsp) ginger juice (*see* p. 357)
1.5 ml (¼ tsp) salt
5 ml (1 tsp) sugar
15 ml (1 tbsp) mushroom soy sauce or thick or dark soy sauce
about 15 ml (1 tbsp) sesame oil

Illustrated on Plate 1.

THESE MOREISH mushrooms, which are attractively shiny black to Chinese eyes, can be prepared in advance and served either at room temperature or cold from the refrigerator. When paired with Drunken Chicken (*see* p. 126), for example, you will have two such memorable starters that your guests are bound to ask to be invited back, and soon!

1 Drain the mushrooms, squeezing out excess moisture but leaving them damp. Save all the liquid.

2 Heat a large saucepan over a high heat until very hot. Add the oil and swirl it around several times to cover the entire bottom. Add the mushrooms, stir about a dozen times as they sizzle in the oil. Splash in the wine or sherry, continuing to stir a few more times, then add the ginger juice and stir again. Pour in the soaking liquid. When it comes to the boil, reduce the heat to low. Season with the salt, sugar and soy sauce. Add the lid and simmer for 10–15 minutes or until almost all the juices have been absorbed, taking care, however, not to let the mushrooms become burned. Transfer to a serving dish and arrange them, cap side up.

3 Serve either at room temperature or cold from the refrigerator, where they keep well, covered, for 2–3

days. Just before serving, brush the caps with the sesame oil, which will instantly enhance the fragrance of the mushrooms.

Spicy
Cucumber

THESE CUCUMBER titbits, rooted in the spicy Sichuanese tradition, are one of the most popular dishes I have ever devised, and have universal appeal. Intensely yet harmoniously salty, sweet, vinegary and spicy-hot, they have to be experienced by the palate as they defy description. Fortunately, they are easy to make, and will keep for weeks, if not for ever, in the refrigerator. They are a sure winner for a drinks party.

SERVES 10–12

2 large cucumbers, each about 450 g (1 lb), rinsed
20 ml (4 tsp) salt
90 ml (6 tbsp) sugar
60 ml (4 tbsp) Chinese rice vinegar or 45 ml (3 tbsp) white wine vinegar
30 ml (2 tbsp) sesame oil
15 ml (1 tbsp) peanut oil
3–6 dried red chillies (depending on size and your tolerance of spiciness), deseeded and cut into pieces

Illustrated on Plate 1.

1 Quarter the cucumbers lengthways. Scoop out and discard the seeds, then cut each strip crossways into about 2 cm (¾ in) cubes. Put them into a clean, grease-free bowl, sprinkle with the salt and stir to mix, then leave to stand at room temperature for 2–3 hours. During this time moisture from the cucumber will be drawn out while the saltiness will sink in.

2 Drain the cucumber pieces but do not rinse with water. One handful at a time, squeeze out excess moisture without overdrying them. Transfer to a clean bowl, add the sugar and vinegar, and mix well.

3 Heat the oils in a small saucepan until smoke rises. Remove the pan from the heat and wait for a few seconds until the smoke has disappeared before adding the chilli flakes – otherwise they will burn. Let the chilli sizzle in the oil, then pour into the bowl with the cucumber. Mix well.

4 Leave the cucumber to stand in a cool place for at least 6 hours, covered, during which time the different flavours will become harmonized in the juices. Thereafter, keep in the refrigerator. Serve cold; eat with fingers or cocktail sticks.

HOT STARTERS

I F cold starters are more of a northern way of eating, hot first courses are very
southern indeed. In a traditional Cantonese banquet menu, the first group of dishes
are called 'yitfun'. 'Yit' in Cantonese simply means hot, but 'fun' is the opposite of
vegetarian dishes, so that 'yitfun' together means hot, non-vegetarian dishes. What
they are, in fact, are light, delicate stir-fries, often using ingredients that are in season,
and they are intended to whet the diners' appetite for the 'big dishes' that are to come.
Vegetables themselves are often used in yitfun to complement other ingredients, such
as poultry, fish or shellfish, to provide a contrasting texture, or to add colour.

Generally speaking, until the 1950s, it was customary to serve four yitfun or
stir-fries, in groups of two at a time. Some of the most sought after dishes were
bamboo fungus with deboned duck's webs, cock's testicles with just a few pieces of
vegetables, pigeon eggs with straw mushrooms, scrambled eggs with loose shark's
fin and minced quail with dried oyster wrapped in crisp lettuce. These dishes are still
served at banquets, but two yitfun are the general rule now rather than four, while
pigeon eggs and cock's testicles are not so readily available.

But in Taiwan, during the last two to three decades, it has become very fashionable to serve a Shanghai banquet with 'four small hots', so much so, in fact, that at
times they are even more welcome than the traditional cold starters. These hot dishes
may be a mixture of stir-fries, deep-fries, steamed buns and the like: for example,
fresh broadbeans – if in season – stir-fried in rendered chicken fat, fuyung chicken
slices, Shanghai spring rolls and prawn balls with shredded dried scallop.

When planning a dinner at home, it is necessary to take into account such
considerations as time, labour and cost. Fortunately, among the vast repertoire of the
Chinese cuisine as a whole, there are many dishes suitable for first courses, and it is
possible to serve just one to set the tone of the dinner. Of course, if you wish to serve

two, by all means do so. Deep-fried and sautéed dishes, with their crisp texture and fragrance, are certainly very moreish, and hence are always welcome as a first course. Stir-fries, with their subtle flavours, could not be more suitable. But in general, a stir-fried meat dish, such as pork or beef, would be deemed too heavy, while poultry and seafood are just light enough. Sometimes, special festival foods more readily fit the bill, such as the 'go' or 'puddings' in this chapter.

Shanghai Spring Rolls

THESE DAYS spring rolls are eaten all over the world, and there are Thai and Vietnamese ones, besides the Chinese, from which they all evolved. Few, perhaps, are familiar with the story of their origin. One of the first important dates in the Chinese lunar calendar, which is geared to the agricultural cycle of sowing and harvesting of crops, is called Lichun or 'the beginning of spring', which falls around 5 February. By the Tang dynasty (AD 618–907), it was customary to mark the day with chunpan or 'spring cakes', which were thin wheat dough wrappers stuffed with lettuce, chives or other vegetables, and symbolised a new season of growth and prosperity. People not only enjoyed eating them, poets like Du Fu wrote poems to celebrate both the food and the occasion. By the Song dynasty (960–1279), these spring cakes had found their way from the home into street markets and delicatessens. The name chunjuan or spring roll, with its sausage shape as we know it now, was not adopted until a few hundred years later, and by the Qing dynasty (1644–1911), its popularity as a celebratory food went far beyond the beginning of spring, and they were being eaten throughout the year. Some people in Peking still make the traditional spring cakes on the day of Lichun as a fun thing to mark the occasion.

The main distinguishing feature between Cantonese and Shanghai spring rolls is in the stuffing. Whereas the stuffing of the former is on the dry side, that of the latter is

上海春卷

MAKES ABOUT 50

900 g (2 lb) raw shrimps in the shell, (50–60 shrimps per 450 g/ 1 lb), shelled and de-veined (see p. 353)

350 g (12 oz) thin pork escalopes, cut into matchstick-sized strips

180 ml (12 tbsp) peanut or vegetable oil

24 medium dried Chinese black mushrooms, reconstituted (see p. 353) and cut into thin strips

225 g (8 oz) canned bamboo shoots, blanched (see p. 353) and cut into matchstick-sized strips

2 kilos (4 lb) Chinese celery cabbage (Chinese leaves), cut crossways into 3 mm (⅛ in) wide slivers, stalk and leafy parts separated

10 ml (2 tsp) salt

about 50 ml (2 fl oz/¼ cup) stock or mushroom soaking liquid (see p. 353)

50–60 large spring roll wrappers, about 21–23.5 cm (8¼–9¼ in) square

lightly beaten egg white

vegetable oil for deep-frying

FOR THE SHRIMP MARINADE:
5 ml (1 tsp) salt
10 ml (2 tsp) cornflour
30 ml (2 tbsp) egg white

FOR THE PORK MARINADE:
2.5 ml (½ tsp) salt
10 ml (2 tsp) thin or light soy
  sauce
10 ml (2 tsp) Shaoxing wine or
  medium dry sherry
10 turns peppermill
5 ml (1 tsp) tapioca or potato flour
15 ml (1 tbsp) water
30 ml (2 tbsp) peanut or vegetable
  oil

FOR THE SAUCE:
about 60 ml (4 tbsp) tapioca or
  potato flour
60 ml (4 tbsp) chicken stock
15 ml (1 tbsp) thin soy sauce

so moist that it is slightly soupy when you bite into the roll. The secret of how to achieve this was shown to me by the Shanghai chef Chu Te-an. Since making these rolls is always a lot of work, one may as well make a large quantity at a time. Fortunately, they freeze well.

1 Marinate the shrimps. Put the shrimps in a large bowl, add the salt and stir in the same direction for about 30 seconds until they feel elastic. Add the cornflour and egg white and stir until evenly coated. Leave in the refrigerator, covered, for 1–2 hours.

2 Marinate the pork. Put the pork in a bowl. Add the salt, soy sauce, wine or sherry, pepper, flour and water and stir to coat. Leave for 15–20 minutes. Blend in the oil to separate the strips.

3 Prepare the sauce. Put the flour in a small bowl. Gradually add the stock, stirring to dissolve it. Stir in the soy sauce.

4 Heat a wok over a high heat until smoke rises. Add 90 ml (6 tbsp) of the peanut or vegetable oil and swirl it around to cover a large area. Add the shrimps and, going to the bottom of the wok with the wok scoop, toss, turn and separate the shrimps until they turn pink. Remove the wok from the heat and scoop up the shrimps with a perforated spoon on to a dish, draining the oil back into the wok.

5 Wash and dry the wok. Reheat over a high heat until smoke rises. Add 30 ml (2 tbsp) oil and swirl it around. Add the pork, stirring as before until it becomes opaque. Remove on to another dish.

6 Wash and dry the wok. Reheat over a high heat until smoke rises. Add the remaining 60 ml (4 tbsp) oil and swirl it around. Add the Chinese mushrooms. Stir until the aroma is released; add the bamboo shoots and the stalk parts of the cabbage. Season with the salt, which will draw out the water from the cabbage. Continue to cook over a moderate heat for about another 5 minutes or until quite a lot of water has oozed out of the cabbage. Add the leafy parts, stir to mix. Add about 50 ml (2 fl oz/¼ cup) stock or mushroom liquid and continue to cook, covered, for another 5–10 minutes until the cabbage is limp and tender and the water has oozed out. Gradually pour in the well-stirred sauce, which is the thickening agent, return the pork and mix. Scoop this

mixture, which should be held together with no excess water and yet not gluey, on to a large dish and let cool to room temperature. Sometimes you will need to add more thickening agent than specified, sometimes less. The consistency of this filling eventually gives the soupy result in the deep-fried rolls.

7 Wrap the spring rolls. Carefully tear off 1 wrapper at a time from a pile, which should be kept constantly covered with a damp cloth to prevent the wrappers from becoming dry. Arrange the wrapper on a flat surface in a diamond shape. Put about 45 ml (3 tbsp) of the filling just off the centre and spread it out to about 12.5 cm (5 in) wide. Top with 2 shrimps, one on each side. Tucking in the filling, fold up the bottom flap and start rolling. Midway, fold the 2 side flaps towards the centre, brush the remaining flap with the egg white and fold it up to seal the spring roll tightly. Repeat until all are done. Place the rolls under a cloth to prevent them drying out.

8 Fry the spring rolls. Half fill a wok over a wok stand or deep-fryer with oil. Heat over a high heat to a temperature of 190°C (375°F). Carefully add 8–10 rolls at a time or however many will float freely and deep-fry for 4–5 minutes or until pale golden in colour, turning periodically. Remove with a large hand strainer or perforated disc and drain on kitchen paper. (After this first deep-frying, the rolls can be frozen.) To crisp, reheat the oil to 190°C (375°F) and deep-fry a second time for 1–2 minutes or until golden. Drain and serve hot.

NOTE: To crisp frozen spring rolls, heat the oil until it reaches 180°C (350°F). Add the rolls direct from the freezer, i.e. without letting them defrost at all, and deep-fry for 5–6 minutes or until they are golden. Drain and serve hot.

Bean Curd
Skin Rolls

MAKES ABOUT 24 ROLLS;
SERVES UP TO 12

350 g (12 oz) small raw shrimps in
the shell (37–45 shrimps,
without heads, rinsed, drained
well, then shelled, or 225 g/8 oz
already shelled)
115 g (4 oz) pork escalopes, cut
into matchstick-sized strips
90 ml (6 tbsp) peanut or vegetable
oil for frying
2.5–5 ml (½–1 tsp) finely chopped
garlic
8 spring onions, trimmed, cut
into 3.5 cm (1½ in) sections,
then shredded
15 small dried Chinese black
mushrooms, reconstituted (see
p. 353) then cut into very thin
strips
450 g (1 lb) bean sprouts, topped
and tailed if patience and time
permits
2.5 ml (½ tsp) salt
15 ml (1 tbsp) tapioca or potato
flour dissolved in 30 ml (2 tbsp)
mushroom soaking liquid or
water
30 ml (2 tbsp) oyster sauce
12 sheets bean curd skin (see
introduction above)
vegetable oil for sautéing

MARINADE FOR THE SHRIMPS:
2.5 ml (½ tsp) salt
2.5 ml (½ tsp) cornflour
7.5 ml (1½ tsp) egg white

LARGE DRIED sheets of bean curd skin are available in Chinese supermarkets, carefully wrapped in wax paper, then enveloped in substantial plastic bags. The almost transparent sheets, delicate to look at and brittle when dry, are surprisingly pliant and durable once sprayed with cold water, and hence are easy to use.

The process of making them is fascinating to watch, although the conditions in which the workers operate are often hard. Two years ago, when I was in Hong Kong, I was taken by three vegetarian chefs to Cheung Chau – an off-shore fishing port known to Europeans, because of its shape, as 'Dumbbell' – for the express purpose of seeing how these sheets were made. We were taken to a house where a middle-aged Chinese woman had turned her home into a 'factory' which provided for the livelihood of her entire family, consisting of a gambling husband and four children. Half of a small room was occupied by a huge cauldron in which simmered, ever so gently, the milky liquid of ground soy beans. The woman sat on a stool by the cauldron, clad in a sleeveless singlet and shorts in order to ward off the intense heat and humidity caused by the fire, and held with one hand a thin bamboo stick, less than a metre in length. A small electric fan, hovering over the cauldron, blew directly on to the surface, cooling off the gathering and thickening ripples that shot up to form a skin. At the moment she judged most opportune, the woman lowered the stick into the liquid, then gradually but decisively lifted it up to mid-air, and a thin, half circular sheet of bean curd skin was seen hanging on it. This she then hung up on one side of the room for the skin to set more firmly and returned to her stool with another bamboo stick. The simmering bean liquid, in the meantime, was gathering its ripples again, as if in anticipation of madame's next rich picking. This magical performance was done with such aplomb and ease that we felt encouraged to have a go, and she smilingly handed over the stick to us. We all tried our hands at it, but soon realised that, as we lifted the stick, the wind from the electric fan played havoc with our skins, and we didn't have much to show for our efforts. To comfort us, she told us she had been at it for more than ten years so that even the wind obeyed her command; now that she had trained her eldest daughter, aged 18, who manned another cauldron in the next room, they were able to cope with the orders, mostly from restaurants in Hong Kong and Kowloon. She explained that the work begins with the choice of soy beans, making sure that they are of the sort that will yield rich skins when processed. The next step is cooking the beans then grinding them to extract the milk, and what we saw was the end of the process. Before we left, she treated us to fresh soy bean milk; it was so refreshing and sweet that we felt we would never ask for cow's milk again.

1 Marinate the shrimps. Put the shrimps into a bowl, add the salt and stir in the same direction for 30–60 seconds until they feel elastic. Add the cornflour and egg white and stir until evenly coated. Refrigerate, covered, for 30 minutes or longer. The shrimps, when cooked, should have a firm yet succulent texture.

2 Marinate the pork. Put the pork into a bowl, add the salt, sugar, soy sauce, ground pepper, wine or sherry and tapioca or potato flour and stir to coat the pork. Leave to stand for 15–20 minutes. Blend in the oil.

3 Make the filling. Heat a wok over a high heat until smoke rises. Add 90 ml (6 tbsp) peanut or vegetable oil and swirl it around over a large area and heat until smoke rises. Add the shrimps, stir and turn with the wok scoop, separating them, for about 30 seconds or until they curl up and turn pinkish. Remove with a perforated disc, draining the oil back into the wok.

Reheat the oil in the wok until smoke rises. Add the garlic, stir a few times, then add the pork. Turn and toss for about 1 minutes or until the pork becomes opaque. Remove with a perforated disc and put together with the shrimps.

Reheat the remaining oil in the wok, adding 15–30 ml (1–2 tbsp), more, if necessary. Add the spring onion, stir a few times, add the mushrooms and stir about a dozen times to enhance their aroma. Add the bean sprouts, season with the salt and, going to the bottom of the wok with the wok scoop, turn and toss for about 2 minutes until any water has oozed out and the bean

MARINADE FOR THE PORK:
1.5 ml (¼ tsp) salt
1.5 ml (¼ tsp) sugar
10 ml (2 tsp) thin or light soy sauce
8 turns peppermill
5 ml (1 tsp) Shaoxing wine or medium dry sherry
2.5 ml (½ tsp) tapioca or potato flour
10 ml (2 tsp) peanut or vegetable oil

Illustrated on Plate 3.

sprouts become quite limp. Gradually pour in the well-stirred dissolved tapioca or potato flour to thicken the sauce, which should just hold the mixture together without being either gluey or watery. Sometimes you'll need more thickening agent than specified, and sometimes less. Scoop up and put together with the shrimps and pork. Season with the oyster sauce, mixing well. Leave this filling to cool down to room temperature.

4 Wrap the rolls. Put 1 sheet of fan-shaped bean curd skin on a flat surface and spray it all over with cold water until quite wet. Leave for about 30 seconds until it becomes pliable, then cut vertically into 2 pieces. Place in the centre of the wider end of 1 piece about 30 ml (2 tbsp) filling including 2–3 shrimps, fold up this end to cover the filling, fold the 2 side ends towards the centre and start rolling away from you until the remaining end self–adheres to seal the roll you have made. If the uneven 'bony' lines or knots in the skin make the wrapping difficult, spray with a little more water to soften them. Even holes can be mended by sticking a small wet piece of skin on top. Place the roll on a tray and cover with a moist cloth, then make another roll in the same way with the other piece of skin. Repeat the procedure until all are done.

5 Fry the rolls. Heat a large, flat frying pan until hot. Add sufficient oil to cover the entire pan and heat until hot. Add the rolls, one by one next to each other, and fry over a medium heat for 1½–2 minutes or until golden. Turn them over and fry the other side. Remove, drain on kitchen paper and put on to a serving dish. Fry the remaining rolls as before. Serve hot. No sauce is necessary.

Shredded Chicken
with Edible Jellyfish

I FIRST tasted this dish in which the tender chicken contrasts with the slightly bouncy jellyfish, cooked by the Shanghai chef, Chu Te-an, in his restaurant, the Country Club, in Harrow-on-the-Hill. As your guests go into the dining room, you can slip into the kitchen and make this stir-fry as the first course, having prepared the jellyfish and marinated the chicken beforehand. During the course of the five-minute cooking, the atmosphere becomes aromatic with the wok fragrance, which stimulates your guests' tastebuds so that they can't wait to taste your offering.

1 Prepare the jellyfish. If the jellyfish comes in sheets, shake then rinse off with cold water the large grains of salt used to preserve them. Soak them in plenty of cold water. Change the water 10–12 times at 30–60-minute intervals, each time squeezing the sheets with your hands to get rid of the saltiness and the sea odour. If you are not in a hurry, the soaking can be spread over 1–2 days until they are totally bland and devoid of odour.

   Drain, then cut the sheets into thin strips about 5 mm (⅕ in) wide. Squeeze out excess water then pat dry.

2 Marinate the chicken. Put the chicken in a bowl, add the salt, soy sauce, wine or sherry and pepper and stir to mix. Sprinkle on the cornflour, add the egg white and stir until absorbed. Leave to stand for about 15–20 minutes. Stir in the sesame oil.

3 Prepare the sauce. In a small bowl add the soy sauce to the two mustards and stir to mix well. Stir in the sesame oil.

4 Heat a wok over a high heat until smoke rises. Add the oil and swirl it around to cover a large area. Add the garlic, stir and let sizzle for 2–3 seconds, then add the chicken. Going to the bottom of the wok with the wok scoop, turn and toss for about 30 seconds, partially cooking the chicken. Splash in the wine or sherry around the edges of the wok, continuing to stir. When the sizzling subsides, reduce the heat to the minimum and remove the chicken, cooked by now, with a slotted spoon on to a serving dish, leaving the oil behind.

SERVES 4–6

450 g (1 lb) dried edible jellyfish
2 chicken breast fillets, 225 g (8 oz), skinned and boned, cut into strips
60 ml (4 tbsp) peanut or vegetable oil
5 ml (1 tsp) finely chopped garlic
15 ml (1 tbsp) Shaoxing wine or medium dry sherry

FOR THE MARINADE:
2 ml (⅓ tsp) salt
10 ml (2 tsp) thin or light soy sauce
10 ml (2 tsp) Shaoxing wine or medium dry sherry
8 turns peppermill
5 ml (1 tsp) cornflour
7.5 ml (1½ tsp) egg white
15 ml (1 tbsp) sesame oil

FOR THE SAUCE:
30–45 ml (2–3 tbsp) thin or light soy sauce
5 ml (1 tsp) hot made-up English mustard
7.5 ml (1½ tsp) Dijon mustard
15 ml (1 tbsp) sesame oil

Illustrated on Plate 3.

5 Lift the wok from the heat and add the jellyfish and stir. The strips should start to curl up with the impact of the heat; take care therefore that the heat is not too intense, lest the jellyfish becomes chewy instead of pleasantly bouncy. Add the sauce and mix evenly. Scoop on to the serving dish and mix with the chicken. Serve warm.

NOTE: This dish is also delicious served cold, if you add 15–22.5 ml (1–1½ tbsp) Chinese rice vinegar just before serving, and mix well.

Sautéed Jumbo Prawns

SERVES 4–6

12 jumbo raw prawns in the shell, with heads, about 450 g (1 lb)
45–60 ml (3–4 tbsp) peanut or vegetable oil
10 ml (2 tsp) finely shredded ginger
1.5–2.5 ml (¼–½ tsp) tapioca or potato flour dissolved in 15 ml (1 tbsp) water
1 small bunch coriander leaves, rinsed and trimmed
15–22.5 ml (1–1½ tbsp) sesame oil

FOR THE SAUCE:
60 ml (4 tbsp) stock
1.5 ml (¼ tsp) salt
30 ml (2 tbsp) thin or light soy sauce
15 ml (1 tbsp) Chinese rice vinegar or Chinkiang vinegar (or balsamic vinegar)
7.5 ml (1½ tsp) sugar
15 ml (1 tbsp) Shaoxing wine or medium dry sherry
5 ml (1 tsp) Worcestershire sauce
15–30 ml (1–2 tbsp) tomato ketchup
10 ml (2 tsp) tomato paste

IF THE twin prawns of Shandong are available (*see* p. 83), use them; otherwise, use any jumbo prawns. This East-meets-West sauce, known among professional Chinese chefs as Western or 'capital' – why capital no one is quite sure – sauce, can be made according to one's own taste, mixing Western sauces such as A1, tomato ketchup and/or Worcestershire with Chinese ingredients such as Chinese rice vinegar or Chinkiang (Zhenjiang) vinegar, soy sauce and the like.

1 Using a pair of scissors, clip off the eye of each prawn, leaving the rest of the head intact. De-vein the prawns: hold a prawn with one hand and, using a satay stick or a strong needle with the other hand, pierce the flesh at the joints of the shell section and remove the black vein bit by bit. Wash the shells of the prawns, rubbing with your fingers. Pat dry.
2 Prepare the sauce. In a small bowl, combine the stock, salt, soy sauce, vinegar, sugar, wine or sherry, Worcestershire sauce, tomato ketchup and tomato paste and stir to mix.
3 Heat a wok or a large sauté pan over a high heat until smoke rises. Add the oil and swirl it around to cover a large area. Add all the prawns and spread them out in one layer, fry for 20 seconds until the shells turn pinkish, turn them over one by one and fry the other sides

for another 20 seconds. Sprinkle the ginger on top, then pour in the well-stirred sauce. Reduce the heat to prevent the sauce from splashing and bring to a simmer. Add the wok cover or sauté pan lid, continue to cook over a moderate heat for 2 minutes. Remove the cover, turn the prawns over, replace the cover and continue cooking the other sides for another 1–2 minutes. The prawns should now be cooked, having absorbed much of the flavour of the sauce. Add the dissolved tapioca or potato flour, stirring until the sauce thickens slightly. Remove everything to a serving plate and arrange the prawns. Garnish with the coriander leaves and sprinkle on the sesame oil. Serve hot.

4 To eat, use either chopsticks and suck the shell, take a bite then spit out the shell as the Chinese do, or use fingers but still suck the shell.

Illustrated on Plate 2.

Prawns with Chillies and Spiced Salt

A SOUTHERN dish adored by seafood lovers all over the country. For the Chinese, half of the fun of eating these prawns is in sucking the taste in the shell before gently spitting it out. But to shell a chunk of a prawn inside one's mouth is a Chinese habit – acquired from childhood – not necessarily appreciated by other nationals. You may therefore like to simply peel the prawns with your fingers and then enjoy them in the manner to which you are accustomed. Finger bowls or wet towels will come in handy. If you wonder why the prawns are not shelled beforehand, it is because the shell acts as a shield to protect the flesh inside against the intense heat while being deep-fried, thereby making the cooked prawns that much more succulent.

1 Rinse the prawns well, rubbing the shells with your fingers so that they are clean enough for sucking when cooked. Drain.

2 De-vein. Stand a prawn on a board, belly side down. With the pointed end of a knife, saw through the shell

椒
盐
虾

SERVES 6

450 g (1 lb) medium raw prawns in the shell, without heads (25–30 prawns)
2.5 ml (½ tsp) salt
10–15 ml (2–3 tsp) cornflour
vegetable oil for deep-drying
30 ml (2 tbsp) peanut or vegetable oil
1 large clove garlic, peeled and cut into slivers
2 long red or green chillies, cored and deseeded, cut into small rounds
3 spring onions, trimmed and cut into small rounds, white and green parts separated
5 ml (1 tsp) Shaoxing wine or medium dry sherry
15 ml (1 tbsp) spiced salt (*see* p. 360)

along the back, shallowly cutting into the body. Remove the black vein, if any. Remove the feet attached to the belly, if preferred (many Chinese actually leave them on). Place on kitchen paper to absorb excess moisture. Repeat until all are done. Put all the prawns into a dish.

3 Mix the salt and cornflour together. Add to the prawns and mix together. Pick up the prawns, shake off excess flour and put on to another dish.

4 'Let prawns go through oil.' Half fill a wok over a wok stand with oil and heat over a high heat until it reaches 180°C (350°F). Put all the prawns on a large perforated disc and carefully slip them into the oil. They will instantly begin to curl up and turn pinkish in colour. Stir them around once, then immediately remove with the disc and put on kitchen paper to absorb excess grease. Keep nearby. The prawns are just slightly underdone at this point. Leave the oil for future use after it has been strained.

5 Using another wok or frying pan, heat over a high heat until smoke rises. Add the peanut or vegetable oil and swirl over a large area. Add the garlic, stir and let sizzle, add the chillies, stir, then add the white spring onion and stir a few more times, to release the aroma. Splash in the wine or sherry, then add 5–7.5 ml (1–1½ tsp) of the spiced salt and stir a couple of times to mix. Return the prawns to the wok and, going to the bottom of the wok with the wok scoop, flip and turn for about 30–60 seconds, adjusting the heat to medium. The prawns should be thoroughly cooked by now. Sprinkle on the green spring onion, then remove the prawns from the wok or frying pan and put on a serving plate. Serve hot. Put the rest of the spiced salt on the table for dipping to taste – not that the prawns really need it.

Butterfly Prawns
in Red Bean Curd Cheese

SEVERAL years ago, Chef Wu Kwun of Fung Shing in Soho created these prawns which, on a whim, he named Yunnan prawns, even though, as he himself said, they have nothing to do with either the cuisine or any of the special products from that province. I loved eating them so much in his restaurant that I asked him for the secret, which he most generously revealed to me. I share it with you and hope you will find the prawns as delectable as I do.

SERVES 6–8

450 g (1 lb) medium raw prawns in the shell, without heads (25–30 prawns)
120–150 ml (8–10 tbsp) tapioca or potato flour or cornflour
vegetable oil for deep-frying

FOR THE MARINADE:
2 square cakes (4 cm/1½ in each) red bean curd cheese, mashed, yielding about 22.5 ml (1½ tbsp)
15 ml (1 tbsp) juice from the jar containing the bean curd cheese
10 ml (2 tsp) Shaoxing wine or medium dry sherry
2–2.5 ml (⅓–½ tsp) five-spice powder
7.5 ml (1½ tsp) puréed or very finely chopped garlic

1 Shell the prawns. Stand them on a flat surface, one by one, and make butterfly prawns; cut each along the back downwards to within 1 cm (½ in) of the tail without splitting it into 2 halves. Remove the black vein, if any. Put prawns into a large dish.

2 Marinate the prawns. Put the mashed red bean curd cheese in a bowl and stir in the juice, wine or sherry, five-spice powder and garlic until smooth. Add this marinade to the prawns and mix evenly to coat, taking care not to split the butterfly prawns into two. Leave to stand for 15–30 minutes.

3 Put the tapioca or potato flour or cornflour in a bowl or dish. Press each prawn, first one side then the other, on the flour to coat thinly and evenly, smoothing with fingers to avoid lumps forming and to get rid of any excess flour. There is no need to use up all the flour.

4 Half fill a wok with oil, and heat over a high heat until it reaches 180°C (350°F). Lower all the prawns into the oil and deep-fry for about 30–45 seconds, separating them with chopsticks or tongs if they stick together. The prawns should be cooked by now. Remove with a large hand strainer and drain on kitchen paper.

5 Reheat the oil to the same temperature as before and deep-fry the prawns a second time for about 10–20 seconds to crisp the outside. Remove with the hand strainer and drain on kitchen paper. Put on a serving dish and serve hot. As the red bean curd cheese gives the predominant taste, there is no need to provide any other dipping sauce.

Stir-fried
Scallops with Mange-tout

8 large scallops, about 350 g
   (12 oz)
salt
5 ml (1 tsp) cornflour
15 ml (1 tbsp) egg white, lightly
   beaten
225 g (8 oz) mange-tout, topped
   and tailed, rinsed
60 ml (4 tbsp) peanut or vegetable
   oil
4–6 thin slices ginger, peeled
3–4 spring onions, trimmed and
   cut into 5 cm (2 in) sections,
   white and green parts separated
10 ml (2 tsp) Shaoxing wine or
   medium dry sherry

DIPPING SAUCES:
oyster sauce
chilli sauce

Illustrated on Plate 2.

WHEN scallops are fresh, they have the subtlest xian (fresh) and tian (sweet) flavours which require only a little bit of salt to bring them out, but not a whole lot of other condiments. For this light stir-fry, therefore, make sure to use fresh scallops. It makes a very tempting small hot dish with which to stimulate the palate.

1 Wash the scallops, remove and discard the hard muscle on the side. Separate the corals from the white scallops, leaving the corals whole. Pat dry. Place each scallop on its side and, depending on the size, slice into 2–3 pieces. Pat dry again and put both the corals and the scallop pieces into a bowl.

2 Add 2.5 ml (½ tsp) salt to the cornflour and sprinkle on the scallops and corals. Add the egg white and stir to coat.

3 Blanch the mange-tout. Half fill a medium-sized saucepan with water and add 5 ml (1 tsp) salt. Bring to the boil, add 22.5 ml (1½ tbsp) of the oil. Add the mange-tout and give them a thorough stir. Leave for about 10 seconds but before the water returns to the boil, pour into a colander and drain thoroughly.

4 Heat a wok over a high heat until smoke rises. Add the remaining 37.5 ml (2½ tbsp) oil and swirl it around to cover a wide area. Add the ginger and the white spring onion and let them sizzle for a few seconds to release their aromas, stirring a few times. Add the scallops and corals and, going to the bottom of the wok with the wok scoop, rapidly toss and turn for about 20 seconds, partially cooking the scallops. Splash in the wine or sherry, continue to stir as it sizzles. Scoop the ingredients on to a perforated disc and rest it over a bowl to catch the juices that will continue to ooze out. Return the corals to the wok, turn the heat to medium and continue to cook them for about 1 minute or until they are just cooked. Pour in the juices as well.

5 Add the mange-tout and the green spring onion to the wok and stir with the corals until very hot again. Sprinkle with a pinch of salt, if liked. Scoop on to a

8

serving dish. Add the white scallop pieces on top. Serve
hot immediately. The dipping sauces are for dipping to
individual taste, but for those who prefer the inherent
sweet flavour of the scallops and the mange-tout, the
sauces are superfluous.

White Radish Pudding
(Law Baak Go)

A RECIPE that the southern Chinese adore, so
much so that they make it at home, in restaurants
as a dimsum, for Chinese New Year and other
festive occasions. In the olden days, when it was
quite common for a family to have a stone-grinder
in its possession, rice was ground with water to
make the liquid starch as the basis for the pudding.
These days, the rice starch comes in a flour form,
and the success of the pudding depends on working out
the proportion between rice flour, water and white radish,
seasoned by the filling mixture.

SERVES 10–12

16 medium dried Chinese black
  mushrooms, rinsed and
  reconstituted in 250 ml (8 fl oz/
  1 cup) water (*see* p. 353)
115 g (4 oz) dried shrimps, rinsed
15 ml (1 tbsp) Shaoxing wine or
  medium dry sherry
225 g (8 oz) or 6 wind-dried pork
  sausages, rinsed
2.3 kilos (5 lb) white radish
  (moolie) without the green tops,
  peeled
15 ml (1 tbsp) peanut or vegetable
  oil
20–25 g (¾–1 oz) Chinese brown
  brick sugar, or 15–20 ml
  (3–4 tsp) brown sugar
5–7.5 ml (1–1½ tsp) salt
2.5–5 ml (½–1 tsp) ground white
  pepper
450 g (1 lb/3 cups) rice flour
  (sometimes labelled powder)
30 ml (2 tbsp) cornflour dissolved
  in 30 ml (2 tbsp) water
45–60 ml (3–4 tbsp) roasted white
  sesame seeds (*see* p. 359)
small bunch coriander leaves,
  rinsed and torn up
oyster sauce or soy sauce as
  dipping sauce

1 Drain the mushrooms and chop into pieces the size of
   matchstick heads. Reserve the soaking liquid.
2 Soak the dried shrimps in 50 ml (2 fl oz/¼ cup) warm
   water and wine or sherry for 30–60 minutes. Drain and
   chop roughly.
3 Dice the wind-dried sausages into small cubes.
4 Shred the radish into fine julienne strips and put into a
   container, keeping any juices that have oozed out. This
   can be done effectively in a food processor.
5 Prepare the filling mixture. Heat a wok over a high heat
   until smoke rises. Add the peanut or vegetable oil and
   swirl it around. Add the wind-dried sausages, stir a few
   times until the fat begins to ooze out. Add the mushrooms, stir, then add the dried shrimps and stir together
   for about 1–2 minutes until fragrant. Scoop the mixture
   into a container and keep nearby.
6 Reduce the heat to medium, add 50 ml (2 fl oz/¼ cup)
   water to the wok and bring to the boil. Add all the
   radish and the sugar, which will remove the odour from
   the radish. Add the salt, which will help draw out the

water from the radish. Add also the ground white pepper. Gently cook the white radish, covered, for about 15 minutes or until the julienne strips are soft. Remove the wok from the heat, leaving the radish in it.

7   Mix the rice flour. Add the rice flour to a very large mixing bowl and make a well in the centre. Gradually stir 500 ml (16 fl oz/2 cups) cold water (including the mushroom soaking liquid) into the flour, drawing it in to mix and blend with a wooden spatula. Unlike wheat flour, rice flour does not tend to become lumpy. The consistency of the mixture should be like runny double cream. Add the well-stirred dissolved cornflour and stir to mix well.

8   Reheat the white radish until piping hot and its juices simmering again. Using a ladle, scoop the radish and the juices, a ladle at a time, into the rice flour mixture and stir to mix. The hot radish gradually thickens the rice flour mixture, partially cooking it as well. The new mixture should look a gluey mess. Add the filling mixture and stir to mix well. Scoop into a large round well-oiled cake tin or enamel dish, about 30 cm (12 in) in diameter and 6 cm (2½ in) high, or one with a comparable capacity.

9   Place the dish into a steamer and steam over a high heat (*see* p. 355) for 1 hour until the pudding is well cooked. Test by inserting a chopstick; if it goes in easily and comes out quite clean, it is ready. Remove the steamer from the heat. If too much water from the circulating steam has accumulated on the surface of the pudding, tip the tin or dish to get rid of it, but a small amount of moisture will not affect the pudding at all. Sprinkle on the sesame seeds and scatter the coriander leaves on top. Remove the dish from the steamer. Let the pudding set for 5–10 minutes before serving.

10   To serve, quarter the pudding, then halve each quarter. Cut crossways into pieces at 1 cm (½ in) intervals and serve hot. There should be more than 70 slices. White radish pudding is delicious as it is, but oyster sauce can be used as a dipping sauce. There is no need to consume the pudding at one sitting, as it can be sautéed the next day (*see* following recipe).

Sautéed
White Radish Pudding

WHILE white radish pudding is served hot, it is often allowed to become cold and firm overnight in the refrigerator and is then served sautéed in a small amount of oil. Sautéed white radish pudding features in the repertoire of dimsum in Cantonese restaurants, but, alas, more often than not, it lacks the necessary depth of taste and flavour because not enough moolie and filling mixture are used. The home-made pudding is so much superior that it warrants the expense, time and labour involved. It also makes for an unusual first course.

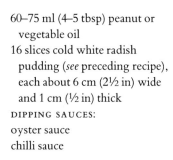

SERVES 4–5

60–75 ml (4–5 tbsp) peanut or
  vegetable oil
16 slices cold white radish
  pudding (*see* preceding recipe),
  each about 6 cm (2½ in) wide
  and 1 cm (½ in) thick
DIPPING SAUCES:
oyster sauce
chilli sauce

1 Heat a large flat frying pan over a high heat until very hot. Add 15–22.5 ml (1–1½ tbsp) of the oil and swirl it to cover the whole of the pan. Reduce the heat. Put half of the pudding slices, one by one, into the pan, allowing a space between them. Fry slowly for about 2–3 minutes or until the bottom is lightly brown. You can peep by lifting a corner of each slice to check the colour. Turn the slices over, one by one, drip in another 7.5–15 ml (½–1 tbsp) oil and fry the other side for about the same time. Remove the slices to a serving dish and keep warm nearby.
2 Turn up the heat and add another 15 ml (1 tbsp) oil and swirl it around to cover the whole pan. Reduce the heat and add the remaining slices, one by one, and fry as before until lightly brown on both sides. Remove and add to the serving dish. Serve hot. Oyster sauce and chilli sauce should be served on separate saucers for individual dipping, if required.

Steamed Taro Pudding
(Wu Tow Go)

SERVES 10–12

115 g (4 oz) dried shrimps, rinsed

15 ml (1 tbsp)) Shaoxing wine or medium dry sherry

1.2 kilos (2½ lb) peeled taro, cut into slices about 1 cm (½ in) thick

4 wind-dried pork sausages, or about 140 g (5 oz), rinsed

170 g (6 oz) wind-dried belly pork, rind removed

30 ml (2 tbsp) peanut or vegetable oil

450 g (1 lb/3 cups) rice flour

1.2 litres (2 pints/5 cups) cold water

7.5 ml (1½ tsp) salt

2.5 ml (½ tsp) ground white pepper

5 ml (1 tsp) five-spice powder

45–60 ml (3–4 tbsp) roasted white sesame seeds (*see* p. 359)

1 bunch coriander, leaves only, rinsed and patted dry

deseeded red chilli rounds for garnish

LIKE WHITE radish pudding, this is Cantonese Chinese New Year food. It can, of course, be made at other times when there is taro around. The success of the recipe depends on having the right proportion of taro, rice flour and water, as well as the techniques of mixing them and steaming the pudding. Bianca Fu was inspiring on the technique, and we had great fun making the dish together.

1 Soak the dried shrimps in 50 ml (2 fl oz/¼ cup) warm water and the wine or sherry for 30–60 minutes. Chop roughly and mix with any remaining soaking liquid.

2 Put the taro in a heatproof dish with raised edges and put into a steamer and steam over a high heat (*see* p. 355) for 30 minutes. Remove from the steamer, let cool, then dice the taro.

3 Dice the wind-dried sausages into small cubes. Dice the wind-dried belly pork into small cubes.

4 Prepare the filling mixture. Heat a wok over a high heat until smoke rises. Add the oil and swirl it around. Add the wind-dried sausages and belly pork and stir for about 1 minute or until the fat oozes out. Add the dried shrimps and stir for about 1 more minute or until fragrant. Scoop the mixture into a dish and keep nearby.

5 Mix the rice flour. Put the rice flour into a very large mixing bowl and make a well in the centre. Gradually add the cold water, drawing in the rice flour to mix with a wooden spatula. Unlike wheat flour, rice flour does not tend to become lumpy. As the water is added, the consistency of the mixture becomes more and more watery, as it should. Add the taro, stir to mix. Add the salt, pepper and five-spice powder and stir to mix. Add all but 105–120 ml (7–8 tbsp) of the filling mixture, stirring to mix. The entire mixture is still watery after the mixing. Pour everything into a large round cake tin or enamel dish, already well oiled, about 30 cm (12 in) in diameter and 6 cm (2½ in) high, or one with a comparable capacity.

6 Put the dish into a steamer and steam (see p. 355) for 15 minutes. Remove the lid of the steamer and, using a

wooden spatula or a pair of strong chopsticks, stir and turn the mixture in the dish thoroughly. Some of the taro dice will become mushy. Use the spatula or a palette knife to smooth the surface. Scatter evenly on the surface the filling mixture that has been kept back. Replace the lid of the steamer and continue to steam for 1 hour until the pudding is cooked. Remove the lid, sprinkle the sesame seeds on the pudding and scatter on top the coriander leaves as well as the red chilli rounds. Remove the dish from the steamer, let the pudding set for 5–10 minutes before serving.

7 To serve, quarter the pudding then halve each quarter. Cut crossways into pieces at 1 cm (½ in) intervals and serve hot. There should be more than 70 slices which, however, need not be consumed in one sitting. In fact, most people save some to serve sautéed the following day (*see* following recipe).

Sautéed Taro Pudding

As the Chinese New Year approaches, Cantonese families busy themselves making steamed taro puddings, which they put away in the refrigerator (formerly the cold larder). To entertain New Year callers, they cut up the pudding into slices, fry it and then serve it with tea. Like white radish pudding, taro pudding is even more scrumptious after it has been shallow-fried in a small amount of oil. It, too, makes a novel first course.

SERVES 4

45 ml (3 tbsp) peanut or vegetable oil
12 slices cold taro pudding (*see* preceding recipe), each about 6 cm (2½ in) wide and 1 cm (½ in) thick

1 Heat a large flat frying pan over a high heat until very hot. Add 15 ml (1 tbsp) of the oil and swirl it to cover the whole of the pan. Reduce the heat. Add half of the pudding slices, one by one, into the pan, allowing a space between them. Fry slowly for about 2–3 minutes or until the bottom is partially brown. You can peep by lifting a corner of each slice to check the colour. Turn the slices over, one by one, drip in 15 ml (1 tbsp) oil and fry the other side for about the same time. Remove the slices to a serving dish and keep warm nearby.

2 Turn up the heat and add another 15 ml (1 tbsp) oil and swirl it around to cover the whole pan. Reduce the heat and add the remaining slices, one by one, and fry them as before until partially brown on both sides. Remove and add to the serving dish. Serve hot.

Three Threaded Friends

SERVES 6

2 skinned and boned chicken
  breasts, about 285 g (10 oz)
salt
170 g (6 oz) canned bamboo
  shoots in solid pieces
170 (6 oz) boiled or roasted ham
  in slices, each about 2.5 mm
  (¹/₁₀ in) thick
1 large round Chinese dried black
  mushroom, reconstituted (*see*
  p. 353)
30 ml (2 tbsp) Shaoxing wine or
  medium dry sherry
about 250 ml (8 fl oz/1 cup)
  chicken stock
10 ml (2 tsp) potato or tapioca
  flour dissolved in 15 ml (1 tbsp)
  water
about 12 pieces mange-tout

A WELL-KNOWN Jiangsu and Zhejiang dish famed for its decorative looks and served on festive occasions at home. The three ingredients are always ham, chicken and bamboo shoots. Very often, shredded pork is used as a filler in the centre, but I have decided to keep faith with the title and use only three ingredients. The ham used in eastern China is inevitably Jinhua ham, which has no match for its intense depth of flavour and fragrance, and is therefore used in smaller quantities than either the chicken or bamboo shoots. As Jinhua ham is not easily available in the West, we have to use a large amount of cooked ham in the hope that quantity makes up for flavour.

1 Put the chicken breasts into a heatproof dish and sprinkle on 2.5 ml (½ tsp) salt. Put into a steamer and steam (*see* p. 355) for 15–20 minutes or until just cooked. Remove from the steamer and let cool, saving the liquid in the dish. When the chicken is cold and firm, cut into slices, then shred into strips about 5–6 cm (2–2½ in) long.
2 Cut the bamboo shoots into slices, then shred into strips about the same size as the chicken. For best results, blanch the strips in boiling water for about 1 minute to rid them of any odour from the can. Rinse in cold water and drain well.
3 Cut the ham into strips about the same size as the chicken and bamboo shoots.
4 Place the mushroom, black side down, in the bottom of a heatproof bowl. A Chinese noodle bowl about 15–17.5 cm (6–7 in) in diameter and 5–6 cm (2–2½ in) deep would be ideal. Slightly overlapping the side of the

mushroom, line one-third of the ham strips upwards along the slope of the bowl, occupying one-sixth of the slope space. Repeat on the opposite side with another one-third of ham. On one side of the ham, line one-third of the chicken strips in the same way, repeating on the opposite side. Next to the chicken line one-third of the bamboo strips in the same way, repeating on the opposite side.

5 Mix together the remaining one-third of ham, chicken and bamboo shoots and add them, in any fashion, so that they fill up the centre of the bowl and come up more or less to the top. Sprinkle on top 2.5 ml (½ tsp) salt, add the wine or sherry and 100–150 ml (4–5 fl oz/ ½–⅔ cup) stock including the liquid from steaming the chicken. Place the bowl in a steamer and steam (see p. 355) for about 20 minutes. Remove the bowl from the steamer.

6 Put a plate on top of the bowl, tilt it to pour out all the juices into a small saucepan. Add stock to make up to about 250 ml (8 fl oz/1 cup). Stir in the well-stirred dissolved potato or tapioca flour and bring the sauce to a simmer. Season with salt to taste.

7 Briefly blanch the pieces of mange-tout. Drain before the water returns to the boil.

8 Remove the plate on top of the bowl. Cover the bowl with a large plate with sloping sides. Holding on tightly to both the bowl and plate, invert them. Remove the bowl and you will find the three threaded friends beautifully moulded in the centre of the plate with the black mushroom on top, black side up. Place the mange-tout around the mould, adding vividness to the dish. Return the sauce to a simmer, then carefully pour it over the mould.

9 Serve hot. It may be a pity to break the mould, but the three threaded friends should be eaten together for contrast of taste and texture.

SOUPS

MANY Chinese soups, made mainly with leafy vegetables or gourds, are very thin and watery; others, made mainly with meat or poultry, are like consommés.

In southern China, where the climate is sub-tropical and the heat and humidity so oppressive they sap the appetite, the watery, clear type of soup is the daily fare. Even today, when people at both ends of the social scale drink beer, and serving wine with a meal is considered quite a smart thing to do, especially among city people who are exposed to Western culture, a bowl of thin broth is still considered the best beverage to accompany rice. It is often served at the beginning of the meal 'to wet the mouth', as the saying goes, or it may be served simultaneously with the meal. In the latter case, a bowl of soup is simply placed next to the rice bowl, so that the diner can have spoonfuls of soup to go with the rice, in much the same way as one may sip wine with food. Sometimes, at the end of the meal, more of this watery broth is served as an aid to digestion.

Everywhere in China, whatever the climate or region, particular soups are regarded not only as tonics which benefit many parts of the body but also as panaceas for all ills. After simmering for hours, these soups, which consist of both yin and yang ingredients, are thought to remedy any imbalance between the cooling and heating elements in the body, so that a state of good health results. Lotus root and watercress, both cooked for a long time with pork, are two such soups, and, since they are also delicious, I have included them for everyone's benefit. Others, using such common ingredients as chicken or duck, as well as the more exotic water turtle, are believed to strengthen, or even restore, vital energy, and cure impotence. One celebrated example is the Sichuanese duck soup, which I have also included in this chapter.

More substantial soups are often given another name, geng, and usually consist of a stock, slightly thickened by tapioca starch (or cornflour), with a medley of ingredients swimming in it. Geng is sometimes referred to as a thick soup, but whereas a Western thick soup is often arrived at by liquidising the ingredients to give a puréed texture, a Chinese geng is never prepared this way. Geng, originally meaning a stew-like dish, dates back more than three thousand years. By Han times (206 BC–AD 220), there were both meat geng and vegetable geng, which accompanied rice and other cereal foods. I have described how, during the latter half of the Song dynasty (1127–1279), Mrs Song earned herself a place in culinary history by selling fish geng (*see* p. 17). The exotic southern snake soup is also traditionally referred to as geng (see p. 97).

As for Shark's Fin Soup and Bird's Nest Soup (the *crème de la crème* of Chinese soups), neither the word soup nor geng is included in their Chinese titles, as if to say that dishes so special need no other explanation. Even though they have featured in banquets since the Ming dynasty (1368–1644), and are without doubt classic soups, I have included neither in this book. My justification is that they are extremely time-consuming and laborious to prepare, requiring 2–3 days for shark's fin and at least 1 day for bird's nest. Whilst they are prepared at home from time to time, they really belong to the category of luxurious treats in restaurants. Furthermore, the poor quality of both the uncooked, dried shark's fin and bird's nest that are available abroad is such that it warrants neither the enormous expense nor the intensive labour involved.

Watercress
Soup

SERVES 6

1 kilo (2¼ lb) pork, including lean
    meat and spareribs
2.5–3 litres (4½–5 pints/10–12
    cups) water
25–30 g (1 oz) ginger, peeled and
    bruised
4 Chinese honeyed dates or dried
    figs
about 450 g (1 lb) or 4–5 bunches
    watercress
salt to taste

THIS SOUP is thought to possess harmonious properties beneficial to many parts of the body, including the throat, the lungs, the stomach and the innards, and is hence considered conducive to good health for all ages. Ever since the introduction of watercress to southern China in the 19th century, the Chinese have believed that it helps to reduce blood pressure and aid bowel movements. If it is a yin food with cooling elements, the scale is tipped by the pork and the long hours of simmering, restoring enough yang or heating elements to result in an efficacious balance.

Besides being health-enhancing, the broth is full of delicate flavours, achieved not least by the addition of the dates or figs, which temper the tangy edge of the watercress. If you find honeyed dates too sugary, use figs, for they are dried without the addition of sugar.

1   Cut the lean pork into large pieces and trim off the fat in the spareribs. Put into a stockpot and add the water. Bring to the boil, then spoon off the scum that continues to surface until the water is quite clear.

2   Add the ginger, dates or figs and watercress and bring to the boil again, skimming off any more impurity which foams up.

3   Cover with a lid, leaving, however, just a small gap. Reduce the heat to the lowest and continue to maintain a gentle simmer for about 4 hours, at the end of which the liquid, tinted beigey green and full of a subtly sweet flavour, is reduced to no more than 1.75 litres (3 pints/ 7 cups). Add salt to taste, starting with 2.5 ml (½ tsp).

4   Serve the soup hot. The soup can be served on its own, or with some of the pulpy but flavourful watercress added to each bowl. Alternatively, the watercress, drained of soup, can be served as a side dish. The same goes for the pork, even though all its flavour and its juices have been imparted to the soup. If it is served, you can always use some thin or light soy sauce as a dipping sauce.

Oxtail Soup

A SOPHISTICATED Sichuanese rustic dish which has all the ingredients that fit the bill. The chicken meat serves to enhance the flavour of the soup, while the dipping sauce for the oxtail, which is peppery and stimulating, provides the characteristic touch of the regional cuisine.

清湯牛尾

SERVES 6

1 oxtail, about 1.2 kilos (2½ lb), cut into sections
550 g (1¼ lb) chicken drumsticks and thighs
2.5 litres (4½ pints/10 cups) water
25 g (1 oz) ginger, peeled, cut into sections and bruised
10 ml (2 tsp) Sichuan peppercorns
25 g (1 oz) dried Chinese wolfberries, rinsed (optional)
30 ml (2 tbsp) Shaoxing wine or medium dry sherry
salt to taste

FOR THE DIPPING SAUCE:
30 ml (2 tbsp) broadbean paste
15 ml (1 tbsp) thick or dark soy sauce
15 ml (1 tbsp) sesame oil

1 Submerge the pieces of oxtail in a large pot of cold water for 20 minutes. The water will gradually turn pink as some of the blood is drained out of the oxtail. Drain, discarding the water.

2 Put the oxtail in a heavy-bottomed saucepan or flameproof casserole. Add the chicken and the water and bring to the boil over a high heat. When the scum foams to the surface, spoon it off continuously for about 5 minutes until the water is relatively clear again.

3 Add the ginger, Sichuan peppercorns, Chinese wolfberries, if used, and wine or sherry. Simmer fast, semi-covered, for 2½–3 hours until the oxtail is very tender, and the meat comes away from the centre bone even though not completely severed from it.

4 Remove the oxtail and chicken from the soup, picking off any peppercorns or ginger that may be stuck to them. Discard the chicken because all the taste will have been extracted from it by now.

5 Drain the soup through a fine wire sieve (if necessary, lined with cheesecloth). Discard the solids, save for the wolfberries, if possible. There should be about 1.5 litres (2½ pints/6 cups) soup.

6 Prepare the dipping sauce. In a bowl or dish mix together the spicy broadbean sauce and soy sauce, then stir in the sesame oil.

7 Return the soup and the oxtail to the saucepan and gently reheat until very hot. Taste the soup and season with salt to taste. Remove the oxtail to a serving dish and serve with the dipping sauce. Serve the soup hot simultaneously.

Mustard Greens
with Salt-cured Egg Soup

SERVES 6

2 salt-cured duck eggs
about 1.75 litres (3 pints/7 cups)
  water
4 slices ginger, peeled
45 ml (3 tbsp) peanut or vegetable
  oil
800 g (1¾ lb) mustard greens,
  trimmed and cut into lengths
  about 7.5 cm (3 in)

Illustrated on Plate 13.

AN EASY and healthy family soup that is also quick to make. Salt-cured duck eggs are readily available in Chinese supermarkets these days, but they are not actually difficult to make (*see* recipe p. 360), even though it takes four to six weeks for them to mature. The depth of savouriness they add to this soup makes it worth one's while either to go to the supermarket or to make them oneself.

1 Crack the eggs into a bowl. Cut up each egg yolk (already solidified during the salting process) into 6–8 bits. Lightly mix the egg yolk and egg white together so as to break the gel. Keep nearby.
2 In a large pot bring the water to a rolling boil. Add the ginger and the oil. Add the mustard greens and return to a simmer, lowering the heat.
3 Pour in the eggs, stirring as the whites solidify. Continue to simmer, either covered or uncovered, for about 3 minutes until the egg yolk is thoroughly cooked. Transfer the soup mixture into a soup tureen or into individual bowls. Serve hot.

Silver Ears
with 'Milk' Stock

SERVES 8

115 g (4 oz) dried silver ears
1 knob ginger, about 2.5 cm
  (1 in), peeled and cut into thick
  slices
about 2 litres (3½ pints/8 cups)
  'milk' stock (*see* p. 362)
salt to taste

ALSO KNOWN as white ears and snow ears, these fungi are whitish, semi-transparent masses of folds grown in the wild on dead wood in damp forests. During the Qing dynasty, they were considered an aristocratic food, and were served at posh banquets, but since their successful cultivation in the 1970s, which resulted in a big drop in their price, they have become easily accessible to many people. That they are a good tonic benefiting high blood pressure and cholesterol levels makes them the more welcome as an ingredient.

This soup is a northern dish, for northern Chinese have

a penchant for using a whitish stock, which they call 'milk' stock.

1   Reconstitute the silver ears. Put the fungi in a large mixing bowl. Pour a kettle of boiling water over them and leave to soak for 30–60 minutes. The fungi will expand into large floral shapes.

Pour into a colander and drain. Break up the whole fungi and, with a pair of scissors, clip off and discard the hard, often yellowish centres, retaining the white and ruffly parts. Rinse these in water, removing any dirt or other impurities. Drain.

Bring a pot or half a wokful of water to the boil. Add the ginger then the fungi and blanch briskly for 10 minutes. Pour into a colander and drain. The fungi are now fully reconstituted and ready to be used as an ingredient.

2   Put the creamy stock in a saucepan and bring to the boil. Add the silver ears and simmer for 10–15 minutes if you wish them to retain a crinkly bite, or about 30 minutes if you prefer them tender and viscous. Season with salt to taste. Serve hot.

Lotus Root
with Pork Knuckle Soup

DURING THE summer in China, one of the gastronomic pleasures, for both its crunchy texture and subtle taste, is fresh lotus root, thinly sliced and stir-fried. As the rhizome is rich in starch, as well as vitamin C, it is often combined with pork to make a soup that is regarded by the Chinese as a tonic which has a harmonious effect on the viscera. When fresh lotus roots are not available, the dried product, packaged in slices, is a very good substitute in making the soup.

SERVES 4–6

115 g (4 oz) dried lotus root pieces
  or 350 g (12 oz) fresh lotus root
1 small pork knuckle, about
  675 g (1½ lb)
1 knob ginger, about 4 cm
  (1½ in), peeled and bruised
5 ml (1 tsp) salt or to taste
thin or light soy sauce as dipping
  sauce

1   Soak the dried lotus root in plenty of water to cover for 30–60 minutes. Drain and discard the water. If fresh root is used, trim the ends, scrape off the skin with a knife, then cut into chunks.

2 Pour 2.25 litres (4 pints/9 cups) water into a large saucepan, add also the lotus root, the pork knuckle and the ginger. Bring to a rolling boil, then skim off the scum that surfaces, until the liquid is relatively clear.

3 Reduce the heat and continue to cook, maintaining a strong simmer, for about 3 hours or until the liquid is reduced to 1.3–1.5 litres (2¼–2½ pints/5½–6 cups). Remove the pork and the ginger; keep nearby.

4 Degrease by spooning off the fat on the surface. Better still, leave the saucepan in the cold larder or refrigerator for a few hours or overnight, then remove the coagulated fat on the surface. Reheat until piping hot, season with about 5 ml (1 tsp) salt or to taste.

5 To serve, ladle the soup into individual bowls and add 2–3 pieces lotus root. The pork can also be served as a side dish with soy sauce as a dipping sauce, even though most of its taste has been imparted into the soup.

'Chicken Bean' Soup

SERVES 6–8

285 g (10 oz) skinned and boned chicken breast fillet
6 small egg whites (size 3)
30 ml (2 tbsp) cornflour, dissolved in 30 ml (2 tbsp) water
250 ml (8 fl oz/1 cup) clear stock or water
5 ml (1 tsp) salt
white ground pepper to taste
15 ml (1 tbsp) sesame oil
1.2–1.3 litres (2–2¼ pints/5–5½ cups) chicken stock
4 large leaves mustard greens or Cos lettuce, rinsed
15 ml (1 tbsp) vegetable oil
10 ml (2 tsp) chopped ham

A CHINESE cook often loves to play this game: to make one ingredient imitate another. He may not even use a cheaper ingredient to mock an expensive one, either; often it is the other way round, as in this sophisticated Sichuanese soup. Much ingenuity is applied before chicken breast takes on the appearance of a popular and inexpensive dish made with ground beans, which every family can afford.

1 Prepare the chicken purée. Trim the chicken fillets, removing and discarding membranes, tendons and fat. Put into a food processor and process very finely. Put into a deep bowl, add one-sixth of the egg white at a time, and stir vigorously until homogenised before adding another sixth. Gradually dribble in the dissolved cornflour, stirring all the time to blend well. Pour in the clear stock or water, a quarter at a time, stirring until well absorbed before pouring in more. Add the salt and

pepper to the thin pastelike purée. Blend in the sesame oil.

2 Add the chicken stock to a large saucepan and slowly bring to a simmer. Remove from the heat.

3 Gradually pour the chicken purée into the saucepan containing the stock, stirring with a wooden spoon all the time so that the purée, which will turn opaque and become solidified as it meets the hot stock, does not stick to the bottom of the saucepan. Place the saucepan over a very low heat, cover with a lid and bring the soup to a gentle simmer. Continue to simmer for another 5 minutes until the chicken is well cooked.

4 Break up the mustard greens or lettuce into large pieces and plunge into a pot of boiling water laced with the oil. Return to the boil, then pour into a colander to drain.

5 To serve, add a few pieces of mustard greens or lettuce to each bowl, then ladle in the soup. Sprinkle ¼–⅓ tsp chopped ham on top. Serve hot.

NOTE: The soup can be prepared ahead of time to step 3 when the soup is brought to a gentle simmer. When about ready to eat, finish the remaining procedures.

Silver Ears
with Chicken Velvet Soup

THIS is a very successful dinner party soup. Pretty to look at, harmonious in flavour, it can also be prepared ahead of time, to be slowly reheated at the appropriate moment. The reheating will not spoil the chicken velvet, though the silver ears will become pleasantly more glutinous in texture the longer they soak in the soup. At my own dinner parties I have had huge success with this soup, when many a guest has asked for seconds, if not thirds!

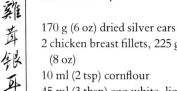

SERVES 12–14

170 g (6 oz) dried silver ears
2 chicken breast fillets, 225 g
  (8 oz)
10 ml (2 tsp) cornflour
45 ml (3 tbsp) egg white, lightly
  beaten
24–30 quail eggs
salt
3 litres (5 pints/12 cups) chicken
  stock

Illustrated on Plate 8.

1 Reconstitute the silver ears as on p. 161, step 1.
2 Prepare the chicken velvet. Trim the chicken fillets, removing and discarding the membranes, tendons and fat. Put into a food processor and mince very finely. Put into a bowl, add the cornflour and egg white and stir

FOR THE MARINADE:

5 ml (1 tsp) salt

1.5 ml (¼ tsp) sugar

2.5 ml (½ tsp) white ground pepper

10 ml (2 tsp) thin or light soy sauce

10 ml (2 tsp) Shaoxing wine or medium dry sherry

15 ml (1 tbsp) sesame oil

vigorously in the same direction until a light purée – the velvet – is achieved.

3 Marinate the chicken velvet. Add the salt, sugar, ground pepper, soy sauce, wine or sherry and stir to mix thoroughly. Leave for 15–20 minutes. Blend in the oil.

4 Put the quail eggs in plenty of salted cold water in a saucepan, bring to the boil and continue to cook over a moderate heat for about 2–3 minutes until the eggs are hard-boiled. Pour into a colander, refresh under cold running water, then submerge them in plenty of cold water for about 30 minutes before peeling them. You will find this makes the peeling much easier.

5 Pour the stock into a large saucepan and heat. As soon as it is fairly warm but not overly hot, pour about 250–300 ml (8–10 fl oz/1–1¼ cups) into the chicken velvet, stirring slowly but continuously to make the latter smooth without forming any lumps.

6 Add the silver ears and eggs to the stock and bring slowly to the boil. Pour in the liquidy chicken velvet, stirring to integrate with the soup. Return to the boil, at which point the chicken velvet will be cooked and the fungi still crunchy. Add salt to taste. The soup is ready to be served. But should you prefer the fungi to be soft and slippery, simmer them in the stock for about 15–20 minutes before adding the eggs and chicken velvet.

Fish Maw
with Dried Scallop Geng

SERVES 6–8

115 g (4 oz) dried eel maws or fish maws, already 'exploded'

8 large, about 85 g (3 oz), dried scallops

6 thick slices ginger, peeled

575 ml (1 pint/2½ cups) prime stock (*see* p. 361)

THIS soup is the embodiment of a geng, for it is thickened and the ingredients are substantial, leaving not much excess liquid. Fish maw, or the swim-bladder from such large fish as shark and large eels, is dried then 'exploded' by heat – deep-fried or put in the oven – before it is sold in shops. Fish maws are slippery in texture, but eel maws are slightly bouncy as well, and as such they are the perfect foil to the tender and savoury-sweet dried scallops.

This geng makes a very presentable dish at an elegant dinner.

If fish or eel maw does not appeal to you, or you can't get hold of it, you can still proceed with this soup. Just use the scallops, doubling the quantity if possible, and continue with the rest of the recipe.

1 Reconstitute the fish maws. Put the tubular eel maws or the fish maws in a colander and pour a kettle of boiling water all over them in order to help rid them of their greasy rank odour.

Fill a large pot with cold water and add the eel or fish maws, which will float to the surface. To weigh them down so that they will gradually absorb and eventually be submerged in water, put a plate over them. Leave to soak for 24 hours, at the end of which they will have become sodden and fully expanded.

2 Steam the scallops. Rinse the scallops and put them on a heatproof dish with sloping edges. Add about 100 ml (4 fl oz/½ cup) water. Place the dish on a steamer and steam (see p. 355) for 1½ hours until the scallops are tender. Remove from the steamer, discard the muscles from the scallops but save the precious juice. Shred the scallops either with your fingers or chopsticks or forks. Put aside.

3 Drain the eel maws or fish maws but leave damp. Cut them up into 1 cm (½ in) cubes.

4 Bring a large pot of water to the boil, add the ginger and the fish or eel maw cubes and return to the boil. Reduce the heat and simmer, covered, for 15–30 minutes. Test by tasting if a cube is tender enough. Pour into a colander and refresh under cold water, discarding the ginger. Drain and squeeze out excess moisture. By now, any greasy rank odour should have disappeared.

5 Add the stock and the fish or eel maw to a large saucepan and slowly bring to a simmer. Continue to simmer, covered, for 10 minutes. Stir in the shredded dried scallops and their juices and return to a simmer. Season with the salt and soy sauce, testing for taste. The soup is now ready and can be left until such time as you are ready to serve it. Refrigerate it if it is left overnight.

6 Just before serving, bring the soup to a simmer again. Thicken it by stirring in the well-stirred dissolved tapioca or potato flour, stirring continuously as the

4–5 ml (¾–1 tsp) salt
15 ml (1 tbsp) thin or light soy sauce
15 ml (1 tbsp) tapioca or potato flour dissolved in 30 ml (2 tbsp) water
white or black ground pepper to taste

liquid thickens slightly. Serve hot immediately. Ground white or black pepper should be added to individual taste.

Hot and Sour Squid Soup

SERVES 4

450 g (1 lb) squids
8 large crisp lettuce leaves, cut into strips
salt
15–30 ml (1–2 tbsp) vegetable oil
850 ml (1½ pints/4 cups) stock
7.5–10 ml (1½–2 tsp) ginger juice (*see* p. 357)
4 spring onions, trimmed and cut into small rounds, white and green parts separated
22.5–30 ml (1½–2 tbsp) Chinese rice vinegar
ground black pepper

THE SICHUANESE hot and sour soup, made with bean curd, cloud ears, golden needles and pork, and thickened with beaten egg and tapioca or potato flour, can have counterparts using ingredients from another province. I myself find this hot and sour squid soup a very pleasant change indeed.

1 Clean the squids. Cut off the heads of the squids from the body pouches. Cut off and discard the eyes. Cut the tentacles into 4 cm (1½ in) lengths.

Slit the body pouches open lengthways as far as the innards. Pull them out and discard. Remove the transparent bones and peel off the reddish skin; discard.

Turn the body pouches inside out and lay them flat on a board. Using a pointed knife, score a criss-cross pattern on the surface of each pouch then cut into pieces about 2 × 4 cm (¾ × 1½ in).

Rinse the pieces in cold water, clean of ink and impurity.

6 Blanch the squids. Bring a pot of water to the boil, immerse the squids for about 5 seconds – an in-and-out action – when they will begin to curl up. Pour into a colander and rinse under cold running water. This makes the squids at once crisp and tender. Drain thoroughly.

3 Blanch the lettuce. Bring another pot of water to the boil. Add about 5 ml (1 tsp) salt and 15 ml (1 tbsp) oil. Add the lettuce; as soon as the water is returned to the boil, pour into a colander and drain thoroughly. Divide into 4 portions and line the bottom of the serving bowls. Keep nearby.

4 Bring the stock to a simmer in a saucepan or a wok. Season with the ginger juice, white spring onions,

vinegar and about 2.5 ml (½ tsp) salt, or to taste. Add the squids, return to a simmer and maintain it for 30–60 seconds until the squids are curled up, being just cooked. Remove from the heat, add the green spring onions and give the soup a stir.

5 Scoop the soup into the bowls. To give the soup the hot-and-sourness it warrants, give each bowl a minimum of 12 rounds of black pepper from the peppermill. More vinegar can also be added to individual taste. Serve hot immediately.

Lemon Sole
Geng

IN CHINA when you make a fish soup – often called fish geng – you will use, more often than not, a freshwater fish, such as a grass carp if you live in the Yangzi River delta, or a dace if you live in the south. But in Europe and America, it is more realistic to use a less bony white fish and prepare the soup in the Chinese manner. Lemon sole, reasonably priced and subtle in flavour, is the easy answer.

1 Marinate the fish. Cut the lemon sole into pieces about 2.5 cm (1 in) square. Put into a bowl, add the salt, soy sauce, wine or sherry, pepper, ginger, tapioca or potato flour and egg white and stir to coat. Leave to stand for 15–20 minutes, then blend in the oils.

2 Add the stock to a saucepan or a wok and heat to a rolling boil. Add the fish, stirring to separate the pieces. As soon as the stock returns to a simmering boil, remove the saucepan or wok from the heat. The fish is just cooked by now. Scatter in the spring onions or coriander leaves, give the soup a stir, then taste for saltiness. Add salt to taste, if necessary. Add also ground white or black pepper to taste. Transfer either into a large serving tureen or individual bowls. Serve hot.

SERVES 6

1 lemon sole, about 675 g (1½ lb), cleaned and gutted, filleted and skinned
1.5 litres (2½ pints/6 cups) clear chicken stock
3 spring onions, trimmed and cut into rounds or leaves from several stalks of coriander leaves
salt to taste
ground white or black pepper to taste

FOR THE MARINADE:
2.5 ml (½ tsp) salt
5 ml (1 tsp) thin or light soy sauce
5 ml (1 tsp) Shaoxing wine or medium dry sherry
6 turns peppermill
5–10 ml (1–2 tsp) finely shredded ginger
5 ml (1 tsp) tapioca or potato flour
15 ml (1 tbsp) egg white
15 ml (1 tbsp) peanut or vegetable oil
10 ml (2 tsp) sesame oil

Cordyceps and Duck Soup

SERVES 6–8

1 cleaned duck, about 2.3 kilos (5 lb)
24–32 cordyceps
10 ml (2 tsp) salt
45 ml (3 tbsp) Shaoxing wine or medium dry sherry
8 thick slices ginger, peeled
4 large spring onions, trimmed and halved
1.5–1.75 litres (2½–3 pints/6–7 cups) stock

CALLED dongchong xiacao in Chinese, which means winter-worm-summer-grass, *Cordyceps sinensis* are caterpillar fungi trailing grass ends. They abound in Sichuan province, and are much treasured by the Chinese, both the young and the old, who use them as a tonic. They are believed to benefit the lungs and kidneys, stop bleeding and dispel phlegm, and they can also correct impotence, seminal emissions, and ease aches and pains in the loins and knees. Usually put in soups, as in this renowned dish, they have a crisp texture. Whatever you may think of cordyceps, this soup, prepared by closed-steaming with duck, is fabulously scrumptious.

1 Make sure to remove remnants of innards from the cavity of the duck, as well as the glands from the tail. Rinse well.

2 Place the duck on a rack of a very hot oven preheated to 240–260°C (475–500°F) Gas Mark 9 with a tray of hot water underneath. Roast for 30 minutes, turning over halfway, so that excess fat from the skin will ooze out and drip down to the tray and be discarded. Remove the duck from the oven, taking care not to lose the juices that have gathered inside the cavity. Put it into a heat-proof lidded bowl or container, large enough to hold it.

3 Meanwhile, soak the cordyceps in warm water for about 20 minutes. Rub with your fingers in the soaking water to rid the grass ends of dirt and impurities. Drain, then rinse once more.

4 Rub the salt and wine or sherry all over the skin and cavity of the duck. Place it breast side up and, with a pointed instrument, pierce holes at regular intervals into the skin and flesh of the breasts, then insert into each hole about three-quarters of the body end of a cordycep. Put half the ginger and spring onions inside the cavity and the remainder on the breast. Add two-thirds of the stock to the bowl or container and put on the lid.

5 Put this lidded bowl or container into a steamer and steam (*see* p. 355), covered, over a high heat for 2½ hours or until the flesh of the duck comes away from the

drumsticks. Make sure to check from time to time that there is plenty of water in your steamer!

6 Remove the bowl or container from the steamer. Degrease the soup inside. The easiest way is to refrigerate it for several hours or overnight until the fat on the surface congeals, then just remove the fat. This dish can be prepared hours or even a day or two in advance up to this point.

7 Just before the duck is ready to serve, add the remaining one-third stock to the lidded bowl or container and resteam for 30 minutes until very hot. Transfer the duck and the soup into a serving tureen. Discard the ginger and spring onions.

8 To serve, break up the duck with a pair of chopsticks (or knife and fork); the meat should be so tender that it comes off the bone at the command of the chopsticks. Put both soup and some duck meat in individual bowls, as well as a few cordyceps.

170

VEGETARIAN DISHES

CHINESE vegetarianism, which is closely associated with Buddhism, in fact preceded the spread of Buddhism into China during the 1st century AD. Vegetarianism had been formulated during the Zhou dynasty (11th century–221 BC) as a means for rulers to prepare themselves spiritually before they were considered fit to make sacrifices to heaven or to their ancestors. As abstinence was a prerequisite to achieving this state of purity, several days prior to the major events rulers would stay in seclusion, away from their wives and concubines, refrain from eating meat and drinking wine, and instead undergo ritual ablutions and eat only vegetables and grain foods. Unfortunately, there is no detailed information on the vegetarian dishes they ate.

The first glimpse we have of ancient Chinese vegetarian dishes is from the chapter entitled Vegetarian Food in the cookery section of Jia Sixie's encyclopaedia on agriculture, *Qimin Yaoshu* (*see also* p. 21), written in the 6th century AD. Totalling eleven dishes, the main ingredients featured spring onions and chives, celery, soy beans, laver, winter gourd and other gourds, white rice, ginger, aubergine and mushrooms, and the seasoning condiments included salt, spring onions, shallots, ginger, ground huajiao or fagara, tangerine peel, black beans, honey, sesame oil and jiang or fermented relishes. Although garlic was not mentioned, the other 'odorous' condiments of spring onions, chives and shallots – which are proscribed foodstuffs in Buddhist vegetarian dishes – were used generously in the recipes. Furthermore, su or animal fat (su is usually translated as butter) was used in two recipes. In a rice dish, Jia wrote: 'Add one pint of su; if there is no su, add two pints of vegetable oil.'

Buddhism came from India during the later half of the Han dynasty, in the 1st century AD. At first, following the example set by its founder, Gautama Buddha (Prince Sakyamuni) and his disciples, every morning Chinese monks would take their begging bowls to their patrons and eat whatever was put into them, whether meat or vegetables. As time went by and more and more temples were built, it became impracticable to continue with this practice, so that kitchens were built to cater for the monks. Even then, they ate whatever they could produce from the land and trawl from the sea. The person who was credited with successfully advocating and enforcing Buddhist vegetarianism was King Wudi of Liang who, in the early 6th century, for political reasons, himself retreated three times to a temple where he observed a stringent vegetarian diet. Since then, it has become the prescribed diet for Buddhist monks and nuns, even though believers themselves need only observe it at certain times or on certain days, or indeed not at all.

In the Buddhist diet, all flesh, be it of warm-blooded animals, poultry and birds or of cold-blooded fish and shellfish, is forbidden, since all life is sacred. The allowable ingredients for Buddhist vegetarian cuisine are, therefore, vegetables and legumes, mushrooms and other fungi, bean curd and its related products, and also wheat gluten, which is what remains after the starch of wheat flour has been washed off. All the herbal plants that are considered to have an odour – or a fragrance, depending on your viewpoint – notably garlic, spring onions and onions, chives, leeks and coriander, are also forbidden. The reason for this is that these herbs are thought to arouse the sensuous desires of a person, and Buddhist monks and nuns are required to remain celibate and abstain from alcohol. Similarly, wine is also out of bounds for them. The rhizome, ginger root, is not, however, on the proscribed list, and hence is much used in the cuisine.

For hundreds of years, especially since the Ming and the Qing dynasties (AD 1368–1644, 1644–1911), Buddhist temples have been, and continue to be, the centres where vegetarian food is served. As most temples are up in the mountains, many people, whether they are believers or tourists, visit them as much for an outing as to burn incense in worship. Whatever their motives, however, at the end of their visit, most people will have enjoyed a vegetarian meal or a banquet in the dining room or the restaurant attached to the temple. The temple kitchen which caters for visitors has for a long time been called the Xiangji Chu or Fragrant Vegetarian Kitchen, a name which has been borrowed by many a commercial vegetarian restaurant all over China. What is interesting about the menu served in these places is the list of meat or poultry dishes which carry the prefix 'zhai' or 'vegetarian' next to them, the most popular being zhai roast goose, zhai roast duck, zhai chicken and even zhai gizzard and zhai pig's stomach. In fact, these dishes contain no meat and are made of wheat gluten or bean curd skins. Others, such as zhai fish, are made of taro, and zhai shark's fin soup is really just glass noodles and vegetables. While the psychology behind these make-believe names is debatable, such dishes go back a thousand years to the Song dynasty (AD 960–1279), and seem to derive more from taverns and food shops than from temples.

In this chapter, most of my recipes adhere to the Chinese Buddhist vegetarian rules, and I have refrained from using even cooking wine. A sprinkling, however, with the additional inclusion of spring onions and the like, will appeal to vegetarians of other persuasions as well. In preparing vegetarian food, oil, especially sesame oil, is used and in understandably generous quantities in order to provide the necessary nutritional value, as well as fragrance and flavour. Another indulgence is the frequent application of deep-frying – of vegetables, bean curd and wheat gluten – in order to enhance the aroma and the richness of the ingredients.

Vegetarian Stock

YIELDS ABOUT 2.25 LITRES
 (4 PINTS)

30 ml (2 tbsp) peanut or vegetable oil
6 thick slices ginger, peeled
1.35 kilos (3 lb) yellow soy bean sprouts, rinsed and drained
675 g (1½ lb) kohlrabi, peeled and cut into slices
45–55 g (1½–2 oz) dried mushroom stalks, washed
25 g (1 oz) dried straw mushrooms (if available), well washed
10 ml (2 tsp) dried longan

素
上
湯

AMONG the ingredients suitable for making vegetarian stock, the most efficacious are fresh soy bean sprouts and dried straw mushrooms, the former exuding a natural sweetness and the latter a more intense flavour, on account of being a reconstituted dried product. Unfortunately, dried straw mushrooms are seldom available in the West, so that I have to resort to the next best thing: the stalks from dried Chinese black mushrooms. Also good are certain legumes, such as kohlrabi, broccoli and carrots. Sometimes, to add sweetness, a very small amount of dried longan can be used.

1 Heat a wok over a high heat until smoke rises. Add the oil and swirl it around to cover a large area. Add the ginger and let sizzle for a few moments to release the aroma. Add the soy bean sprouts and, going to the

bottom of the wok with the wok scoop, turn and toss repeatedly until the water, which oozes from the sprouts, has been absorbed again. This takes about 10 minutes and adds a fragrance to the sprouts. Transfer to a stockpot.

2 Add the kohlrabi, mushroom stalks, straw mushrooms (if used) and longan to the stockpot. Add 3.5 litres (6 pints/14 cups) water and bring to the boil. Skim off any scum that surfaces, then reduce the heat to maintain a fast simmer, partially covered, for about 2 hours.

3 Pour the stock into a container through a wire sieve. Add the solid ingredients to the sieve, batch by batch, and press out additional stock before discarding them. Keep the stock in the refrigerator or the freezer in the normal way.

Shanghai Small Baak Choi

THESE squat cabbages, with white stalks and green leaves – some with pale green stalks – are less than half as long as the common baak choi. Living up to the idea that 'small is beautiful', they possess a more refreshing and subtle sweetness, and have a crisper texture than their larger cousins. They used to be native to just Shanghai and its environs, but are now grown in Europe and America, to the delight of Chinese abroad.

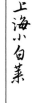

SERVES 6 WITH 3–4 OTHER DISHES

675–900 g (1½–2 lb) Shanghai small baak choi
90–120 ml (6–8 tbsp) peanut or vegetable oil
6–8 slices ginger, peeled
5–7.5 ml (1–1½ tsp) salt or to taste
1½ ml (¼ tsp) sugar
15 ml (1 tbsp) thin or light soy sauce

1 Rinse the baak choi whole, making sure to rinse off any dirt embedded in the leaves.

2 Place each cone of baak choi on a board and halve it lengthways with a knife, showing the heart. Leave the tiny ones whole.

3 Heat a wok over a high heat until smoke rises in abundance. Add the oil, swirl it around and heat for about 1 minute or until very hot. Add the ginger, which will sizzle. Add all the baak choi, which will cause some explosive noises because of the moisture meeting hot oil. Going to the bottom of the wok with the wok scoop, turn and toss the baak choi vigorously 6–8 times.

Add the salt, continuing to toss and turn for about 1 minute, until moisture starts to be drawn out from the cabbage. Reduce the heat if the cabbage begins to burn, and continue to stir and turn for another 2 minutes or longer, depending on how crunchy you would like your baak choi. Taste for crispness and saltiness. Remove from the heat. Using a slotted disc or spoon, scoop up the cabbage and ginger on to a serving dish, leaving the excess water behind in the wok. Sprinkle on the soy sauce and serve hot.

NOTE: This dish can be prepared 1–2 hours in advance up to the point of initially stirring the baak choi for 1 minute and adding the salt in step 3. When about ready to serve, proceed with the rest of the stir-frying.

Cooked
Wheat Flour Gluten

MAKES SUFFICIENT FOR 2 DISHES

1.5 kilos (3½ lb/14 cups) white strong flour
15 ml (1 tbsp) salt
5 ml (1 tsp) bicarbonate of soda (optional)
about 850–900 ml (30–32 fl oz/ 3¾–4 cups) tepid (or cold) water

THIS IS one of the mainstays of Chinese Buddhist vegetarian cuisine, providing fodder for numerous mock meat dishes. Its viscous texture, especially after soaking in stock or sauce, harmonises the mushrooms and fungi and contrasts the crisp vegetables that are cooked with it. It also provides tasty bulk to satisfy the appetite. In China, Taiwan and Hong Kong it is produced commercially as a basic ingredient, which is then used by home cooks, delicatessen and restaurant chefs in umpteen dishes, with varying flavours. In a delicatessen, for example, it is sold in various mock guises: firm and spicy gizzard cubes, soft and sweet and sour pig's stomach pieces and savoury abalone, to name but the most popular. After the gluten is extracted from the flour, the remaining product, revived as wheat starch, is used as a binding agent or as dimsum shells. Whereas wheat starch is sold in packets in the West, gluten is thus far not available except in cans which, unfortunately, are of poor quality. Fortunately, it is quite easy to make at home, and the following recipe gives you enough to make more than two of the most delicious vegetarian dishes.

1 Sift the flour into a very large and deep mixing bowl. Add the salt and bicarbonate of soda (if used). Add 575 ml (1 pint/2½ cups) of the water and stir to mix with a rolling pin or large wooden spoon. Gradually add the remaining water and work into a dough, which should be firm but not hard.

2 Knead the dough. If you use your hands, knead, pull, punch and throw on to a hard surface. If you use a dough hook fitted to a domestic food mixer, divide the dough into 2 pieces. Following the instructions for making bread dough, knead each piece for 4–6 minutes, stopping after every minute lest the motor becomes overheated. In either case, knead until the dough is very, very smooth and elastic so that the maximum amount of gluten can be produced.

3 Put all the dough back into the bowl and cover the bowl with a damp cloth. Leave for several hours or overnight until the dough has become soft and, when you pull it, is very elastic indeed.

4 Pick up the dough, place it in a colander and stand the colander in a sink under cold running water. With both hands, start pressing and squeezing the dough in order to wash off the milky starchy substance. At the end of about 10–12 minutes, most of the starch will have been washed away, and you can feel that what is left in the colander is a soft and spongy mass, the wheat gluten. When some of the excess water is squeezed out, it weighs about 550–675 g (1¼–1½ lb). (Instead of running water, the process can be done in several changes of water, with the sink plug in. Towards the end, the water will become almost clear.) For the best result, leave this gluten lump to prove in a bowl for 2–3 hours, or in the refrigerator, covered, overnight. Drain off the water that has oozed out.

5 With a knife, halve the gluten mass into 2 lumps. Use one half to make deep-fried gluten and the other half steamed gluten.

6 Make deep-fried gluten pieces. Pull with your fingers to break off from 1 gluten lump 1 piece of dough at a time, about the size of a small chestnut. Holding it between one thumb and the first two fingers, pull out some of the dough and then fold back to the centre with the other hand 8–10 times, rotating the piece until it becomes rounded. Put on a flat plate. Repeat until the

gluten is used up. You should be able to make about 34 pieces.

Half fill a wok on a wok stand with vegetable oil and heat over a high heat to a temperature of 190°C (375°F). Add half the gluten pieces from the side of the wok, 1 piece at a time. They will sink to the bottom, then come up to the surface, inflating and puffing bubbles all over. With a long pair of bamboo or wooden chopsticks, turn them over repeatedly for about 2 minutes until light brown in colour. Remove with a large hand strainer and drain on kitchen paper.

Reheat the oil to the same temperature and deep-fry the remaining pieces as before. They can be kept in the refrigerator for 7 days and they freeze well.

7 Make steamed gluten. Put the other lump of gluten mass, in 1 piece, in a lightly oiled heatproof dish with slightly raised edges. Put into the steaming container of a steamer and steam (*see* p. 355) for 1 hour, at the end of which time the steamed gluten will feel spongy and airy. Remove from the steamer and let cool. It can be kept in the refrigerator for 2 days and it freezes well.

You now have the basic flour gluten ingredient to be used in dishes.

Hongshao Kaofu

SERVES 6 WITH 3–4 OTHER
DISHES

1 portion steamed gluten (*see* step 7 above)
vegetable oil for deep-frying
170 g (6 oz) drained canned bamboo shoots, rinsed and cut into wedges
10 medium dried Chinese black mushrooms, reconstituted in 300 ml (10 fl oz/1¼ cups) water (*see* p. 353)

红
烧
烤
麸

THIS dish of red-braised steamed gluten or kaofu in Shanghaiese is a favourite of the Shanghai people, whether or not they keep a vegetarian diet. Characteristic of Shanghai food, it is rich and sweet, but it is also moreish. A vegetarian friend of mine from Shanghai, Sylvia Sung, showed me how to make this dish.

1 Cut the steamed gluten into 22 pieces and squeeze out excess moisture from each piece. (If the steamed gluten has been frozen and defrosted, blanch the whole piece in boiling water for 20–40 seconds. Refresh in cold water, then cut into pieces and squeeze out excess moisture.)

2 Half fill a wok over a stand with vegetable oil and heat to a temperature of 200°C (400°F). Add all the gluten pieces, which will foam at once. Deep-fry them for about 2 minutes until the edges are golden, moving them around periodically with a pair of long bamboo or wooden chopsticks or a wooden spoon. Remove with a hand strainer or perforated spoon and put on kitchen paper to absorb excess grease. Transfer to a large saucepan.

3 Reheat the oil to the same temperature. Add the bamboo shoots and deep-fry for about 5 minutes until the edges are pale golden. Remove and add to the saucepan.

4 Halve the Chinese mushrooms and add to the saucepan.

5 Clip and discard the hard ends of the golden needles. If you do not mind the trouble, tie each into a loop, but this customary practice can be dispensed with. Add to the saucepan.

6 Break the cloud ears into lobes, discarding the hard nobs. Add to the saucepan.

7 Add 45 ml (3 tbsp) oil from the wok to the mixture in the saucepan. Season with the mushroom soy sauce, thin or light soy sauce, salt, and sugar and add the stock, which should just cover the ingredients. Give everything a big stir, then bring to the boil over a high heat. Reduce the heat to maintain a fast simmer, covered, for 25–30 minutes or until most of the liquid has been absorbed. Stir in the sesame oil and simmer for a few more minutes. (If the juices have not been absorbed, turn up the heat to reduce them.) Transfer the mixture to a serving dish and serve hot while the kaofu is full of aroma.

25 g (1 oz) golden needles, reconstituted (*see* p. 353)

5 g (⅕ oz) cloud ears, reconstituted (*see* p. 353)

45 ml (3 tbsp) mushroom soy sauce or thick or dark soy sauce

5 ml (1 tsp) thin or light soy sauce

1.5 ml (¼ tsp) salt

15 ml (1 tbsp) sugar

about 450 ml (15 fl oz/2 cups) vegetarian stock (*see* p. 172) and mushroom soaking liquid together

30 ml (2 tbsp) sesame oil

Broccoli
with Ginger Juice

450 g (1 lb) broccoli spears or
   Chinese broccoli spears, washed
6.5 ml (1¼ tsp) salt
60 ml (4 tbsp) peanut or vegetable
   oil
4 thickish slices ginger, peeled
15 ml (1 tbsp) ginger juice (*see*
   p. 357)
1.5–2.5 ml (¼–½ tsp) sugar
22.5 ml (1½ tbsp) thin or light soy
   sauce
30 ml (2 tbsp) sesame oil

FOR this simple and easy dish you can use either Chinese broccoli or the ordinary broccoli, even though the Chinese themselves, understandably so, have a penchant for the former, which is reminiscent of asparagus in flavour. For the gourmet palate, it is also customary to use only the central spears which, needless to add, are the most tender.

As broccoli, Chinese or otherwise, is good basic material to make vegetarian stock, the remaining parts can be fed into the stockpot, and hence not wasted.

1 Bring a large pot or wokful of water to the boil, add 5 ml (1 tsp) salt and 30 ml (2 tbsp) oil. Add the broccoli or Chinese broccoli spears, return to the boil, then continue to boil for about 2 minutes. The spears will still be very crunchy. Pour into a colander and drain. (If you are not proceeding with the following steps straight away, run cold water over the broccoli spears until they are cool so that their vividness can be retained for up to 2 hours.)

2 Heat a wok over a high heat until smoke rises. Add the remaining 30 ml (2 tbsp) oil and swirl it around to cover a large area. Add the ginger slices, stir and let sizzle for a few moments. Return the spears to the wok and toss and turn until very hot again. Sprinkle with 1.5 ml (¼ tsp) of the salt and the ginger juice, stirring to mix. Add the sugar and soy sauce, continuing to stir over a medium heat until the sauce is absorbed. Test to see if the spears are sufficiently tender for your liking, yet still crisp. If too hard, add about 30 ml (2 tbsp) water and continue to cook them, covered, for another 1–2 minutes. Remove the cover, add the sesame oil and stir to mix. Place on a serving dish and serve hot.

Vegetarian
Fish

THESE fish, made of taro, are a great favourite on Chinese vegetarian menus. They make a tantalising first course, but can also be served as a main course together with some other dishes. They may seem difficult to make but are actually quite easy if you follow this foolproof recipe. The secret of how to achieve success was shown to me by a Chinese chef in Soho, who prefers to remain anonymous, but he knows he has my thanks.

SERVES 4 AS FIRST COURSE:
  8–10 WITH 4–5 OTHER DISHES

500 g (1 lb 2 oz) well-peeled taro
6 medium dried Chinese black
  mushrooms, reconstituted (*see*
  p. 353)
30 ml (2 tbsp) sesame oil
5 ml (1 tsp) thin or light soy sauce
about 75 g (3 oz/⅔ cup) wheat
  starch
about 60 ml (4 tbsp) boiling hot
  water
4 ml (¾ tsp) salt
2.5 ml (½ tsp) five-spice powder
vegetable oil for deep-frying
4 garden peas, lightly blanched
  and patted dry
DIPPING SAUCES:
chilli sauce
Worcestershire sauce

Illustrated on Plate 7.

1 Steam the taro. Cut up the taro into slices about 1 cm (½ in) thick. Put them directly on to the steaming basket or container of the steamer and steam (*see* p. 355) for 40–45 minutes until the taro is thoroughly soft. Transfer to a dish or bowl and leave to cool completely so that any extra moisture will dissipate.

2 Drain the mushrooms and cut into very thin slices. Heat a wok over a high heat until smoke rises. Add 15 ml (1 tbsp) of the sesame oil and swirl it around. Add the mushroom and stir for about 30 seconds. Lower the heat, season with the soy sauce and stir until absorbed. Remove to a dish and let cool.

3 Put the wheat starch into a small bowl. Add 45 ml (3 tbsp) of the boiling water and stir immediately with a pair of chopsticks. Using your fingers, work it into a firm dough. If necessary, gradually add the remaining water, but as soon as all the starch is drawn in, cover the bowl and leave it to stand for about 10 minutes.

4 In the meantime, mash the taro pieces with a spoon until totally smooth. Season with the salt and five-spice powder. Pick out and discard any hard bits.

5 Add the wheat starch dough to bind the mashed taro, incorporating the former into the latter evenly. (The resultant taro dough should be easily pliable but not sticky. If it is, it means there is too much moisture and you will have to add a little wheat starch to absorb it.) Divide into 4 equal portions.

6 Make the 4 fish. Take 1 portion at a time with your hands and break off a quarter (or just under) and put aside. Halve the remaining three-quarters. Shape into 2

thin oval sheets 11.5–12.5 cm (4½–5 in) long and no more than 7.5 cm (3 in) wide, tapering at the tail end. Put them on a cool worktop. Place on top of 1 sheet the mushroom strips in 1 layer, stopping before the edges. Put the other sheet on top and pinch the edges to seal the body of the fish completely.

Halve the remaining quarter of taro dough. Shape 1 half into an arc to make the fish-tail and attach it to the tapering end of the fish. Halve the other half of dough and shape into 2 fins, then attach 1 to each side of the body (you may have 1 fin if by any chance you don't have enough dough to make 2).

Now, with the pointed end of a small knife, carve a semi–circle to indicate the fish head. To etch the scales below the head, indent with the pointed end across the body, row by row. Etch a few lines on the head and a small hollow to indicate the eye. Etch also lines on the tail and the fins. Leave the completed fish flat on a cool surface, lightly oiled, to ensure non-stickiness. Make the other 3 fish as before.

7 Deep-fry the fish. Half fill a wok placed on a stand with vegetable oil and heat over a high heat until it reaches 200°C (400°F). Before the oil becomes hot, dip a large hand strainer momentarily into the oil, then leave it nearby. Holding a metal pastry scraper against one side of a fish, slide it underneath to lift the whole fish and then slip it on to the hand strainer. If you wish the fish-tail to curl upwards, place it near the edge of the strainer. When the oil is hot enough, lower the hand strainer into the oil, submerging the fish for deep-frying. The fish will foam instantly, but after 20–30 seconds, it will float away from the hand strainer. Remove the strainer from the oil, let cool momentarily, then place another fish on it and deep-fry it as the first one. Continue to deep-fry the first one for about 5 minutes or until the fish, scales et al, turn beautifully golden and, when you tap it lightly with long chopsticks or a wooden spoon, you can feel the crispness and hear a hollow sound. Remove with the hand strainer and put on to kitchen paper to absorb excess grease. Continue to deep-fry the other fish until ready.

Deep-fry the remaining 2 fish as before. Just before serving, don't forget to place 1 garden pea into each eye

Top left: Braised Pigeons (p. 303).
Right: Cantonese Chow Mein with Prawns (p. 242).
Bottom left: Water Spinach with a Robust Sauce (p. 194).

PLATE 5

Top: Stir-fried Cucumber and Bean Sprouts (p. 181).
Bottom: Lohan Zhai (p. 182).

PLATE 6

socket of the fish. Serve hot. The dipping sauces cater to individual tastes, but I myself love it neat, so that I can enjoy contrasting the crispy outside with the soft inside.

NOTE: The stuffed and sculpted fish, wrapped in cling film, can be left in the refrigerator overnight before they are deep-fried. If you do not wish to stuff the fish, instead of dividing the dough to make 2 sheets in step 6, just make 1 sheet and proceed.

Stir-fried Cucumber and Bean Sprouts

CUCUMBERS were introduced to China from the Middle East during the early Christian era. Bean sprouts, on the other hand, are native to China and have, during the 20th century, become very popular in the West. Stir-fried together, they are pretty to look at, crunchy, and also healthy.

黄瓜豆芽

SERVES 4 WITH 2–3 OTHER DISHES

225–350 g (8–12 oz) bean sprouts
1 long cucumber, about 450 g (1 lb)
45 ml (3 tbsp) peanut or vegetable oil
2 thin slices ginger, peeled
3 spring onions, trimmed and cut into 5 cm (2 in) sections, white and green parts separated
2.5 ml (½ tsp) salt or to taste

Illustrated on Plate 6.

1 If the bean sprouts do not look as pristine as they should be, rinse them. Drain thoroughly; better still, put into a salad spinner and spin off excess moisture.
2 Rinse the cucumber and halve lengthways. Remove the seedy pulp in the centre, cut each half on the diagonal at about 3 mm (⅛ in) intervals, resulting in crescent slices.
3 Heat a wok over a high heat until smoke rises. Add the oil and swirl it around to cover a large area. Add the ginger, let sizzle, then add the white spring onion and stir for a few seconds to release the aroma. Add the bean sprouts and cucumber and season with the salt. Going to the bottom of the wok with the wok scoop or a spatula, turn and toss continuously for about 3 minutes until the vegetables are cooked but still crisp, and much of the water that exuded has disappeared owing to the high heat. Add the green spring onion and stir to mix. Scoop everything on to a serving plate and serve hot.

Lohan Zhai

SERVES 12 WITH 5 OTHER
DISHES

20 g (⅔ oz) dried hair moss

15–20 g (½–⅔ oz) dried bamboo
fungi

120 ml (8 tbsp) peanut or
vegetable oil

9 slices ginger, peeled

12 medium dried Chinese black
mushrooms, reconstituted (*see*
p. 353)

25 g (1 oz) golden needles,
reconstituted (*see* p. 353)

10 g (⅓ oz) cloud ears,
reconstituted (*see* p. 353)

50 g (2 oz) silver or white ears,
reconstituted (*see* p. 161)

30–37.5 ml (2–2½ tbsp) mashed
red bean curd cheese

2.5 ml (½ tsp) salt or to taste

5 ml (1 tsp) sugar

30 ml (2 tbsp) thin or light soy
sauce

575–850 ml (1–1½ pints/2½–4
cups) vegetarian stock (*see*
p. 172)

170 g (6 oz/1½ cups) canned
drained gingko nuts

20 pieces deep-fried gluten (*see*
p. 175, step 6)

15–30 ml (1–2 tbsp) sesame oil

170 g (6 oz) mange-tout, rinsed,
topped and tailed

Illustrated on Plate 6.

LOHAN, or Arahats, were the personal disciples of Buddha, as well as guardians and defenders of the faith. This time-honoured dish, named after them, is often eaten on Chinese New Year's Day when many, especially in southern China, prefer to observe a vegetarian diet. It combines ingredients that can vary in kind, number and quantity, as long as they fit into the Buddhist vegetarian category. With this recipe as a guideline, you can make up your own Lohan Zhai, using such variables as carrots, bamboo shoots, or other fungus, and bean curd puffs as substitutes for (or additions to) the more exotic and less accessible hair moss and bamboo fungi. Whilst the ingredients in this recipe are those popularly associated with the dish, I chose them to provide the widest contrast of textures. This was not lost on an English friend and food journalist, Vicky Hayward, who enthused: 'Never have I tasted a dish in which texture is so important. Every ingredient has something viscous about it, and yet each one has something quite different. The silver fungus between the teeth and the nuts and hair moss on the tongue are quite wonderful and so different from anything in the Western tradition.'

1 Reconstitute the hair moss. Wet the lump of hair moss with water and put it in a fine sieve. Dribble over 15 ml (1 tbsp) of peanut or vegetable oil and start squeezing it to bring out the dirt and muddy impurities embedded between the hairy strands. Rinse under slowly running water. After a few moments, add another 15 ml (1 tbsp) of oil and continue the squeezing and rinsing process until the water is clear and the hair moss clean.

2 Reconstitute the bamboo fungi. Soak the fungi in plenty of warm water for about 15 minutes until they are soft. Rubbing gently with your fingers, remove sandy impurities from them. Drain, then change the water, which will have become yellowish, several times, repeating the rubbing action until the water is clean and the fungi clean.

3 Cure the hair moss and bamboo fungi. Bring half a pot of water to the boil. Add 3 slices of ginger and 15 ml

(1 tbsp) oil. Add the hair moss in a lump and the bamboo fungi and blanch for 2 minutes to refresh them. Drain through a fine sieve and discard the ginger. Divide the lump of hair moss into small bunches to facilitate serving later. Cut each fungus into about 3 pieces.

4 Drain the black mushrooms, reserving the soaking liquid. Halve them.

5 Drain the golden needles. Clip and discard the hard ends.

6 Drain the cloud ears and break up into lobes, discarding the hard knobby ends.

7 Drain the silver ears and break them up into large pieces. With a pair of scissors, clip and discard the yellow hard centres.

8 Heat a large casserole or saucepan over a high heat until very hot. Add 75 ml (5 tbsp) oil and heat until hot. Add the remaining ginger, stir and sizzle for a few seconds, then add the red bean curd cheese and stir a few more times. Add the black mushrooms, stir half a dozen times, add the golden needles, continuing to stir another half a dozen times. Add the cloud ears, the silver ears and the bamboo fungi and continue to stir to mix, lowering the heat to medium, lest the cloud ears jump out of the pot! Season with the salt, sugar and soy sauce. Pour in the stock, add the gingko nuts and the deep-fried gluten pieces and bring to the boil. Turn down the heat and simmer, covered, for about 20–25 minutes. Give all the ingredients a big stir, then add the hair moss, submerging it. Simmer for another 5 minutes, when the hair moss will become tender and yet not overly so. Most of the stock should be absorbed; if too dry, add a little more stock. This zhai or vegetarian dish can be prepared in advance up to this point. The flavour actually improves overnight.

9 Just before serving, stir in the sesame oil and reheat to a simmer. Add the mange-tout and stir to mix. Continue to simmer for 1–2 more minutes or until the mange-tout are just cooked yet still very green and crunchy. Remove from the heat and scoop the mixture into a large serving dish. Serve hot.

NOTE: If there is any left over, Lohan zhai can be reheated in the normal way or served cold. Surprisingly, it is quite delicious eaten cold.

Vegetarian
'Shark's Fin' Soup

SERVES 5–6

100 g (3½ oz) cellophane or glass
  noodles
6 medium or large black Chinese
  mushrooms, reconstituted (*see*
  p. 353)
4 g (⅛ oz) wood ears,
  reconstituted (*see* p. 353)
30 ml (2 tbsp) peanut or vegetable
  oil
225 g (8 oz) carrots, peeled and
  shredded into very fine julienne
  strips
5 ml (1 tsp) salt
1 litre (1¾ pints/4 cups)
  vegetarian stock (*see* p. 172)
15 ml (1 tbsp) thin or light soy
  sauce
15 ml (1 tbsp) potato or tapioca
  flour dissolved in 30 ml (2 tbsp)
  water
15 ml (1 tbsp) sesame oil
ground pepper to taste

Illustrated on Plate 7.

As ALL fish and shellfish are forbidden in the Buddhist vegetarian diet, real shark's fin is, of course, out of the question for anyone adhering to it. But cellophane or glass noodles are allowed, and when cut into shorter lengths, they can, especially at a quick glance, give the impression of being shark's fin needles.

1 Using a pair of scissors, cut the glass noodles into 5 cm (2 in) lengths and put into a large bowl. Pour over them plenty of very hot water and leave to soak for about 20 minutes or longer. Pour into a colander. Drain.

2 Drain the mushrooms and cut them into the thinnest possible strips. Set aside.

3 Drain the wood ears and cut into the thinnest possible threads. Set aside.

4 Heat a wok over a high heat until smoke rises. Add the peanut or vegetable oil and swirl it around to cover a wide area. Add the mushrooms, stir about a dozen times, add the wood ears, continuing to stir with, however, reduced heat, lest the wood ears jump out of the wok! Add the carrots and stir to mix a few more times. Season with 2.5 ml (½ tsp) of the salt. Transfer the mixture into a bowl and keep nearby.

5 Put the glass noodles into a saucepan and add the stock. Season with the remaining 2.5 ml (½ tsp) salt and the soy sauce. Bring to the boil, then simmer over a low heat for 10–15 minutes. Add the mushroom mixture and return to the simmer.

6 Give the dissolved flour a good stir, then gradually pour into the saucepan to thicken the soup, if ever so slightly, stirring all the time to prevent lumps from forming as the soup continues to simmer. Remove from the heat. Stir in the sesame oil, add ground pepper to taste, then pour into a large serving soup bowl. Serve hot.

Red-in-Snow
and Bamboo Shoots

RED-IN-SNOW is a variety of mustard plant grown in Zhejiang province which, being very resistant to cold, sprouts up its red shoot in the spring snows. It is mostly used as a pickled vegetable to season other ingredients in stir-fries and soups.

1 Blanch the bamboo shoots in a pot of boiling water for about 2 minutes to get rid of any canning odour. Pour into a colander and refresh under cold running water. Drain well.

2 Heat a wok over a high heat until smoke rises. Add the oil and swirl it around. Add the red-in-snow and stir a few times to enhance its fragrance. Add the sugar, stirring a few more times. Add the bamboo shoots and stir to mix. Pour in the stock, bring to the boil, then reduce the heat and simmer, covered, for about 5 minutes so that the stock will absorb the savouriness of the pickled red-in-snow which, in turn, will season the bamboo shoots.

3 Pour in the well-stirred dissolved flour and continue to stir as the sauce thickens. Remove the mixture to a serving dish. Sprinkle on the sesame oil and serve hot.

SERVES 4–6 WITH 2–3 OTHER DISHES

450 g (1 lb) drained canned slender bamboo shoots, halved
30 ml (2 tbsp) peanut or vegetable oil
115 g (4 oz) drained canned red-in-snow, roughly chopped
2.5–5 ml (½–1 tsp) sugar
75 ml (3 fl oz/⅓ cup) vegetable stock or water
2.5 ml (½ tsp) tapioca or potato flour dissolved in 10 ml (2 tsp) water
15 ml (1 tbsp) sesame oil

Broadbean Relish

NINGBO people in eastern China love to have this as a side dish, and they eat it either hot or cold. In the summer, when broadbeans are in season, fresh ones are a great treat, but to my pleasant surprise, frozen broadbeans, which retain much of the texture, are a more than satisfactory substitute.

1 Shell the fresh broadbeans, which usually contain only 3–5 seeds each. Remove the husk enveloping each seed with your fingers. You will find that this is not difficult to do with fresh broadbeans. Shelled and husked, the seeds will yield only about 375–400 g (13–14 oz). If frozen broadbeans are used, plunge into a large

SERVES 10–12 AS A SIDE DISH

1.8 kilos (4 lb) fresh broadbeans in their shells or 600 g (1 lb 5 oz) frozen
about 300 ml (10 fl oz/1¼ cups) water or less
45 ml (3 tbsp) peanut or vegetable oil
200 g (7 oz) drained canned red-in-snow or Shanghai pickled vegetable, finely chopped by hand or in a processor
7.5–10 ml (1½–2 tsp) sugar

pot of boiling water, return to the boil, then pour into a colander and refresh under cold water. Remove the husks with your fingers or a small knife; the seeds weigh about 400 g (14 oz).

2 Put the husked beans in a saucepan, add the water which should just about cover them. Add also 15 ml (1 tbsp) of the oil and bring to the boil. Reduce the heat to medium and fast-simmer, covered, for 20–25 minutes or until the water is all but absorbed and the beans are soft enough to be crumbled up. Remove from the heat. Using a wooden spoon to push the beans against the sides of the saucepan, mash them, leaving, however, some lumps for chewing and for giving an uneven texture.

3 Heat a wok over a high heat until smoke rises. Add the remaining 30 ml (2 tbsp) oil and swirl it around. Add the chopped red-in-snow, stir and turn to mix with the oil. Reduce the heat to medium, add the sugar and continue to stir until the sugar is melted, which will take only 10–20 seconds. Remove the wok from the heat.

4 Add the red-in-snow vegetable to the saucepan containing the broadbean mixture and stir to mix thoroughly. Scoop on to one or two dishes with sloped edges and smooth the surface with a palette knife. Leave to cool or keep in the refrigerator, covered. Serve cold as a side dish. It keeps well in the fridge for several days.

Vegetarian Lettuce Wraps

SERVES 8

50 g (2 oz) dried lotus root slices or about 170 g (6–8 oz) fresh lotus root
45 ml (3 tbsp) peanut or vegetable oil
4–6 spring onions, trimmed and cut into small rounds, white and green parts separated

BEAN CURD, commercially produced in factories in the West, is known popularly as tofu, and is quite easily available in health food shops as well as large supermarkets. Compared to Chinese bean curd, Western tofu is much thicker and firmer in consistency, and the soy bean aroma, which is very attractive to the Chinese, but not to Westerners, is nullified. Western tofu is used in this recipe.

If Buddhist vegetarians wish to use this recipe, all they need to do is to drop the use of spring onions.

1 If using dried lotus root soak in plenty of water to cover for 15–30 minutes. Drain the lotus roots and put into a saucepan. Add about 850 ml (1½ pints/4 cups) water and bring to the boil, then simmer for about 1 hour until the roots are fully expanded and crunchily tender. Pour into a colander to drain, then cut into small dice or thin, small slices.

   If using fresh lotus root, trim the ends, scrape off the skin with a knife and cut into dice. Add water to cover and blanch for 10–15 minutes until crunchily tender.

2 Prepare the sauce: put the dissolved flour into a small bowl, add the stock or water and the soy sauce. Stir to mix.

3 Heat a wok over a high heat until smoke rises. Add the oil and swirl it around. Add the white spring onion rounds and stir to release the aroma. Add the lotus roots, grass mushrooms and water chestnuts and stir for about 1 minute. Add the tofu and stir to mix until thoroughly hot. Season with the salt. Lower the heat to medium, push the ingredients to the sides, leaving a space in the centre of the wok. Add the well-stirred sauce and slowly bring to a simmer, stirring as it thickens. Fold the surrounding mixture into the sauce and stir to mix. Add the green spring onion rounds and the sesame oil. Stir to mix, then scoop everything on to a serving dish.

4 To serve, place the lettuce leaves on 1 or 2 plates and put them on the dining table. Put the vegetarian dish on the table as well. Let each individual take 1 lettuce leaf on to their plate, spoon some vegetarian mixture on the leaf, wrap it up and pick it up to eat with their fingers.

225 g (8 oz) canned drained grass mushrooms, each quartered
225 g (8 oz) canned drained water chestnuts, cut into small dice or slices
225 g (8 oz) firm tofu, cut into small dice
2.5 ml (½ tsp) salt
15 ml (1 tbsp) sesame oil
1–2 heads crisp lettuce, leaves separated and trimmed into cup shapes

FOR THE SAUCE:
7.5 ml (1½ tsp) potato or tapioca flour dissolved in 15 ml (1 tbsp) water
75 ml (5 tbsp) vegetable stock or water
30 ml (2 tbsp) thin or light soy sauce

Shandong Cabbage

XIE BAOCHEN (1850–1926), a late Qing court official who became a herbal doctor, wrote an important vegetarian cookbook, *Sushi Shuolue* or *A Summary of Vegetarian Food*, which was published in the 1920s. He advocated vegetarianism, not so much for reasons of health but because the first Buddhist Precept forbids slaying 'that which hath life'. His book, comprising more than one hundred dishes, many of which are simple and straightforward,

SERVES 4 WITH 2 OTHER DISHES

675 g (1½ lb) Chinese celery cabbage (Chinese leaves)
45 ml (3 tbsp) sesame oil
30 ml (2 tbsp) mushroom soy sauce or thick or dark soy sauce
10 ml (2 tsp) Chinkiang vinegar

reflects the vegetarian food of Peking and the neighbouring province, Shanxi, during the 19th century. This recipe, which is both simple and delicious, is a particularly fine example.

'Cut the white cabbage into rectangular sections and stir-fry with sesame oil. Add soy sauce and mature vinegar and braise until well done without, however, adding any water. They are rich yet crisply pleasant, delectable served both hot and cold. Restaurants in Chinan [capital of Shandong] excel in this dish, and hence it is so named.'

1 Rinse the 2–3 outer leaves that need cleaning. Shake off excess moisture. Cut all the leaves into long strips about 7.5 cm (3 in) long and 2.5 cm (1 in) wide.
2 Heat a wok over a high heat until very hot. Add the sesame oil and swirl it around to cover a wide area. Add the cabbage and, going to the bottom of the wok with the wok scoop, turn and toss for about 1 minute to incorporate the oil, reducing the heat to medium if it begins to burn. Add the soy sauce and the vinegar, continuing to stir to mix. Cover with the lid and braise between low and medium heat for 12–15 minutes or until the cabbage is well done. Much moisture will have oozed from the cabbage. Turn up the heat until most of it is absorbed. Scoop on to a serving dish and serve hot. If you wish to serve it cold, let it cool or keep in the refrigerator before serving. It is delicious served either way.

Red-braised Bean Curd

SERVES 4 WITH 2 OTHER DISHES

4 cakes bean curd, refreshed (see p. 354)
6 medium dried Chinese black mushrooms, reconstituted (see p. 353)
vegetable oil for deep-frying
30 ml (2 tbsp) peanut or vegetable oil

红
烧
豆
腐

THIS is a very popular dish served both in restaurants and at home, and prepared both in a vegetarian or non-vegetarian way. Speaking for myself, whenever I'm asked to choose a bean curd dish from a restaurant menu, more often than not I choose this one, even though I'm fond of all bean curd dishes. What attracts me is the combination of the slightly crisp skin of the bean curd with the meltingly soft centre and the overall effect of the topping made with shredded ginger, mushrooms and bamboo shoots. When the dish is made in a non-vegetarian way, a small amount of shredded pork is added to the topping.

1 Cut each cake into about 4 rectangular pieces and pat dry with kitchen paper.
2 Drain the mushrooms, but leave them damp. Reserve the soaking liquid for making the sauce. Cut the mushrooms into very thin slices.
3 Prepare the sauce. Put the dissolved tapioca or potato flour in a small bowl. Stir in the mushroom liquid or stock. Add the salt, sugar, soy sauces (or oyster sauce) and stir to mix.
4 Half fill a wok sitting over a wok-stand with vegetable oil and heat over a high heat until it reaches 210–220°C (410–425°F) in temperature. Put the bean curd pieces in a large, lightly oiled hand strainer and then add to the oil and deep-fry for 2–3 minutes. The bean curd will foam fiercely at first and then will swell up slightly. Remove with the hand strainer and put on kitchen paper to absorb excess grease.
5 Heat a second wok or a frying pan over a high heat until smoke rises. Add the peanut or vegetable oil and swirl it around to cover a large area. Add the ginger, stir 12 times, then add the mushroom and stir a few more times. Add the bamboo shoots, stir another dozen times, then season with the salt and stir again. Return the bean curd to the wok and stir to mix until very hot. Reduce the heat, make a well in the centre of the wok and pour in the well-stirred sauce. As the sauce thickens, stir in the other ingredients to absorb it. Transfer to a serving dish and serve immediately. Use chilli sauce optionally as a dipping sauce.

15–22.5 ml (1–1½ tbsp) shredded ginger
50 g (2 oz) drained canned bamboo shoots, shredded into strips then blanched (*see* p. 353)
1.5 ml (¼ tsp) salt
chilli sauce (optional)

FOR THE SAUCE:
5 ml (1 tsp) tapioca or potato flour dissolved in 15 ml (1 tbsp) water
45–60 ml (3–4 tbsp) mushroom soaking liquid or vegetarian stock
1.5 ml (¼ tsp) salt
1.5 ml (¼ tsp) sugar
10 ml (2 tsp) thick or dark soy sauce (or 15 ml/1 tbsp oyster sauce)
5 ml (1 tsp) thin or light soy sauce

Sour and Spicy
Bean Curd Cubes

SERVES 4–6 WITH 2–3 OTHER
DISHES

6 large cakes bean curd, refreshed
  (*see* p. 354)
vegetable oil for deep-frying
30 ml (2 tbsp) thin or light soy
  sauce
22.5–30 ml (1½–2 tbsp) Chinese
  rice vinegar
2.5–5 ml (½–1 tsp) chilli powder

AMONG Xie Baochen's ten recipes in the chapter on bean curd in his *Summary of Vegetarian Food*, he bubbles with enthusiasm over this one, leaving no doubt that it is his favourite.

'Cube the bean curds and deep-fry them. Then cook them with soy sauce, vinegar and chilli powder, and they are crisply pleasant to the palate. I am addicted to this dish!'

1 Pat dry the bean curd, then cut each cake into about 2 cm (¾ in) square cubes. As moisture will continue to ooze out, put on changes of kitchen paper to get them dry.

2 Put a wok over a wok-stand and half fill it with vegetable oil. Heat over a high heat until it reaches 200°C (400°F) in temperature. Meanwhile, put the bean curd cubes in an oiled hand strainer or perforated disc and put into the oil. The cubes will foam straight away and will swim away from the hand strainer or disc. Remove it from the oil and deep-fry the cubes for about 4–5 minutes until they are floating and the foaming has disappeared. Scoop up with the strainer or disc and put over a bowl to catch any juices from the bean curd that may still ooze out.

3 Heat a saucepan or another wok over a high heat until hot. Add 15–30 ml (1–2 tbsp) of the deep-frying oil and swirl it around. Add the deep-fried bean curd cubes, stir a few times, add the soy sauce, the vinegar and the juice in the bowl and stir until they are absorbed. Sprinkle on the chilli powder, stir to mix and scoop on to a serving dish. Serve hot.

VEGETABLES

IN her excellent book, *Oriental Vegetables*, Joy Larkcom asserts that 'vegetables are enormously important in China: the average vegetable consumption per head is said to be higher than in any western European country or the USA. They are the warp and woof of Chinese cookery, found in some form in most dishes.' She is absolutely right. Furthermore, many of the vegetables, notably brassicas, bamboo shoots and bean sprouts, give Chinese dishes their distinctive texture and flavour.

The brassicas are the most characteristic Chinese vegetables, and they are nutritious and healthy as well. The most common among them – these days also the most well known outside of China – are the Chinese cabbages which, despite their confusing names in different countries and continents, can be divided into two main groups. The celery cabbage (*Brassica rapa var pekinensis*), known as Chinese leaves in Great Britain and napa cabbage in the States, is the most popular in northern China. From October onwards, you can see mountains of these cabbages piled up on city pavements, as they are harvested to sustain a large population during the winter. Among their different types, the cylindrical Tianjin cabbage (wong nga baak in Cantonese) is the sweetest and most sought after, not only by northern Chinese but by southern Chinese as well. The Chinese leaves grown in Israel and the West are of the more barrel type and, although less succulent compared to wong nga baak, are sweet and juicy and hence a welcome addition to the selection of Western vegetables.

Those of the other main group, better known by their universally accepted Cantonese name, baak choi or pak choi, meaning white cabbage (*Brassica rapa var chinensis*), have white stalks, which graduate to broad green leaves. Within this group, there is the Shanghai 'small' type, a miniature baak choi 10–15 cm (4–6 in) long, half the size of the ordinary ones. There is also the green baak choi, whose stalks and leaves are both a light green colour. The latter two are known to be crisper and more delicate in flavour. All are now available in Chinese supermarkets.

In south China, there is choi sum (*Brassica rapa var para-chinensis*), which means the heart of the vegetable. It is sometimes called Chinese flowering cabbage, since it has yellow flowers which complement the green leaves, and is the favourite of the Cantonese. Their next favourite is gai laan or Chinese broccoli (*Brassica oleracea var alboglabra*), which has a more blue-green, waxy look and carries (usually) white flowers. Its distinctive flavour is reminiscent of asparagus.

The mustard greens are the next most popular of the Chinese brassicas. There are many types, but the most commonly available in the West are the leaf mustards (*Brassica juncea var foliosa*), with their pleasantly pungent flavour. Sometimes, the wrapped heart mustard, so called because the leaves curl inward to form a heart in the centre, are seen in the shops, and they are more delicate and less tangy in flavour. But the special Chaozhou (Swatow) large-headed mustard, famed for its pungent flavour, has yet to be available abroad.

Whereas the above are mostly eaten fresh, two other types of mustard green are better known as preserved and pickled vegetables, and are used as a seasoning for other ingredients. One is the xuelihong or red-in-snow type (*Brassica juncea var multiceps*) found in the Shanghai region, which is so called because its reddish stem can be seen sprouting through the spring snow. The other type (*Brassica juncea var zhacai*), which has swollen nodules on the stems, is grown in Sichuan province. The former is pickled in salt, and the latter in salt and chilli powder.

Bean sprouts, or sprouts from mung beans (*Phaseolus aureus*), together with Chinese leaves, are arguably the two Chinese vegetables that have become part and parcel of the Western diet. The soy bean sprouts (*Glycine max*), which are essential in making vegetable stock for vegetarian cuisine, are becoming more and more visible in the West, and I expect it won't be too long before they become regular stock items in many supermarkets. Fresh Chinese water chestnuts (*Eleocharis dulcis*), the ebony-coloured corm of the plant, are sometimes available, but the same cannot be said of the different kinds of bamboo shoots (*Dendrocalamus latiflorus*), which arrive in the West as a canned product.

Other more exotic Chinese vegetables – from the Western point of view – such as the chrysanthemum greens (*Chrysanthemum coronarium*), the edible amaranth (*Amaranthus gangeticus*) and Chinese matrimony vine (*Lycium barbarum*) are now available in Chinese supermarkets. The latter two are mostly used in soups. Another, water spinach or kangcong (*Ipomea aquatica*), which is very popular with Southeast Asian people, is also easily obtainable. But others, such as water shield (*Brasenia schreberi*) and Chinese clover (*Medicago hispida*), are not seen in the West, and even in China are confined to the eastern or Shanghai region.

The Chinese use the simplest techniques when cooking this splendid array of vegetables. They blanch them until they are just done yet still crunchy, or in Chinese cookery parlance, until the raw rankness of vegetables is gone and their fresh fragrance brought out. They simmer them for a long time to make delicious and health-giving soups. They braise them for a more intense flavour. And they stir-fry them, until just cooked , rendering them ever so crisp, and at the same time adding a special fragrance to their freshness. This last method reaps the bonus of retaining the vitamins that are vital to good health. Sometimes, two techniques are employed together in order to achieve the desired effect: for instance, before beans and broccoli are stir-fried, they are blanched for a short time to make them just sufficiently tender.

As vegetable dishes are just as an important accompaniment to boiled plain rice as any other dishes, they are frequently seasoned with a small amount of meat so as to enhance their taste. By the same token, meat, fish, shellfish and poultry dishes are often cooked with some vegetables as a means to break up the monotony of ingredients or to save cost, but, above all, to make them ever more interesting in terms of looks, taste, texture and fragrance.

A brief mention should be made of gourds or melons. The Chinese wax gourd, more commonly known as the winter melon (*Benincasa hispida*), which can be round or oblong and can weigh up to 45 kilos (100 lb) or more, is the most popular among the Chinese. Those that are perfect in size and shape are often reserved by restaurants to make Winter Melon Pond, a sophisticated soup, which is made using delicacies to replace the pips and pulp in the melon and then close-steamed for several hours. There is hairy or fuzzy melon (*Benincasa hispida chieh-kua*), which is firmer in texture and is usually braised with flavour-imparting ingredients, such as mushrooms or pork. There is also silk gourd or sigua (*Luffa acutangula*), which has striped skin and must be eaten young. Lastly, there is bitter melon (*Momordica charantia*), whose bitterness is an acquired taste. But those who have acquired it, can't have enough of it.

Now that Western cooks increasingly use Chinese vegetables, especially bean sprouts and celery cabbage, in salads one may well ask why the Chinese themselves traditionally cook their vegetables rather than eat them raw. In fertilising the vege-table fields, human waste has always been used, and, as a safeguard against parasites, the Chinese developed the habit of always cooking their vegetables. Stir-frying them in intense heat for a short time is the delicious answer: it kills the parasites, but retains the crisp quality of the vegetables.

Water Spinach
with a Robust Sauce

SERVES 4 WITH 2 OTHER DISHES

675 g (1½ lb) water spinach, rinsed
22.5–30 ml (1½–2 tbsp) shrimp paste or 45 ml (3 tbsp), about 6 pieces, mashed, fermented white bean curd cheese (with chilli flakes in the jar)
15 ml (1 tbsp) Shaoxing wine or medium dry sherry
60–75 ml (4–5 tbsp) peanut or vegetable oil
5–7.5 ml (1–1½ tsp) finely chopped garlic
1–2 red or green chilli peppers, deseeded and cut into small rounds
2.5 ml (½ tsp) sugar

Illustrated on Plate 5.

ALSO known as hollow spinach, since the stems are hollow, this popular vegetable is basically quite mild and insipid in taste, so the Chinese use a very robust sauce to flavour it. Fermented bean curd cheese is one popular sauce (especially among vegetarians), but shrimp paste remains the favourite, despite the inescapably heady atmosphere it generates when the vegetable is being cooked, which may not endear you to your neighbours. If they happen to be from Malaysia or Thailand, you can relax, for they, too, love this vegetable, which they call kangcong, and they use the concentrated shrimp paste in a brick, known as balachan, to cook it. On the other hand, by all means use the bean curd cheese sauce, which is just as delicious.

1 Cut off and discard about 2.5 cm (1 in) of the tough end of the stems, then cut the remaining stems into 6.5–7.5 cm (2½–3 in) sections. Separate them from the leafy parts.
2 Put the shrimp paste or bean curd cheese into a small bowl and add the wine or sherry. Stir to mix.
3 Heat a wok or a heavy bottomed saucepan (if you wish to contain the splashing in this instance) over a high heat until very hot. Add the oil and swirl it around several times, add the garlic, stir as it sizzles, add the chilli rounds and the shrimp paste or bean curd cheese and stir a few more times. Add the stems of the spinach, stirring and turning to mix with the sauce. Lower the heat to medium, cover with the lid and continue to cook for about 2 minutes. Replace the lid, add the leafy parts and stir to mix well. Add the sugar, which will round off the

saltiness of the shrimp paste or bean curd cheese. Continue to cook, covered or uncovered, for about another 2 minutes or longer until the leaves are limp and the stems tender but still crunchy. Transfer to a serving dish and serve hot.

Dry-fried
Shredded White Radish

THE Sichuanese love frying vegetables until they are withered and dry, and they don't seem to mind spending a long time to effect the drying in a wok over a low heat. The most notable dish in this category is perhaps Dry-fried Four Seasonal Beans, in which dry-fried beans are seasoned with chopped dried shrimps, spicy hot preserved Sichuan vegetable and vinegar to add to the complexity of the tastes. In the case of white radish, beef is used to make it into a well-balanced meat and vegetable dish seasoned, not surprisingly, with the heady and spicy hot bean paste. Instead of stir-frying for a long time in the traditional way, I have opted for the modern method of deep-frying the ingredients to achieve the desired effect.

SERVES 6 WITH 3 OTHER DISHES

350 g (12 oz) beef, rump or topside
1 kilo (2¼ lb) long white radishes (moolie), peeled
1 large, about 225 g (8 oz), red pepper, trimmed
vegetable oil for deep-frying
15 ml (1 tbsp) peeled and finely shredded ginger
8–10 spring onions, trimmed and cut into 5 cm (2 in) sections, white and green parts separated
15–30 ml (1–2 tbsp) hot bean paste
15 ml (1 tbsp) Shaoxing wine or medium dry sherry
2.5 ml (½ tsp) salt or to taste
1.5 ml (¼ tsp) sugar

FOR THE MARINADE:
5 ml (1 tsp) roasted ground Sichuan peppercorns (see p. 359)
2.5 ml (½ tsp) salt
5 ml (1 tsp) cornflour
10 ml (2 tsp) peanut or vegetable oil

1 Cut the beef into rope-like lengths about 7.5 cm (3 in) long and 4 mm (⅕ in) thick. Put into a bowl.
2 Marinate the beef. Add the Sichuan peppercorns, salt and cornflour to the beef and stir vigorously to coat. Leave to stand for about 20 minutes. Stir in the oil to separate the beef.
3 Cut the radishes into sticks about 7.5 cm (3 in) long and as thick as a chopstick.
4 Halve, core, and deseed the red pepper. Cut lengthways into strips.
5 Half fill a wok over a wok stand with the oil and heat over a high heat until the oil reaches the temperature of 200°C (400°F). Add the beef, spread it out and fry for about 30 seconds until firm. Remove with a large hand strainer or perforated disc and drain on kitchen paper.
6 Reheat the oil to 200°C (400°F). Add the white radishes which will foam. Deep-fry for about 10 minutes until

many of the bubbles have disappeared. Remove and drain on kitchen paper.

7 Add the red pepper to the oil and dry for about 2 minutes. Remove and drain on kitchen paper.

8 Pour the oil into a heatproof container, leaving about 30 ml (2 tbsp) in the wok.

9 Reheat the oil over a high heat until smoke rises. Add the ginger, stir a few times, then the white spring onion and stir a few more times, then the hot bean paste. Return the beef, radish and red pepper to the wok and stir to mix. Splash in the wine or sherry around the edges of the wok, and, when the sizzling subsides, add the salt and sugar, stirring continuously. Add the green spring onion, stir, then remove everything to a serving dish. Serve hot.

Stir-fried Beans and Straw Mushrooms

SERVES 4 WITH 2 OTHER DISHES

225 g (8 oz) fine beans or French beans or sugar snaps
1 can straw mushrooms, drained weight 225 g (8 oz), rinsed and drained
salt
67.5 ml (4½ tbsp) peanut or vegetable oil
10 ml (2 tsp) finely chopped garlic
22.5–30 ml (1½–2 tbsp) oyster sauce

A GOOD combination of the slippery straw mushrooms, which inevitably come in a can, and green beans. Sugar snaps or other larger beans can also be used as long as, when you blanch them, you make sure they are neither underdone nor overcooked.

1 Top and tail the beans. Rinse.

2 Halve the straw mushrooms so that they will absorb the seasoning more easily, although you can leave them whole if you wish.

3 Blanch the beans. Half fill a wok with water and bring it to the boil. Add 5 ml (1 tsp) salt and 22.5 ml (1½ tbsp) oil. Add the beans, return to the boil and continue to cook for 2 minutes if using fine or French beans, and for 1 minute if using sugar snaps. Pour the contents into a colander and refresh with cold water which will keep the beans vivid in colour. This step can be done a couple of hours in advance.

4 Dry the wok and reheat over a high heat until smoke rises. Add the remaining 45 ml (3 tbsp) oil and swirl it around to cover a large area. Add the garlic, stir, let it sizzle but, before it becomes burned, add the beans and

the straw mushrooms. Going to the bottom of the wok with the wok scoop, turn and toss for about 1 minute or until piping hot. Lower the heat, add the oyster sauce and stir to mix. Taste and, if need be, add a pinch of salt. Scoop on to a serving dish and serve immediately.

Sichuan
Aubergine

AUBERGINES, or eggplants, can be round or cylindrical and come in different colours – white, green and purple – but perhaps the most common ones we find in markets are elongated, egg-shaped and dark magenta-purple. The Sichuanese fish-fragrance sauce, with its spicy overtone tempered by the ever so slight sweet-and-sour suggestion, makes this one of the most sensuous dishes in any cuisine. If you add the optional cloud ears, which the Sichuanese certainly do, you will experience a contrasting yet complementary texture to the aubergine.

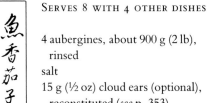

In preparing this dish, Chinese cooks will habitually add some dissolved tapiocal or potato flour at the end as a thickening sauce. I have purposely omitted it, for I prefer the purer effect here.

1 Remove and discard the hard tops of the aubergines, but leave the skin on. Quarter each aubergine lengthways, then cut breadthways into pieces at about 4–5 cm (1½ in) intervals. Put the pieces on to one or two platters, skin side down.
2 Sprinkle about 12.5 ml (2½ tsp) salt evenly over the exposed side of the aubergine. Leave for about 45 minutes, during which time the bitter juices will ooze out. Put all the pieces into a colander and drain, then rinse thoroughly with cold water. Drain well. Lay the pieces on kitchen paper to absorb excess moisture.
3 Rub the cloud ears with your fingers to rid them of mud and impurities. Pluck off the hard knobs. Rinse and drain, then break up the pieces and keep nearby.
4 Deep-fry the aubergine. Put a wok over a wok-stand and half fill it with oil. Heat over a high heat to a

SERVES 8 WITH 4 OTHER DISHES

4 aubergines, about 900 g (2 lb), rinsed
salt
15 g (½ oz) cloud ears (optional), reconstituted (*see* p. 353)
vegetable oil for deep-frying
10 ml (2 tsp) finely chopped garlic
7.5 ml (½ tsp) finely chopped ginger
6–10 medium dried red chillies, deseeded and roughly chopped
22.5 ml (1½ tbsp) Shaoxing wine or medium dry sherry
7.5 ml (1½ tsp) sugar
30 ml (2 tbsp) thin or light soy sauce
22.5 ml (1½ tbsp) Chinese rice vinegar or 15 ml (1 tbsp) white wine vinegar
about 30 ml (2 tbsp) clear chicken stock or water
4 spring onions, trimmed and cut into small rounds
15 ml (1 tbsp) sesame oil

temperature of 200°C (400°F). Put in all the aubergine pieces and deep-fry for 2–2½ minutes until soft but not overly limp. Remove with a large perforated disc or spoon and drain well on kitchen paper. The oil can be used again.

3 Heat a second wok (or sauté pan or saucepan) over a high heat until smoke rises. Add 30 ml (2 tbsp) oil and swirl it around. Add the garlic, stir a few times, add the ginger, stir a few more times, then add the chillies and stir a few more times. Add the cloud ears and return the aubergine to the wok, stir until very hot. Splash in the wine or sherry around the edges of the wok, stirring as it sizzles. Season with 2.5 ml (½ tsp) salt, the sugar, soy sauce and vinegar. Add the stock, reduce the heat to medium, put on the wok lid and cook for 5–8 minutes until the pieces are tender and the liquid absorbed. Remove to a serving dish. Add the spring onion rounds to the wok, stir a few times, then remove and scatter on to the aubergine. Sprinkle the sesame oil on top, then serve immediately.

NOTE: This dish can be cooked hours or even a day in advance and reheated just before serving. Furthermore, it is equally delicious served cold.

Stir-fried Yard-long Beans with Pork Slivers

SERVES 4 WITH 2 OTHER DISHES

115 g (4 oz) trimmed lean pork, cut into thin slivers
225 g (8 oz) long beans, topped and tailed and cut into 2.5 cm (1 in) lengths
salt
60 ml (4 tbsp) peanut or vegetable oil
5 ml (1 tsp) finely chopped garlic

季豆肉片

YARD-long beans really do live up to their name and are about 45–60 cm (1½–2 ft) in length, so that you have to cut them into convenient lengths before cooking them. In this dish, the pork is used to season the beans, in the typical Chinese way of stir-frying vegetables.

1 Marinate the pork. Put the pork into a bowl. Add the salt, soy sauce, ground pepper, wine or sherry and tapioca or potato flour and stir to mix. Add the water and stir vigorously until absorbed; this makes the

pork light and velvety. Leave to stand for about 15 minutes. Blend in the oil.

2 Prepare the sauce. In a small bowl add the dissolved tapioca or potato flour to the stock or water. Blend in the oyster sauce. Leave aside.

3 Blanch the beans. Half fill a wok with water, add 5 ml (1 tsp) salt and 15 ml (1 tbsp) of the oil and bring to a rolling boil over a high heat. Add the beans, return to the boil, then continue to cook for 1 more minute or until the beans are at once tender but retain a bite to them. Pour into a colander and rinse under cold running water. Drain. Dry the wok.

4 Reheat the wok over a high heat until smoke rises. Add 15 ml (1 tbsp) oil and swirl it around. Return the beans to the wok, stir to incorporate the oil over a medium heat for about 30 seconds, sprinkling with a pinch of salt. Scoop on to a dish and keep nearby.

5 Reheat the wok over a high heat until smoke rises. Add the remaining 30 ml (2 tbsp) oil and swirl it around several times. Add the garlic, stir a few times but before it gets burned, add the white spring onions and stir a few more times to release their aroma. Add the pork and, going to the bottom of the wok with the wok scoop, turn and toss for 20–30 seconds until the pork slivers are turning opaque. Splash in the wine or sherry around the edges of the wok, continue to stir as it sizzles. Pour in the sauce and, when it thickens, reduce the heat, return the beans to the wok and stir to mix. Add the green spring onions, give another stir, then scoop on to a serving dish. Serve hot immediately.

NOTE: French beans or fine beans can be used instead of long beans. In that case, keep them whole or halve them lengthways and blanch them 1 minute or more longer.

3 spring onions, trimmed and cut into 2.5 cm (1 in) lengths, white and green parts separated
7.5 ml (1½ tsp) Shaoxing wine or medium dry sherry

FOR THE MARINADE:
1.5 ml (¼ tsp) salt
5 ml (1 tsp) thin or light soy sauce
6 turns peppermill
5 ml (1 tsp) Shaoxing wine or medium dry sherry
2.5 ml (½ tsp) tapioca or potato flour
7.5 ml (1½ tsp) water
5 ml (1 tsp) sesame oil

FOR THE SAUCE:
2.5 ml (½ tsp) tapioca or potato flour dissolved in 15 ml (1 tbsp) water
30 ml (2 tbsp) stock or water
15 ml (1 tbsp) oyster sauce

Stir-fried
Oyster Mushrooms

SERVES 4 WITH 2 OTHER DISHES

300 g (10 oz) oyster mushrooms
45 ml (3 tbsp) peanut or olive oil
4–5 ml (¾–1 tsp) finely chopped
   garlic
1–2 spring onions, cut into 2.5 cm
   (1 in) sections
2–2.5 ml (⅓–½ tsp) salt
ground white pepper to taste
   (optional)
15 ml (1 tbsp) finely chopped ham

Illustrated on Plate 14.

IN 1986 my sister Yan-ho and I visited the capital of Yunnan, Kunming, renowned for its geological wonders, the stone forests. Unexpectedly, we were told of a food street off a side street in the centre of town. We sauntered there one evening and found ourselves in the midst of a myriad stall-restaurants, many of which were no more than tricycles turned back to front, decked out to become food counters. On them were numerous ingredients ready for stir-frying at a moment's notice when passers-by ordered them. What allured us were the off-white wild oyster mushrooms, looking fresh and pretty in bamboo baskets, so we put in a double order and watched the lightning stir-frying on top of a charcoal brazier. We then sat on wooden stools by a table and wolfed down the mushrooms, which were made the more delicious by the red specks of Yunnan ham scattered over them.

I mustn't forget to mention that as we sipped the dark Yunnan Pu'er tea afterwards, still at the table watching the milling crowd do their choosing and eating, we felt the long journey from Hong Kong had been worth it.

1 Do not wash the mushrooms, which generally are very clean. Instead, use a damp cloth to wipe off any dirt or impurity. Cut up into large pieces.

2 Heat a wok over a high heat until smoke rises. Add the oil and swirl it around. Add the garlic, stir a few times and, before it becomes burned, add the spring onions and stir a few more times. Add the mushrooms and, going to the bottom of the wok with the work scoop, flip and turn for about 2 minutes, seasoning with the salt. Moisture that oozes from the mushrooms will be reabsorbed. Reduce the heat, continue to stir for another 1–2 minutes. Season with ground white pepper, if used, then scoop on to a serving dish. Sprinkle with the ham. Serve hot.

House of Confucius
Stuffed Mushrooms

NOT that the sage Confucius himself ate these mushrooms. The name derives from his descendants, who still live in the estate where he was born more than two thousand years ago, where they have maintained a kitchen renowned for its sophisticated and refined dishes. This example uses quite ordinary ingredients and yet achieves an elegant result by applying some thoughtful craftsmanship.

SERVES 6 WITH 3 OTHER DISHES

16 medium dried Chinese black mushrooms reconstituted (*see* p. 353)
150 ml ((5 fl oz/⅔ cup) prime stock (*see* p. 361)
2 slices ginger, peeled
115–170 g (4–6 oz) chicken breast fillet, finely minced
vegetable oil in a small dish
sesame oil

FOR THE MARINADE:
2 ml (⅓ tsp) salt
5 ml (1 tsp) Shaoxing wine or medium dry sherry
5 ml (1 tsp) tapioca or potato flour
30 ml (2 tbsp) egg white
10 ml (2 tsp) sesame oil

FOR THE SAUCE:
45 ml (3 tbsp) peanut or vegetable oil
5 ml (1 tsp) puréed or very finely minced garlic
5 ml (1 tsp) puréed or very finely minced ginger
25 g (1 oz) dried shrimps, pulverised in a liquidiser
15 ml (1 tbsp) Shaoxing wine or medium dry sherry
5 ml (1 tsp) tapioca or potato flour dissolved in 75 ml (5 tbsp) prime stock (*see* p. 361)

1 Drain the reconstituted mushrooms. Clip off the stalks, taking care to keep the caps whole.
2 Put the mushrooms into a saucepan, add the stock and the ginger slices and bring to a simmer. Continue to simmer, covered, for 30 minutes or until the stock is absorbed. Remove the mushrooms to a platter and let cool. Discard the ginger.
3 While the mushrooms are simmering, marinate the chicken in a bowl. Add the salt, wine or sherry, tapioca or potato flour and egg white to the chicken and stir-beat the mixture for 30–60 seconds or until light and fluffy. Stir in the sesame oil.
4 Stuff the mushrooms. Using a small palette knife, scoop up 5–7.5 ml (1–1½ tsp) minced chicken to fill the inside of 1 mushroom cap. Dip the palette knife into the dish of oil, then smooth over the stuffing. Repeat until all are done.
5 Place the stuffed mushrooms, stuffing side up, on a heatproof dish with slightly raised edges and put into a steamer and steam (*see* p. 355) over a high heat, for about 5 minutes until the stuffing is cooked, looking whitish. Remove the steamer from heat but keep the mushrooms inside. This dish can be prepared up to this point in advance and resteamed until hot before the next step.
6 Prepare the sauce. Heat a wok over a high heat until smoke rises. Add the oil and swirl it around. Add the garlic and ginger, stir once or twice, then add the shrimps, continuing to stir until very hot. Splash in the wine or sherry around the side of the wok and let sizzle for a few seconds. Reduce the heat, add the dissolved

and well-stirred tapioca or potato flour, stirring as it thickens.

7 Arrange the mushrooms on a serving dish, stuffing side up. Spoon some of the sauce on top of each cap, then sprinkle a few drops of sesame oil on it. Serve hot.

Braised Chinese Celery Cabbage and Chestnuts

SERVES 6 WITH 3 OTHER DISHES

170 g (6 oz) shelled frozen whole
    chestnuts
salt
1 Chinese celery cabbage (Chinese
    leaves), about 675 g (1½ lb),
    rinsed
90 ml (6 tbsp) peanut or vegetable
    oil
10 ml (2 tsp) sugar
5 ml (1 tsp) finely chopped ginger
15 ml (1 tbsp) chopped white
    spring onion
15 ml (1 tbsp) Shaoxing wine or
    medium dry sherry
30 ml (2 tbsp) thin or light soy
    sauce
150 ml (5 fl oz/⅔ cup) chicken
    stock

栗
子
白
菜

WHEN you cook this famous Shandong dish, you can use either fresh chestnuts, which no doubt are used there, or frozen ones. If you choose the former, do the usual thing of inserting a cross into the skin with a pointed knife, then boil them for about 20–25 minutes, refresh them and then shell them. As I loathe this procedure with a passion, I have opted for the easy way out, having discovered that in some supermarkets it is possible to buy excellent, whole but already shelled chestnuts in frozen packets.

1 Bring a pot of salted water to the boil and plunge the frozen chestnuts into it. Return to the boil and continue to cook for about 5–6 minutes until the chestnuts are just done yet still *al dente*. Pour into a colander and refresh under cold running water. Leave to drain well. Halve each chestnut crossways.

2 Halve each celery cabbage leaf lengthways, then cut crossways into about 5 cm (2 in) long pieces. Separate the white stalk parts from the leafy parts.

3 Heat a wok over a high heat until smoke rises. Add 60 ml (4 tbsp) of the oil and swirl it around several times. Add the chestnuts and fry them for about 2 minutes, moving them around from time to time and adjusting the heat if they become burned. Using a perforated disc or spoon, remove them to a bowl, leaving as much oil behind in the wok as possible.

4 Add the white parts of cabbage and stir. Sprinkle with 2.5 ml (½ tsp) salt and continue to stir for about 2 minutes. Add the remaining leafy part of cabbage, continuing to stir for another 3 minutes, during which time more water will have oozed out. Transfer to a wire sieve

lodged over a bowl to catch the moisture which will continue to exude. Wash and dry the wok.

5 Reheat the wok over a high heat until hot. Add the remaining 30 ml (2 tbsp) oil. Add the sugar, stirring as it melts in the oil. Reduce the heat to medium and continue to caramelise the sugar until it turns russet brown. Immediately add the ginger and the white spring onion and stir to release their aroma. Splash in the wine or sherry and return the chestnuts to the wok, stirring to mix with the sauce. Add the cabbage, continue to stir to mix. Add the soy sauce, pour in the chicken stock and bring to the boil, stirring to mix. Cover with the wok lid and continue to braise for about 10 minutes over medium to low heat, at the end of which time most of the sauce should have been absorbed. Scoop on to a serving dish and serve hot.

Baby Leeks
with Wind-dried Belly Pork

A VERY easy family dish that finds favour with Hunanese people. The fat that oozes from the wind-dried pork during frying will be used to fry the baby leeks while the pork slices will flavour them. Wind-dried belly pork imparts a special cured flavour to the leeks and it is quite easily available in Hunan, and indeed, throughout China. Outside China, it is not so easily available. Fortunately, streaky bacon, smoked or unsmoked, is a very good substitute, so do use it, if need be.

SERVES 4 WITH 2 OTHER DISHES

115 g (4 oz) wind-dried belly pork (or use streaky bacon as substitute), cut crossways into thin slices
350 g (12 oz) baby leeks, trimmed and cut diagonally into slivers at 6 mm (¼ in) intervals

1 Heat a wok over a medium heat until hot. Add the wind-dried pork (or streaky bacon) and fry until cooked, the fat becoming transparent. Remove with a slotted spoon, leaving the melted fat behind in the wok.
2 Add the leeks to the wok and stir, first over a high heat for about 10 seconds, then over a low/medium heat for 2–3 minutes until the leeks are tender.
3 Return the wind-dried pork (or bacon) to the wok and stir to mix with the leeks. Scoop on to a serving dish and serve hot.

Stir-fried Baak Choi with Chopped Garlic

SERVES 4–6 WITH 2–3 OTHER
DISHES

900 g (2 lb) baak choi, rinsed and
  drained
45–60 ml (3–4 tbsp) peanut or
  vegetable oil
10 ml (2 tsp) finely chopped garlic
5 ml (1 tsp) salt or to taste

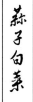

THE odour of garlic is dissipated during the quick stir-frying while its aroma, imparted to the cabbage, gives it a unique fragrance no other herbs can surpass. Take care, however, not to overcook the baak choi, lest it becomes rather stringy, having oozed out most of its water content. Cutting up the stalks into short sections does the trick.

1 Cut the baak choi stalks (and leaves) crossways into short lengths at 2.5–4 cm (1–1½ in) intervals. Separate the white stalk from the green parts.

2 Heat a wok over a high heat until smoke rises. Pour in the oil and swirl it around. Add the garlic, stir, but before it gets burned, add the white baak choi. Going to the bottom of the wok with the wok scoop, toss and turn vigorously for about 1 minute, seasoning with the salt as well. Any water that exudes from the baak choi is likely to be absorbed, so take care not to burn it. Add the green parts and continue to turn and toss for about another minute. Reduce the heat, keep on stirring, but less vigorously, for 1–2 more minutes. By now the leaves should be limp while the stalk parts are still crisp to the bite. Remove either with the wok scoop or a perforated spoon on to a serving dish. Serve hot.

VARIATION: Whole Shanghai Small Baak Choi Stir-fried with Chopped Garlic. Use the same amount of Shanghai small baak choi but leave them whole after rinsing them. Instead of step 1, bring a large potful of water to the boil, add 15 ml (1 tbsp) vegetable oil. Blanch the baak choi for no more than 1 minute after the water returns to the boil, then refresh under cold running water and drain well. Follow step 2, taking care, however, when turning and tossing the baak choi, to be more gentle, so that it can be kept whole and crisp.

Three-coloured Vegetables

THE three colours are gold, white and green corresponding to carrots, bean sprouts and mange-tout. This clean-looking and pretty stir-fry is designed to use the juices which exude from the bean sprouts to cook the carrots and mange-tout. This last vegetable originates from Europe, and the Chinese refer to it as Holland pea, even though the rest of the world regards it as Chinese now.

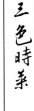

SERVES 4 WITH 2 OTHER DISHES

2 carrots, each about 50 g (2 oz)
350 g (12 oz) bean sprouts
115 g (4 oz) mange-tout
45 ml (3 tbsp) peanut or vegetable oil
4 slices ginger, peeled
3–4 spring onions, trimmed and cut diagonally at 2 cm (¾ in) intervals, white and green parts separated
2.5 ml (½ tsp) salt
10 ml (2 tsp) soy sauce

Illustrated on Plate 15.

1 Peel the carrots. Make a diagonal cut at one end and then cut, either by hand or using a food processor, into slices as thin as the mange-tout.

2 Bean sprouts are usually packed in pristine condition, but if you need to wash them, spin off excess moisture.

3 Top and tail the mange-tout. Wash them, rubbing off any impurities, then drain well.

4 Heat a wok over a high heat until smoke rises. Add the oil and swirl it around to cover a large area. Add the ginger, let sizzle, then add the white spring onion and stir several times to release the aroma. Add the bean sprouts and, going to the bottom of the wok with the wok scoop, turn and toss. Sprinkle over the salt, stir to mix, then add the carrots and the mange-tout and continue to stir vigorously, uncovered. The water that oozes from the bean sprouts will cook the carrots and mange-tout. After stirring for 3–4 minutes, the juices should be absorbed again, and the vegetables cooked yet very crunchy. Add the soy sauce, stir a few more times, add the green spring onions and stir to mix. Transfer to a serving dish and serve hot.

Stir-fried Cucumber
with Cloud Ears

SERVES 4 WITH 2 OTHER DISHES

5 g (⅕ oz) or 45 ml (3 tbsp) cloud
  ears, reconstituted (*see* p. 353)
450 g (1 lb) long or small
  cucumbers, trimmed
30–37.5 ml (2–2½ tbsp) peanut or
  vegetable oil
4 thin slices ginger, peeled
1 medium onion, peeled and cut
  lengthways
3 spring onions, trimmed and cut
  into 4 cm (1½ in) sections, white
  and green parts separated
2.5 ml (½ tsp) salt or to taste
15 ml (1 tbsp) oyster sauce or
  10 ml (2 tsp) thin or light soy
  sauce

A QUICK and easy family dish that cuts across regions and provinces, providing delight to vegetarians and non-vegetarians alike. For Buddhist vegetarians, the spring onions can be omitted. For those who would like to play around with other ingredients, either add 225 g (8 oz) bean sprouts and proceed with step 3 or use them as a substitute for cloud ears.

1 Drain the cloud ears, breaking up large pieces. Pour over plenty of boiling water to cover and soak for another 30–45 minutes so that they will be tender. Drain well.

2 Roll-cut the cucumbers. Make a diagonal cut on one end of a cucumber, roll it a quarter turn towards yourself and make another diagonal cut, then continue rolling and cutting into wedges.

3 Heat a wok over a high heat until smoke rises. Add the oil and swirl it around. Add the ginger, stir to release the aroma, add the onion and white spring onion and stir for about a minute. Add the cloud ears, stir for a few times, then add the cucumber. Season with the salt and, going to the bottom of the wok with the wok scoop, turn and toss for about 2 minutes until the cucumbers are very hot but still crunchy. Add the oyster sauce or soy sauce (or both), stir, add the green spring onions, stir, then scoop on to a serving dish and serve hot.

Choi Sum
with Oyster Sauce

NOT for nothing is this green flowering cabbage called choi sum, which means the heart of the vegetable, for it is only the stalk in the centre that is tender and delicious to eat while the outer stalks, belying their green looks, are stringy and tough. You can expect to lose one third to one half of the weight of choi sum in the cooking. Wasteful as they may seem, the Cantonese adore choi sum for their delicate taste; more often than not, they simply blanch them and lace them with oyster sauce.

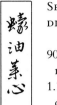

SERVES 4–6 WITH 2–3 OTHER DISHES

900 g (2 lb) choi sum, trimmed of most of the outer stalks, rinsed
1.75–2 litres (3–3½ pints/7–8 cups) boiling water
10 ml (2 tsp) salt
60 ml (4 tbsp) peanut or vegetable oil
30 ml (2 tbsp) oyster sauce

Illustrated on Plate 8.

1 Cut the choi sum into about 15 cm (6 in) long lengths.
2 Pour the boiling water into a wok or a large saucepan. Add the salt and 30 ml (2 tbsp) of the oil. Submerge the choi sum in the water and return to the boil over a high heat, uncovered, then continue to cook for about 1 more minute until they are tender yet retaining a bite. Pour into a colander and drain.
3 Arrange the choi sum on a serving dish. Lace with the remaining 30 ml (2 tbsp) oil and oyster sauce.

VARIATION: Chrysanthemum greens with Oyster Sauce. As there is no waste in chrysanthemum greens, just rinse them and halve the very long lengths. Use about 675–900 g (1½–2 lb) of them and proceed as in step 2. But as soon as the water returns to the boil, pour into a colander and drain, for the greens are already tender enough to eat. Do not overcook them. Proceed with step 3.

BEAN CURD DISHES

CHINA'S alternative to dairy products, and an invaluable staple, especially for vegetarians, is bean curd (doufu in Mandarin, dowfu in Cantonese and tofu in Japanese). It is made from soy bean (*Glycine max*), one of the five staple cereals grown in China since the Zhou dynasty (11th century–221 BC). As a source of protein, soy bean outweighs not only all other crop plants, including rice, wheat, millet and barley, but also all animal meat, including beef. Whereas soy bean contains 57.6 g of protein per 100 g, lean beef of the same weight contains only 20.3 g and silverside beef 32.9 g. But although economical and nutritious, soy bean, unlike rice, is not easily digestible in its simply cooked form. The solution to this problem was found in the invention of bean curd, the ivory white, milky curd which results from processed soy beans.

Theoretically, to make bean curd, soy beans are soaked in plenty of water for up to 10 hours until tender – the length of time depending on the room temperature and the type of beans. They are then ground with water into a liquid (for a small amount, an electric blender is an ideal implement). This liquid is then strained through muslin, which separates the soy milk from the residue, the latter being ideal fodder for pigs and other animals. The milk is then boiled, and a setting agent – originally brine but now more commonly, and effectively, sodium sulphate (gypsum) – is stirred into it, producing the coagulated curd. A weight is put on the curd to squeeze out excess water, and the resultant product is bean curd. Whether it turns out to be velvety or hard, silkenly loose or dense in texture, depends on the proportion of water to beans for the grinding, the amount of setting agent used, and the weight applied to the curd. Only a skilled bean curd master will be able to achieve the desired quality.

The basic bean curd is an ivory cake-like curd, usually about 6–6.5 cm (2¼–2½ in) square and 3 cm (1¼ in) thick, but its size can vary. It is usually available in slabs of 2–4 cakes, with ridges on the surface for delineation. Fragile and easily breakable, it is nevertheless possible to cook it in all manner of ways: by boiling, steaming, braising, stir-frying, deep-frying, sautéing, smoking or fermenting. When bean curd cakes are quartered and deep-fried in hot oil until golden and crisp on the outside and hollow inside (about 12 minutes), they become bean curd puffs.

There is also the drier shredded bean curd, which is denser in texture; and also the five-spice dried bean curd in which bean curd pieces have been marinated in spices and soy sauce and sugar, then baked slowly. In Shanghai and its environs, the street hawkers, who carry their movable food stalls on their shoulders, balanced on the two ends of a bamboo pole, call out loudly and unabashedly 'chou doufu' or 'stinking bean curd', which is perhaps the most notorious bean curd product, loved by some and abhorred by others. They are, in fact, bean curd pieces fermented in brine and salted vegetables until very 'high' and then deep-fried. This method has been in use at least since the 18th century. A couple of years ago, I was finally able to taste some from a Shanghai food stall on the pavement. When I wondered why they did not 'stink' half as highly as an overripe French Camembert cheese, the stall keeper explained that the aroma depends on the weather – the hotter it is when the bean curd pieces are fermented, the more 'stinking' they will become.

A more universally acceptable fermented bean curd, marinated primarily in a combination of salt, sugar, yeast and wine, is bean curd 'cheese', which comes in square pieces. The two common kinds are ivory white (plain or spiced with chilli) and red, which is also known as 'southern'. The ivory white kind is smaller in size and, whether plain or spicy, is sometimes served as a side dish to go with boiled rice, and very often used as a sauce to cook bland vegetables. The red or 'southern' kind, larger in size, is too strong to be served as a side dish to go with rice; it is used in marinades and in sauces to enhance the flavours of meat and poultry.

Then there is the soy bean milk itself, which, in northern China, is often served warm for breakfast, accompanied by the oily deep-fried dough strips or youtiao (*see* p. 80). It is also sold in bottles or cartons, and, as a cold drink, is becoming increasingly popular with health-conscious people in both the East and West. And there is the slippery doufu hua or bean curd junket, popular throughout China, which is soy bean milk before it has had a weight applied to it. Made fresh everyday in shops or street stalls, it is spooned into a bowl and eaten hot or cold with a sugary syrup.

Last, but not least, there are bean curd skins. To make these, soy bean milk is boiled, then reduced to a constant simmer in a large cauldron. The skin formed on the surface is then skimmed off, piece by piece, by a skilled hand using a thin, tubular bamboo stick about 45 cm (18 in) long. The skin is then hung up to dry, but, while still moist, is wrapped up, also piece by piece, to be sold. Dried bean curd sheets and bean curd sticks are also made commercially and sold in packets. The names are at times frustratingly confusing for people who cannot read the Chinese labels.

When was this versatile food – and all its related products – which plays such a vital role in the Chinese and Japanese diets invented? The popular Chinese belief is that bean curd was invented by a Daoist (Taoist) prince in the 2nd century BC during the Han dynasty. This belief is based on the authoritative, though uncorroborated statement made by the famous 16th-century scholar and botanist, Li Shizhen, in his encyclopaedia on medicinal plants, *Bencao Gongmu*. 'The way of making bean curd originated from the Duke of Huainan, Liu An, in the Han dynasty,' begins the chapter on bean curd. But Liu An makes no mention of bean curd in any of his work, nor, as pointed out by the Japanese historian on Chinese food, Shinoda Osamu, and agreed with by many Chinese historians, is there any mention of bean curd in any Chinese literature up to the end of the 9th century AD.

Around the mid-10th century, the writer Tao Gu made the first mention of bean curd by way of extolling the virtue of a Mr Shi Ji, the frugal magistrate of a town south of the Yangzi River. In administrating the town, Mr Shi set himself up as an example of thriftiness in his everyday life, including his diet. Rather than indulging in meat dishes as befitted his station in life, he chose to eat meat only rarely. Instead, he encouraged the daily consumption of bean curd. To his delight, the people actually found it succulent and delicious, so much so that they called it tenderly cooked lamb.

Not surprisingly, its popularity soon spread. By the end of the Song dynasty (AD 960–1279), bean curd had caught on among the poor and rich alike, and was enjoyed by both meat eaters and Buddhist vegetarians. It didn't take long for it to migrate to Japan and, by the 12th century, it was featuring in an Imperial banquet. By the 16th century, it had become popular throughout Japan, where it was known as tofu, a name borrowed from the Chinese language. In China itself, it was to assume the importance of milk and cheese in the West, but minus the cholesterol risk. Today, it continues to hold sway over the Chinese table and, in recent years, has become an indispensable part of the diet for Western vegetarians.

Soy Bean
Milk

EVEN though soy bean milk is available in cartons in Chinese stores, more and more Chinese who live abroad prefer to make their own at home, since all that is required is an electric blender or liquidiser and a bag made of muslin, say about 25 × 30 cm (10 × 12 in), with the opening on the shorter side. They spread the word from continent to continent and show each other how to make it. I myself was shown the way by a Peking friend, Paula Yao, who now lives in Hong Kong and the United States, where she makes it for her family all the time. As soy bean milk is rich in calcium, it is the answer for many Chinese who suffer from lactic intolerance and cannot easily digest cow's milk.

YIELDS ABOUT 1.75 LITRES (3 PINTS/7½ CUPS) MILK

200 g (7 oz) yellow soy beans in weight, or 250 ml (8 fl oz/1 cup) in volume
cold water
about 75–90 ml (5–6 tbsp) sugar or to taste

1 Wash the soy beans several times in cold water to get rid of impurities, rubbing with your fingers. Drain.
2 Put the soy beans into a large bowl and add plenty of cold water to cover them with a margin of about 2.5 cm (1 in) from the surface. Leave the beans soaking for 12 to 24 hours, changing the water several times as it will foam on the surface. A longer soaking period will do the beans no harm as long as the water is changed periodically. Pour into a colander and drain.
3 Scoop 1 cup of soaked beans and place in the electric blender. Add 2½ cups water and grind fast for 2 minutes, at the end of which there will be lots of foam on the surface of the liquid inside the blender. Skim off and discard the foam, which will amount to several spoonfuls. Pour the remaining liquid into a muslin bag placed inside a large and clean saucepan. Pick up the bag, gather up the opening and gently squeeze the milk into the saucepan. As the residue is left inside the bag, squeeze hard to get all the milk. Most probably there will still be foam on the surface of the milk; if so, skim it off. Remove the bag, turn it inside out and remove and discard the residue. Wash the inside of the bag to remove any remaining residue, wring it dry. Repeat the whole procedure until all the beans are ground and the milk extracted.

4 Place the saucepan over a medium heat and bring the milk to a gentle boil. Be careful lest it, like cow's milk, boils over. A skin which will form on the surface can be removed (it is actually delicious to eat, seasoned with a tiny bit of salt). Gently bring the milk back to the boil and remove the second layer of skin. This second boiling will help dissipate any excess bean odour as well as preserve the milk longer.

5 Add the sugar. Give the milk a couple of stirs to help dissolve the sugar. The milk is now ready to be served hot. But as most people prefer it to be a cold drink, pour the milk into a container or a large jug and refrigerate until cold before serving. The milk will keep for 2–3 days.

VARIATION: Savoury Soy Bean Milk. Northern Chinese love to make soy bean milk savoury and drink it almost like a soup. To proceed, steps 1 and 2 are the same. In step 3, add 2 cups instead of 2½ cups of water to every cup of soaked beans, which will yield about 1.5 litres (2½ pints/6 cups) milk instead of 1.75 litres (3 pints/7½ cups), with a slightly thicker consistency. Step 4 remains the same. In step 5, instead of adding sugar, add condiments such as salt, soy sauce, chopped dried shrimps, vinegar, chilli hot oil as follows.

5 Put into each bowl .75 ml (⅛ tsp) salt or to taste, 5 ml (1 tsp) thick or dark soy sauce, 5 ml (1 tsp) rice vinegar, 5 ml (1 tsp) chopped dried shrimps and 5 ml (1 tsp) chopped spring onions. Pour in 250 ml (8 fl oz/1 cup) very hot soy bean milk and give it a stir. The salt and vinegar are likely to make the milk curdle, producing a semi-bean curd effect. Chilli hot oil can be added to taste.

Clockwise from top right: Vegetarian 'Shark's Fin' Soup (p. 184), Red-braised Bean Curd (p. 188), Vegetarian Fish (p. 179).

PLATE 7

Clockwise from top right: Silver Ears with Chicken Velvet Soup (p. 163),
Stir-fried Prawns with Broadbeans (p. 259), Muichoi Moulded Pork (p. 311),
Choi Sum with Oyster Sauce (p. 207).

PLATE 8

Bean Curd
with Scrambled Egg

Two high-protein ingredients make this dish a truly nutritious and delicious treat to give to children, not that the grown-ups will not enjoy it as well.

蛋炒豆腐

SERVES 4 WITH 2 OTHER DISHES

4 cakes bean curd, refreshed (*see* p. 354)

4 large eggs, lightly beaten with 2 ml (⅓ tsp) salt and 10 ml (2 tsp) Shaoxing wine or medium dry sherry

90 ml (6 tbsp) peanut or vegetable oil

100 ml (4 fl oz/½ cup) chicken stock

10 ml (2 tsp) Shaoxing wine or medium dry sherry

2–2.5 ml (⅓–½ tsp) salt

2–3 spring onions, trimmed and cut into small rounds

1 Cut the bean curd into 1 cm (½ in) cubes. Pat dry with kitchen paper.

2 Scramble the eggs. Heat a wok over a high heat until smoke rises. Add the oil and swirl it around over a large area several times until it is hot but not burning. Pour in the egg and, sliding the wok scoop to the bottom of the wok, keep turning and letting the liquid egg go under in layers, so it blends with the oil and sets softly. Lower the heat if the egg is getting burned. As soon as all the egg is just set, remove the wok from the heat, transfer the egg to a dish and keep nearby. There is no need to wash the wok, as there should be no egg stuck to it, just a film of oil.

3 Pour the stock into the wok, add the wine or sherry and salt and gently bring to the boil. Add the bean curd and cook over a high heat until the stock is almost absorbed. Return the egg to the wok, stir and turn with the wok scoop for about 30 seconds or until some of the egg has folded over the bean curd. Sprinkle with the spring onions and remove this soft egg and bean curd mixture to a serving dish. Serve hot.

'Bless the Old
and the Young'

SERVES 6 WITH 3 OTHER DISHES

4 cakes bean curd, refreshed (*see* p. 354) then puréed
1 large cod steak, about 350 g (12 oz), skinned, boned and finely minced
22.5 ml (1½ tbsp) cornflour
1 large egg white
6.5 ml (1¼ tsp) salt
1.5 ml (¼ tsp) white ground pepper (optional)
3 spring onions, trimmed and cut into small rounds

A CANTONESE family dish for all three generations, grandparents, parents and children who, very often, still live under one roof in China. Since it is cholesterol-free, nutritious and easily digestible it couldn't be a safer or more healthy dish to serve to both the old and the young. Dace is usually used by the Cantonese, but as it is not easily available abroad, cod is used as a satisfactory substitute. If you wish to add finely chopped ham or dried shrimp in the mixture, feel free.

1 Put the minced fish in a bowl, add the cornflour and egg white. Stir vigorously in the same direction for about 30 seconds. Add the salt and stir again for about 10 seconds until you feel it is difficult to continue. Stir in the pepper, if used. Stir in also the spring onion.
2 Add the puréed bean curd to the fish and mix until homogeneous. Pour into either a lightly oiled heatproof dish with raised edges or into the top receptacle, lightly oiled, of a double boiler.
3 Either put the heatproof dish into a steamer and steam (*see* p. 355) for about 12 minutes or place the receptacle over the double-boiler base and double-boil over a high heat for about 25 minutes. In either case, insert a chopstick or a fork into the mixture; if it comes out clean, the bean curd mixture is set and ready. Remove the dish from the steamer and serve hot or scoop the bean curd on to a plate and serve hot.

NOTE: If you wish to make this dish more exciting, carry on from where we've left off. Let the set bean curd mixture cool completely, then refrigerate for about 2 hours to firm it. Cut into 1 cm (½ in) slices and shallow-fry them in 45–60 ml (3–4 tbsp) of peanut or vegetable oil for 2–3 minutes until both sides are golden.

Braised
Bean Curd Puffs

A CASSEROLE dish one can cook ahead of time and leave until the following day, when it will taste even better. For pot-luck, more ingredients than given below can be added, as long as they either complement them in kind, such as prawns, or contrast with them in texture, such as bamboo shoots. To enrich the casserole, slices of roasted belly pork can also be added. Because the cellophane noodles (glass noodles) are so bland as to need a very strong stock, a chicken or vegetable stock cube may be added to the home-made stock. Cod fish balls and bean curd puffs are available in Oriental supermarkets, already cooked.

SERVES 6–8 WITH 3–5 OTHER DISHES

12–16 dried Chinese black mushrooms, reconstituted in 300 ml (10 fl oz/1¼ cups) water (*see* p. 353)
50–85 g (2–3 oz) cellophane or glass noodles, reconstituted (*see* p. 184, step 1)
60–90 ml (4–6 tbsp) peanut or vegetable oil
8–10 thin slices ginger, peeled
4 spring onions, trimmed and cut into 5 cm (2 in) sections, white and green parts separated
450–675 g (1–1½ lb) Chinese celery cabbage (Chinese leaves), rinsed, cut crossways at 5 cm (2 in) intervals, stalk and leafy parts separated
2.5 ml (½ tsp) salt, or to taste
575–850 ml (1–1½ pints/2½–3¾ cups) chicken stock
1 chicken or vegetable stock cube, mashed
9–12 bean curd puffs, halved
225 g (8 oz) precooked cod fish balls
15 ml (1 tbsp) thin or light soy sauce, or to taste
white or black ground pepper to taste
small bunch coriander leaves, rinsed, trimmed and torn up (optional)
10–15 ml (2–3 tsp) sesame oil

1 Drain the black mushrooms, reserving the liquid.
2 Drain the cellophane noodles, discarding the water.
3 Heat a large casserole or saucepan over a high heat until hot. Add the oil and swirl it around to cover the entire bottom and heat until hot. Add the ginger and white spring onion, stir and let sizzle for a few seconds. Add the mushrooms and stir and turn for about 10 times to enhance the fragrance. Add the stalky parts of the cabbage, continuing to turn for another dozen times. Season with the salt.
4 Lower the heat to medium. Pour in the stock and add the stock cube. Add the cellophane noodles, bean curd puffs and fish balls and bring slowly to the boil. Reduce the heat to low and continue to simmer, covered, for 10 minutes. Add the remaining leafy parts of cabbage, stir to submerge the leaves and cook for another 5–10 minutes. Test for taste, then add the soy sauce and ground pepper. Remove the casserole from the heat and, if time allows, leave for about 1 hour so that the flavours will be absorbed.
5 When ready to serve, reheat until piping hot. Add the green spring onion and coriander leaves, if used. Scoop into a deep bowl, and add the sesame oil.

Sautéed Bean Curd
with Spinach

SERVES 6 WITH 3 OTHER DISHES

550–675 g (1¼–1½ lb) spinach
4 cakes bean curd, refreshed (*see*
　p. 354)
salt
120 ml (8 tbsp) peanut or
　vegetable oil
100 ml (4 fl oz/½ cup) prime stock
　(*see* p. 361)
15 ml (1 tbsp) thin or light soy
　sauce

Illustrated on Plate 12.

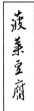

A TRADITIONAL Hangzhou dish which Yuan Mei in the 18th century referred to in his renowned *Cookery Lists of Suiyuan* (*see* p. 38). The Hangzhou people likened the fried bean curd to 'white jade inlaid with gold', an image Yuan was impressed with. True to form as a purist, Yuan made it a point to keep the ingredients to bean curd and spinach only, without adding 'bamboo tips and mushrooms'.

1　Wash the spinach thoroughly to get rid of sand and impurities. If the stalks are thick, make a 5 cm (2 in) long split from the end of each to ensure even cooking of the spinach.

2　Cut each cake of bean curd into 4–5 rectangles. Pat dry with kitchen paper.

3　Bring a large pot of water to the boil. Add 5 ml (1 tsp) salt and 30 ml (2 tbsp) of the oil. Add the spinach, submerging every stalk under the water. As soon as the water returns to a simmer, pour into a colander and rinse with cold running water. Drain thoroughly.

4　Heat a large flat frying pan (or wok) over a high heat until smoke rises. Add the remaining 90 ml (6 tbsp) oil, swirl it around to cover the entire surface of the pan and heat until smoke rises. Add the bean curd, piece by piece, to the oil and fry for 2–3 minutes until golden on both sides, turning them over at half-time. Reduce the heat, pour in the stock, season with the soy sauce and salt to taste and cook for about another minute so that the bean curd can absorb the stock. Remove to a dish and keep warm nearby, leaving as much liquid and oil in the frying pan as possible.

Return the spinach to the frying pan and cook until very hot. Remove to a serving dish, then arrange the bean curd pieces on top. Serve hot immediately.

Braised Bean Curd with Bean Sauces

PEOPLE in Hunan province use a lot of chillies in their food. In this dish, the dried chillies, interacting with the black beans and garlic, provide a very potent sauce. However, for those with a delicate palate, the bean curd will taste just as good without the spiciness.

1 Quarter each cake of bean curd, then halve each piece again. Pat dry with kitchen paper.
2 Prepare the sauce. Rinse the black beans and partially mash them in a bowl. Add the sweet bean sauce and soy sauce and stir to mix.
3 Heat a wok over a high heat until smoke rises. Add the oil and swirl it around to cover a large area. Add the garlic, stir a few times until it takes on colour, then add the chillies and stir a few more times. Add the bean curd and, sliding the wok scoop to the bottom of the wok, toss and turn the cubes for about 1 minute to allow excess water to be absorbed. Pour in the sauce, stir and mix for another minute. Add the stock, continuing to cook fast so that the stock is absorbed. Sprinkle on the spring onion rounds, stir, then remove to a serving dish and serve hot.

SERVES 6 WITH 3 OTHER DISHES

4 cakes bean curd, refreshed (*see* p. 354)
45 ml (3 tbsp) peanut or vegetable oil
3 large cloves garlic, peeled, cut into thin slivers then shredded
6–12 medium dried chillies (about 5 cm/2 in long), trimmed but left whole
50 ml (2 fl oz/¼ cup) prime or vegetable stock (*see* p. 361 or p. 172)
2 spring onions, trimmed and cut into small rounds

FOR THE SAUCE:
45 ml (3 tbsp) fermented black beans
15 ml (1 tbsp) sweet bean sauce (*see* p. 362)
15 ml (1 tbsp) thick or dark soy sauce

Stir-fried Bean Curd
with Minced Dried Shrimp

YUAN MEI liked this dish served in Mr Zhang's home so much that he included it in his cookbook, *The Cookery Lists of Suiyuan*. To use the flavour from the dried shrimp to season the bland bean curd is common sense to most cooks, but to take the trouble of mincing the shrimp will enhance the overall flavour of the dish tenfold.

1 Cut the bean curd into 1 cm (½ in) cubes. Pat dry with kitchen paper.
2 Put the dried shrimps into a small bowl, add the wine or sherry and leave them to marinate for about 30 minutes.

SERVES 6 WITH 3 OTHER DISHES

4 cakes bean curd, refreshed (*see* p. 354)
40 g (1½ oz) dried shrimp
15 ml (1 tbsp) Shaoxing wine or medium dry sherry
75 ml (5 tbsp) peanut or vegetable oil
2 large cloves garlic, peeled and crushed
3 spring onions, trimmed and cut into small rounds

3 Heat a wok over a high heat until smoke rises. Add 30 ml (2 tbsp) of the oil and swirl it around several times. Add the garlic, stir and let sizzle, taking on colour and releasing the aroma. Add the shrimps, stir for about 1 minute over a medium heat.

4 Remove the shrimps to a liquidiser and process until finely minced. Remove to a dish and put nearby.

5 Rinse and dry the wok. Reheat it over a high heat until smoke rises. Add the remaining 45 ml (3 tbsp) oil and swirl it around. Add the spring onion rounds and stir several times. Add the bean curd cubes and, going to the bottom of the wok with the wok scoop, turn and toss carefully for about 1–2 minutes or until piping hot. Sprinkle on three-quarters of the dried shrimp, continuing to stir to mix. Scoop on to a serving dish. Sprinkle the remaining shrimp on top. Serve hot.

Mapo Doufu

SERVES 4–6 WITH 2–3 OTHER DISHES

4 cakes bean curd, refreshed (*see* p. 354)
50 g (2 oz) lean pork
60 ml (4 tbsp) peanut or vegetable oil
3 cloves garlic, peeled and finely chopped
20–25 g (¾–1 oz) zhacai or Sichuan preserved vegetable, rinsed, patted dry and finely chopped
15–30 ml (1–2 tbsp) spicy-hot soy bean paste or broadbean paste
5 ml (1 tsp) thin or light soy sauce
2.5–5 ml (½–1 tsp) sugar
5–10 ml (1–2 tsp) hot chilli oil (*see* p. 357)
5–10 ml (1–2 tsp) sesame oil

UNDOUBTEDLY the most famous Sichuanese bean curd dish, which reflects the earthy regional sense of humour. Mapo actually means a woman scarred with pock marks on her face. This particular pock-marked woman, a Sichuanese Mrs Chen of the late-19th century, happened to be a superb cook who worked side by side with her husband, a chef of some repute. But it was Mrs Chen's bean curd dish, with its lingering spicy and slightly numbing effect on the palate, that has turned the rather unkind nickname into an everlasting tribute to her. The restaurant in Chengdu, the capital of Sichuan province, where Mapo was believed to have sold her bean curd, has become a tavern proudly displaying the sign in four Chinese characters: Ma Po Dou Fu. The dish I wolfed down there in 1986 was made with bean curd with a succulent and soft texture that is difficult to find outside of China, and the intensity of the flavours made an indelible mark on my mind. I often cook this dish myself, especially on a wintry evening when hot chilli flavours seem even more alluring.

1 Cut the bean curd into 1 cm (½ in) cubes. Pat dry with kitchen paper.

2 Marinate the pork: add the salt, sugar, soy sauces, wine or sherry and oil to the pork. Stir to coat well. Leave to stand for 15–30 minutes.

3 Prepare the sauce: in a small bowl add 15 ml (1 tbsp) of the stock to the potato flour and stir until dissolved. Gradually stir in the remaining stock. Leave aside.

4 Heat a wok over a high heat until smoke rises. Add the oil and swirl it around. Add the garlic, stir a few times, then add the pork and, using the wok scoop or a metal spatula, turn and toss until partially cooked. Add the Sichuan vegetable, bean paste, soy sauce and sugar, continuing to turn and toss to let the sauce permeate the pork.

5 Add the bean curd and stir gently so as not to break up the cubes. Blend in the well-stirred stock sauce and slowly bring to the boil over a moderate heat. Continue to simmer for about 2 minutes to absorb both the flavours of the pork and the sauce. Remove to a serving dish.

6 Add the hot oil and sesame oil; sprinkle with the ground Sichuan peppercorns and spring onion. This garnish adds a pretty red and green contrast as well as subtle flavouring. Serve piping hot.

VARIATION: Family Bean Curd. Known as the non-spicy twin of Mapo bean curd, it is made the same way and with the same ingredients except that it omits the spicy ones – i.e. the Sichuan preserved vegetable, the soy bean or broadbean paste and the hot chilli oil.

2.5 ml (½ tsp) roasted ground Sichuan peppercorns (*see* p. 359)
2 spring onions, green parts only, cut into tiny rounds

FOR THE MARINADE:
.75 ml (⅛ tsp) salt
.75 ml (⅛ tsp) sugar
5 ml (1 tsp) thin or light soy sauce
5 ml (1 tsp) thick or dark soy sauce
7.5 ml (1½ tsp) Shaoxing wine or medium dry sherry
5 ml (1 tsp) sesame oil

FOR THE SAUCE:
150 ml (5 fl oz/⅔ cup) prime stock (*see* p. 361)
5 ml (1 tsp) potato flour

Guotie
Bean Curd

SERVES 4–6 WITH 2–3 OTHER
DISHES

4 cakes bean curd, refreshed (*see* p. 354)
15 ml (1 tbsp) plain flour
1 large egg, lightly beaten
2 ml (⅓ tsp) salt
ground white pepper to taste
75–90 ml (5–6 tbsp) peanut or vegetable oil
15 ml (1 tbsp) peeled and finely shredded ginger
5 ml (1 tsp) finely chopped garlic
4 large spring onions, trimmed, cut into 5 cm (2 in) lengths then shredded finely, with white and green parts separated
15 ml (1 tbsp) sesame oil

FOR THE SAUCE:
1.5 ml (¼ tsp) potato flour
15 ml (1 tbsp) Shaoxing wine or medium dry sherry
15 ml (1 tbsp) thin or light soy sauce
2.5 ml (½ tsp) salt
1.5 ml (¼ tsp) sugar
60–75 ml (4–5 tbsp) vegetable or chicken stock

A FAMOUS Peking dish which, because it is easy to make, is served as much at home as in local restaurants, where, more often than not, the chefs come from the neighbouring Shandong province. The name means little more than 'pan-fried', but 'guotie' has a much more Chinese ring to it.

1 Quarter each cake of bean curd, then halve the thickness of each piece. Pat dry with kitchen paper.

2 Prepare the sauce. In a small bowl mix together the potato flour, wine or sherry, soy sauce, salt, sugar and stock and put to one side.

3 Sift the flour into a small bowl. Gradually add the egg, stirring vigorously so it mixes to a thick and smooth batter. Add the salt and pepper.

4 Heat a large frying pan over medium heat until hot. Add 45–60 ml (3–4 tbsp) of the oil and swirl it around. Using a pair of chopsticks or tongs, dip the bean curd pieces, one at a time, into the egg batter and coat on both sides. Remove gently, put into the frying pan and fry for about 1 minute or until golden yellow before turning over to fry the other side. Transfer to a dish, and repeat until all the bean curd is battered and fried. You will find that the first piece is ready for removal from the pan before the last one has been dipped into the batter.

5 Heat a wok (or you can use a frying pan if you don't mind the splashing) over a high heat until smoke rises. Add the remaining 30 ml (2 tbsp) oil and swirl it around. Add the ginger and garlic, stir and let sizzle, then add the white spring onion and stir them together to release their aroma. Pour in the well-stirred sauce and slowly bring to a simmer over a lower heat.

6 Return the bean curd to the wok and cook in the sauce for 1–2 minutes or until most of it is absorbed. Transfer to a serving dish. Sprinkle on the sesame oil and arrange the green spring onion on top as a garnish. Serve immediately.

Green
Egg Bean Curd

NOT only is this Shanghai dish, which is much sought after in the summer, easy to make, but it can also be prepared in advance, so that it is an ideal first course. The creamy yolks and the jelly-like brownish whites of the preserved duck eggs complement the texture of the bean curd while the dried shrimps and preserved Sichuan vegetables quicken one's taste buds from one mouthful to the next. The crux of the recipe is in the right proportion of the ancillary ingredients, which I have worked out for you.

SERVES 8

4 cakes bean curd, refreshed (*see* p. 354)
25 g (1 oz) dried shrimps, rinsed
15 ml (1 tbsp) Shaoxing wine or medium dry sherry
50–85 g (2–3 oz) Sichuan preserved vegetable (zhacai), rinsed
60 ml (4 tbsp) sesame oil
3 preserved green duck eggs
1.5–2.5 ml (¼–½ tsp) salt, or to taste

1 Put the bean curd on several layers of kitchen paper to absorb excess water.
2 Put the dried shrimps in a bowl. Add the wine or sherry, add also about 15 ml (1 tbsp) water to barely cover the shrimps. Leave to soak for 1 hour or longer to soften the shrimps. Drain, then chop them finely.
3 Chop the Sichuan vegetables finely.
4 Mix together the dried shrimps and the Sichuan vegetables. Add the sesame oil and stir to mix.
5 Crack and discard the shells of the green eggs. Rinse and pat dry. Cut up roughly into small pieces, then mix thoroughly with the shrimp mixture.
6 When ready to serve, transfer the bean curd cakes to a serving bowl or a dish with raised edges. Roughly break up the bean curd into small pieces. Add the seasoning mixture and mix together thoroughly. Add 1.5 ml (¼ tsp) salt, mix and taste before adding more, if necessary.

Iced Bean Curd
Casserole

4 cakes bean curd, refreshed (*see* p. 354)

6 medium dried Chinese black mushrooms, reconstituted (*see* p. 353)

30 ml (2 tbsp) peanut or vegetable oil

85–115 g (3–4 oz) canned drained bamboo shoots, cut into wedges then blanched (*see* p. 353)

salt

10 ml (2 tsp) thin or light soy sauce

1.5–2.5 ml (¼–½ tsp) sugar

575 ml (1 pint/2½ cups) prime stock (*see* p. 361)

15 ml (1 tbsp) sesame oil

'ICE the bean curd cakes overnight,' begins one of Yuan Mei's bean curd recipes, 'then cut them into square cubes and blanch them to get rid of the bean odour. Add chicken stock, ham stock and meat stock to braise them. Before bringing the dish to the table, discard the chicken, ham etc., retaining only the fragrant mushrooms and winter bamboo shoots. When bean curd cakes are braised for a long time, they will loosen up to form beehives, similar to icing them.'

Yuan Mei's words made a noticeable impact on cookery books in the 19th century, for more than one of them made reference to the beehive effect that occurs to bean curd if it is left to freeze. At that time, during the winter in northern China, people used to put bean curd cakes on the tiled roofs in order to freeze them. Nowadays, we can put them in the freezer compartment of a refrigerator, or in a freezer itself. When they are frozen overnight, or, better still, over two nights, a beehive effect is formed inside.

1 Put the bean curd cakes in a covered plastic bag or a freezer bag. Put into the freezer and freeze for 1–2 nights – the beehive effect on the bean curd will be more pronounced for the longer time. Defrost thoroughly. Squeeze out excess water from the bean curd cakes, then cut into large cubes, say 12 to each cake.

2 Drain the mushrooms. Halve or quarter them.

3 Heat a heavy-based saucepan or casserole over a high heat until very hot. Add the peanut or vegetable oil and swirl it around. Add the mushrooms, stir a few times, then add the bamboo shoots. Season with 2.5 ml (½ tsp) salt or to taste, the soy sauce and the sugar, continuing to stir for another minute over medium heat. Pour in the stock, then add the bean curd and gently bring to the boil. Continue to cook, maintaining a simmer for about 30 minutes so that the stock can be absorbed by the ingredients. If necessary, turn up the heat to reduce some of the stock. Taste for saltiness, adding salt to taste. Add the sesame oil and stir to mix. Transfer to a serving dish or bowl and serve.

RICE
AND
NOODLES

FOR over a thousand years, rice, with its high nutritional value, has been the most popular and favoured staple food of the Chinese, both in the north and in the south. There are two main types of rice, the common or non-glutinous (non-sticky) kind, and the glutinous (sticky) kind. The non-glutinous has two varieties: indica or xian, the long-grained rice which is favoured by the Chinese for everyday consumption, and japonica or geng, the short-grained rice which is favoured by the Japanese. The most commonly grown glutinous rice is the white variety, followed by the black, but there are also rarer varieties, such as that known as 'blood-glutinous', a pinkish-red rice grown in small quantities along the Yangzi (Yangtze) River. The modern trend, however, particularly in Taiwan and the Philippines, has been to produce 'miracle' rices – hybrids between the long-grain and the short-grain rices which are considered to have the perfect balance of texture and also produce larger yields. Another variety which has found favour with southern Chinese in recent years is Thai rice, which is also known as 'fragrant' rice because of the sweet scent it imparts when cooked.

Recent archaeological finds show that Chinese farmers in Hemudu, a village in Yuyao county of the eastern coastal province of Zhejiang, were already planting both indica or xian and japonica or geng varieties of rice as early as 5000 BC. The remains found at the site yield evidence of cultivated rice grains, as well as stalks and leaves of rice plants. Although it is a moot point whether the Chinese pictorial script for paddy or rice (dao) first appeared in the oracle bones (tortoiseshells or other animal bones used in ancient China for divination) of the Shang dynasty (16th–11th century BC), it is clear that rice had already become a main crop in southern China (south of the

Yangzi River) by the Zhou dynasty (11th century–221 BC), due to the warmer climate there favouring its growth. Indeed, in the lists of 'five grains' used to classify the main cereals since that time, rice has always been included, and considered the most superior, while soy bean, millet, wheat, hemp and barley have made up the variables.

The cold climate in northern China has always favoured the growth of millet and wheat, so much so that from the Zhou dynasty, and right through the Han (206 BC–AD 220), Tang (AD 618–907) and the beginning of the Song (AD 960–1279) dynasties, they remained the chief staples, while rice could only be afforded by the rich. The popularity of rice, however, progressively increased with each succeeding dynasty until, midway through the Song, its consumption in both the north and the south took off dramatically. Eventually, by the Ming dynasty (AD 1368–1644), it reached the level at which it has remained until today. What brought about this revolution in eating habits was the introduction of new strains of rice from Champa, now in modern Vietnam, in the 11th century.

Throughout the history of China, the emperors had always concerned themselves with agriculture and the distribution of basic staples to the people. Their annual prayers and sacrifices to the gods for bumper harvests were not, however, solely motivated by their love for their subjects, but were driven, equally if not more so, by self interest, since it was through the collection of taxes from the peasants who grew the crops that the emperors filled the Imperial coffers. The emperor responsible for introducing the new drought-resistant, early maturing rice was Zhenzong, the Song emperor who reigned during the early 11th century (AD 999–1022). What prompted him to take urgent action was a severe drought in the Fujian and Guangdong provinces – the rice-growing region – which resulted in a famine that spread like wildfire. In 1011 he sent an envoy to Champa to bring back the rice via Fujian. Experimental growth was carried out immediately and was found to be hugely successful, so much so that the emperor summoned his ministers to taste the new crop and he, himself, composed poems in praise of it. Within a year, it was being grown over a wide area and, furthermore, it enabled double-cropping of rice in the south, as well as the gradual spread of rice growing northward beyond the Yangzi River.

That rice was becoming a basic need for every family, rich and poor, was summed up in a phrase coined in the 13th century by the southern Song writer, Wu

Zimu, who reminisced about the good old days in Hangzhou. 'The seven things with which to open the family door were,' he wrote, 'firewood, rice, salt, cooking oil, soy sauce, vinegar and tea.' To this day, the saying rolls off every Chinese tongue.

And yet, even today, there are differences between the southern and the northern Chinese diets. Polished white rice is eaten twice a day in the south, while wheat products, such as noodles, wontons, steamed buns and the like are enjoyed as occasional foods or as snacks. In north China, however, noodles and steamed buns (mantou) are very much daily staples, while rice is the ideal alternative.

Cooked rice in Chinese is called fan, both in Mandarin and Cantonese. Fan is of such paramount importance to the Chinese that when two Chinese meet, irrespective of where they come from, after the initial 'How are you?', they greet each other with the words 'Have you eaten fan?' Fan in its wider sense also means a meal, and a Chinese meal consists of cooked rice (boiled or steamed) and dishes made up of different ingredients, called generically in Mandarin cai, and in Cantonese, sung.

To eat rice, a Chinese picks up the bowl with one hand and places it between his lips. Then, holding the chopsticks with the other hand, he shovels the rice into his mouth, so neatly, though, that the grains do not fall on to his lap. He is not supposed to pick up only a few grains at a time, since rice is considered a blessing and he had better shovel it all in rather than pick at it! Whereas it doesn't matter if any of the other dishes served at a meal are left unfinished, the rice grains in the bowl must all be eaten up. In the olden days, when a young girl was fearful of her beauty being marred by smallpox, it was said that a grain left in the bowl would invoke the curse of one pock mark on the face. And what chance of a good marriage would she have with a scarred, albeit pretty, face?

Beyond good table manners, Chinese writers and poets throughout the ages have appreciated the hard toil of the peasants in producing rice, stressing how we should treasure every resultant grain. The sentiment poignantly overflows in the poem, 'Women Rice-Planters', written in the early 19th century by Chen Wenshu. Chen's poem is, in fact, an echo of another poem written by a much earlier poet in the Tang dynasty, Li Shen, who, in describing the hardship endured by the peasants, asked the question:

'Who would have thought the rice in the bowl
Every grain is full of bitter sweat'

Below is my translation of Chen's 'Women Rice-Planters':

In the morning I see women planting rice
In the evening I see women planting rice

They know not the cold from pouring rain
They know not the heat from burning sun

Their feet, like wild ducks and sea gulls
Are steeped all day on muddy banks

To grow one field of rice
Ten fields more are sown

Worries over seedlings withering in shallow water
Fears of seedlings rotting in deep water

On high terraces the wheat already threshed
On low ground the corn yet to be planted

The fourth month arrives followed by the fifth
Still hoping for more Dragon rains

Swaddled babes are left on roadsides
No leisure spared to feed a son

Now I believe: 'the rice in the bowl
Every grain full of bitter sweat'

Many Chinese folk sayings and proverbs are based on rice. They range from the banal to the profound, but they reflect the Chinese sense of humour and their down-to-earth approach to life, as seen in these examples.

'Even a clever wife cannot make dinner without rice' is a saying used all the time to underline the fact that, as with money, a lack of the key ingredient makes the situation hopeless.

'The rice is cooked' means it's a *fait accompli*, or what is done cannot be undone. It's a favourite saying of resigned parents whose children have eloped, married undesirable partners or, worse still, had a child outside of wedlock.

'A rice bucket' has a derogatory ring to it, so don't refer to anyone by that term unless you really wish to say he or she is lazy and stupid to boot. More insulting still is 'the big worm who eats into rice'; he or she is good for nothing and beyond the pale.

'An iron rice bowl' means a guaranteed life-long livelihood, a term often used by civil servants to describe, even if with a touch of irony, their own jobs which, though none too stimulating, are nevertheless always there.

'To eat soft rice' is used to describe a man living off a woman, but never a woman living off a man as, traditionally, women have the right to be provided for, either by a father or a husband. It does not necessarily apply to a pimp living immorally on the earnings of prostitutes, but often to a young man who has married or is living with an older and richer woman.

Even though wheat as a grain food is just as important in northern China as rice, there are virtually no folk sayings derived from its products. Noodles, however, have always carried the significance of longevity, so much so that they are known as 'longevity noodles'. For everybody, whatever their age, it is important for them to have a bowl of noodles on their birthday. If a dinner is given to celebrate the birthday, the sequence of dishes will end with a large bowl or plate of noodles; all those who share the noodles with the birthday celebrant will, by implication, be blessed with longevity as well. As if to emphasise the point, the person serving the noodles will lift the noodles high up from the serving bowl or plate before putting them into individual bowls. For the birthdays of elders, besides savoury longevity noodles, sweet, peach-shaped longevity buns, made with white flour and stuffed with lotus paste, are also served.

Boiled
Rice

SERVES 4–6 WITH OTHER
DISHES

375 g (13 oz/2 cups) long-grain
  white rice
20 ml (4 tsp) peanut or vegetable
  oil
575 ml (1 pint/2½ cups) water

CHINESE boiled rice, the daily staple, is done in such a way that when the rice is cooked, all the water is absorbed, and hence the natural fragrance and taste of rice is retained. The crux of the matter is, therefore, the correct proportion of water to rice. What is known as the near-foolproof Chinese method of measuring the right amount of water goes like this: put the rinsed rice in a saucepan, stand an index finger on the surface of the rice, then add cold water until it comes up to about the first joint. You should also know whether the rice you are using is a water-absorbing type or not, as, for example, the American patna rice is more water-absorbent than the Thai fragrant. According to individual taste, some Chinese like their rice firmer (or softer) than others, but whatever their preference, they all insist on thoroughly cooked rice rather than rice having a slightly chalky centre, as European salad rice is often served. While boiled rice should not be mushy, the grains do stick together; only when it comes to fried rice should you expect the grains to be more separated.

Below is a guideline for the amount of water to rice:

RICE	WATER	OIL	COOKED RICE
1 250 ml (8 fl oz) cup or 190 g (6½ oz)	1½ cups or 350 ml (12 fl oz)	10 ml (2 tsp)	3 loose cups
2 cups or 375 g (13 oz)	2½ cups or 600 ml (20 fl oz)	20 ml (4 tsp)	6 loose cups
3 cups or 540 g (19½ oz)	3¼ cups or 800 ml (26 fl oz)	30 ml (6 tsp)	9 loose cups

1 Rinse the rice in cold water, rubbing the grains gently with your fingers to get rid of impurities. Drain.
2 Put the rice into a saucepan, preferably with a copper bottom. Add the oil and water. The oil enhances the natural flavour of the rice; it also helps prevent the rice sticking to the bottom.

3 Add the lid and bring to the boil. Stir thoroughly with a wooden spoon and continue to boil, either covered or uncovered, until most of the water is absorbed, leaving only tiny 'eyelets' around the rice. Reduce the heat to a minimum.

4 Place a metal heat diffuser under the saucepan (the French *diffuseur/mijoteur* with a flexible handle is ideal), and leave the rice to simmer with the lid on for 12–15 minutes.

5 Replace the lid, fluff up the rice with a spoon or chopsticks. Either scoop all the rice into a large bowl, from which everyone takes their portion, or scoop some rice into individual rice bowls. Serve hot.

Moist Noodles with Chicken Breast

IF YOU can find noodles that are white in appearance and labelled 'Shanghai Noodles' – they are available – use them. Otherwise, use other white ones, or Italian tagliatelle.

1 Put the chicken on a heatproof dish with raised sides. Rub 5 ml (1 tsp) of the salt, the ginger juice and the wine or sherry over the chicken. Place the dish in a steamer and steam (*see* p. 355) over a high heat for 10–12 minutes until the chicken is just done, having turned opaque. Remove the dish from the steamer, cut the chicken breadthways into thin (3 mm/⅛ in) slices and keep nearby. Save the steaming liquid from the chicken.

2 Heat a wok over a high heat until smoke rises. Add the oil and swirl it around. Add the ginger and white spring onions and stir about half a dozen times to release their aroma. Add the Chinese cabbage, season with 2.5 ml (½ tsp) salt and stir-fry over a medium heat for about 5 minutes until much of its water content has been yielded up. Discard the ginger slices; add the green spring onions.

3 Bring a large pot of water to the boil. Add the noodles, return the water to the boil and continue to cook over a

SERVES 2 AS LUNCH

2 chicken breast fillets, 170–225 g (6–8 oz)
7.5 ml (1½ tsp) salt
5 ml (1 tsp) ginger juice (*see* p. 357)
5 ml (1 tsp) Shaoxing wine or medium dry sherry
45 ml (3 tbsp) peanut or vegetable oil
2 thick slices ginger, peeled
3 spring onions, trimmed and cut into 3.5 cm (1½ in) sections, white and green parts separated
275–350 g (10–12 oz) Chinese celery cabbage (Chinese leaves) cut crossways into 6 mm (¼ in) strips
225 g (8 oz) dried noodles (*see* introduction above)
300 ml (10 fl oz/1¼ cups) chicken stock

medium-high heat for 5–10 minutes (depending on the noodles) until quite tender, as this is the way Shanghai people like their noodles. Pour into a colander to drain, then divide the noodles and put into 2 large serving bowls.

4 Bring the stock to a gentle boil. Meanwhile, halve the portions of cabbage and chicken and put them, cabbage first then chicken on top, on to the noodles in the bowls. Pour half of the stock on to each bowl of noodles, which will absorb it. Serve immediately.

Stir-fried
Shanghai Rice Pudding

SERVES 8

500 g (1 lb 2 oz) Shanghai rice pudding in thin pieces (if frozen, thoroughly defrosted)
225–285 g (8–10 oz) lean pork, trimmed and cut into matchstick-sized strips
90 ml (6 tbsp) peanut or vegetable oil
675 g (1½ lb) Chinese celery cabbage (Chinese leaves), cut crossways at 6 mm (¼ in) intervals, stalk and leafy parts separated
2.5 ml (½ tsp) salt
15 ml (1 tbsp) Shaoxing wine or medium dry sherry
thick or dark soy sauce to taste

SHANGHAI rice pudding is made of the common or non-glutinous kind of rice, which is processed in such a way that the end product is white and has a viscous texture when it is cooked. When you buy it in Chinese stores, it often comes frozen, in thin slices (about 5 mm/⅕ in thick), and in a vacuum-sealed plastic bag. Shanghai people prepare it as a savoury dish and serve it in lieu of noodles, often at the end of the meal. It is a popular food during the Chinese New Year, as its Chinese name, nian gao, suggests.

1 Soak the rice pudding pieces in plenty of cold water to cover for about 2 hours.

2 Marinate the pork. Put the pork in a bowl, add the salt, sugar, ground pepper, soy sauce and wine or sherry and stir to mix. Sprinkle on the tapioca or potato flour and stir vigorously to coat. Leave to stand for about 20–30 minutes. Blend in the seasame oil.

3 Drain the rice pudding pieces, which may have expanded a little bit in size but will still feel quite hard to the touch.

4 Heat a wok over a high heat until smoke rises. Add 45 ml (3 tbsp) of the oil and swirl it around to cover a large area. Add the pieces of cabbage stalk, stir and turn for about 30 seconds but, before they become burned, reduce the heat to medium. Add the salt and continue to stir for about 1 minute, when water from the cabbage

will be oozing out. Add the leafy parts of the cabbage and continue to cook for about 5 minutes until tender. Transfer to a bowl, retaining the juices as well. Rinse and dry the wok.

5 Reheat the wok over a high heat until smoke rises. Add the remaining 45 ml (3 tbsp) oil and swirl it around to cover a large area. Add the pork and, going to the bottom of the wok with the wok scoop, stir and toss for about 30 seconds. Splash in the wine or sherry around the edges of the wok, continuing to stir a few more times. Reduce the heat to low and return the cabbage and its juices to the wok, stir to mix and spread out to cover a large area. Add the rice pudding slices on top, spreading them over the mixture. Add the wok cover and cook over a medium heat for about 5–7 minutes until the steam inside has softened the pudding. Replace the lid, stir and mix the ingredients until piping hot and the juices from the cabbage are absorbed. (Inevitably, slices will stick together in clusters; separate some with the wok scoop.) Scoop on to a serving dish and serve hot. Individuals may like to add a little dark soy sauce to their own bowls.

NOTE: Refrigerate any leftovers in the normal way. The rice pudding pieces will harden but, when you reheat them in the wok, they will soften instantly. Sprinkle on a few drops of water for the reheating, if necessary.

FOR THE MARINADE:
2.5 ml (½ tsp) salt
5 ml (1 tsp) sugar
12 turns white or black peppermill
15 ml (1 tbsp) thick or dark soy sauce
10 ml (2 tsp) Shaoxing wine or medium dry sherry
5 ml (1 tsp) tapioca or potato flour
15 ml (1 tbsp) sesame oil

Lotus
Leaf Rice

Serves 6–8 AS SIDE DISH;
2–3 AS MAIN COURSE

255 g (8 oz) raw prawns in the
    shell, without heads (13–15
    prawns), peeled and de-veined
    (*see* p. 353)
115 g (4 oz) garden peas, fresh or
    frozen
7.5 ml (1½ tsp) salt
90 ml (6 tbsp) peanut or vegetable
    oil
1 large dried lotus leaf
2 large eggs, size 2
about 425–620 g (15–22 oz/3–4½
    cups) cooked rice, firm rather
    than mushy in texture (*see*
    p. 228)
4 spring onions, trimmed and cut
    into small rounds
85–115 g (3–4 oz) cooked ham,
    cut into small cubes

FOR THE MARINADE:
2.5 ml (½ tsp) salt
2.5 ml (½ tsp) cornflour
7.5 ml (1½ tsp) egg white

Illustrated on Plate 9.

'*Ten miles of lotus ponds by the temple*
Where early morning maidens flock, busy at picking
Not lotus flowers they pick but the leaves
Rice wrapped in lotus leaf more fragrant than the flower'

THIS CANTONESE ditty in praise of this celebrated dish explains why lotus leaves are used to wrap rice. In Canton, where fresh leaves are used in spring and summer, cooked rice – made the more tasty with such things as meat and shrimps – is wrapped and steamed for about 20 minutes or until the fragrance of the leaves is imparted to the rice. As we have to use dried lotus leaves abroad, stir-frying the rice first helps to enhance the fragrance.

1 Marinate the prawns. Put the prawns into a bowl, add the salt and stir vigorously in the same direction for about 30 seconds until the prawns feel firm and gelatinous. Add the cornflour and egg white, and stir again for about 30 seconds or until totally absorbed. Leave in the refrigerator, covered, for 1 hour or longer to make the texture of the prawns bouncy and crisp. Just before cooking, loosen them up.

2 Blanch the peas. Bring a pot of water to a rolling boil. Add 5 ml (1 tsp) of the salt and 15 ml (1 tbsp) of the oil. Add the peas and cook for about 5 minutes (if fresh) or 1 minute (if defrosted). Pour into a colander and drain thoroughly.

3 Soak the lotus leaf in warm water for 10 minutes or until pliable again. Shake off or wipe off excess moisture.

4 Make 1 egg crêpe. Lightly beat 1 egg. Heat a wok over a medium heat until very hot. Add 15 ml (1 tbsp) oil and swirl around to cover a large area. Pour in the egg. When it begins to set, tip the wok to let the still runny egg set. Remove from the heat and transfer the lightly done egg crêpe to a dish. Cut it into pieces and keep nearby. The wok should be so clean that it does not need rinsing.

5 Stir-fry the prawns. Reheat the wok over a high heat until smoke rises. Add 30 ml (2 tbsp) oil and swirl it

around several times. Loosen the prawns in the bowl and add to the wok. Stir for 20–30 seconds as they turn pinkish in colour, being just cooked or slightly under-done. Remove to a plate and cut into about 2 cm (¾ in) sections. Rinse and dry the wok.

6 Stir-fry the rice. Lightly beat the remaining egg, adding 2.5 ml (½ tsp) salt. Reheat the wok over a high heat until smoke rises. Add the remaining 30 ml (2 tbsp) oil and swirl it around several times, covering a large area. Add the spring onion which will sizzle. Pour in the egg and let it set partially for a few seconds. Pour in the loosened rice and, going to the bottom of the wok with the wok scoop, flip and turn to mix the egg and oil with the rice for about 2 minutes or until the rice is hot. Add the ham and peas, continuing to turn and stir until hot again. Return the prawn and egg pieces to the wok, stirring until piping hot again., Remove the wok from the heat.

7 Wrap the rice. Open the lotus leaf. Add the rice mix-ture, scoopful by scoopful, into the centre of the leaf. Make a parcel by folding top and bottom sides toward the centre, then folding the right and left sides likewise, making sure they overlap each other. Turn the parcel over. The recipe can be prepared several hours in advance up to this point. When ready to serve, steam the wrapped rice until piping hot.

8 Put the parcel, folds side down, in a bowl or dish and then put into a steamer and steam (see p. 355) for about 15–20 minutes until the rice inside is faintly flavoured by the fragrance of the lotus leaf.

9 Remove the bowl or dish from the steamer and transfer the parcel to a serving plate. To serve, use a pair of scissors and cut open the top. Scoop out the rice inside and serve in individual bowls.

VARIATION: *Prawn Fried Rice.* If you don't have a lotus leaf, you can follow the recipe up to step 6 and serve the rice as fried rice.

Cantonese
Beef Chuk

170 g (6 oz/¾ cup) Thai or
  fragrant rice (or short-grain
  rice), rinsed
2.5–4 ml (½–¾ tsp) salt
15 ml (1 tbsp) peanut or vegetable
  oil
3 litres (5¼ pints/12 cups) boiling
  hot water
350 g (12 oz) rump steak,
  trimmed and cut into
  rectangular pieces, about 2 ×
  4 cm (⅓ × 1½ in) and 5 mm
  (⅕ in) thick
leaves of heart of a crisp lettuce,
  cut crossways at 2.5 cm (1 in)
  intervals

FOR THE MARINADE:
2.5 ml (½ tsp) salt
1.5 ml (¼ tsp) sugar
15 ml (1 tbsp) thin or light soy
  sauce
12 turns white or black peppermill
5 ml (1 tsp) Shaoxing wine or
  medium dry sherry
7.5 ml (1½ tsp) tapioca or potato
  flour
10 ml (2 tsp) finely shredded
  ginger julienne strips
1 large egg, lightly beaten
30 ml (2 tbsp) peanut or vegetable
  oil

FOR as long as the Chinese have eaten boiled rice, they have also enjoyed rice congee – zhou in Mandarin and chuk in Cantonese – boiled for a much longer time than cooked rice. By Chinese standards, zhou or chuk is not a soup, for it is made with rice, while soups are not made with rice. As a meal, it makes a hot and soothing breakfast, it is also a good luncheon dish, accompanied by fried noodles, and it is suitable for a light supper, since it is easily digestible and can be eaten just before bedtime. It is also something to resort to when you are not feeling well, in the same way that one eats soup rather than solid food.

With the regional diversities, the consistency of rice congee as well as what is put into it, can vary a great deal. In the north, what is referred to as xifan or thin rice is accompanied by pickles, roasted peanuts and fermented bean curd cheese, etc. Southern Chinese, on the other hand, habitually make chuk to a much smoother consistency. When the water and rice have become integrated, they add anything from meat to poultry to fish and shellfish; in fact, there are easily more than three to four dozen possible combinations. As long as you have made the basic plain chuk successfully, you can add various ingredients as a seasoning as well as to make it more substantial. In this recipe, for example, instead of beef, you can use chicken.

1 Put the rinsed rice into a large saucepan, add the salt and the oil. Boil a kettle, then pour 1 litre (1¾ pints/4½ cups) boiling hot water over the rice. Put the saucepan over a high heat and continue to boil the rice for about 10 minutes so as to open up the grains. Add the remaining 2 litres (3½ pints/9 cups) water, return to the boil, give the rice a big stir, then reduce the heat. Place a pair of chopsticks across the rim of the pan, set apart, before putting the lid on top. Leaving a gap between the saucepan and the lid in this way will prevent the congee from boiling over. Continue to simmer fast for 1½–2 hours until the rice and water look smooth and integrated.

2 While the chuk is simmering, marinate the beef. Add

the salt, sugar, soy sauce, ground pepper, wine or sherry and stir to mix until absorbed. Add the tapioca or potato flour and stir to mix until well coated. Add the ginger and mix well. Leave to stand for about 20 minutes. When the chuk is almost ready, stir in the egg and the oil; mix well.

3 Add the beef and the lettuce to the simmering chuk and, using a wooden spoon, give a couple of big stirs so that the beef is submerged. Add the lid, turn off the heat and leave for about 3 minutes until the beef is just cooked. Ladle into individual bowls and serve hot.

Shanghai Cabbage Rice

SHANGHAI people love this and they make it with small baak choi, the cabbage with white stalks and green leaves. To serve it as a meal on its own, they would put dice of salted pork with the cabbage, but otherwise they would use just the cabbage as in this recipe.

上海菜飯

SERVES 6

1.1–1.35 kilos (2½–3 lb) small Shanghai baak choi, rinsed and drained

60 ml (4 tbsp) peanut or vegetable oil

4 slices ginger, peeled

7.5 ml (1½ tsp) salt

2.5 ml (½ tsp) sugar

15 ml (1 tbsp) Shaoxing wine or medium dry sherry

550 g (1¼ lb/3 cups) long-grain white rice

15 ml (1 tbsp) melted lard or sesame oil

1 Chop off the hard ends and cut the cabbage crossways at no more than 1 cm (½ in) intervals. If you are worried about the bulk, don't be, for it will be reduced considerably when cooked.

2 Heat a wok over a high heat until smoke rises. Add 45 ml (3 tbsp) of the oil and swirl it around to cover a large area. Add the ginger and fry for about 30 seconds to season the oil. Add the cabbage, stir and turn with the wok scoop to mix with the oil. Add the salt and sugar, continuing to stir to draw out the water. Splash in the wine or sherry. Reduce the heat to medium and continue to cook for 4–5 minutes until the cabbage is tender. Remove the wok from the heat. Pick out the ginger and discard. Remove the cabbage, scoopful by scoopful, to a wire sieve over a bowl, pressing down on the cabbage with the wok scoop to squeeze out excess moisture before transferring it to another bowl. Keep the cabbage warm; retain the cabbage liquid. The cabbage can be cooked several hours in advance, but if

so, it must be reheated before it is added to the rice in step 3.

3 Rinse the rice several times with cold water, rubbing it with your fingers and picking out impurities. Drain, then put the rice into a large saucepan, preferably with a heavy bottom. Add about 725 ml (26 fl oz/3¼ cups) liquid made up of water and the cabbage liquid. Add the remaining 15 ml (1 tbsp) oil. Cover the saucepan and bring to the boil over a high heat. Stir the rice thoroughly and continue to boil, covered or uncovered, until most of the water is absorbed, leaving only tiny 'eyelets' around the rice. Reduce the heat to low, add the warm cabbage and leave the rice and cabbage to simmer, covered, for 12–15 minutes until the rice is thoroughly cooked.

4 Replace the lid, add the lard or sesame oil on top to enhance the fragrance (leave this out if you prefer not to use lard). Stir to mix the cabbage with the rice. Serve hot into individual bowls.

Yunnan
Laifen

SERVES 2 AS LUNCH

225 g (8 oz) lean pork, minced

450 g (1 lb) fresh laifen (or 325 g/ 11 oz dried laifen)

1 litre (¾ pints/4 cups) chicken stock

170 g (6 oz) canned pickled mustard greens (the salty and sour type labelled salted mustard greens on the can), coarsely chopped

115–170 g (4–6 oz) Chinese chives, trimmed and cut into 2 cm (¾ in) lengths

4–5 stalks coriander leaves, washed, topped and coarsely chopped

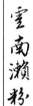

LAIFEN refers to the tubular rice noodles, which are much thicker than the wiry rice vermicelli (being about 2 mm/$^1/_{10}$ in in diameter), even though sometimes, on the packets, the label in English is the same. The texture, too, is different, for whereas laifen literally give you a bouncy sensation on your teeth as you chew, rice vermicelli are soft and delicate. Fresh laifen, which is now available in Chinese shops, is predictably better than the dried product which, nevertheless, is not bad. The Cantonese eat it in a light broth seasoned with slices of char siu or Cantonese roast pork, but the Yunnanese prefer a more earthy approach, with more intense and intermingled flavours. A friend of mine from Hong Kong, Dorcas Hu, whose husband is originally from Yunnan, describes how they and their sons love to eat this dish at home, prepared by their amah.

1 Marinate the pork. Put the minced pork in a bowl, add the salt, sugar, soy sauce, ground pepper and tapioca or potato flour and stir to mix. Add the water and stir again vigorously until absorbed. Leave to stand for 15–20 minutes. Blend in the oil.

2 Heat about 1.75 litres (3 pints/7½ cups) or more water in a large saucepan or a wok until it comes to the boil. Add the fresh laifen and when the water returns to a rolling boil, pour into a colander and rinse with hot water to rid the rice noodles of excess starch, and hence prevent cloudiness in the soup later. (If dried laifen is used, boil for about 10 minutes or go by the instructions on the packet.) Drain. Divide the laifen into 2 portions, put into 2 large serving bowls and keep warm nearby. Rinse the saucepan or wok.

3 Pour the chicken stock into the saucepan or wok and gradually bring to the boil. Add the pork, stir to break up lumps, return to the boil, then reduce the heat and simmer for about 1 minute or until the pork is just cooked. Add the mustard greens, stir to mix and continue to simmer for another minute. Add the chives, stir to mix thoroughly, then add the coriander and give a big stir. Scoop half of this mixture into each bowl and serve hot.

FOR THE MARINADE:

2 ml (⅓ tsp) salt

1.5 ml (¼ tsp) sugar

22.5 ml (1½ tbsp) thick or dark soy sauce

ground white or black pepper to taste

5 ml (1 tsp) tapioca or potato flour

15 ml (1 tbsp) water

30 ml (2 tbsp) peanut or vegetable oil

Illustrated on Plate 4.

Ngormaigai

THE special food for the Dragon Boat or Double Fifth Festival is called zong in Mandarin or chung in Cantonese (*see* p. 56), and is made of white glutinous rice wrapped in bamboo or other leaves into a triangular parcel and boiled for 4–5 hours, if not longer. A simpler version of it – and much easier to prepare – is what the Cantonese call ngor-maigai, which is glutinous rice wrapped in lotus leaf and often served as a dimsum during the luncheon hours.

MAKES 6; SERVES 12

900 g (2 lb) white glutinous rice, Thai or Chinese

5 ml (1 tsp) salt

75 ml (5 tbsp) peanut or vegetable oil

850–900 ml (30–32 fl oz/1½–1⅔ pints/3¾–4 cups) water

40 g (1½ oz) dried shrimps, rinsed

450 g (1 lb) boned but not skinned chicken thighs

continued

1 Rinse the glutinous rice a couple of times until the water is relatively clear. Drain. Put the rice into a lightly oiled, heatproof dish with raised edges, add the salt and 30 ml

16 medium dried Chinese black
mushrooms, reconstituted in
250 ml (8 fl oz/1 cup) water (*see*
p. 353)

15 ml (1 tbsp) Shaoxing wine or
medium dry sherry

115 g (4 oz) canned bamboo
shoots, diced and blanched (*see*
p. 353)

2.5–5 ml (½–1 tsp) tapioca or
potato flour dissolved in 15 ml
(1 tbsp) water

salt

115 g (4 oz) roast belly pork, cut
into 18–24 pieces

6 medium or 3 large dried lotus
leaves, rinsed

FOR THE MARINADE:

2.5 ml (½ tsp) salt

5 ml (1 tsp) sugar

30 ml (2 tbsp) thick or dark soy
sauce

10 ml (2 tsp) ginger juice (*see*
p. 357)

8–10 turns black peppermill

5 ml (1 tsp) five-spice powder

5 ml (1 tsp) tapioca or potato flour

15 ml (1 tbsp) sesame oil

Illustrated on Plate 9.

(2 tbsp) of the oil and mix. Add 850 ml (30 fl oz/1½ pints/3¾ cups) water for Thai rice and 900 ml (32 fl oz/ 1⅔ pints/4 cups) for Chinese rice. Place the dish in a steamer and steam (*see* p. 355) for 30 minutes until the rice is thoroughly cooked, but not mushy. Remove from the steamer. When cool enough to handle, divide into 6 portions.

2 Soak the dried shrimps in 45 ml (3 tbsp) warm or hot water for 1 hour or longer. Drain, saving the soaking liquid.

3 Marinate the chicken. Remove the skin from the chicken and cut into 2 cm (¾ in) cubes. Put into a bowl, add the salt, sugar, soy sauce, ginger juice, pepper, five-spice powder and tapioca or potato flour and stir to coat. Leave for about 20 minutes, then blend in the sesame oil.

4 Drain the Chinese mushrooms, saving the soaking liquid. Quarter them.

5 Make the stuffing. Heat a wok or saucepan over a high heat until very hot. Add the remaining 45 ml (3 tbsp) oil and swirl it around to cover a large area. Add the dried shrimps and mushrooms and stir about a dozen times. Add the chicken skin and the chicken, continuing to stir for about 30 seconds. Splash in the wine or sherry, and when the sizzling subsides, add the bamboo shoots and stir to mix. Add the shrimp soaking liquid and the mushroom soaking liquid and bring to the boil. Reduce the heat and simmer, covered, for about 15 minutes or until much of the liquid is absorbed. Pick out and discard the chicken skin. Stir in the dissolved tapioca or potato flour to thicken the sauce slightly. Test for taste, add about 2.5 ml (½ tsp) salt, if liked. Transfer to a dish, scraping out the sauce and the oil as well. Add the belly pork, then divide this stuffing into 6 portions.

6 Make the ngormaigai. Soak the lotus leaves in hot water for 5–10 minutes until pliable. Drain and wipe off excess moisture. Open 1 leaf (or half of 1 large one) and lay it on a work surface. With your hands lightly oiled, pick up 1 portion of the rice and divide it into 2 halves. Press 1 half into a square shape about 10 cm (4 in) and put on or near the centre of the leaf. Spoon 1 portion of the stuffing (with the sauce and oil) on top of the rice square, leaving a little space at the edges. Press the other half of rice to more or less the same size and place on top

of the stuffing. Fold the top and bottom flaps of the
lotus leaf tightly towards the centre, then fold the right
and left flaps towards the centre. If the leaf is too large,
trim it with scissors as you fold, leaving plenty of
margin, however, for the folds to overlap each other.
There is no need to tie the ngormaigai at all, but simply
place it folds side down. Repeat until all 6 are made. The
recipe can be prepared up to this point several hours in
advance. At this stage, they can also be frozen in the
normal way.

7 Steam the ngormaigai. When ready to serve, put the
ngormaigai directly on the perforated container of a
steamer and steam over a high heat for about 25 minutes
(longer if from the freezer) until piping hot.

8 To serve, open the folds of the ngormaigai and serve the
rice and stuffing inside. Each ngormaigai fills about 2
rice bowls.

NOTE: If your steamer is small, you can make half of the
recipe. Roast belly pork can be bought from some Cantonese restaurants, but for those who do not wish to include
pork, it can be left out.

Mantou

THIS is the steamed bread people in northern
China, a wheat-growing region, eat as a staple in
lieu of rice. From the crack of dawn, steaming hot
mantou is sold on street stalls, in taverns and in
restaurants, and it is eaten in the same way, accompanied by dishes, as one eats rice. For better or
worse, mantou is always made with light, white
flour rather than wholewheat flour, just as Chinese
people eat polished white rice rather than brown rice.

MAKES 20–24; SERVES 10

25 g (1 oz) dried yeast
2.5 ml (½ tsp) salt
25–85 g (1–3 oz/2–6 tbsp) sugar
about 500 ml (16 fl oz/2 cups)
  tepid water
750 g (1 lb 10½ oz/5¼ cups) light
  plain white flour
30 ml (2 tbsp) peanut or vegetable
  oil

'To make mantou at home is as commonplace an
activity as it is easy', says a family friend, Dr Willian Fong,
who showed me with aplomb the easy way he learned
from his mother when they lived in Peking. The size of the
mantou is flexible, so that it can be worked out according
to the size of your own steaming basket or container. Dr
Fong likes to add a lot of sugar in the dough, but you can
use less.

1 Mix the yeast, salt and sugar in a bowl. Add a little of the tepid water and stir to dissolve the yeast so that it will not get lumpy. Stir in the rest of the water. Leave on a warm surface for about 15 minutes or until the liquid becomes very frothy.

2 Sieve the flour into a very large mixing bowl or a basin. Make a well in the centre and gradually pour in the liquid, drawing in the flour to make into a dough. While it is not necessary to overknead the dough, it should be worked for about 2 minutes until it is soft and smooth, and the bowl or basin cleaned of flour. Add the oil and work it into the dough, which will become soft and elastic.

3 Cover the bowl or basin with a damp cloth or cling film and leave it on a very warm surface or in a very warm atmosphere for 1½ hours or until the dough has doubled in size.

4 Pick up this spongy dough and divide it into 2 halves. Divide each half into 10–12 pieces.

5 Put 1 piece of dough at a time in the palm of one hand. With the other hand gather the rough edges on top and twist to hide the folds so that the bottom end (near the palm) will be smooth. Turn the dough over, smooth side up, and put it on a surface. Put your palms vertically on its right and left sides and roll it between your palms several times. Give the dough a firm yet gentle punch and then roll it again between your palms. Repeat this procedure 3–4 times, then put it on a piece of greaseproof paper about 5 × 5 cm (2 × 2 in) in size, still the smooth side up. Repeat until all are done.

6 Place the dough pieces in two large bamboo steaming baskets or metal steaming containers, leaving a space between them. Leave the basket or containers on a very warm surface or in a very warm atmosphere for about 30 minutes for the dough to rise again. Take care that it does not go over the top.

7 Stack the baskets or containers on top of each other and steam (*see* p. 355) for 12–15 minutes until the mantou is cooked. To test, insert a satay stick, if it comes out clean, the mantou are cooked.

8 Serve the mantou hot to go with soup or other dishes. Mantou can be frozen and resteamed.

Fujianese
Fried Rice

WHEREAS Cantonese fried rice has an overall dry texture, Fujianese fried rice is topped with slightly thickened sauce, so that the rice has a moistened finish. Another distinguishing feature is the use of a large amount of eggs. Reflecting the products of the Fujianese coastal area, all sorts of seafood, such as clams and squid, can be used, even though in this recipe only prawns are used.

福
建
炒
飯

SERVES 2 AS LUNCH OR DINNER

225 g (8 oz) raw prawns in the
  shell, without heads (13–15
  prawns), peeled and de-veined
  (*see* p. 353)
115 g (4 oz) garden peas or petits
  pois
7.5 ml (1½ tsp) salt
75 ml (5 tbsp) peanut or vegetable
  oil
3 large eggs, lightly beaten
about 450 g (1 lb/3 cups) cooked
  rice (*see* p. 228)

FOR THE MARINADE:
2.5 ml (½ tsp) salt
2.5 ml (½ tsp) cornflour
7.5 ml (1½ tsp) egg white

FOR THE SAUCE:
175 ml (6 fl oz/¾ cup) chicken
  stock
6.5 ml (1¼ tsp) cornflour
10 ml (2 tsp) thin or light soy
  sauce
ground pepper to taste

Illustrated on Plate 13.

1 Marinate the prawns. Put the prawns in a bowl, add 2.5 ml (½ tsp) of the salt and stir vigorously in the same direction for about 30 seconds until the prawns feel firm and gelatinous. Add the cornflour and egg white and stir again until totally absorbed. Leave in the refrigerator for 30 minutes or longer to firm the texture of the prawns.

2 Blanch the peas. Bring a pot of water to a rolling boil. Add 5 ml (1 tsp) salt and 15 ml (1 tbsp) of the oil. Add the peas or petits pois and cook for about 5 minutes (if fresh) or 1 minute (if defrosted). Pour into a colander and drain.

3 Prepare the sauce. Pour about 15 ml (1 tbsp) chicken stock on to the cornflour to dissolve it, then add the remaining stock and stir to blend. Add the soy sauce and ground pepper and keep nearby.

4 Heat a wok over a high heat until smoke rises. Add 30 ml (2 tbsp) oil and swirl it around to cover a large area. Add the prawns, stirring for 30–60 seconds until they are cooked and have turned opaque and pink. Remove to a plate and cut into sections. Rinse and dry the wok.

5 Reheat the wok over a high heat until smoke rises. Add the remaining 30 ml (2 tbsp) oil and swirl it around to cover a large area. Season the beaten eggs with 2.5 ml (½ tsp) of salt, then pour into the wok. When it begins to set, stir and turn to scramble into chunky pieces. Add the rice and, going to the bottom of the wok with the wok scoop, turn and toss for about 2 minutes or until the rice is very hot. Add the peas, continuing to stir

until hot. Scoop on to a warm serving dish and keep warm nearby.

6 Pour the well-stirred sauce into the wok and heat over a low heat, stirring as it thickens. Return the prawns to the wok and cook until hot again. Scoop this sauce mixture all over the rice. Serve immediately.

Cantonese
Chow Mein with Prawns

SERVES 2 FOR LUNCH

12 large raw prawns in the shell (about 225 g/8 oz) but without heads
225 g (8 oz) dried or 350 g (12 oz) fresh Chinese egg noodles
150–175 ml (5–6 fl oz/⅔–¾ cup) vegetable oil
225–285 g (8–10 oz) bean sprouts
2.5 ml (½ tsp) salt
105 ml (7 tbsp) peanut or vegetable oil
2 cloves garlic, peeled and finely chopped
4 thin slices ginger, peeled
4–6 spring onions, trimmed and cut into 5 cm (2 in) sections, white and green parts separated

DIPPING SAUCES:
Chinese red vinegar
chilli sauce

MARINADE FOR PRAWNS:
2.5 ml (½ tsp) salt
2.5 ml (½ tsp) cornflour
7.5 ml (1½ tsp) egg white

Illustrated on Plate 5.

CHOW MEIN has always been authentic Cantonese food, and this dish is a very popular example of it. Across the boundaries of regional cooking, there seems to be a national consensus about the best technique of frying noodles (chow mein); the ideal is to achieve a golden-brown toasted effect on both sides, while the centre remains moist and tender.

1 Shell the prawns and pat dry. Stand them, one at a time, on a board and, using a sharp knife, halve them along the back, removing and discarding the black veins at the same time. Put the prawns into a large bowl.

2 Marinate the prawns. Add the salt, cornflour and egg white to the prawns and stir vigorously for 30–60 seconds until the marinade is well absorbed. Refrigerate, covered, for 1–2 hours so that the prawns will have a light and crisp texture. Just before you are ready to cook them, loosen them in the bowl.

3 Bring a large pot of water, about 1.75 litres (3 pints/7½ cups), to the boil. Add the noodles, return to the boil and continue to cook, uncovered, until *al dente* (usually about 4 minutes for dried, 1–1½ minutes for fresh noodles, but use your discretion or follow instructions on the packet). Separate them with chopsticks or a fork while boiling. Pour into a colander and refresh immediately under cold running water. Leave to drain and dry for about 1 hour, turning them over once to ensure even drying.

4 Prepare the sauce. In a small bowl add 15 ml (1 tbsp) of the stock to the potato or tapioca flour and stir until

dissolved. Add the remaining stock, soy sauce and oyster sauce and stir to mix. Leave aside.

5 Heat a wok over a high heat until smoke rises. Add 150–175 ml (5–6 fl oz/⅔–¾ cup) vegetable oil and swirl it around. Heat for about 45 seconds or until hot. Add all the prawns and, using a metal perforated spoon, move them around as they curl up almost instantly, turning pinkish in colour as they become cooked. Remove them immediately with the spoon, draining the oil back into the wok.

6 Continue heating the remaining oil, add the bean sprouts to the wok. Sprinkle with 2.5 ml (½ tsp) salt and turn and toss over a high heat for about 2 minutes until the bean sprouts are cooked yet still crunchy. Remove the wok from the heat and pour the bean sprouts into a wire sieve set over a bowl to drain.

7 Heat a large flat frying pan (ideally between 20–25 cm/ 8–10 in in diameter) over a high heat until very hot. Add 60 ml (4 tbsp) of the oil to cover the surface and heat until smoke rises. Add the noodles and arrange them evenly to the edges like a pancake. Fry for about 1 minute or until golden-brown but not burned. Slip the wok scoop or a metal spatula underneath to check the colour and loosen edges. Lower the heat and fry for another minute. Either toss the noodle cake or turn it over with the scoop. Fry the other side in the same way, streaming in 15 ml (1 tbsp) oil along the edges. Remove to a serving plate and keep warm in a cool oven with the door ajar.

8 Heat a wok over a high heat until smoke rises. Add the remaining 30 ml (2 tbsp) oil and swirl it around. Add the garlic, stir until it takes on colour, then the ginger, stir, add the white spring onion and stir several more times. Return the prawns and the bean sprouts to the wok, and stir until hot. Lower the heat, make a well in the centre of the wok and pour in the well-stirred sauce, stirring as it thickens to prevent lumps. Stir in the surrounding prawns and bean sprouts to blend with the sauce, add the green spring onion, then scoop on to the noodle cake. Serve immediately.

9 To facilitate serving, cut up the noodles with a pair of scissors or a knife and fork. Chinese red vinegar and chilli sauce can be served at the table as dipping sauces.

FOR THE SAUCE:

150 ml (5 fl oz/⅔ cup) chicken stock

10 ml (2 tsp) potato or tapioca flour

7.5 ml (1½ tsp) thin or light soy sauce

30 ml (2 tbsp) oyster sauce

Dandan Noodles

MAKES 3–4 BOWLS

225 g (8 oz) pork, finely minced
45 ml (3 tbsp) peanut or vegetable
  oil
3 large cloves garlic, peeled and
  finely chopped
350 g (12 oz) dried noodles (*see*
  introduction opposite)
2 large stalks baak choi (Chinese
  cabbage)
salt
about 450–575 ml (15–20 fl oz/2–
  2½ cups) stock

FOR THE MARINADE:
2.5 ml (½ tsp) salt
15 ml (1 tbsp) thick or dark soy
  sauce
15 ml (1 tbsp) Shaoxing wine or
  medium dry sherry
10 ml (2 tsp) sesame oil

FOR THE SAUCE:
15 ml (1 tbsp) sesame paste
5–15 ml (1–3 tsp) chilli hot oil (*see*
  p. 357)
15 ml (1 tbsp) sesame oil
5 ml (1 tsp) roasted ground
  Sichuan peppercorns (*see* p. 359)
10 ml (2 tsp) Chinese rice vinegar
15 ml (1 tbsp) thick or dark soy
  sauce

Illustrated on Plate 11.

AN earthy, spicy dish, which is typical of Sichaun street food. The noodles used locally are often the hand-drawn kind, made on the spot; after a dramatic performance of 'dancing' and twisting, the well-beaten flour-and-water dough is split, as if miraculously, into several hundreds of strands. These hand-drawn noodles, flat and ribbon-shaped, are available dried in plastic bags in Chinese and Oriental stores, but although the Chinese characters tell you they are hand-drawn, the English label often does not go beyond the word 'noodles'. For a substitute, use strong-textured noodles, such as the Japanese or Korean U-dong.

1 Marinate the pork. Put the pork into a bowl, add the salt, soy sauce, wine or sherry and sesame oil and stir to mix. Leave to stand for about 15 minutes.

2 Prepare the sauce. In a small bowl mix together the sesame paste, hot oil, sesame oil, Sichuan peppercorns, rice vinegar and soy sauce.

3 Heat a wok over a high heat until smoke rises. Add the peanut or vegetable oil and swirl it around. Add the garlic, stir, add the pork and stir and turn with the wok scoop for about 3 minutes until quite dry. Remove from the heat, add the sauce and mix well.

4 Plunge the noodles into a large pot of boiling water, return to the boil and continue to cook for about 5 minutes or until *al dente*. Pour into a colander and drain.

5 Simultaneously, blanch the baak choi in another pot of boiling salted water for 2 minutes. Drain, then chop up.

6 Heat the stock until very hot.

7 Divide the noodles and put into 3–4 bowls. Top the noodles in each bowl with 15–30 ml (1–2 tbsp) chopped baak choi, one third to one quarter of the amount of the minced pork and pour in from the side of the bowl 150 ml (5 fl oz/⅔ cup) of the stock. Serve immediately.

Fried
Amoy Vermicelli

THESE dried cotton-threadlike noodles, hand-made and plaited into thin cakes, come from Amoy, Fujian Province, hence their name. They are very popular in Taiwan and Singapore, as there are many Chinese of Fujianese origin living there. The key to this dish lies in very quickly deep-frying the vermicelli so that they become neither lumpy nor mushy. This can be done hours, or even a day, in advance, as long as they are kept from going rancid.

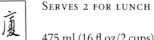

1 Sit a wok on its stand, add the deep-frying oil and heat over a high heat until it reaches 180°C (350°F) in temperature. Add the vermicelli, 1 plait at a time, and let the noodles sizzle in the oil for a few seconds. Turn them over with a large spoon or chopsticks and fry the other side for a few more seconds, until they turn pale gold in colour. Remove with a perforated disc, letting the oil drip off, then put on kitchen paper to drain. Discard the oil. Wash and dry the wok.

2 Marinate the pork. Add the salt, soy sauce, pepper, wine or sherry and tapioca or potato flour to the pork and mix together. Stir in the water until absorbed. Leave for about 15 minutes, then stir in the oil.

3 Reheat the wok over a high heat until smoke rises. Add 22.5 ml (1½ tbsp) of the oil and swirl it around. Add the spring onions and stir to release the aroma. Add the Chinese mushrooms, stir for about a dozen times, then add the pork. Going to the bottom of the wok with the wok scoop, turn and toss for about 20 seconds. Splash in the wine along the edges of the wok, continuing to stir until the pork is cooked, and has turned opaque. Scoop up this mixture on to a dish and keep warm nearby.

4 Add the remaining 30 ml (2 tbsp) oil to the wok and swirl it around. Add the cabbage, first the white parts, stirring for about 30 seconds and seasoning with salt to taste, then the leafy parts and stir for about 1 minute to reduce the bulk. Continue to cook, covered, over a moderate heat until the cabbage is tender and limp and the water has oozed out. Scoop up with a perforated

SERVES 2 FOR LUNCH

475 ml (16 fl oz/2 cups) vegetable oil for deep-frying .
170 g (6 oz), or 3 plaits dried Amoy wheat flour vermicelli
115 g (4 oz) trimmed lean pork, cut into matchstick-sized strips
52.5 ml (3½ tbsp) peanut or vegetable oil
6 spring onions, trimmed, halved lengthways then cut into 5 cm (2 in) sections
6 medium dried Chinese black mushrooms, reconstituted in 300 ml (10 fl oz/1¼ cups) water (see p. 353), cut into very thin slivers
10 ml (2 tsp) Shaoxing wine or medium dry sherry
450 g (1 lb) Chinese celery cabbage (Chinese leaves), shredded crossways
2.5 ml (½ tsp) or salt to taste
600 ml (21 fl oz/2½ cups) chicken stock (or mushroom soaking liquid and water)

FOR THE MARINADE
1.5 ml (¼ tsp) salt
10 ml (2 tsp) thin or light soy sauce
6 turns black peppermill
5 ml (1 tsp) Shaoxing wine or medium dry sherry
2.5 ml (½ tsp) tapioca or potato flour
15 ml (1 tbsp) water
5 ml (1 tsp) peanut or vegetable oil

Illustrated on Plate 4.

spoon and mix with the pork mixture, leaving behind as much juice as possible in the wok.

5 Add the chicken stock to the wok and bring to the boil. Add the deep-fried vermicelli and cook gently for about 3 minutes until they have absorbed almost all the liquid and have become moist. Add a little more water if necessary. Remove to a large serving dish. Add the pork and cabbage mixture on top. Serve hot.

Jiaozi
(Northern Dumplings)

SERVES 6–8 AS A MEAL:
  MAKES 100–120

FOR THE DOUGH:
550 g (1¼ lb/5 cups) plain white
  flour
325–350 ml (11–12 fl oz/1⅓–1½
  cups) cold water
some extra flour

FOR PORK STUFFING A:
1 kilo (2¼ lb) Chinese celery
  cabbage (Chinese leaves),
  trimmed and shredded
  crossways then chopped up
  roughly
10 ml (2 tsp) salt
500–550 g (1⅛–1¼ lb) lean pork,
  finely chopped or minced
40 g (1½ oz) dried shrimps, rinsed
  and soaked in just sufficient hot
  water to cover for 45 minutes,
  then finely chopped, reserving
  the soaking liquid
14 spring onions, trimmed and
  cut into small rounds

FOR northern Chinese, jiaozi (chiao-tzu) or dumplings, which are rich in symbolism, are a must during Chinese New Year (*see* p. 49), but they are also eaten on any special occasion, even when friends and relatives gather together for a meal. There used to be two traditional stuffings, either pork with Chinese celery cabbage or beef with Chinese chives, especially blanched chives. But in recent years, pork with chives has become just as popular as pork with cabbage, while beef stuffing remains popular among Chinese Muslims. I therefore show you the way to prepare all three of them.

1 Prepare the dough. Sift the flour into a large mixing bowl. Gradually stir in the water, reserving about 25 ml (1 fl oz/⅛ cup), and start kneading. Add the remaining water, if necessary. Knead for 1–2 minutes or until the dough is smooth, firm but pliable and not dry. Cover the bowl with a dry towel and leave at room temperature for about 30 minutes in order to relax the gluten in the dough.

2 Prepare one of the three stuffings. To prepare pork stuffing A, put the cabbage into a bowl, add the salt and mix together. Leave for about 30 minutes during which time water will ooze out from the cabbage. Bunch by bunch, squeeze out the excess water from the cabbage but leave damp. Put the pork into a large bowl, add from the marinade the salt, pepper, wine or sherry and water (including the shrimp soaking liquid), and stir

vigorously in one direction for about 1 minute. This lightens the texture of the pork. Add the sesame oil, the dried shrimps, the cabbage and spring onions and stir again until thoroughly mixed. Leave for about 15 minutes.

To prepare pork stuffing B, put the pork into a large bowl, add from the marinade the salt, pepper, wine or sherry and water (including the shrimp soaking liquid) and stir vigorously in one direction for about 1 minute. This lightens the texture of the pork. Add the sesame oil, the dried shrimps and the chives and stir again until thoroughly mixed. Leave for about 15 minutes.

To prepare the beef stuffing, put the beef into a large bowl. Add from the marinade the salt, pepper, egg yolk, wine or sherry and water, and stir vigorously in one direction for about 1 minute. This lightens the texture of the beef. Add the sesame oil and the chives and stir again to mix well. Leave for about 15 minutes.

3 Put the dough on a floured working surface. Knead briefly until smooth and soft. Divide into 4 portions. With both hands, roll out one portion into a long cylindrical roll, about 2.5 cm (1 in) in diameter and then cut into pieces about 1 cm (under ½ in) long. Cover spare dough portions with a dry towel.

4 Make the jiaozi or dumpling skin. One by one, stand each piece upright on the heel of your hand; slightly round off the dough, then flatten with the other hand. Flour them ever so lightly. Using a narrow, floured rolling pin, roll out each piece into a circle about 7 cm (under 3 in) in diameter. Don't worry if the pieces are more oval than circular in shape.

5 Make the jiaozi or dumplings. Place 1 piece of skin in the palm of one hand and put about 7.5 ml (1½ tsp) of the stuffing in the middle. Pinch tightly to seal the top and bottom edges. Now hold the dumpling between the thumbs and index fingers of both hands, seal the right edges by squeezing the thumb and index finger together, pinching and pleating to make one or two tucks simultaneously, then seal the left edges in the same way. Put the dumpling on a floured tray. Repeat until all are done, making sure that they are not stuck to each other on the tray. At this point, the dumplings can be put into takeaway containers and frozen in the normal way.

FOR PORK STUFFING B:
500–550 g (1⅛–1¼ lb) lean pork, finely chopped or minced
40 g (1½ oz) dried shrimps, rinsed and soaked in just sufficient hot water to cover for 45 minutes, then finely chopped, reserving the soaking liquid
400–450 g (14–16 oz) Chinese chives or blanched chives, rinsed, trimmed and cut into small rounds

FOR BEEF STUFFING:
500–550 g (1⅛–1¼ lb) trimmed beef, rump, skirt or flank, or frying steak, minced
400–450 g (14–16 oz) Chinese chives or blanched chives, rinsed, trimmed and cut into small rounds

MARINADE FOR PORK AND BEEF:
7.5–10 ml (1½–2 tsp) salt
12 turns peppermill
1 egg yolk (for beef only)
15 ml (1 tbsp) Shaoxing wine or medium dry sherry
45 ml (3 tbsp) cold water
120–135 ml (8–9 tbsp) sesame oil

FOR THE DIP: EACH PORTION:
10–15 ml (2–3 tsp) finely chopped garlic
10–15 ml (2–3 tsp) finely chopped ginger
60 ml (4 tbsp) Chinkiang vinegar (or balsamic vinegar)
30 ml (2 tbsp) thin or light soy sauce
15–30 ml (1–2 tbsp) sesame oil
10–15 ml (2–3 tsp) chilli hot oil (*see* p. 357) (optional)

6 Prepare the dip. In a small bowl combine the garlic, ginger, vinegar, soy sauce, sesame oil and chilli hot oil (if used) and stir to mix. You may like to make 2 portions and put into 2 small bowls.

7 Cook the dumplings. In a wok (or a large saucepan) bring about 1.75 litres (3 pints/7½ cups) of water to a rolling boil. Put in 6 dumplings and stir so that they do not stick to the bottom of the wok. Add another 16–18 and stir again. Cover the wok and return to the boil. Remove the cover, stir, then cover again, lower the heat and continue to simmer gently for another 8–10 minutes or until the dumplings have floated to the surface. (If the cooking is done on an electric burner where the temperature cannot be controlled instantly, about 250 ml/ 8 fl oz/1 cup cold water should be added twice during cooking to prevent the dumplings from bursting.) Using a hand strainer or perforated spoon, remove the dumplings, draining excess water back into the wok, and put on to a large, lightly oiled serving dish. Discard the cooking water and start with fresh water to cook the next lot of dumplings.

8 Serve hot in bowls or plates. Each person spoons some sauce over the dumplings before eating them.

NOTE: Jiaozi freeze well. To cook frozen jiaozi, do not defrost them but instead put them directly into boiling water and proceed as in step 7. Left-over cooked dumplings should not be reboiled but should be shallow-fried with a small amount of oil for 5–6 minutes or until piping hot and the skin partially coloured and crisp.

Shanghai
Oily Noodles

THESE fresh shiny noodles, which are packaged in plastic bags and sold in Chinese supermarkets, are yellow in colour, round in shape and oily to the touch. They are already cooked, so that it is a matter of making a topping in the manner to which the Shanghaiese are accustomed. One characteristic of Shanghai food is its greasiness, so if you wish to cut down on the oil when frying the ingredients, do so.

SERVES 2 FOR LUNCH

170–225 g (6–8 oz) lean pork, cut into matchstick-sized strips
90 ml (6 tbsp) peanut or vegetable oil
6 spring onions, trimmed, cut lengthways into 5 cm (2 in) sections, then shredded
15 ml (1 tbsp) Shaoxing wine or medium dry sherry
45 ml (3 tbsp) thick or dark soy sauce
450–550 g (1–1¼ lb) Chinese celery cabbage (Chinese leaves), trimmed and shredded into 6 mm (¼ in) wide slivers
2.5 ml (½ tsp) salt or to taste
450 g (1 lb) fresh Shanghai oily noodles

FOR THE MARINADE:
2.5 ml (½ tsp) salt
2.5 ml (½ tsp) sugar
5 ml (1 tsp) thin or light soy sauce
5 ml (1 tsp) Shaoxing wine or medium dry sherry
5 ml (1 tsp) tapioca or potato flour
15 ml (1 tbsp) water
10 ml (2 tsp) sesame oil

Illustrated on Plate 4.

1 Marinate the pork. Put the pork into a bowl, add the salt, sugar, soy sauce, wine or sherry and tapioca or potato flour and stir to mix. Add the water and stir vigorously in the same direction until absorbed. Leave to stand for about 15 minutes. Blend in the oil.

2 Heat a wok over a high heat until smoke rises. Add 30 ml (2 tbsp) of the oil and swirl it around. Add the spring onions, stir a few times to release the aroma. Add the pork and toss and turn with the wok scoop for about 30 seconds until partially cooked. Splash in the wine or sherry along the edges of the wok, continuing to stir, and when the sizzling subsides, reduce the heat and add 15 ml (1 tbsp) of the soy sauce. Remove the mixture to a dish and keep nearby. Rinse and dry the wok.

3 Reheat the wok over a high heat until smoke rises. Add 30 ml (2 tbsp) oil and swirl it around. Add the cabbage, sprinkle with the salt and stir, turning and tossing from the bottom of the wok for about 1 minute until water oozes from the cabbage. Add the wok cover, reduce the heat and cook for about another 2 minutes until the cabbage is tender. Scoop up with the juices on to a dish. Wash and dry the wok.

4 Reheat the wok over a medium heat until hot. Add the remaining 30 ml (2 tbsp) oil and swirl it around. Add the noodles and toss them in the oil with long chopsticks or wooden spoons until hot. Return the pork and the cabbage to the wok, mixing and tossing with the noodles. Mix in the remaining 30 ml (2 tbsp) soy sauce, then scoop everything on to a serving dish. Serve hot.

Spring Onion Cakes

550 g (1¼ lb/5 cups) plain white
    flour
350 ml (12 fl oz/1½ cups) boiling
    water
15 ml (1 tbsp) cold water
5–10 ml (1–2 tsp) sesame oil
salt
about 90 ml (6 tbsp) sesame oil
about 350 g (12 oz) spring onions,
    trimmed and cut into small
    rounds
105–142.5 ml (7–9½ tbsp) peanut
    or vegetable oil for frying

ONE of Peking's best-known 'small eats', 'oily spring onion cakes' are actually quite easy to make. As a warming winter food against the biting wind, they were traditionally made with lard or duck fat which, being so cholesterol laden, would deprive any of us who are health-conscious of the pleasure of eating them. I therefore use sesame oil in this recipe so that we can feel free to enjoy them.

I have kept faith, however, with the traditional technique of frying or sautéing the spring onion cakes rather than deep-frying them, as many restaurants – not in Peking itself – are wont to do nowadays. Sautéing them gives that contrast between the crisp outside and the soft inside, made fragrant by the spring onion.

1 Sift the flour into a large mixing bowl. Gradually pour in the boiling water and mix with a pair of chopsticks or a wooden spoon as you do so. Rub together with the fingers while the flour is still warm. Drip in the cold water and knead to form a dough which should be firm but not hard. Continue to knead for about 2–3 minutes, drawing in all the flour so as to leave the sides of the bowl clean. Cover the bowl with a cloth and leave for 30–45 minutes to relax the gluten in the dough.

2 Oil a working surface with 5 ml (1 tsp) sesame oil. Also oil a rolling pin with a little sesame oil.

3 Transfer the dough to the surface. Knead a few more times and shape into a roll 30 cm (12 in) long. Using a ruler as a guide, cut the dough into 6 equal pieces.

4 Make the cakes. With the oiled rolling pin, roll out 1 piece into a circular shape about 17.5 cm (7 in) in diameter. Sprinkle all over with 2 ml (⅓ tsp) salt. Pour over 15 ml (1 tbsp) sesame oil and spread it all over, stopping just before the edges. Spread on about 75–90 ml (5–6 tbsp) chopped spring onion, stopping before the edges.

5 With both hands, pick up the side nearest you and roll up the cake away from you, taking care to include the spring onion rounds. Pinch in both ends. Then, holding one end in each hand, roll in towards the middle until

the ends meet. Lift one end and put on top of the other and twist, in opposite directions, and then press down to make into a ball.

6 Gently roll out the ball, turn over and roll out the other side. Repeat this process until it forms a circular shape about 15–17.5 cm (6–7 in) in diameter. The surface of the cake is bound to burst during rolling. Do not worry, for it does not make much difference when fried.

7 Fry the cakes. Heat a heavy frying pan until hot, then add 30 ml (2 tbsp) peanut or vegetable oil and swirl around to cover a large area. Put in one cake, lower the heat and fry, covered, for about 3–4 minutes or until spotted golden-brown. Take a peep after 2 minutes so that you can adjust the heat, if necessary. Turn over and fry the other side, covered, for about the same length of time, checking to make sure it does not burn. Transfer to drain on kitchen paper and keep warm on a warm serving plate.

8 Repeat steps 4–6 to prepare another cake while the first cake is being fried. Before frying a second cake, add another 15–22.5 ml (1–1½ tbsp) oil. Repeat until all 6 cakes are fried.

9 To serve, cut each cake into 6–8 pieces and serve hot. If served as an hors d'oeuvre, cut into bite-sized pieces.

NOTE: Spring onion cakes can be made ahead of time. They can be reheated either in a frying pan with a little oil or on a cake rack with a little oil spread over them in a preheated oven at 180°C (350°F) Gas Mark 4 for 10 minutes, or until hot and crisp again. They also freeze well.

FISH
AND
SHELLFISH

THE Chinese culinary approach towards fish, whether it be the species of fish that appeal to the tastebuds or the methods of cooking them, is vastly different from that of the West.

To begin with, the Chinese have a penchant for freshwater fish, harvested from rivers and lakes, or cultivated in ponds. Records show that fish farming goes back a long time. Certainly by the Tang dynasty (AD 618–907), many Chinese farmers were keeping carp in their ponds and hence were getting a cheap form of protein from them, even though they may not have realised it. They found that compared to livestock, it was relatively cheap to farm carp, for they would eat most scraps, including the droppings from silkworms that fed on mulberry leaves hanging over the ponds, not to mention bits and pieces of vegetables and other grain foodstuffs thrown in as their feed. As a result, the Chinese eat more carp than any other peoples in the world, and they wax lyrical about the delicate texture and flavour of these fish, even though other people – except Central and Eastern Europeans – dismiss them as bony, muddy and insipid.

This last point is driven home by one of the twenty-four stories of exemplary filial piety enshrined in Chinese folk literature. Wang Xiang's stepmother loved the xian or fresh taste of carp. But it was winter and so cold that the river had frozen solid, so that for all the money in the world there was no carp to be bought in the market. Even though Wang Xiang knew that Mrs Wang had no love for him because he was not her own son, he nevertheless went to the river, stripped himself completely naked and lay down on the solid ice, in the hope that the warmth from his body would melt it. This extreme filial piety must have moved the gods in heaven, for, suddenly, the ice cracked, and out jumped two lively carp, which Wang caught and took home to his stepmother. This touching gesture brought a complete change of heart on the part of Mrs Wang, who loved her stepson ever after.

Besides the carp, the other popular freshwater fish for the Chinese table are grey mullet (*Mugil cephalus*), snakehead mullet (*Ophiocephalus maculatus*), which is used to make the brothlike fish soup, freshwater bream (*Parabramis pekinesis*), catfish (*Parasilurus anomalus*) and the yellow or paddy field eel (*Monopterus albus*), which the Shanghaiese adore. There are also the seasonal fish, such as the summer shad, which is also considered a great delicacy in America. For northern Chinese, the Mandarin fish, which belongs to the perch family and has a large mouth and black stripes, ranks top of the scale, and the yellow croaker, which, when scored, dipped into a batter, then deep-fried and finished off with a sweet and sour sauce, makes the famous northern dish, the Squirrel Yellow Fish.

Not that the Chinese do not adore the more expensive sea fish, many of which are indeed familiar to the West. Among the flat fish family, sole is graphically called dragon's tongue and plaice is dubbed left-mouth fish. The groupers of the genus *Epinephelus*, whose habitat is warm tropical water, have tremendous appeal to Cantonese palates: the velvety smooth and firm yet not dry texture of the flesh makes them winners. And, in Hong Kong and Canton, the most highly rated is the polka-dot grouper (*Cromileptes altivelis*) which, however, has a much more descriptive local name of rat grouper. For a gourmet dinner or for showy entertaining, a dish of a steamed rat grouper of, say, 2 kilos (4 pounds), which serves about ten people with seven more other dishes, on its own will set you back easily £300! The family of parrot fishes, with their beaklike mouths and colourful skin, which swim among the coral reefs, are also highly regarded. Snappers, red, silver and grey etc., sea bream, sea bass, pomfret and mackerel are also esteemed, to name but a few more.

Turbot, halibut, swordfish and tuna are alien to the Chinese, but those who live abroad and come across them, have taken an instant liking to them and made them into Chinese dishes. As for salmon, they make two special dishes out of the heads, which are either made into a soup boiled with bean curd or halved then grilled or roasted in a hot oven and seasoned with rock salt. The tastiness of the latter dish is in eating the gelatinous substance around the eyes and the fatty skin itself, which, although rich, is low in if not free of cholesterol. Many Chinese hark back to the period from the 1950s to the early 1970s when they used to get their salmon heads free from the fishmongers, who used to think that they were for the cats!

As for shellfish, molluscs and crustaceans, the Chinese eat every kind that is available to them: oysters, scallops, clams and razor clams, mussels, sea slugs, snails, squids and octopuses, abalones, shrimps and prawns, crabs, winkles and crayfish. Freshwater crabs and turtles are also favourites.

The Chinese method of cooking fish could not be more different to that of the West. To steam fish is the main, and the most desirable, Chinese method. A fish is placed on a heatproof dish with slightly raised sides so that the cooked fish juices, which result from the steam, are retained as the natural sauce, to be enriched with just some oil and soy sauce. That the inherent sweetness of the fish will be drawn out while the flesh remains subtly succulent is the main reason for steaming fish; freshness is, therefore, the prerequisite to a successful outcome. By this criterion the fish should ideally be live until just before cooking. This quest for freshness has led to a sky-rocketing price for live fish in restaurants, which keep choice fish such as carp or the rat grouper alive in tanks, to await specific orders from customers.

Steaming is also the preferred method to cook many live or very fresh shellfish and crustaceans, such as crabs, prawns and scallops. Other methods, especially stir-frying, are also used in cooking fish and shellfish, as are reflected in the recipes of this chapter.

When eating fish, the Chinese way is also different to that of the West. Besides the flesh, which the Chinese break up with their chopsticks and share with other diners in the usual manner, they actually also pick up the fins and gnaw on them, sucking away the gelatinous substances before spitting out the hard bony parts. As for the fish head of a big fish, such as grouper or salmon, it is rated such a choice piece that it is usually reserved for the head of the family or for the honoured guest.

The ultimate evidence of the Chinese liking for fish fins is manifest in the exotic dishes of shark's fin soup and braised shark's fin. The first court record of using shark's fin in a state banquet dates back to the middle of the Ming dynasty (AD 1368–1644); ever since then, shark's fin has been a banquet food for those who can afford its ever climbing price. The fins from many species of sharks, the best of which swim in the Pacific Ocean, the China Sea and the Indian Ocean, are dried in the sun and preserved in lime, then graded into different types, according to colour, the size of the fin 'needles' and where the fins themselves originate, whether from the back of the shark, the tail or the sides.

The reason why the Chinese are so mad about shark's fin dishes is twofold. The texture of the fin is uniquely gelatinous, bouncy and viscous at the same time. As a food, it couldn't be more nutritious, containing between 50 and 80 per cent of protein and other properties, such as iron, phosphate and sugar, and is therefore eaten as a lusciously delicious tonic.

The other dried seafood which the Chinese love is dried abalone, which is even more expensive and just as elaborate to prepare. The best abalones are dried and preserved to an ultra-secretive formula by Japanese who cater to the Chinese market. Size is the key to the grading of this product, and the sale lingo is 'so many heads per catty' (one catty is about 550 g/1¼ lb). There is an ocean-gap between the price you pay for the kind of abalone for which you get thirty heads per catty and that for which you get three heads per catty, not to mention that the latter is rarely available.

Stir-fried Whole Scallops
with Quail Eggs

FRESH scallops, newly prised open and rinsed of the embedded sand and dirt, are delicious steamed in the shell for a few minutes until they are barely done, then seasoned with a little oil and soy sauce. The Cantonese often serve them this way. Equally often, however, they will cook them after what is termed the 'oil-explosive stir-fried' fashion, as in this recipe I have prepared.

SERVES 4 WITH 2 OTHER DISHES

12 quail eggs
12 large scallops in the shell,
  opened and rinsed
vegetable oil for deep-frying
60 ml (4 tbsp) peanut or vegetable
  oil
4 thin slices ginger, peeled
4 asparagus, rinsed and cut
  diagonally into thin slices
salt
1 very large clove garlic, peeled
  and thinly sliced
15 ml (1 tbsp) Shaoxing wine or
  medium dry sherry

1 Put the quail eggs in a pot of cold water and slowly bring to the boil. Continue boiling for about 3 minutes when the eggs will become hard-boiled. Pour into a colander and refresh under cold running water for a couple of minutes before immersing the eggs in cold water for 15 minutes or longer. This helps to separate

FOR THE SAUCE:

2.5 ml (½ tsp) potato or tapioca
  flour dissolved in 7.5 ml
  (½ tbsp) water
30 ml (2 tbsp) juice from scallops
  and chicken stock
22.5 ml (1½ tbsp) oyster sauce

the shells from the eggs, and hence makes peeling them much easier. Peel the eggs, rinse to remove all bits of shell, and leave aside for use later.

2 Separate the yellow roes from the white flesh part of the scallops. Cut off and discard the muscles from the flesh. Pat dry. With a pointed small sharp knife, insert a cross into both the top and bottom ends of each scallop.

3 Half fill a wok over a wok-stand with the oil for deep-frying and heat over a high heat until it reaches 180°C (350°F). Place the scallops, both the flesh and the roes, on a large, oiled perforated disc, carefully lower the disc into the oil until the scallops are submerged, then lift the disc from the oil and sit it on a bowl to catch the juices from the scallops. Turn off the heat. The oil can be reused 2–3 more times after being strained.

4 Heat a second wok (or frying pan) over a high heat until smoke rises. Add 15 ml (1 tbsp) of the peanut or vege-table oil and swirl it around. Add 1 slice ginger, stir, then add the asparagus and stir for about 1 minute, sprinkling with a pinch of salt to taste. Scoop on to a dish and leave nearby. Wipe clean the wok.

5 Prepare the sauce: in a small bowl place the potato or tapioca flour. Gradually stir in the juices from the scallops (and chicken stock if necessary). Add the oyster sauce and stir to mix.

6 Reheat the wok over a high heat until smoke rises. Add the remaining 45 ml (3 tbsp) oil and swirl around to cover a wide area. Add the garlic, let sizzle and take on colour, add the remaining ginger which will also sizzle. Add the scallops, both the white flesh and the roes, and, going to the bottom of the wok with a wok scoop, toss and turn for about 30 seconds when the scallops will be partially cooked. Sprinkle with salt to taste. Splash in the wine or sherry around the edges of the wok, and when the sizzling dies down, return the asparagus to the wok and stir to mix. Lower the heat, add the sauce, stirring as the sauce thickens. Scoop on to a serving dish and serve immediately.

Mussels
in Black Bean Sauce

THE versatile black bean sauce is the perfect foil for these molluscs: it brings out their inherent sweetness and adds a tangy zest to their flavour. But for the effort needed in cleaning their muddy shells, one would enjoy this cheap and tasty dish during the season every day, or at least every other day.

豉
椒
淡
菜

SERVES 4–8 WITH 2–4 OTHER DISHES

2 kilos (4½ lb) mussels
75 ml (5 tbsp) fermented black beans, rinsed
10 ml (2 tsp) sugar
90 ml (6 tbsp) peanut or vegetable oil
15–20 ml (3–4 tsp) finely chopped garlic
10 ml (2 tsp) finely chopped ginger
2 fresh green or red chillies, topped, deseeded then roughly chopped (optional)
1 green pepper, about 115 g (4 oz), topped, deseeded and cut into wedges
1 yellow or red pepper, about 115 g (4 oz), topped, deseeded and cut into wedges
30 ml (2 tbsp) Shaoxing wine or medium dry sherry
15 ml (1 tbsp) tapioca or potato flour dissolved in 30 ml (2 tbsp) water
10–15 ml (2–3 tsp) thick or dark soy sauce
30 ml (2 tbsp) sesame oil

1 One by one, wash and scrub the mussels in 3–4 changes of water until they are thoroughly clean. Pull off the 'beards' between the shells of each mussel and knock off any barnacles. Discard those that are broken. Put into a colander and drain.

2 Put the black beans into a bowl and add the sugar. Mash with a spoon until the beans become pasty.

3 Heat a wok over a high heat until smoke rises. Add the oil and swirl it around several times to cover a large area. Add the garlic, stir and let it sizzle, but before it becomes burned, add the ginger and chilli, if used, and stir again. Add the black bean paste and stir to mix. Add the pepper wedges, toss and turn them a couple of times, then add all the mussels. Going to the bottom of the wok with the wok scoop, turn and toss the mussels continuously for about 1 minute. Cover the wok with the lid and continue to cook them over high heat for 2 minutes. Remove the lid and splash in the wine or sherry, stirring and turning the mussels as it sizzles. By now, most of the mussels will have opened their shells and oozed moisture. Cover with the lid again and cook for a further 2 minutes or until all the mussels are open (discard any that remain closed).

4 Remove the lid and reduce the heat to low. Using a perforated disc or spoon, remove the mussels to a serving dish, leaving the juices in the wok.

5 Gradually dribble into the wok some or all of the dissolved tapioca or potato flour, stirring as the sauce thickens to a creamy, but not gluey, consistency. Stir in the sesame oil and remove the wok from the heat. Taste the sauce, add the soy sauce, if necessary. Pour the sauce over the mussels. Serve hot immediately.

Lettuce-wrapped
Minced Prawns

SERVES 6–8 WITH 3–5 OTHER
DISHES

450 g (1 lb) fresh or defrosted
   medium raw prawns in the shell,
   without heads (between 25–30
   prawns), shelled and de-veined
   (*see* p. 353)
1.5 ml (¼ tsp) salt
10 ml (2 tsp) cornflour
30 ml (2 tbsp) egg white
1 head crisp lettuce, Webb or
   Iceberg, trimmed and cleaned
60 ml (4 tbsp) peanut or vegetable
   oil
50 g (2 oz) Sichuan zhacai or
   preserved vegetable, trimmed
   and finely chopped
5 ml (1 tsp) finely chopped garlic

新蝦生菜包

As Sichuan zhacai, the pressed mustard greens pre-served in salt and chilli powder, is intensely salty and spicy, it enhances the natural sweetness of prawns as well as lending taste to the lettuce leaves which add a crispy touch to the dish.

1 Pat dry the prawns, leaving them damp, how-ever. Mince roughly either by hand or in a food processor. Put into a fairly large mixing bowl.

2 Add the salt and stir in the same direction for about 20 seconds. Add the cornflour and the egg white. Stir vigorously again in the same direction until the egg white is absorbed and the prawn mixture elastic – about 60 seconds. Cover the bowl and leave in the refrigerator for 1 hour or longer in order to firm up the texture.

3 Arrange the lettuce leaves, preferably cup-shaped, on a serving plate and place on the dining table.

4 Heat a wok until hot. Add 15 ml (1 tbsp) of the oil and swirl it around. Add the chopped Sichuan preserved vegetable and stir for a few seconds. Scoop on to a small dish and keep nearby. Wipe clean the wok.

5 Reheat the wok over a high heat until smoke rises. Add the remaining 45 ml (3 tbsp) oil and swirl to cover a large area. Add the garlic which will sizzle. Add the prawn and, using the wok scoop, stir, turning as well as breaking up the mass as much as possible. Add the Sichuan preserved vegetable and continue to stir and mix until the prawn has turned pink, indicating that it is cooked. Scoop the mixture on to a serving dish and place next to the lettuce.

6 To eat, each person takes 1 piece of lettuce at a time, spoons some prawn on to the lettuce, wraps it around the prawn, then picks up the package with their fingers.

Stir-fried Prawns
with Broadbeans

YOU can have your own variations of stir-fried prawns as long as you follow the three essential steps: marinating the prawns (step 1), lightly deep-frying them (step 6) and stir-frying them (step 7). For example, you can substitute garden peas for broadbeans, or, in making the sauce, add some oyster sauce as the Cantonese are wont to do, or, just before stir-frying the prawns, use some chopped garlic to season the oil, and, as an extreme measure to make the dish peppery hot, use hot soy bean paste and fresh chillies with the garlic.

SERVES 10 WITH 5 OTHER DISHES

900 g (2 lb) medium raw prawns (25–30 per 450 g (1 lb) in the shell, without heads, peeled and de-veined (*see* p. 353)
450 g (1 lb) frozen broadbeans
salt
150 ml (5 fl oz/⅔ cup) prime stock (*see* p. 361)
60 ml (4 tbsp) peanut or vegetable oil
vegetable oil for deep-frying

FOR THE MARINADE:
5 ml (1 tsp) salt
10 ml (2 tsp) cornflour
30 ml (2 tbsp) egg white, lightly beaten

FOR THE SAUCE:
150–175 ml (5–6 fl oz/⅔–¾ cup) stock, including the drained bean-poaching liquid
10 ml (2 tsp) tapioca or potato flour dissolved in 10 ml (2 tsp) water
salt to taste

Illustrated on Plate 8.

1 Marinate the prawns. Put the prawns in a large mixing bowl, add the salt and stir vigorously in the same direction for up to 1 minute until the prawns feel elastic. Sprinkle with the cornflour and add the egg white. Stir again vigorously until both are absorbed. Cover the bowl and refrigerate for 2 hours or, for best effect, overnight.

2 Blanch the frozen broadbeans in a pot of boiling salted (5–10 ml/1–2 tsp salt) water for about 1 minute. Pour into a colander and refresh under running cold water.

3 Shell the broadbeans: using a pointed knife, make an incision on the seam of each bean and squeeze it out. Discard the husks.

4 Poach the beans. Put the beans into a saucepan. Add the prime stock, salt to taste and 15 ml (1 tbsp) of oil, bring to the boil, then simmer for about 5 minutes so that the beans will absorb the flavour of the stock. Drain, but reserve the liquid.

5 Prepare the sauce. In a small bowl gradually add the stock to the dissolved tapioca or potato flour, stirring to mix. Add salt to taste. Put aside.

6 Half fill a wok on a wok-stand with vegetable oil and heat over a high heat until it reaches 180°C (350°F) in temperature. Meanwhile, loosen the prawns in the bowl, then carefully add them to the oil, separating with wooden chopsticks or spoons. Deep-fry for about 30 seconds or until the prawns have curled up and turned pink. Remove with a large perforated disc and put on to

a dish. Turn off the heat. The oil can be reused 2–3 more times after being strained.

7 Heat a second wok (or frying pan) over a high heat until smoke rises. Add the remaining 45 ml (3 tbsp) peanut or vegetable oil and swirl it around. Return the prawns and stir for about 30–60 seconds, or until very hot. Reduce the heat, then add the well-stirred sauce, stirring and mixing as the sauce thickens. Remove the prawns to a large serving dish, leaving some sauce behind in the wok.

8 Return the broadbeans to the wok and heat until very hot. Scoop them up and arrange them either around the prawns or on the right and left hand sides of them. Serve hot immediately.

Crabmeat Cellophane Noodles

SERVES 6–8 WITH 3–4 OTHER DISHES

170 g (6 oz) cellophane or glass noodles
105 ml (7 tbsp) peanut or vegetable oil
12 thin slices ginger, peeled
675 g (1½ lb) Chinese celery cabbage (Chinese leaves), cut crossways at about 1 cm (½ in) intervals
salt
about 450 ml (15 fl oz/2 cups) chicken stock
4–6 spring onions, trimmed and cut into 3.5 cm (1½ in) sections, white and green parts separated
225 g (8 oz) cooked brown crabmeat (crab roe); if frozen, thoroughly defrosted and drained
225 g (8 oz) cooked white crabmeat; if frozen, thoroughly defrosted and drained

PEOPLE living in southern and eastern China are very fond of eating steamed whole freshwater crabs or using crabmeat, with its inherently sweet taste, to season stir-fried vegetables. When they live abroad and cannot get hold of freshwater crabs, they use crabmeat to season local vegetables, such as asparagus or mange-tout. I am very fond of both cellophane noodles and Chinese celery cabbage, and I find that crabmeat and roe go a long way to make these otherwise totally tasteless noodles very appetising indeed. Furthermore, as this dish is a cross between a stir-fried and a braised dish, you can prepare it ahead of time.

1 Using a pair of scissors, cut the wiry cellophane noodles into shorter lengths, say about 7.5 cm (3 in) for easier handling when eating them. Put them into a large bowl and steep in plenty of very hot or boiling water for 30 minutes or longer. Drain.

2 Heat a large, heavy-bottomed saucepan over a high heat until very hot. Add 45 ml (3 tbsp) of the oil and swirl to cover the entire bottom. Add 5 slices of the ginger, stir and let sizzle to release the aroma. Add the cabbage and

stir for 20–30 seconds, lowering the heat to medium if it starts to burn. Sprinkle on 2.5 ml (½ tsp) salt, stirring to mix. Add the cellophane noodles and pour in the stock. Bring to the boil, then simmer over a low heat, covered, for about 10–12 minutes until some (or most) of the stock has been absorbed. (This dish can be prepared up to this point in advance and reheated just before step 3.)

3 Heat a wok over a high heat until smoke rises. Add the remaining 60 ml (4 tbsp) oil and swirl it around to cover a large area. Add the remaining ginger, stir and let sizzle, then add the white spring onions and stir again to release their aroma. Add the brown crabmeat, stir, then the white crabmeat and stir and mix, incorporating the oil. Reduce the heat and continue to cook for 1–2 minutes until very hot. Season with about 1.5 ml (¼ tsp) salt, the soy sauce and the oyster sauce. Stir to mix and cook for another minute. Add the sesame oil and green spring onions and remove the wok from the heat.

4 Transfer the cellophane noodles and cabbage to a large serving bowl or dish. Add the crabmeat on top. Alternatively, serve in two separate bowls and let people help themselves. Add ground white or black peppercorns to taste. Serve hot.

NOTE: This can also be served as a starter instead of soup, if you wish.

10–15 ml (2–3 tsp) thin or light soy sauce
15–22.5 ml (1–1½ tbsp) oyster sauce
15 ml (1 tbsp) sesame oil
ground white or black peppercorns

Steamed Grey Mullet
with Preserved Lime

A RURAL dish from the Chaozhou region with its distinctive cuisine, which is quite different from the mainstream Cantonese cuisine. The predominant seasoning, lime preserved in brine, would overpower fish with a finer taste and texture, but it works wonders with grey mullet. No surprise then that Chaozhou people love it.

It may be as well to point out that lime in Chinese is 'green lemon', and this may explain why the label on a jar of preserved limes actually reads 'preserved

SERVES 2–4 WITH 1–2 OTHER DISHES

1 grey mullet, about 675 g (1½ lb), scaled and gutted
1–1½ preserved limes in brine
10 ml (2 tsp) ginger juice or purée (see p. 357)
45 ml (3 tbsp) peanut or vegetable oil

lemon in brine', even though the fruit is definitely lime rather than lemon. Sorry about that!

1 Using a fairly strong brush, remove the black membrane lining the cavity of the grey mullet, thereby eliminating the bitter and rank odour. Rinse, then pat dry the fish.
2 Make 3–4 diagonal slashes across both sides of the fish and put it on a heatproof serving dish with slightly raised edges. If your wok or steamer is rather small, the fish can be halved and the two halves laid side by side on the dish.
3 Halve the lime, remove the seeds and core. Shred into thin strips.
4 Rub the ginger juice or purée on both sides of the fish. Put the lime on the skin and crevices of both sides of the fish as well as in the cavity. This can be done 30–60 minutes in advance.
5 Place the dish with the fish in the steamer and steam (*see* p. 355) for about 6 minutes or until cooked, the flesh flaking easily. Turn off the heat and remove the dish from the steamer.
6 Heat the oil in a small saucepan until smoke rises. Dribble it, little by little, on to the fish. Serve immediately.

Clear-steamed
Seasonal Fish

SERVES 6–8 WITH 3–4 OTHER DISHES

1 sea bass or grouper, 1 kilo (2¼ lb) or 1 baby turbot, 1.35–1.5 kilos (3–3½ lb), cleaned, with head left on
2.5–4 ml (½–¾ tsp) salt
2–3 spring onions, trimmed and left whole
15–22.5 ml (1–1½ tbsp) finely shredded ginger

Illustrated on Plate 12.

THE fresher and the more valued the fish, the more likely are the Chinese, both in the north and in the south, to cook it in the simplest yet most sophisticated way. Even though this technique is called clear-steaming, sliced ham or preserved and chopped cabbage are sometimes added to enhance the flavours. In China, mandarin fish and marine groupers are often prepared in this way, and in the West sea bass and baby turbot.

1 Pat the fish dry. Rub the salt all over the skin of the fish. Line a heatproof serving dish with slightly raised sides with the whole spring onions and then place the fish on

top. This will allow a gap for better circulation of the steam to cook the fish. Spread the shredded ginger on the fish (and also the preserved cabbage if using baby turbot). If your steamer is not large enough, you can halve the fish and put the two halves side by side.

2 Place the dish in a steamer and steam (*see* p. 355) over a high heat for 8–14 minutes or until the fish is just cooked and the flesh is flaking from the main bone. Remove the lid of the steamer. If too much water from the steam has collected on the dish, use kitchen paper to dab off about half of it.

3 Spread first the green parts then the white parts of spring onion over the fish.

4 Heat the oil in a small saucepan until smoke rises. Pour it, little by little, over the spring onion. The sizzling oil partially cooks it, releasing the fragrance.

5 Remove the dish with the fish from the steamer. Add the soy sauce. Garnish with the coriander leaves, if used. Serve hot immediately.

25–40 g (1–1½ oz) Tianjin preserved cabbage (for baby turbot only)

7–10 spring onions, trimmed, cut into 5 cm (2 in) sections, finely shredded and white and green parts separated

75–90 ml (5–6 tbsp) peanut or vegetable oil

45–60 ml (3–4 tbsp) thin or light soy sauce

coriander leaves for garnish (optional)

Sea Bream
with Small Clams

EVEN though steaming is the method most frequently used by the Chinese to cook fish, an alternative method is poaching and in this recipe the stock and the clam juice add much sweetness to the bream poached in it.

1 Scrub the clam shells hard, then rinse. Soak the clams in plenty of salted cold water for 2 hours so that the clams will spit out the sand embedded in them. Drain and rinse with cold water. Repeat this process, if necessary, to make sure the clams are clean and free of sand.

2 Using a pointed knife, make 4 diagonal cuts on one side of the bream. Rub the ginger juice over the fish and into the crevices.

3 Heat a wok over a high heat until smoke rises. Add the oil and swirl it around to cover a large area. Add the ginger, let sizzle to release its aroma. Add the clams, stir

鯿
魚
蛤
蜊

SERVES 4–6 WITH 2–3 OTHER DISHES

450 g (1 lb) small clams
salted cold water
1 bream, about 675 g (1½ lb), cleaned
10 ml (2 tsp) ginger juice (*see* p. 357)
45–60 ml (3–4 tbsp) peanut or vegetable oil
4 thick slices ginger, peeled
about 750 ml (1¼ pints/3 cups) prime or seafood stock (*see* p. 361)
salt to taste

and turn for about a dozen times. Pour in the stock, bring to the boil, and continue to cook, covered, for 20–30 seconds or until the clams are cooked. They are cooked when opened. Discard those that remain recalcitrantly closed even after a longer period of cooking. Remove the wok from the heat and scoop up the clams with a slotted spoon, leaving the stock in the wok. Keep the clams warm.

4 Taste the stock and season with salt to taste. Place the fish in the stock which should just cover it. If necessary, add more. Bring to the boil, then poach at a simmer, covered, for about 8–10 minutes until the fish is just cooked, the flesh flaking from the bone. Remove the fish to a large serving dish, arrange the clams on either side then pour the boiling juices over them. Serve hot.

VARIATION: Parrot Fish with Small Clams. A parrot fish is so called because its beaky mouth looks like that of a parrot. As its skin, even after being scaled, is still prettily rainbow-coloured, it makes a visually attractive dish with small clams. Follow the same procedure as above.

Red-braised
Cuttlefish

THIS rich Shanghai dish does our appetite proud in the cold winter, with the strong flavour of the red bean curd cheese mellowed by the Shaoxing wine and sugar.

紅烤墨魚

1 cuttlefish, 1.2 kilos (2½ lb), after cleaning, about 675 g (1½ lb)

170 g (6 oz) pork, leg or other joint, cut into 3 mm (⅛ in) thick slices

1 knob ginger, 1 cm (½ in), peeled and bruised

45 ml (3 tbsp) peanut or vegetable oil

30 ml (2 tbsp) finely chopped ginger

4–5 large spring onions, trimmed and cut into 4 cm (1½ in) sections, white and green parts separated

30 ml (2 tbsp) Shaoxing wine or medium dry sherry

2 cakes (each about 3 cm/1¼ in square) red bean curd cheese, mashed

7.5 ml (1½ tsp) sugar

100 ml (4 fl oz/½ cup chicken) stock

FOR THE MARINADE:

1.5 ml (¼ tsp) salt

5 ml (1 tsp) thick or dark soy sauce

6 turns peppermill

5 ml (1 tsp) Shaoxing wine or medium dry sherry

2.5 ml (½ tsp) tapioca or potato flour

1 Ask your fishmonger to clean the cuttlefish for you. But if you have to do it yourself, use a sharp knife to slit open the body, remove the viscera and bones with your hands. Wash off the ink. Cut into rectangular pieces about 2 × 3.5 cm (¾ × 1½ in) in size, leaving the tentacles whole or in sections.

2 Marinate the pork. Add the salt, soy sauce, pepper, wine or sherry and tapioca or potato flour to the pork and stir to mix well. Leave to stand for 15–20 minutes.

3 Blanch the cuttlefish. Add the knob of ginger to a large pot of water and bring it to the boil. Add the cuttlefish and return to the boil until the scum rises to the surface. Pour into a colander and refresh under cold running water, rinsing off the scum and the ink.

4 Heat a heavy-bottomed saucepan or casserole until very hot. Add the oil and swirl to cover the entire bottom. Add the ginger, stir, add the white spring onion, and stir to release the aroma. Add the pork, stir 6–7 times, then splash in the wine and sherry and let sizzle. Add the mashed bean curd cheese and the sugar, stir to mix. Add the cuttlefish, continuing to stir. Pour the stock into the bean curd cheese bowl, scrape and rinse, then pour into the saucepan. Bring to the boil, reduce the heat and simmer gently, covered, for about 30 minutes, at the end of which both pork and cuttlefish should be succulently tender. While simmering, water will ooze from the cuttlefish so that there is quite a lot of liquid in the pot. Scoop up the fish and pork and reduce the sauce over a high heat until a thickish consistency is achieved. Return the cuttlefish and pork to the sauce and stir to coat, then remove everything to a serving dish and serve hot.

Dry-fried
Dover Sole

SERVES 4 WITH 2 OTHER DISHES

1 large Dover sole, about 800–
    900 g (1¾–2 lb), cleaned and
    skinned on both sides
15 ml (1 tbsp) plain flour
1 egg, lightly beaten
250 ml ((8 fl oz/1 cup) peanut or
    vegetable oil
1–2 large cloves garlic, peeled and
    cut into slivers

FOR THE MARINADE:
10 ml (2 tsp) Shaoxing wine or
    medium dry sherry
15 ml (1 tbsp) sesame oil
10 ml (2 tsp) salt

FOR THE SAUCE:
15–22.5 ml (1–1½ tbsp) finely
    chopped ginger
4–5 spring onions, trimmed and
    cut into small rounds
2.5–5 ml (½–1 tsp) sugar
22.5 ml (1½ tbsp) Shaoxing wine
    or medium dry sherry

DURING one of my visits to Peking, I ate in a Shandong restaurant a sautéed flat fish which rather took my fancy. Using the UK's best, the Dover sole, with its firm texture and subtle flavour, I find that it is a delicious success.

1 Pat dry the fish. With a pointed knife, make large criss-cross lines on both sides of the fish without cutting deep into the flesh.

2 Marinate the fish. Brush both sides of the fish with the wine or sherry and sesame oil, halving the amount for each side. Likewise, sprinkle the salt on both sides. Leave to stand for 1–1½ hours.

3 Prepare the sauce. Mix together the ginger, spring onion, sugar and wine or sherry in a small bowl. Put aside.

4 When ready to cook the fish, sprinkle the plain flour on both sides, then brush all over with the beaten egg.

5 Heat a wok over a high heat until smoke rises in abundance. Pour in the oil, carefully swirl it around to cover a large area, then pour it back into a container, leaving about 30 ml (2 tbsp) behind. This prevents the fish from sticking. Carefully lower the fish into the wok and, tilting the wok in different positions, let the oil reach all over the fish. Lower the heat to medium and fry the fish for 5 minutes or longer until golden. With the wok scoop and perhaps also another spatula turn the fish over. Drip along the edges of the fish another 15–30 ml (1–2 tbsp) oil and fry for another 5 minutes or longer until the other side is also golden. The fish should be cooked by now. Lift the fish on to a serving dish.

6 Wipe clean the wok. Reheat over a high heat until smoke rises. Add 30 ml (2 tbsp) oil and swirl it around. Add the garlic, stir until it takes on colour. Pour in the sauce and cook over a low heat until the sugar is melted. Pour the sauce on to the fish. Serve immediately.

Shanghai
Stir-fried Eel

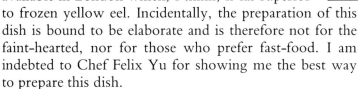

USING yellow or rice paddy field eel, the Shanghai stir-fried eel, with its finishing touch of oil-sizzled minced garlic placed in the centre of the dish, has a fame of its own, unrivalled by any other eel dish in the rest of the country. At the risk of being upbraided by purists, I am reproducing the dish using white eel, or what is available in London which, I think, is far superior to frozen yellow eel. Incidentally, the preparation of this dish is bound to be elaborate and is therefore not for the faint-hearted, nor for those who prefer fast-food. I am indebted to Chef Felix Yu for showing me the best way to prepare this dish.

SERVES 6–8 WITH 3–5 OTHER DISHES

1 white or silver live eel, about 1 kilo (1¼ lb)
225 g (8 oz) bean sprouts, topped and tailed
7.5 ml (1½ tsp) salt
67.5 ml (4½ tbsp) peanut oil
3–4 large cloves garlic, peeled and crushed
4 thick slices ginger, peeled
3 large spring onions, white parts only, cut into 2.5 cm (1 in) sections
15 ml (1 tbsp) Shaoxing wine or medium dry sherry
10–15 ml (2–3 tsp) puréed garlic
22.5 ml (1½ tbsp) sesame oil
7.5–10 ml (1½–2 tsp) Sichuan peppercorns
ground white or black peppercorns

FOR THE SAUCE:
5 ml (1 tsp) tapioca or potato flour dissolved in 15 ml (1 tbsp) water
60 ml (4 tbsp) prime stock (see p. 361)
30 ml (2 tbsp) thick or dark soy sauce

1 Ask your fishmonger to kill and gut the eel for you, chopping off and discarding the head. During the next 1–2 hours, if you touch the eel, it will still respond with jerky muscular reflex movements which may be quite offputting. The best thing to do is to take it home in a well-tied plastic bag and leave it in a cool place for 1–2 hours before tackling it.

2 Debone the eel. Using plenty of dry kitchen paper, rub off some of the slime on the skin of the eel so that you can hold and work with it. Lay it flat on a work surface with its fin facing upward and in the centre and hold it firmly with one hand. With a very sharp boning knife, make a decisive incision along one side of the fin down to the backbone; sliding the knife against the backbone, cut through the skin and flesh and gradually remove one whole side of the eel from the top to the tail end. Do likewise with the other side which is a more difficult task at first, because you have to work without the balance of the other side of flesh. Patience, however, will reward you with 2 strips of eel.

3 Skin the eel. Place 1 strip of eel on the work surface, flesh side up, the tail end close to yourself. Hold the tip of the tail with one hand and with the other hand insert a knife at an angle between the skin and the flesh. Moving the knife forward, separate the flesh from the skin. It is

remarkable how easily the skin comes away from the flesh. Do likewise with the other strip.

4 Cut the eel fillets crossways at 5 cm (2 in) intervals, then cut each piece lengthways into strips about 8 mm (⅓ in) wide.

5 Plunge the strips into a pot of hot (definitely not boiling or even simmering) water for a few seconds to cleanse them of blood and impurities. Pour into a colander to drain.

6 Blanch the bean sprouts. Bring a pot of water to the boil. Add 5 ml (1 tsp) of the salt and 15 ml (1 tbsp) of the oil. Add the bean sprouts and blanch for about 10 seconds. Pour into a colander, drain well, then pat dry.

7 Prepare the sauce. In a small bowl combine the dissolved tapioca or potato flour, the stock and the soy sauce, stirring to blend.

8 Heat a wok over a high heat until smoke rises. Add 45 ml (3 tbsp) of the remaining oil and swirl it around. Add the garlic, let it sizzle and take on colour, add the ginger and the spring onions and fry them until brown, almost burned. With a perforated spoon, remove and discard them, leaving the seasoned oil in the wok.

Add the eel to the oil and, going to the bottom of the wok with the wok scoop, toss and turn for about 20 seconds. Sprinkle with the remaining salt, then splash in the wine or sherry around the sides of the wok. When the sizzling subsides, pour in the well-stirred sauce, stirring as the eel absorbs the thickening sauce. Add the bean sprouts, tossing and turning to mix until very hot. Remove the mixture to a large serving dish. Make a well in the centre of the dish and place the puréed garlic in it.

9 In a small saucepan heat the sesame oil and the remaining 7.5 ml (½ tbsp) peanut oil until smoke rises. Remove from the heat and wait until the smoke has disappeared. Add the Sichuan peppercorns which will sizzle but may also fly out of the saucepan if the oil is still too hot, so please take care. Pour the oil through a small wire sieve on to the garlic which will be partially cooked, exuding a fragrant aroma. Discard the peppercorns. Add as many turns of ground white or black pepper as you wish. Serve hot immediately.

Braised
Conger Eel

In 1988 when I was in Hong Kong, I had the good fortune of being treated to the rarely encountered dish of braised giant eel (dai sin in Cantonese), cooked no less by the 'abalone king' and restaurateur, Chef Yang Koon-yat. As the expert food journalist Willy Mark and I savoured the treat, Mr Yang regaled us with the story of how the giant eel was flooded out of an estuary of the Pearl River into the rice fields and was subsequently caught and shipped to Hong Kong, ending up in the sandpot of his restaurant. The succulence of the flesh, made the more fragrant by the roast belly pork, dried mushrooms, tangerine peel and deep-fried garlic – the usual ingredients Cantonese use to braise eel – defies description and yet is unforgettable.

Back in London, as I hankered after the taste, it occurred to me to try out conger eel (moon sin) as a 'poor man's' substitute. Not that conger eel can ever come anywhere near giant eel, but, to my happy surprise, braising it this way has elevated it from being an ordinary to a gourmet food.

Instead of conger eel steaks, you can also use a live eel, preferably a large one, for the wider the diameter of the body, the richer its taste and the more succulent its flesh.

1 Remove and discard the blood clots and fatty blubber in the centre of the conger eel steaks, if any. Rinse off any blood stains on the eel and pat dry.
2 Remove the black mushrooms from the soaking liquid and halve them. Put aside.
3 Soak the tangerine peel pieces in plenty of cold water for 1–2 hours or until pliable again. Drain. Using a small knife, scrape off the pithy layer on the inside of the peel. Halve each piece and put aside.
4 Put the flour into a small shaker with a wire mesh top. Using the shaker, dust both sides of the eel steaks with a thin film of flour. There is no need to use up all the flour.
5 Half fill a wok over a wok-stand with vegetable oil and heat over a high heat until the temperature reaches

红
烧
海
鳗

SERVES 8 WITH 3 OTHER DISHES

4 large steaks conger eel, each about 2.5 cm (1 in) thick and 350 g (12 oz)
12–15 medium dried Chinese black mushrooms, reconstituted (see p. 353)
1 whole (3 pieces) dried tangerine peel
22.5 ml (1½ tbsp) plain white flour
vegetable oil for deep-frying
2–3 bulbs large-cloved garlic, peeled
30 ml (2 tbsp) peanut or vegetable oil
115 g (4 oz) roast belly pork, cut crossways into strips
15 ml (1 tbsp) Shaoxing wine or medium dry sherry
300 ml (10 fl oz/1¼ cup) chicken stock
15 ml (1 tbsp) thin or light soy sauce
15 ml (1 tbsp) thick or dark soy sauce
15 ml (1 tbsp) oyster sauce

180°C (350°F). Put all the garlic cloves into a wire sieve, lower it into the oil and deep-fry for 1–2 minutes or until the cloves are brown. Lift the sieve from the oil and put aside.

6 Reheat the oil until it reaches 190°C (375°F). Carefully lower the eel steaks into the oil and deep-fry them for about 6–8 minutes, turning them over once. Remove with a large hand strainer or perforated disc to a dish. The oil can be reused 2–3 more times after being strained.

7 Heat a large saucepan or casserole with a heavy bottom until very hot. Add the peanut or vegetable oil and swirl to cover the entire surface. Add the mushrooms and stir 6–7 times, then add the roast pork and stir a few more times. Add the eel steaks, splash in the wine or sherry and pour in the stock. Season with the soy sauces and oyster sauce, add the tangerine peel and bring to a simmer. Reduce the heat to low and continue to simmer for about 25 minutes. Remove the lid, carefully turn the steaks over, check the stock, adding more if necessary. Make room in the centre and add all the garlic. Continue to simmer, covered, for another 10–15 minutes until the garlic melts in the mouth. Remove everything to a serving dish, arranging all the garlic in the centre, and pour the juices over. Serve hot.

Five-willow Fish

SERVES 6–8 WITH 3–4 OTHER DISHES

1 fish with firm flesh such as red snapper, black bream, sea bass, 1–1.1 kilo (2¼–2½ lb) when cleaned
2.5–5 ml (½–1 tsp) salt
10 ml (2 tsp) ginger juice (see p. 357)
about 30 ml (2 tbsp) plain flour
60–75 ml (4–5 tbsp) peanut or vegetable oil for frying

A CANTONESE way of preparing fish with a sweet and sour sauce served both at home or in a restaurant. 'Five-willow' is the poetic name given to herbs and pickles of different hues and flavours used for the sauce. In south China, when you wish to make this dish, you go to a specialty store and ask for the five-willow sauce ingredients, and the store-keeper will make up the proportion for you. I have taken on the role of the store keeper and detailed below the different ingredients, all of which, except for the carrots, are available in a can or jar in Chinese stores, so that all that you need to do is follow the cooking instructions.

1 Make 3–4 diagonal and shallow slits on both sides of the fish. Rub both sides with the salt and ginger juice and leave to stand for about 20 minutes.

2 Prepare the sauce. In a bowl gradually add the stock or water to the tapioca or potato flour, stirring to dissolve it. Stir in the tomato paste, rice vinegar, sugar, salt and soy sauce. Keep nearby.

   Heat a wok over a high heat until smoke rises. Add the oil and swirl it around. Add the spring onions and stir rapidly to release their aroma. Reduce the heat to medium, add the chilli, shallot, ginger and cucumber and stir to mix until hot. Pour in the well-stirred liquid in the bowl and continue to stir as it thickens. Pour into a dish and keep nearby. Wash and dry the wok.

3 Dust both sides of the fish with a thin layer of the flour, covering the head and tail as well.

   Reheat the wok over a high heat until smoke rises. Add 45 ml (3 tbsp) of the oil and swirl it around to cover a very large area. Carefully lower the fish into the wok and brown one side for about 1–2 minutes. Slipping the wok scoop underneath the fish, turn it over and brown the other side for 1–2 more minutes. Reduce the heat, and continue to fry the fish for 10–15 minutes on each side until cooked. Stream in along the side of the wok 15–30 ml (1–2 tbsp) oil during the frying. Remove on to a serving platter. Discard the burned oil left in the wok and wash it.

4 Reheat the sauce in the wok and pour it over the fish. Serve immediately.

FOR THE FIVE-WILLOW SAUCE:

300 ml (10 fl oz/1¼ cups) fish stock or water

45 ml (1 tbsp) tapioca or potato flour

20 ml (4 tsp) tomato paste

60 ml (4 tbsp) Chinese rice vinegar

45–60 ml (3–4 tbsp) sugar

2.5 ml (½ tsp) salt

10 ml (2 tsp) thin or light soy sauce

45 ml (3 tbsp) peanut or vegetable oil

6 spring onions, trimmed, cut into 5 cm (2 in) sections then shredded

2 long red chillies, deseeded and cut lengthways into thin strips

6 large pickled shallots or 3–4 large pickled onions, drained and cut into slivers

50 g (2 oz) pickled ginger slivers, drained and cut into strips

50–85 g (2–3 oz) preserved cucumber in syrup, drained and cut into slivers

Illustrated on Plate 16.

Stir-fried Squid
with Pickled Mustard Greens

1 large squid, about 675 g
   (1½–2 lb) , net weight about
   450 g (1 lb) when cleaned
60 ml (4 tbsp) peanut or vegetable
   oil
1 large red pepper, trimmed,
   cored and cut into wedges
2 large cloves garlic, peeled and
   cut into slices
22.5 ml (1½ tbsp) fermented
   black beans, rinsed and partially
   mashed
3 spring onions, trimmed and cut
   diagonally at 2.5 cm (1 in)
   intervals, white and green parts
   separated
225 g (8 oz) pickled mustard
   greens, rinsed and shredded into
   slices
15 ml (1 tbsp) Shaoxing wine or
   medium dry sherry
2.5 ml (½ tsp) potato or tapioca
   flour dissolved in 30 ml (2 tbsp)
   water

CHINESE pickled mustard greens, even though often labelled salted mustard greens, is actually both salty and sour. It is therefore most effective in adding a zest to ingredients with a subtle taste which needs to be brought out, as in the case of squid. In cooking squid try to achieve a bouncily crisp yet tender texture rather than a chewy, rubber-bandlike one, by following the method below.

1 Remove the reddish membranes covering the squid, if not already done. Slit open lengthways the body pouch of the squid. Remove the transparent bones and any slippery remains of the innards; discard. Rinse in cold water.

2 Turn the body pouch inside out. Lay it flat and, using the pointed edge of a knife, score in a criss-cross pattern. Do likewise to the wing piece. Cut into pieces about 5 × 2.5 cm (2 × 1 in). Cut the tentacles into 4 cm (1½ in) sections.

3 Half fill a wok with cold water and bring it to the boil. Add the squid which will curl up almost instantly. Leave for about 10 seconds, but before the water returns to a boil, pour into a colander, then rinse the squid under cold running water. This will make the squid crisp and tender. Drain thoroughly and pat dry the squid.

4 Rinse and dry the wok, then reheat over a medium heat until hot. Add 7.5 ml (½ tbsp) oil. Add the red pepper and fry for 2 minutes until it is lightly cooked yet retains a bite. Remove to a dish and keep nearby.

5 Wipe clean the wok. Reheat over a high heat until smoke rises. Add the remaining oil and swirl it around to cover a large area of the wok. Add the garlic, let it sizzle and take on colour but before it gets burned, add the black beans and stir 6–7 times. Add the white spring onion, stir, then add the mustard greens, continuing to stir until very hot. Add the squid, flip and turn with the wok scoop and return the red pepper to the wok, continuing to stir and turn until very hot. Splash in the wine or sherry, still stirring as the sizzling subsides. Reduce

the heat to medium, add the dissolved and well-stirred potato or tapioca flour, stirring as it thickens with the juices in the wok. Add the green spring onion, stir a couple more times, then scoop everything on to a large serving dish. Serve hot.

Peking
Vinegary Carp

'MILK' stock is often used in Peking dishes, and so is vinegar. The combination of the two of them, seasoned with a little bit of salt, works subtle wonders for a carp. Common carps are available from Western fishmongers, and they are popular with Eastern Europeans. They are kept, live, in tanks in some Chinese restaurants and markets.

北京醋鯉

SERVES 4–6 WITH 2–3 OTHER DISHES

1 common carp, 550–675 g (1¼–1½ lb), gutted and cleaned
45–60 ml (3–4 tbsp) peanut or vegetable oil
22.5 ml (1½ tbsp) finely chopped ginger
5 spring onions, trimmed and cut into 3.5–5 cm (1½–2 in) sections then shredded
22.5 ml (1½ tbsp) Shaoxing wine or medium dry sherry
450 ml (15 fl oz/2 cups) 'milk' stock (see p. 362)
12 turns white peppermill
5 ml (1 tsp) salt
2 branches coriander leaves, trimmed and torn up
30 ml (2 tbsp) Chinese rice vinegar or to taste
10 ml (2 tsp) sesame oil

1 Put the carp on a chopping board. Using a sharp knife, make 3–4 diagonal criss-cross cuts all the way to the bone on both sides of the fish.
2 Half fill a wok with water, bring to the boil and continue boiling. Holding the fish by the tail, slip it into the water and blanch for about 20 seconds when the criss-cross cuts will become more apparent, revealing the flesh. Remove the fish with a large perforated disc and put on a dish. Discard the water in the wok, wash and dry it.
3 Reheat the wok over a high heat until smoke rises. Add the oil and swirl it around. Add the ginger and stir, then the spring onion and stir together to release their aroma. Splash in the wine or sherry and let sizzle for a few seconds. Reduce the heat and add the stock, gradually bringing it to a simmer. Season with the white pepper and salt.
4 Return the fish to the wok and bring the stock to a simmer again. Put on the wok lid, continue to simmer for 5 minutes; turn the fish over and simmer, covered, for another 5 minutes. The carp should be cooked by now.
5 Remove the fish to a serving dish with curved edges. Arrange the coriander leaves on either side.

6 Gradually stir the vinegar into the sauce still in the wok, tasting for the subtle vinegary flavour coming through the sauce, and adjust the amount accordingly. Pour it over the fish and the coriander leaves. Sprinkle the carp with the sesame oil and serve hot straightaway.

Steamed Grey Mullet
with Puréed Black Bean Sauce

SERVES 4 WITH 2 OTHER DISHES

1 grey mullet, about 675–800 g (1½–1¾ lb), cleaned, head left on
6–8 slices ginger, peeled
3–4 spring onions, trimmed and halved
45–60 ml (3–4 tbsp) peanut or vegetable oil
1–2 branches coriander leaves, trimmed, leaves only

FOR THE BLACK BEAN SAUCE:
45 ml (3 tbsp) fermented black beans
30 ml (2 tbsp) chicken stock
15 ml (1 tbsp) thick or dark soy sauce
2.5 ml (½ tsp) sugar
7.5 ml (1½ tsp) Shaoxing wine or medium dry sherry
8 turns black peppermill

THE black bean sauce is a tasty foil to the grey mullet, which is an affordable fish for everybody.

1 Prepare the black bean sauce. Put the black beans and the chicken stock in a heatproof dish with sloping edges and steam (*see* p. 355) for 15 minutes. Remove from the steamer and mash the beans until reduced to a purée. Push the purée through a fine sieve and discard the husk residue in the sieve. Add the soy sauce, sugar, wine or sherry and ground pepper to the purée, stirring to a smooth consistency. Put aside.

2 Steam the fish. If the grey mullet is too long for the steamer, cut it into 2 halves, then place them side by side on a heatproof serving dish with raised edges. Place the ginger and spring onions inside the cavity of the fish. Put the dish in the steamer and steam (*see* p. 355), over a high heat, for 8–10 minutes or until the fish is just done, the flesh flaking from the main bone. Remove the steamer from the heat. Remove and discard the ginger and spring onion from the fish. Keep the fish warm.

3 Pour 30 ml (2 tbsp) of the fish juice (the result of the steaming) into the black bean sauce. Stir to mix. If there is still too much juice in the fish dish, pour some off.

4 Heat a wok over a high heat until smoke rises. Add the oil and swirl it around. Lower the heat and pour in the black bean sauce, stirring to emulsify. As soon as the sauce simmers, remove from the heat and lace it over the fish. Float the coriander leaves on the sauce on either side of the fish. Serve hot immediately.

Monkfish
with Spicy Bean Paste

EVEN though monkfish is unfamiliar to the Chinese, its firm texture makes it most suitable to be turned into a Sichuan dish with the spicy and penetrating flavours. The dish never fails to awaken the appetite.

豆
辦
和
尚
魚

SERVES 8–10 WITH 5–6 OTHER DISHES

1.1 kilos (2½ lb) monkfish, top end
about 250 ml (8 fl oz/1 cup) vegetable oil
45–60 ml (3–4 tbsp) peanut oil
7.5 ml (1½ tsp) finely chopped garlic
2 long red chillies, deseeded (if preferred), then chopped
15–30 ml (1–2 tbsp) broadbean or hot bean paste
15 ml (1 tbsp) Shaoxing wine or medium dry sherry
10–15 ml (2–3 tsp) sesame oil

FOR THE MARINADE:
2.5–4 ml (½–¾ tsp) salt
10 ml (2 tsp) ginger juice (see p. 357)
10 ml (2 tsp) Shaoxing wine or medium dry sherry

FOR THE SAUCE:
juice from the fish
5–10 ml (1–2 tsp) tapioca or potato flour
15 ml (1 tbsp) thin or light soy sauce

1 Using a pointed knife, remove and discard the centre bone from the monkfish. Cut the resulting 2 fillets crossways at about 8 mm (⅓ in) intervals. Put the pieces into a dish.

2 Marinate the fish. Sprinkle with the salt, ginger juice and the wine or sherry. Stir to mix well. Leave to stand for about 15 minutes, turning the pieces over once for even absorption.

3 Let the fish 'go through oil'. Heat a wok over a high heat until smoke rises in abundance. Add the vegetable oil and swirl it around to cover a large area up the sloping sides of the wok. Continue to heat the oil for about 2 minutes until hot. Add the fish, stir with long wooden chopsticks or spoons for 30–40 seconds until the pieces turn opaque on the surface, and are partially cooked. Remove at once with a perforated disc, perch it on top of a bowl in order to catch the juice which will ooze from the fish during the next 15–20 minutes. Either discard the oil or strain it for reuse. Wash and dry the wok.

The fish can be prepared several hours in advance up to this point.

4 Prepare the sauce. When ready to serve the fish, gradually stir the fish juice into the tapioca or potato flour, allowing about 75 ml (5 tbsp) juice per 5 ml (1 tsp) flour. Add the soy sauce.

5 Heat the wok over a high heat until smoke rises. Add the peanut oil and swirl it around to cover a large area. Add the garlic, stir several times until it takes on colour, add the chillies, stir, add the bean paste, stir to mix, then immediately return the monkfish to the wok. Stir and turn the pieces for 30–60 seconds or until piping hot again. Splash in the wine or sherry along the edge of the

wok. When the sizzling subsides, pour in the well-stirred sauce, continuing to stir as it thickens. Scoop on to a serving dish. Sprinkle with the sesame oil. Serve immediately.

Top: Ngormaigai (p. 237).
Bottom: Lotus Leaf Rice (p. 232).

PLATE 9

Top left: Peking Duck (p. 279).
Top right: Chinese New Year Pudding (p. 342).
Bottom: Bobing or Mandarin Pancakes (p. 281).

PLATE 10

POULTRY AND GAME BIRDS

THE 18th-century gastronome, Yuan Mei (*see* p. 35), who is still thought of by the Chinese as the arbiter of culinary excellence, regarded chicken as the most important of all poultry. Among the forty-seven recipes using poultry in his cookbook, no less than thirty-one feature chicken, including one using eggs and one using gizzards. Ten recipes use duck, one sparrow, one quail, two goose and two pigeon.

Then, as now, as highlighted by Yuan, chicken occupied an elevated position on the Chinese table. The Chinese mythical bird, the phoenix, which is the emblem of royalty as well as feminine beauty, is personified in food by the chicken. Traditionally, chicken is a celebratory food, served always at festivals, on people's birthdays, at wedding banquets or just when there is a guest for dinner. For Chinese trading firms or hong where the boss and his employees eat lunch and dinner together and food is regarded as part of the wages, twice a month, on the first and the fifteenth, it is customary to have a special dinner with a more elaborate menu than the everyday fare. Whereas the day-to-day soup may be the watery broth made with gourds or vegetables, for those fortnightly dinners, a soup made with pork will be served, and a whole chicken, prepared in different ways by the chef, is the standard treat.

It has always been part of the Chinese agricultural scene for farmers to keep some chickens – free-range, of course – which run around during the day feeding on grains (and earthworms) and rest in a coop at night. Even in town, as long as there was a yard in the front or at the back of the house, many people used to keep a few chickens at home, which they fattened for special occasions. But to keep ducks, a nearby stream, or a man-made pond, is usually needed, and so it has always been more of a specialised business. Thus, the easier availability of chickens explains why they have always been a more common treat than ducks. This is not to say, however, that Chinese recipes for duck are not as numerous as for chicken. Furthermore, it is the distinctive Chinese ways of preparing ducks that have made an indelible impact on the world. Arguably, Peking Duck is as prestigious as The Great Wall; only that the former is much more accessible! The other bird that the Chinese raise in sizable amounts for domestic consumption is pigeon, which they either deep-fry or braise in a herb sauce.

When the Chinese eat poultry, they generally prefer the dark meat to the white, which is just the opposite of the Western preference. Like Westerners, they, too, often cook the poultry whole, but the parting of the ways follows when they carve the bird, be it chicken, duck, pigeon or quail. A Chinese cook places the whole bird on a thick chopping board in the kitchen and, wielding a large chopper, hacks it with steady precision through the skin and bones into small pieces, which he then reass-embles on a serving dish before he brings it out to the dining room. Children will be served the white meat while the grown-ups much prefer to gnaw at the bony pieces where the meat is considered to be much more tasty and succulent. The drumsticks are often piled on to the bowl of honoured guests while the wings are eyed by fellow diners who politely offer them to each other.

Again, typical of the Chinese culinary approach, every single part of the bird – the heart, the liver and the gizzard – is used. Perhaps the most unusual, if not also unpalatable, from the Western point of view, are what the Chinese consider gourmet dishes prepared from chicken's feet and duck's webs. Having grown up to love the special soup made with chicken stock and chicken's feet, I was never so surprised when an American friend of mine remarked to me in the 1960s in Hong Kong, 'I love to eat everything Chinese, but I loathed the sight of these chicken feet floating in the bowl at the Wong banquet the other evening.' The words gave me food for thought about culinary cultural differences between peoples. By the same token, in the 1970s, an English journalist who had been invited to China and been entertained officially by the Chinese authorities, asked me out of the blue after his return, 'Where in London can I find this scrumptious dish, braised duck's webs?' He then went on to describe how he adored their gelatinous texture, which went so well with the sauce and the accompanying black mushrooms, and all were downed with Maotai wine. In the 1980s, I found that a sprinkling of my non-Chinese friends would actually seek out chicken and duck feet dishes, while the majority would continue to eye them with polite respect. In the early 1990s, I am content with the thought that one people's gourmet dishes are another's abhorrent rejects.

Peking Duck

THIS, China's most prestigious duck dish, has been gaining fame since the middle of the 19th century (*see* p. 82). Since the 1970s, thousands of people have flocked to Peking to eat this dish served in restaurants specialising in it. During my own visits, I saw rows of them hanging up to dry before being roasted, and also suspended vertically, in a specially constructed oven. Fortunately, it can also be made in a simple way, as in this recipe, with remarkably good results.

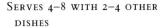

1 Melt the honey in the hot water in a cup. Keep warm.
2 Put the duck in a colander. Scald it with the boiling water from the kettle, turning over several times to ensure even scalding. As the water is poured on to the duck, the skin shrinks at once, becoming shiny. Wipe off excess water but leave damp. Put into a large mixing bowl.
3 Pour the honey mixture all over the skin, including the wings, neck and tail. Return the liquid to the cup and repeat the process once more. To ensure even distribution, dip a pastry brush into the liquid and smear over less accessible spots as well.
4 Hang the duck on either a special Chinese 3-pronged duck hook or on 2 butcher's 'S' meat hooks, 1 each securing the shoulder joint and wing. Hang in a windy place for 10–24 hours until the skin is parchment dry. Do not prick the skin. Alternatively put the duck in the refrigerator, uncovered, on a cake rack, for the same duration of time until the skin is parchment dry.
5 Place the duck breast side up on a wire rack in the middle of the oven with a tray of hot water underneath to catch the cooking juices. Roast in a preheated oven at

SERVES 4–8 WITH 2–4 OTHER DISHES

30 ml (2 tbsp) honey
300 ml (10 fl oz/1¼ cups) hot water
1 plump cleaned and oven-ready duck, 2–2.3 kilos (4½–5 lb)
1 kettle boiling water, about 1.75–2 litres (3–3½ pints/7½–8 cups)
12 spring onions, white parts only
1 large cucumber, cut into matchstick-sized pieces
sweet bean sauce (*see* p. 362) or hoisin sauce
25–30 bobing or Mandarin pancakes (*see* p. 281)

Illustrated on Plate 10.

180°C (350°F) Gas Mark 4 for 20 minutes, at the end of which the skin will have turned golden-brown. With a wooden spoon or spatula held in one hand and another spoon put inside the cavity, turn the duck over and roast the other side for 25–30 minutes. Turn over once more, breast side up again, and roast for another 20 minutes. If the skin is becoming too dark a red, lower the heat to 170°C (325°F) Gas Mark 3; if too pale, raise to 190°C (375°F) Gas Mark 5 for part of the rest of the roasting time. Do not prick the skin during the roasting; the fat which would ooze out would spoil both the colour and the crispness of the skin. Remove from the oven and put on a wire rack to cool for a few minutes before carving.

6 While the duck is being roasted, cut the spring onions into 5 cm (2 in) sections. Shred each section lengthways into strips. Arrange on 1 or 2 dishes. Arrange the cucumber on 1 or 2 dishes.

7 Put 15–30 ml (1–2 tbsp) sweet bean sauce or hoisin sauce into individual saucers for each person.

8 Steam (*see* p. 355) the bobing or Mandarin pancakes for 10 minutes.

9 Just before carving, pour all the juice in the duck cavity into a container. Show the duck whole to the family or friends if you wish, as it is always done in a restaurant. Carve the skin into pieces about 5 cm (2 in) square or into rectangular shapes of approximate size. Carve the meat in a similar manner. Place the skin and meat on 2 serving plates.

10 Bring the warm pancakes to the table.

11 To eat, put a pancake on a plate (rather than in a bowl), smear on some sauce and top with 1 or 2 pieces of skin, either on their own or with meat as well. Add 1 or 2 pieces of cucumber and spring onion before rolling it up. Pick up this roll with either chopsticks or your fingers and eat.

Bobing or Mandarin
Pancakes

THESE pancakes and the Peking Duck are insepar-able. Even though nowadays one can always buy frozen packets of them in Chinese supermarkets, which are perfectly round and thin, home-made ones as in this recipe are much superior in texture – what pancakes are all about – so that it is worth one's while to take the trouble to make them. If two people work together for steps 6–8, one doing the rolling and the other doing the frying, the task will be much easier, not to mention more fun. As the pancakes freeze well at the end of step 8, they can always be made ahead of time.

薄
餅

MAKES 32; SERVES 6–8

450 g (1 lb/3 cups) plain white flour
about 350 ml (12 fl oz/1½ cups) boiling water
15 ml (1 tbsp) cold water
little extra flour
10–15 ml (2–3 tsp) sesame oil

Illustrated on Plate 10.

1 Make the dough. Sift the flour into a mixing bowl. Pour in the boiling water gradually, stirring vigorously with a wooden spoon or a pair of chopsticks until well mixed. Depending on the climate and type of flour you may need either a little more or less water. Then stir in the cold water, which will give the pancakes what Peking people call jing or the firmness they look for in these pancakes. As soon as your hands can withstand the heat, form the mixture into a dough (it should come away clean from the sides of the bowl) and knead lightly either in the bowl or on a lightly floured board or cool work surface for 3–4 minutes or until soft and smooth. Allow to stand in the bowl for 25–30 minutes; cover the bowl with a cloth.

2 Make the pancakes. Transfer the dough to a lightly floured board or work surface. Divide into 2 equal portions and knead a few more times until smooth again. Use as little extra flour on the board as possible or the pancakes will taste floury – the usual pitfall of mass-produced pancakes.

3 Using both hands, roll each portion of dough into a 40 cm (16 in) long roll. Then, using a clean ruler as a guide, divide each roll into 16 pieces, each 2.5 cm (1 in) long, making a total of 32.

4 One by one, stand each piece upright on the heel of your hand, slightly round off the dough, then flatten with the

other hand, into a circle of about 5–6 cm (2–2½ in) diameter.

5 Using a pastry brush, paint the whole surface of half of the pieces with sesame oil, taking care not to use an excessive amount. Place the remaining pieces on the oiled surfaces, making 16 pairs. Shape each pair of circles as evenly as possible. (This film of oil makes it possible to separate the pancakes after they are fried.)

6 Using a lightly floured thin rolling pin or piece of dowel, roll out each pair into thin pancakes about 15–16 cm (6–6¼ in) in diameter. To ensure even thickness and roundness, rotate the circles quite frequently, turning them over as well.

7 Fry the pancakes. Heat an unoiled, flat heavy frying pan or griddle over a medium heat until hot. Put in 1 pair of cakes at a time and fry for about 1 minute or until light brown spots appear underneath. Lift the edges to check the spots. Turn over to fry the other side. In less than 1 minute part of the surface will puff up, indicating that they are done.

8 Remove the pair from the frying pan and, while they are still hot, separate the 2 thin pancakes with the fingers. Put on a dish and cover with a dry cloth to prevent them from drying out. Repeat until all are done.

9 Steam the pancakes. Put them in 2 batches in a bamboo basket, then put it into a steamer and steam (*see* p. 355) for 5–10 minutes before serving.

Pipa Duck

SERVES 8 WITH 4 OTHER DISHES

1 cleaned duck, 2–2.5 kilos
  (4½–5½ lb)
1 kettle boiling water, about 1.75
  litres (3 pints/7½ cups)
30 ml (2 tbsp) honey dissolved in
  300 ml (10 fl oz/1¼ cups) hot
  water

A SOPHISTICATED Cantonese dish that is supposed to resemble the Chinese balloon guitar, the pipa. To achieve the resemblance, even by some stretch of the imagination, one has to split lengthways the breast side of the duck and break some of the rib bones so that the duck can lie flat. This also facilitates the smearing of the marinating sauce all over the cavity, thereby ensuring the characteristic taste and flavour of the duck.

1 Prepare the marinade: in a bowl mix together the salt, hoisin sauce, yellow bean sauce, five-spice powder and minced garlic. The marinade should be thick rather than liquid.

2 Remove with your hands fatty oil sacs, wind pipes, lungs and whatever other undesirable innards are still attached to the cavity of the duck.

3 Pour the boiling water all over the skin of the duck to scald it. The skin contracts and becomes shiny as the water is poured over it. Wipe off excess water but leave damp. Put into a large bowl.

4 Pour the honey liquid all over the skin, including the wings, neck and tail. Dip a pastry brush into the liquid and smear all over the skin once more to ensure even distribution. Remove the duck from the bowl and discard the liquid.

5 With a pair of scissors slit the duck lengthways from end to end on the breast side. Pull back the top shoulder end with your hands, breaking the top ribs on both sides of the cavity. Pat dry the cavity if there is excess moisture.

6 Smear the marinade all over the cavity. If necessary, make shallow slits on the flesh so as to accommodate the marinade.

7 Insert an arclike wire with two small side-turn hooks into the shoulder end of the cavity in order to give the duck the support of the pipa shape. This gadget, spanning about 17.5–20 cm (7–8 in) from hook to hook, can be made from a wire hanger with a spanner.

8 Hang the duck on either a special Chinese 3-pronged duck hook or on 2 butcher's 'S' meat hooks, 1 each securing the shoulder joint and wing. Hang in a windy place for 10–24 hours until the skin is parchment dry. Some of the marinade may drip off. Do not prick the skin, lest the fat that oozes out spoils the result when roasted.

9 Remove the duck hook but leave the wire gadget in the cavity. Place the duck, skin side up, on a wire rack in the middle of the oven with a tray of hot water underneath to catch the cooking grease and juices. Roast in a preheated oven at 180–190°C (350–375°F) Gas Mark 4–5 for 20 minutes, at the end of which time the skin will have turned golden-brown. With tongs and a spatula turn the duck over and roast on the cavity side for 15 minutes at

FOR THE MARINADE:
10 ml (2 tsp) salt
37.5 ml (2½ tbsp) hoisin sauce
37.5 ml (2½ tbsp) ground yellow bean sauce
5 ml (1 tsp) five-spice powder
30–45 ml (2–3 tbsp) minced garlic

a lower temperature of 170–180°C (325–350°F) Gas Mark 3–4. Turn the duck over again, skin side up, and roast for another 10–15 minutes for final crisping of the skin. Do not prick the skin during the roasting; the fat which would ooze out would spoil both the colour and the crispness of the skin. Remove from the oven and put on a wire rack to cool for a few minutes before carving.

10 Carve the duck through the skin and bones into 2.5 cm (1 in) (or larger sized) pieces and arrange them on a serving dish in the shape of a duck.

11 Serve hot or at room temperature. No sauce is needed as the marinade has imparted a very subtle fragrance and taste to the duck.

Chaozhou
Braised Duck

SERVES 6–8 WITH 3–4 OTHER DISHES

1 cleaned duck, about 2.3 kilos (5 lb), and its giblets
salt
30 ml (2 tbsp) fine sea salt mixed with 5 ml (1 tsp) five-spice powder
85 g (3 oz) galangal, skin scraped and cut into thin slices
10 cm (4 in) piece weighing about 55 g (2 oz) Chinese brown sugar, chopped into bits
105 ml (7 tbsp) mushroom soy sauce
30–45 ml (2–3 tbsp) sesame oil

FOR THE DIPPING SAUCE:
10 ml (2 tbsp) puréed garlic
60 ml (4 tbsp) Chinese rice vinegar

ONE of the most famous dishes of the Chaozhou cuisine is a goose braised in a herb sauce. Since the geese in Chaozhou are much more like Western ducks than geese in size and texture, Chaozhou natives who live abroad use ducks instead to make the dish, and they find the result more than satisfactory.

Our Chaozhou neighbours in Hong Kong Mrs Ng and her aunt, once showed me how they made this duck. Thank you, Mrs Ng.

1 Remove and discard oil sacs near the tail of the duck. Clean the cavity well and pat dry. For cleansing the gizzard, heart and livers, rub over with salt, rinse thoroughly then pat dry.

2 Rub the skin and the cavity evenly with the sea salt and five-spice powder mixture. Put into the cavity half of the galangal slices. Leave to stand for about 1 hour.

3 Heat a wok over a moderate heat until hot. Add the sugar, let it melt gradually. When it bubbles all over, add the soy sauce and stir to mix, lowering the heat so that the sauce becomes aromatic rather than burned. Add the remaining galangal slices and about 175 ml (6 fl

oz/¾ cup) water, stir to incorporate and gradually bring to a simmer.

4 Put in the duck, breast side up, and, if necessary, add sufficient water so as to half submerge the duck. Adjust to a moderate heat and gradually bring to the boil, spooning the sauce all over the duck to give the skin an even colour. Add 15 ml (1 tbsp) of the sesame oil to enhance the flavour.

5 Put on the lid, adjust the heat to maintain a simmer for about 15 minutes. Remove the lid, check how much liquid has evaporated, add 50–100 ml (2–4 fl oz/¼–½ cup) water as replenishment, turn the duck, either breast side down or on the side, and simmer again, covered, for another 15 minutes. Repeat this process 3–4 more times, giving a total cooking time of 1¼–1½ hours to the duck. Add the gizzard and heart half-way through the cooking but the livers during the last 15 minutes so that the latter will be tender but not hard. To test, pierce the thighs with a chopstick or fork; if it goes in easily with no pink juices oozing out, the duck is cooked.

6 Remove the duck with the giblet pieces from the wok and let cool. Brush all over with the remaining sesame oil to heighten the aroma.

7 Pour the sauce into a small saucepan. If too thin, it should be reduced to about 250–300 ml (8–10 fl oz/1–1¼ cups).

8 Carve the duck. Using a pair of scissors, cut out the 2 breasts, then debone with a knife. Slice the meat at an angle into thin and large slivers. Chop the rest of the duck through the skin and bones into rectangular pieces about 2.5 × 4 cm (1 × 1½ in). Arrange them on an oval serving dish in the shape of a duck, placing the boneless breast pieces on top. Slice the gizzard into thin pieces and put also on to the serving dish. The carving can be done in advance and the dish kept in a cool place but not refrigerated.

9 Prepare the sauces. When about ready to serve, reheat the cooking sauce. Pour some of it over the duck and some into small saucers for individual dipping at the table.

   Divide the puréed garlic into 2 saucers or small bowls. Add half the rice vinegar to each and stir to mix. This dipping sauce is meant to offset the grease of the duck, thereby aiding digestion.

Sichuan
Smoked Duck

SERVES 6–8 WITH 3–4 OTHER
DISHES

1 plump cleaned duck, about
  2.3 kilos (5 lb)
27.5 ml (1¾ tbsp) salt
4.5 ml (1 scant tsp) saltpetre
  powder
115 g (4 oz/¾ cup) plain flour
115 g (4 oz/½ cup) sugar
60 ml (4 tbsp) tea leaves, such as
  Keemun, Orange Pekoe,
  Jasmine
2 knobs ginger, each about
  1.25 cm (½ in), peeled and
  bruised
4 spring onions, trimmed
1 whole star anise (8 segments)
7.5 ml (1½ tsp) Sichuan
  peppercorns
30 ml (2 tbsp) Shaoxing wine or
  medium dry sherry
vegetable oil for deep-frying
15 ml (1 tbsp) sesame oil

THIS is by far the most distinguished poultry dish of Sichuanese or Western cuisine, with its distinctive smoked and aromatic flavour. Originally, to make the real McCoy, leaves, twigs and wood from the camphor tree were burned and used as the smoking agents, but as this method is not very realistic, a simpler way has been evolved, making it possible to prepare the duck at home. The fourfold cooking process may seem elaborate, but the duck is one of the most sophisticated dishes and would grace any gourmet table. Besides rice, it also goes well with steamed buns.

1 Marinate the duck. Rub the salt thoroughly over the skin of the duck and inside the cavity, and then rub the cavity only with the saltpetre. (As in curing ham or bacon, saltpetre loosens the fibres of the meat, but it must be used sparingly.) Leave the duck in a cool place for about 10 hours or overnight.
2 Rinse the cavity of the duck with warm water. Wipe dry. The duck is now ready for smoking.
3 Smoke the duck. Line a large wok with double-layer foil and add the flour, sugar and tea leaves as smoking ingredients. Put in the centre a metal trivet or bamboo stand on top of which place 4 wooden chopsticks, making a criss-cross to reinforce the stand. Place the duck on top, breast side up, and make sure that there is a gap between it and the smoking ingredients so as to allow free circulation of smoke. Put the wok cover on tightly.
4 Turn the heat to high until you see smoke escaping, then adjust it, making sure, however, that plenty of smoke continues to come out. Smoke for 15 minutes, remove the lid, and you'll see that the duck is partially coloured. Turn the duck over, breast side down, and continue to smoke, covered, for another 15 minutes. Remove the wok from the heat.
5 Transfer the duck to a large heatproof dish, breast side up. Put half of the ginger, spring onion, star anise,

peppercorns and wine or sherry into the cavity; put the other half on the breast.

6 Steam the duck. Put the dish in a steamer and steam (*see* p. 355) for 1–1¼ hours. Take care not to overcook it, lest it be difficult to handle when deep-fried later.

7 Transfer the duck to a rack and leave to cool. Remove and discard all the condiments. Wipe dry the cavity (and the skin, if necessary) with kitchen paper.

8 Deep-fry the duck. Half fill a wok over a wok-stand with vegetable oil and heat to a temperature of 190°C (375°F). Using a large hand strainer, carefully lower the duck into the oil, breast side down, and deep-fry for 3–4 minutes or until brown. Holding a wooden spoon in one hand and another inside the cavity in the other hand, turn the duck over and deep-fry the other side until brown. Hot oil can also be carefully ladled over the skin. Remove to a chopping board. Brush the sesame oil over the breast to enhance the fragrance.

9 To serve, either carve the duck into small pieces the Chinese way or by the method to which you are accustomed. The duck is moist and aromatic and needs no sauce or condiments. Serve warm.

Ni Zan's Duck (Yunlin Goose)

ORIGINALLY, this was a novel way used to cook a goose, devised by the Yuan painter and gastronome, Ni Zan (*see* p. 29). Several hundred years later, in the 18th century, Yuan Mei, in incorporating the recipe into his celebratory cookbook (*see* p. 35), remarked that the same method could be used to prepare a duck, with delectable results. The novelty is in using the steam from an equal portion of wine and water, seasoned with salt, Sichuan peppercorns and honey, to cook the duck, which is placed on a rack inside a large pot. Having combined Ni's and Yuan's recipes and cooked the duck myself, I can vouch for the succulence of the flesh and the sweetness of the sauce.

SERVES 6 WITH 3 OTHER DISHES

1 cleaned duck, 2 kilos (4½ lb)
5 ml (1 tsp) roasted ground
  Sichuan peppercorns (*see* p. 359)
15 ml (1 tbsp) fine sea salt
8–10 spring onions, trimmed
15 ml (1 tbsp) Shaoxing wine
30 ml (2 tbsp) runny honey
300 ml (10 fl oz/1¼ cups)
  Shaoxing wine
300 ml (10 fl oz/1¼ cups) water

1 Clean well and pat dry the cavity of the duck, removing any oil sacs.

2 Put the duck in a colander. Bring a large kettle of water to the boil, then pour it all over the duck to scald the skin, which will shrink instantly, becoming shiny. Wipe off excess water but leave damp.

3 Mix the Sichuan peppercorns with the salt. Using your fingers, smear the mixture all over the cavity of the duck, taking care not to miss any nook or cranny.

4 Stuff the spring onions, preferably whole, into the cavity.

5 Add the 15 ml (1 tbsp) Shaoxing wine to the honey and stir to mix. Brush this mixture all over the skin of the duck.

6 Make a 2.5 cm (1 in) high platform inside a large, deep casserole – an enamel one with a cast-iron bottom would be ideal – using one or two metal or bamboo stands, reinforced on top with several chopsticks, if necessary. Pour in the rest of the Shaoxing wine and the water.

7 Place the duck, breast side up, on the platform, making sure that no part of it is in direct contact with the liquid underneath. Slowly bring to the boil, then immediately reduce to a simmer and cover the casserole with the lid. To ensure more airtight steaming inside, paste strips of Chinese flax tissue paper (or baking paper) moistened with water all around the surface where the lid meets the sides of the casserole. Maintain a slow simmer for about 50 minutes, moistening the tissue strips whenever they get too parched.

8 Remove the paper and replace the lid. Turn the duck over, back facing up on the stand, and continue to simmer, covered and papered as before, for another 45–50 minutes.

9 Remove the duck and place it on a large serving platter. Remove the spring onions from the cavity, place them around the duck, and keep warm nearby. Spoon off the fat in the casserole, then pour the juices over the duck. Serve it whole. The flesh, so meltingly tender, should fall off the bones when picked at by chopsticks, as Chinese are wont to do. But if you prefer to serve it carved in the manner to which you are accustomed, by all means do so.

Sweet and Sour
Duck Liver with Cucumber

THIS dish brings back pleasant memories of summer days in Hong Kong where I grew up. Whenever a duck was served at home, more often than not there would be the accompanying dish of the liver cooked with a light, appetising sweet and sour sauce. I used to love it – and still do.

糖
醋
鴨
肝

SERVES 4 WITH 2 OTHER DISHES

1 long or 2 small cucumbers,
    about 450 g (1 lb)
2.5 ml (½ tsp) salt
duck livers from 1 large duck,
    about 115 g (4 oz), trimmed and
    cut into very thin slices about
    2 mm (¹/₁₀ in) thick
52.5 ml (3½ tbsp) peanut or
    vegetable oil
2 cloves garlic, peeled and cut into
    slices
4 thin slices ginger, peeled
3 spring onions, trimmed and cut
    into 2.5 cm (1 in) sections, white
    and green parts separated
7.5 ml (½ tbsp) Shaoxing wine or
    medium dry sherry

FOR THE MARINADE:

1 pinch salt or .75 ml (⅛ tsp)
2.5 ml (½ tsp) thin or light soy
    sauce
4 turns black peppermill
2.5 ml (½ tsp) Shaoxing wine or
    medium dry sherry
2 ml (⅓ tsp) potato or tapioca
    flour
5 ml (1 tsp) sesame oil

FOR THE SWEET AND SOUR
SAUCE:

5 ml (1 tsp) potato or tapioca flour
    dissolved in 10 ml (2 tsp) water
.75 ml (⅛ tsp) salt
2.5 ml (½ tsp) thin or light soy
    sauce
10 ml (2 tsp) caster sugar
22.5 ml (1½ tbsp) Chinese rice
    vinegar or 15 ml (1 tbsp) white
    wine vinegar
60 ml (4 tbsp) chicken stock

1 Wash and pat dry the cucumbers. Halve lengthways. Using a small knife, remove the seeds, then cut the cucumbers diagonally into very thin slices, about 2 mm (¹/₁₀ in) thick.

2 Put the slices into a bowl and sprinkle on the salt. Mix together and leave for about 30 minutes so as to draw out excess water. Strain the cucumber in a sieve, then squeeze out excess water by hand, a handful at a time.

3 Marinate the duck liver. Add the salt, soy sauce, black pepper, wine or sherry, potato or tapioca flour and stir to mix. Leave to stand for 15–20 minutes. Stir in the sesame oil.

4 Prepare the sweet and sour sauce. Put the dissolved potato or tapioca flour in a small bowl. Add the salt, soy sauce and sugar and stir to mix. Stir in the vinegar and stock.

5 Heat a wok until smoke rises. Add 7.5 ml (½ tbsp) oil and swirl it around. Add the cucumber and stir over a medium heat for about 1 minute or until hot. Scoop on to a dish and keep warm nearby. Wipe clean the wok.

6 Reheat the wok over a high heat until smoke rises. Add the remaining 45 ml (3 tbsp) oil and swirl it around to cover a large area. Add the garlic which will sizzle, then the ginger and white spring onion and stir to release their aroma. Add the duck liver and, going to the bottom of the wok with the scoop, turn and toss for about 20 seconds until the liver is partially cooked. Splash in the wine or sherry along the sides of the wok. When the sizzling subsides, pour in the well stirred sauce, stirring as it thickens. Return the cucumber to the wok and add the green spring onion, stirring to mix. Scoop on to a serving dish and serve immediately.

NOTE: Instead of duck livers, chicken livers can be used to the same effect.

Stir-fried Chicken
with Cashewnuts

SERVES 4 WITH 2 OTHER DISHES

2 skinned and boned chicken
breasts, about 350 g (12 oz)
75 ml (5 tbsp) peanut or vegetable
oil
5 large spring onions, trimmed,
cut into 5 cm (2 in) sections,
white and green parts separated
2 small cucumbers or 1 large, cut
into wedges
2 ml (⅓ tsp) salt or to taste
2–3 large cloves garlic, peeled and
finely chopped
15 ml (1 tbsp) Shaoxing wine or
medium dry sherry
50–75 g (2–3 oz/½–¾ cup)
roasted cashewnuts

FOR THE MARINADE:
2 ml (⅓ tsp) salt
10 ml (2 tsp) thin or light soy
sauce
8 turns white peppermill
5 ml (1 tsp) Shaoxing wine or
medium dry sherry
5 ml (1 tsp) cornflour
15 ml (1 tbsp) egg white
5 ml (1 tsp) sesame oil

FOR THE SAUCE:
5 ml (1 tsp) potato or tapioca flour
dissolved in 10 ml (2 tsp) water
60 ml (4 tbsp) chicken stock
10 ml (2 tsp) oyster sauce
5 ml (1 tsp) thin or light soy sauce

Illustrated on Plate 14.

THIS dish is the archetypal Cantonese stir-fry, loved by both the Chinese and the non-Chinese, for it combines all the winning elements: a contrast of texture between the tender chicken and the crunchy nuts, harmonious flavouring and wok fragrance. Add to this the nutritious yet healthy quality of every ingredient, and the dish will continue to be popular. Instead of cashew nuts, you can use pine nuts or, at a pinch, even peanuts.

1 Cut the chicken into large cubes about 2 cm (¾ in) square. Put into a bowl.
2 Marinate the chicken: add the salt, soy sauce, pepper, wine or sherry, cornflour and egg white to the chicken and stir to coat thoroughly. Leave to stand for 15–20 minutes. Stir in the sesame oil.
3 Prepare the sauce: put the dissolved potato or tapioca flour in a small bowl and add the stock, oyster sauce and soy sauce. Stir to mix.
4 Heat a wok over a high heat until smoke rises. Add 15 ml (1 tbsp) of the oil and swirl it around. Add the white part of 1 spring onion and stir a few times. Add the cucumber wedges, turn and toss with the wok scoop for about 1 minute. Sprinkle with the salt, lower the heat to medium and continue to stir for another 2 minutes or until the cucumber is cooked though still retaining much of its crunchiness. Scoop on to a dish and keep warm nearby. Wash and wipe dry the wok.
5 Reheat the wok over a high heat until plenty of smoke rises. Add the remaining oil and swirl it around to cover a large area. Add the garlic which will sizzle. Add the remaining white spring onion and stir a few times. Add the chicken and, going to the bottom of the wok with the wok scoop, turn and toss for about 30 seconds. Splash in the wine or sherry around the edges of the

wok; when the sizzling subsides, lower the heat to medium, continuing to stir the chicken for another 30 seconds or until it is cooked and has turned opaque. Alternating between higher and lower heat will ensure that the chicken does not become chewy and dried when cooked. Add the well-stirred sauce to the bottom of the wok and continue to stir it while it thickens. Return the cucumber to the wok, add the cashewnuts and green spring onion, stirring and turning to mix. Scoop everything on to a serving dish. Serve immediately.

Stir-fried
Chicken with Pear

YUAN Mei's recipe for this famous Hangzhou dish reads: 'Cut tender chicken breasts into slices. Fry them first of all in 3 taels of lard until cooked, stirring three to four times. Add 1 ladle of sesame oil and 1 teaspoon each of thickening starch, salt, ginger juice and ground fagara. Add also thin slices of pear and small wedges of fragrant mushrooms and stir-fry 3–4 more times. Scoop from the wok and place on to a five-inch dish.' I have adapted it, however, so that it uses peanut oil rather than lard.

SERVES 2 AS MAIN COURSE

150 ml (8 tbsp) peanut or vegetable oil
2 chicken breasts, about 225 g (8 oz), cut crossways into thin slices
5 ml (1 tsp) cornflour
5 ml (1 tsp) salt
5 ml (1 tsp) ginger juice (see p. 357)
5 ml (1 tsp) roasted ground Sichuan peppercorns (see p. 359)
30 ml (2 tbsp) sesame oil
1 large Tianjin or William pear, quartered, skinned and cored, then cut into thin slices
6–8 small dried Chinese black mushrooms, reconstituted (see p. 353), and cut into small wedges

1 Heat a wok over a high heat until smoke rises. Add the peanut or vegetable oil and swirl it around several times to cover a large area. Lower the heat. Add the chicken and separate the slices straightaway with either the wok scoop or wooden chopsticks. Turn the pieces over 3–4 times so that they cook in the warm oil, turning white. Using a perforated disc or spoon, scoop them into a bowl. Discard all but 30–45 ml (2–3 tbsp) of the oil in the wok.
2 Add the cornflour, salt, ginger juice and ground Sichuan peppercorns to the chicken and stir to mix well. Add the sesame oil and the pear and mix again.
3 Reheat the oil in the wok over a high heat until hot. Add the mushrooms and stir until hot. Return the chicken and pear mixture to the wok and stir vigorously until everything is piping hot. Scoop on to a serving dish. Serve hot.

Chicken Braised
in Hongzao

SERVES 6 WITH 3 OTHER DISHES

1 cleaned chicken, about 1.35–1.5
  kilos (3–3½ lb)
2–3 large bunches (20–30) spring
  onions with plenty of green,
  trimmed
45 ml (3 tbsp) peanut or vegetable
  oil
1 large knob ginger, about 4 cm
  (1½ in), peeled, cut into wedges
  and bruised
90 ml (6 tbsp) hongzao (*see* p. 358)
30 ml (2 tbsp) Shaoxing wine or
  medium dry sherry
175–250 ml (6–8 fl oz/¾–1 cup)
  chicken stock
5 ml (1 tsp) salt or to taste
2.5 ml (½ tsp) sugar
about 5 ml (1 tsp) tapioca or
  potato flour dissolved in 10 ml
  (2 tsp) water

The Fujianese love to season poultry with hongzao (hungjo in Cantonese) which is made of fermented glutinous rice and red yeast, with a resultant sweetness all of its own. When I visited Singapore two years ago, Mrs Mok, who is a Fujianese, cooked this dish for me, and she emphasised the importance of the large amount of spring onions in it.

1 Chop the chicken through the skin and bone into pieces about 4 cm (1½ in) square in size. Put the breast meat separately from the dark meat and giblets.

2 Take 2 spring onions and tie them together into a large knot. Repeat until all are done.

3 Heat a wok or a large saucepan over a high heat until smoke rises. Add the oil and swirl it around. Add the ginger and let it sizzle for a few seconds before adding the spring onions. Stir for about a dozen times, then add the hongzao and stir to incorporate the oil. Add the chicken, the dark meat and giblets first, turn and toss for about 1 minute, then add the white meat and continue to stir for about another 30 seconds. Splash in the wine or sherry along the edges of the wok or saucepan; when the sizzling dies down, add the stock and season with the salt and sugar. Bring to the boil, lower the heat and continue to simmer, covered, for about 10 minutes when the white meat should be cooked. Remove the lid and take out the white meat to prevent it from being overcooked. Continue to simmer, covered, for another 15 minutes when the dark meat should be tender. (The dish can be prepared in advance up to this point.)

4 Remove the dark meat, turn up the heat to reduce the sauce. If preferred, stir in the dissolved flour to thicken the sauce a little over a low heat.

5 Return all the chicken to the wok or saucepan, turn the pieces around to absorb some of the sauce. Remove everything to a serving dish and serve hot.

Shandong
Chicken Drumsticks

A Shandong dish that calls for several cookery techniques which, needless to say, require time and effort. Fortunately, much of the preparation can be done ahead of time. In any case, the resultant complex and intriguing tastes that satisfy not only your own palate but all those who have eaten with you will make you forget the hard work and remark with pleasure, 'It has been worth it!'

SERVES 6 WITH 3 OTHER DISHES

12 large chicken drumsticks, each 115–140 g (4–5 oz)
22.5 ml (1½ tbsp) thick or dark soy sauce mixed with 7.5 ml (1½ tsp) Shaoxing wine or medium dry sherry
vegetable oil for deep-frying
30 ml (2 tbsp) peanut or vegetable oil
37.5 ml (2½ tbsp) sugar
15 ml (1 tbsp) Shaoxing wine or medium dry sherry
175 ml (6 fl oz/¾ cup) chicken stock
15 ml (1 tbsp) Chinese rice vinegar
7.5–10 ml (1½–2 tsp) salt
6 slices ginger, peeled
6 spring onions, trimmed and quartered
15–30 ml (1–2 tbsp) sesame oil

1 Brush the skin and exposed flesh of each drumstick thoroughly with the soy sauce and wine or sherry mixture and leave to stand for about 15 minutes.

2 Sit a wok on the wok-stand and half fill it with vegetable oil and heat over a high heat until it reaches 190°C (375°F). Carefully lower all the drumsticks into the oil and deep-fry them for 4–5 minutes. Remove with a perforated disc on to a dish. Turn off the heat.

3 Heat a casserole until hot. Add the peanut or vegetable oil and swirl it around. Add 22.5 ml (1½ tbsp) of the sugar and heat until the melted sugar turns nut-brown. Add the wine or sherry which will splash so also add quickly the chicken stock.

4 Return the drumsticks to the casserole. Season with the vinegar, salt and the remaining 15 ml (1 tbsp) sugar, scraping in the remaining mixture of soy sauce and wine or sherry. Add also the ginger and spring onions. Bring to a gentle boil, then reduce the heat and simmer, covered, for about 30 minutes until the drumsticks are tender. This dish can be prepared in advance up to this point.

5 When ready to serve, remove the drumsticks and keep nearby. Discard the ginger and spring onions. Reduce the sauce over a high heat to a thickish consistency. Reduce the heat and return the drumsticks to the casserole, coating them with the sauce. Remove to a serving dish and sprinkle drops of sesame oil over them. Serve hot.

NOTE: If you abhor the idea of deep-frying in step 2, you can brown the drumsticks in the normal way in 45–60 ml (3–4 tbsp) of oil for 4–5 minutes.

Sichuanese Chicken Thighs
with an Exotic Sauce

SERVES 8 WITH 4 OTHER DISHES

18 chicken thighs, about 675 g
  (1½ lb), skinned and boned
60 ml (4 tbsp) peanut or vegetable
  oil
7.5 ml (1½ tsp) finely chopped
  garlic
10 ml (2 tsp) finely choppped
  ginger
6 large spring onions, white parts
  only, trimmed and cut
  diagonally into sections
30 ml (2 tbsp) Shaoxing wine or
  medium dry sherry
50 ml (2 fl oz/¼ cup) chicken
  stock
7.5 ml (1½ tsp) tapioca or potato
  flour dissolved in 15 ml (1 tbsp)
  water
50–115 g (2–4 oz/½–1 cup)
  roasted peanuts

FOR THE SAUCE:
30 ml (2 tbsp) sesame paste
7.5 ml (1½ tsp) broadbean paste
  or hot bean paste
30 ml (2 tbsp) thick or dark soy
  sauce
15 ml (1 tbsp) Chinese rice
  vinegar
7.5 ml (1½ tsp) sugar
5 ml (1 tsp) roasted ground
  Sichuan peppercorns (see p. 359)
15 ml (1 tbsp) sesame oil

One would expect this dish to be Sichuanese, for
the ingredients that make up the sauce call for
almost every Chinese condiment in your cup-
board. The reward is a range of exotic flavours
which assault your tastebuds in sequence, and you
are at once surprised and delighted by them.

Dark, rather than white, chicken meat is used
because it stands up to the intensity of the sauce so
much better.

1 Cut the chicken thighs into cubes about 2 cm (¾ in)
   square.
2 Prepare the sauce. In a small bowl mix together the
   sesame paste, bean paste, soy sauce, vinegar, sugar,
   Sichuan peppercorns and sesame oil.
3 Heat a wok over a high heat until smoke rises. Add the
   oil and swirl it around over a large area. Add the garlic,
   stir several times, add the ginger, stir several more
   times, then add the spring onion and continue to stir a
   few more times to release the aroma. Pour in the sauce,
   scraping all from the bowl. Reduce the heat, stir to
   incorporate the sauce, the oil and the spices.
4 Add the chicken, turn up the heat to high, and stir and
   turn for 1–2 minutes. Splash in the wine or sherry
   around the edges of the wok and let sizzle. When the
   sizzling dies down, pour in the stock, stir to mix and
   bring to a simmer. Lower the heat, add the wok cover
   and cook for about 2 more minutes until the chicken is
   cooked. Replace the lid, add the dissolved tapioca or
   potato flour, stirring continuously as the sauce thickens.
   Scatter in the peanuts, stir to mix, then remove everything to a serving dish. Serve hot immediately.

Hainan
Chicken Rice

This dish may have originated from Hainan, the offshore island in the south of Guangdong province, but in recent decades it has become the trademark of Singapore cuisine, and is extremely popular among the Chinese there as well as in Hong Kong. When a dish travels from one country to another, where it takes root, it is inevitably adapted to reflect local tastes and this is what has happened here. To poach a chicken then use a salt and grated ginger dipping sauce is basically Cantonese, but to cook the rice subsequently in the seasoned liquid as well as to add a chilli dipping sauce makes it Singaporean.

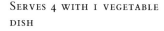

SERVES 4 WITH 1 VEGETABLE DISH

1 cleaned chicken, about 1.5 kilos (3½ lb)
chicken stock (or water with 2 chicken stock cubes dissolved in it)
45 ml (3 tbsp) peanut or vegetable oil (or rendered chicken fat)
10 ml (2 tsp) very finely chopped or puréed garlic
375 g (13 oz/2 cups) long-grain white rice, rinsed and drained
salt

FOR THE GINGER SAUCE DIP:
10–15 ml (2–3 tsp) grated ginger
2.5 ml (½ tsp) salt
15 ml (1 tbsp) peanut or vegetable oil

FOR THE FRESH CHILLI SAUCE DIP:
4 long fresh red chillies, deseeded then pulverised
5 ml (1 tsp) puréed garlic
30 ml (2 tbsp) Chinese rice vinegar
5 ml (1 tsp) salt
5–10 ml (1–2 tsp) sugar

FOR THE SOY SAUCE DIP:
45 ml (3 tbsp) thick or dark soy sauce

1   Remove from the cavity of the chicken oil sacs which can be fried until the fat is rendered for use in step 4.
2   In a large pot put sufficient chicken stock (or water with chicken cubes dissolved in it) to submerge the chicken and bring to a rolling boil. Add the chicken and, inserting a wooden spoon into the cavity, turn it over several times while the water is returned to the boil. Lower the heat to maintain a gentle simmer, add the lid to the pot and continue to simmer gently for about 45 minutes, at the end of which time the chicken should be thoroughly cooked.
3   Remove and rinse the chicken under a stream of running cold water for about 45 minutes, turning it over periodically for even rinsing. Alternatively, submerge it in water with plenty of floating ice cubes. This ensures that the skin of the chicken has the crisp texture characteristic of this dish. Wipe dry the chicken which is now ready for carving.
4   Cook the rice. Heat a wok over a high heat until smoke rises. Add the oil (or rendered chicken fat) and swirl it around. Add the garlic, let it sizzle and take on colour, but before it is burned add the rice. Going to the bottom of the wok with the scoop, turn and toss and stir over a medium heat for about 3 minutes, or until just dried and fragrant. Remove the wok from the heat.

Add the rice to a saucepan, preferably with a copper bottom, and season with salt to taste (up to 5 ml/1 tsp).

Pour in 800–900 ml (28–32 fl oz/3½–4 cups) poaching stock from the pot and bring to the boil, covered, over a high heat. Stir thoroughly with a wooden spoon and continue to boil, covered or uncovered, until most of the water is absorbed, leaving only tiny 'eyelets' around the grains. Reduce the heat to a minimum. Place a metal heat diffuser under the saucepan and leave the rice to simmer with the lid on for 12–15 minutes. Remove the saucepan from the heat. The rice should be cooked through by now with no chalky centres in the grains.

5   Prepare the ginger sauce dip. In a small bowl mix together the ginger, salt and oil and put on to 2 saucers.

6   Prepare the fresh chilli sauce dip. In a bowl mix together the chilli, garlic, rice vinegar, salt and sugar and put into 2 saucers.

7   Carve the chicken. Cut off the wings, place one on either side of a serving dish. Cut off the legs and thighs through the joints and remove the bones in them. Using a pointed sharp knife, cut from near the wing, then along one side of the breastbone down to where the leg was. Simply lift the breast meat off the bone. Do likewise on the other side. Turn the chicken over and remove the flesh from the back. Cut all the chicken meat into pieces and arrange them on the serving dish with the breast meat neatly in 2 rows on top of the other meat. The bones can be saved for making stock.

6   To serve, place the cold chicken on the table and scoop the hot rice into individual bowls. The dips are for the chicken which goes with the rice.

Hand-torn
Chicken

THIS dish, based on that for East River Salt-baked Chicken (*see* p. 101) which is prepared by burying the whole chicken in red-hot coarse salt until it is cooked, is adapted from the recipe of Mrs Choi, the consummate cook of the Golden Chopstick restaurant in South Kensington. She very kindly allowed me into her kitchen and showed me her way.

SERVES 6 WITH 3 OTHER DISHES

1 large cleaned chicken, about
  1.7–1.8 kilos (3¾–4 lb)
1 large knob ginger, peeled and
  bruised
15 ml (1 tbsp) salt
150 ml (5 fl oz/⅔ cup) peanut or
  vegetable oil
100 ml (4 fl oz/½ cup) sesame oil
100 ml (4 fl oz/½ cup) stock or
  water from the poaching liquid
15 ml (1 tbsp) ginger powder
white parts only of 4–6 spring
  onions, cut into 5 cm (2 in)
  lengths, then shredded
3 branches coriander leaves,
  trimmed and torn up

Illustrated on Plate 16.

1 Poach the chicken. Put the chicken in a large saucepan or stockpot. Add sufficient water to submerge the chicken – this can be as much as 4 litres (7 pints/17½ cups). Add the ginger. Bring to the boil over a high heat, then reduce the heat to maintain a simmer for 25–30 minutes with the lid on. The chicken should be just cooked by now, or slightly underdone. Remove from the poaching liquid which, if preferred, can be used as the basis for your stockpot. Rinse under cold running water in order that the texture of the skin becomes crisp. Pat dry.

2 Debone the chicken. Using your hands and with the help of a pointed knife, remove the bones, save for the wings. As long as large chunks of flesh are torn from the chicken, there is no need to fuss over how perfect they look. The bones can be saved for the stockpot. This dish can be prepared up to this point several hours in advance. If so, cover the chicken pieces to prevent them from drying out.

3 Heat a wok over a medium heat until hot. Add the salt and stir for about 2 minutes until it takes on a silvery grey colour. Remove the wok from the heat and let cool for 1–2 minutes. Add the peanut or vegetable oil and the sesame oil and reheat until very hot. Remove the wok from the heat and let cool for 2–3 minutes. Add the stock or poaching liquid and the ginger powder and reheat over a gentle heat until the sauce comes to a simmer, stirring a few times to blend the ingredients. Add the dark meat of the chicken, move the pieces around gently to absorb the flavours and poach for several minutes until well done. Add the white meat and poach until it is very hot and has absorbed the flavour.

4 Remove the chicken together with some of the sauce on to a large serving dish already lined with some of the spring onions in the centre. Break up into pieces and arrange in your own studied haphazard manner. Scatter the coriander leaves on top. Put the remaining spring onions into 2–3 saucers and spoon over some of the sauce. Serve hot. The chicken should already have sufficient flavour; the extra sauce is used for dipping to individual taste.

Huadiao Chicken

SERVES 4 WITH 2 OTHER DISHES

1 cleaned chicken, 1.25–1.35 kilos (2¾–3 lb)
22.5 ml (1½ tbsp) honey dissolved in 15 ml (1 tbsp) warm water
25 g (1 oz/2 tbsp) pork fat, cut into 2–3 slices
1 knob ginger, about 2.5 cm (1 in), peeled and cut into slices
6 spring onions, trimmed and quartered
150 ml (5 fl oz/⅔ cup) Shaoxing Huadiao wine
150–175 ml (5–6 fl oz/⅔–¾ cup) chicken stock
15–22.5 ml (1–1½ tbsp) salt

IN 1988 when I visited Canton, I met Chef Li He, who for many years was the head chef at Guangzhou Restaurant. Among the numerous famous dishes synonymous with his name was this chicken one made in a sandpot with the best Shaoxing wine, called Huadiao. Even as I was trying to envisage its looks and sniff its aroma, the chicken was placed on the table and we ate the chopped pieces with gusto. As I had the good fortune of sitting next to Chef Li, he talked me through the procedure of how the chicken was made. As soon as I returned to Hong Kong, I made it and fêted my family, all of whom grunted their approval between the bites.

1 Bring a large pot of water to the boil. Plunge the chicken momentarily into it twice. The skin will become shiny. Pat dry.
2 While the skin is still warm, brush all over with the honey solution. Hang up the chicken and let dry for about 30 minutes.
3 In a sandpot or clay pot – a casserole can be used as a substitute – fry the pork fat over a medium heat until most of the grease has oozed out. Add the chicken and fry, turning it from side to side, until brown all over. Add the ginger and spring onions, stir them in the fat for a few seconds. Turn the heat up to high and immediately splash in half of the wine which will sizzle. When the sizzling dies down, add the stock and the salt

and bring to the boil. Laying the chicken on the thigh and covering the pot with the lid, continue to cook over a medium high heat for 15 minutes. Turn the chicken over to lie on the other thigh, cook for another 10 minutes before adding the remaining half of the wine and cook for another 5–10 minutes. The wine, added at this stage, enhances the fragrance. The chicken should be cooked by now, with some sauce in the pot. To test, insert a chopstick through the thigh of one leg; if no pink juices ooze out, the chicken is done.

4 Remove the chicken on to a board and chop it through skin and bones into rectangular pieces about 2 × 4 cm (¾ × 1½ in) and arrange on to a serving dish. However, if you wish to carve it in the manner to which you are accustomed, the taste of the chicken will be the same.

5 Reheat the sauce in the pot and pour it over the chicken. Serve hot immediately.

Rendezvous of Quails and Quail Eggs

ORIGINALLY this Sichuanese dish called for pigeons rendezvous-ing with pigeon eggs. But pigeon eggs, rare enough for the table in China these days, are almost unheard of in the West. Inspired by the idea, however, I have used quails and their eggs, both of which are easily available and not very expensive either.

Because quail meat is delicate, it can taste dry and pulpy if overcooked, and this pitfall often occurs when quails are roasted in the oven. Deep-frying them, on the other hand, seals in the juices and renders the birds deliciously moist.

子母會

SERVES 4 AS MAIN COURSE OR 8 WITH 4 OTHER DISHES

8 cleaned quails, each 115–140 g (4–5 oz)
15 ml (1 tbsp) honey
100–150 ml (4–5 fl oz/½–⅔ cup) hot water
about 40 ml (8 tsp) spiced salt (see p. 360), 20 ml (4 tsp) as seasoning, 10–20 ml (2–4 tsp) as dipping sauce
18 quail eggs
vegetable oil for deep-frying

1 Put your hand inside the cavity of each quail, feel for the viscera and remove the organs – lungs, heart, etc. Rinse the cavity, then pat dry thoroughly. Also pat dry the skin, if wet.

2 Put the honey in a small bowl and pour in the hot water to dissolve the honey.

3 While the honey is still warm, brush the skin of each

quail with the honey fluid, not missing wings or leg crevices.

4 Using your fingers, smear 2.5 ml (½ tsp) spiced salt throughout the cavity of each quail. This seasoning makes the quails delicious when deep-fried.

5 Hang the quails up to dry for about 4 hours. This can be done by tying string around the wings of each quail, then hanging the string on to a horizontal pole.

6 Meanwhile, place the quail eggs in a saucepan, add cold water to cover completely. Gently bring to the boil and cook for 2–3 minutes until the eggs are hard-boiled. Pour into a colander and refresh thoroughly under cold running water, then soak them in cold water for 20 minutes or longer. This facilitates the peeling of the eggs. Peel them and keep nearby.

7 When ready to serve the quails, half fill a wok over a wok-stand with oil and heat over a high heat to 190–200°C (375–400°F) in temperature. Add 4 quails (strings removed and discarded!) and deep-fry, laying them on the leg side for 2–2½ minutes. Turn them over with tongs or chopsticks and continue to deep-fry lying on the other leg side for another 2–2½ minutes. The quails should be just cooked by now but still juicy. Remove with a hand strainer and drain on kitchen paper. Deep-fry the other 4 quails as before.

8 To serve, either leave the quails whole or halve them then arrange them skin side up on a dish. Arrange the eggs around them, Spiced salt can be used as dipping sauce for both the eggs and the quails.

Scrambled Eggs
with Blanched Chives

SERVES 4 WITH 2 OTHER DISHES

50 g (2 oz) blanched chives
4 large eggs, size 1 or 2
1.5 ml (¼ tsp) salt or to taste
ground white or black pepper to
    taste
75 ml (5 tbsp) peanut or vegetable
    oil

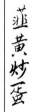

CHINESE chives are green, but blanched chives, having been shielded from light during their growth, are tenderly yellow. Compared to green chives, which have a decidedly stout flavour, blanched chives are much more subtle, and hence sought after by the Chinese. I love them so much that I can never have enough of them. For this reason, I'm using a lot in this recipe.

Fresh duck eggs can be used instead of chicken eggs. As they are usually large in size, use 3 instead of 4. Also Chinese green chives can be substituted for blanched chives, if necessary.

1 Rinse the blanched chives in plenty of cold water, picking out impurities and discarding wilted ends. Cut into 2.5 cm (1 in) lengths. Dry very well: for best effect, use a salad spinner to spin off excess moisture first, then pat dry with a tea towel or kitchen paper.
2 Beat the eggs in a large bowl until well blended and frothy. Add the salt, pepper and the chives and beat for a few more seconds to mix.
3 Heat a wok over a high heat until smoke rises. Add the oil and swirl it around until hot. Add the char siu and stir a few times. Pour in the egg mixture. Sliding the wok scoop to the bottom of the wok, keep turning and letting the liquid egg go to the bottom of the wok to be blended with the oil and become solidified. As soon as all the egg is set, remove the wok from the heat, then scoop the mixture on to a serving dish. Serve hot immediately.

50–85 g ((2–3 oz) char siu or Cantonese roast pork cut into small dice (*see* p. 307)

House of Confucius
Fried Eggs

IN THE family kitchen of the Kong House (the descendants of Confucius) in Shandong, eggs are used for everyday fare. But instead of preparing the egg whites and egg yolks together, they are fried separately, then seasoned in stock again. This thoughtful way in which ingredients, however ordinary, are prepared in order to maximise visual and taste effects, is a typical hallmark of Kong cuisine. The question of diet may not have been uppermost in the minds of the cooks, but those who wish to avoid egg yolks because of cholesterol, can easily do so but still enjoy the dish.

1 Soak the dried shrimps in 15 ml (1 tbsp) hot water and 15 ml (1 tbsp) of the wine or sherry for about 30 minutes. Mince finely in a food processor with the soaking liquid. Keep nearby.

SERVES 6 WITH 3 OTHER DISHES

25 g (1 oz) dried shrimps, rinsed
30 ml (2 tbsp) Shaoxing wine or medium dry sherry
8 water chestnuts, peeled and rinsed (if canned, drained)
6 large eggs, size 2
2–2.5 ml ((⅓–½ tsp) salt
75–90 ml ((5–6 tbsp) peanut or vegetable oil
3 spring onions, trimmed and cut into small rounds
150 ml (5 fl oz/⅔ cup) chicken stock

孔
府
炒
蛋

2 Mince finely the water chestnuts. Keep nearby.

3 Crack the eggs, separating the yolks from the whites, into 2 separate bowls. Add half the salt to each bowl. Beat the egg white lightly until frothy and the gels are completely broken. Beat the egg yolks until blended.

4 Heat a wok over a high heat until smoke rises. Add 30 ml (2 tbsp) of the oil and swirl it around to cover a large area. Pour in the egg white to form a circular cake about 15 cm (6 in) in diameter. Reduce the heat to medium and, sliding the wok scoop or a metal spatula to the bottom of the wok, let the still runny egg white go under to be fried. Flip over this egg-white cake and fry until all the egg white is set. Remove the cake to a dish and keep nearby.

5 The wok should be quite clean so that there is no need to wash it. Turn up the heat, add 30 ml ((2 tbsp) of the oil and swirl it around. Pour in the egg yolk to form a circular cake about 12.5 cm (5 in) in diameter and fry as above into a cake. Remove to a dish and keep nearby.

6 Heat the wok over a high heat again, add the remaining oil and swirl it around. Add the spring onion, stir a few times, then add the minced dried shrimps and turn and flip about 10 times. Add the minced water chestnuts and stir to mix until hot. Splash in the remaining wine or sherry and when the sizzling subsides, pour in the stock. Reduce the heat and bring the stock to a simmer. Return the egg cakes to the wok, placing the egg yolk one on top and cook them slowly until most of the stock is absorbed. Scoop the cakes on to a serving plate, spoon some of the seasoning mixture on top. Serve hot.

Braised Pigeon

In China, pigeons are usually prepared in one of two ways. They are either deep-fried or braised. For the former, they are hung up until the skin, which has been brushed with a honey liquid, becomes very dry and they are then deep-fried until the skin is crispy and russet and the flesh succulent. For the latter, they are braised in good soy sauce made aromatic by herbs, as described below.

4 pigeons or squabs with giblets (not wood pigeons), each about 450 g (1 lb)
30 ml (2 tbsp) peanut or vegetable oil
¾ star anise, or 6 segments
10 ml (2 tsp) thick or dark soy sauce

FOR THE HERBED SAUCE:
15 ml (1 tbsp) peanut or vegetable oil
45 g (1½ oz) pork fat, cut into small pieces
30 ml (2 tbsp) Mei Kuei Lu wine or gin
1½ star anise, or 12 segments
5 ml (1 tsp) Sichuan peppercorns
2.5 ml (½ tsp) cloves
2.5 cm (1 in) cinnamon stick, broken up
25 ml (1 fl oz) thick or dark soy sauce
25 ml (1 fl oz) thin or light soy sauce
1.5–2.5 ml (¼–½ tsp) salt
10 g (⅓ oz) Chinese rock sugar, or sugar
100 ml (4 fl oz) chicken stock or more

Illustrated on Plate 5.

1 Make sure to remove the giblets from the cavity of the pigeons, clean the gizzards, hearts and livers well and put aside. Remove also the lungs and discard. Rinse the pigeons, both the skin and the cavity, and pat dry.
2 Brown the pigeons. Heat a wok over a high heat until smoke rises. Add 30 ml (2 tbsp) of the oil and swirl it around. Add also 6 segments of star anise. Add 2 pigeons to brown for about 1½–2 minutes, turning over periodically so that the skin becomes brown all over. Remove from the wok and put on to a dish. Add the remaining 2 pigeons and repeat the browning procedure. Discard the burned oil and the star anise.
3 Using a small pastry brush, brush the skin of the pigeons with the thick or dark soy sauce in order to add some colour to it.
4 Prepare the herbed sauce. Heat a Chinese sandpot or a thick-bottomed casserole until hot. Add the oil and then add the pork fat to render the lard over a medium heat, uncovered, until most of it has oozed out. Remove the sandpot or casserole from the heat. Scoop out the rendered pork fat pieces, divide into 4 portions and put them into the cavities of the pigeons.

   While the melted lard is still hot, add the wine or gin. Add the star anise, Sichuan peppercorns, cloves and cinnamon. Add the soy sauces, salt, sugar and the stock. Slowly bring to a simmer and continue to simmer, covered, for 5 minutes in order to bring out the flavour of the herbs.
5 Add the 4 pigeons, breast side up, their gizzards and hearts to the sauce and return to a simmer. Continue to simmer gently, covered, for about 10 minutes. Check

the sauce and, if much has evaporated, add some more stock. Turn the pigeons over, ladle the sauce over them, then simmer for another 10 minutes. Add the livers and simmer for another 5 minutes. The pigeons are just about cooked, which is the way the Chinese like to eat them. Transfer the pigeons and their giblets to a warm dish.

6 Turn up the heat to reduce the sauce until it looks thickish. Strain it through a fine sieve, discard the herbs.

7 Either serve 1 pigeon per person with its giblets or chop the pigeons into pieces and cut the giblets into slices and put on to a serving dish. If the former, put the sauce into a bowl and let everyone help themselves; if the latter, pour some of the sauce over the pigeons.

PORK

PORK is to the Chinese what beef is to Europeans and Americans. More of it is eaten per capita than any other meat, and there is no part of the pig, from the head to the trotter, that the Chinese have not rendered into a delectable dish.

The significance of pork as a valued meat goes back a long way, at least to the time of Confucius, in the 5th century BC. The Master himself probably had a weakness for it, but even if he didn't, he certainly fell victim at least once to its being used as a strategic ploy to gain access to him. A scheming minister, Yang Huo, who had usurped power from his master, the reigning duke of Lu (modern Shandong), wanted to be received by Confucius, so as to appear to have gained the support of the sage. When Confucius refused to see him, he sent as a present a steamed piglet, but at a time when he knew that Confucius would not be in the house. At the time, etiquette required that if a minister sent a present to a scholar who was not at home to receive it, the latter would be obliged to acknowledge it by calling upon the former in person. In discharging his obligation, Confucius chose a time when he reckoned the minister would not be at home either. But, as fate would have it, he came across Yang on the way, who immediately cornered him for a face-to-face discussion, firing at him questions that he had to answer.

The liking for pork in north China must have continued unabated from that time, or at least hand in hand with the other valued meats, such as lamb and beef. A thousand years later, in the 6th century AD, the consumption of pork and the different methods of cooking it were detailed by the agriculturist Jia Sixie in his book, *Qimin Yaoshu* (*see* also p. 21). He talked about cooking lamb in the same vein as cooking pork; he gave a recipe for steaming a bear, which was followed by a similar one for steaming a pig; and he discussed how to cook pig's trotters and make pickled pork, using cooked rice as the fermenting agent. But most significantly, in the chapter on roasting, the emphasis centres on the pig, even though other animal meats, such as lamb, beef, venison and roebuck, are also mentioned. But the vivid description of the roasting of a suckling pig (*see* p. 23) leaves no doubt in anyone's mind as to what a delicious meat it was considered at the time.

This high regard for pork was not just limited to the Chinese. Their northeastern neighbours, the Manchus, who eventually fulfilled their ambition of ruling China from 1644 to 1911, had a long tradition of rearing pigs for food, as they, too, adored its taste. Furthermore, when they made sacrifices to the gods, they chose pigs with uniformly black hair and plump and weighty bodies as the sacrificial animals. After the ceremonies, the pork was distributed as the meat of blessing, and eaten in large quantities, as it was supposed to bring luck to the consumers.

The value of taste apart, the Chinese have also, by tradition, regarded pork as a health-enhancing food and source of protein. Thus, in many recipes for nutritious soups, lean pork is the meat used. But none can match the medicinal effect contained in the post-natal tonic dish of pig's trotters and ginger, which Cantonese and Fujianese women eat for one month after they give birth. This dish, prepared as far in advance as a month, consists of three large bottles of dark sweet vinegar to one of black vinegar, 2.3 kilos (5 lb) of peeled ginger cut into chunks, four large, meaty pig's hind trotters, chopped through the skin and bones into round pieces, and a dozen large eggs boiled in their shells, which is simmered in a sandpot for 4–5 hours until both the meat and the ginger are very tender. The new mother is expected to eat about three large bowlfuls of this daily as a form of food-medicine, because it is believed to be beneficial to her speedy recovery. The ginger rhizomes, which are known to have warming properties, are thought to increase blood circulation and help the contraction of the uterus, thus preventing prolonged bleeding afterwards. Being a stimulant, they also relieve wind in the bowel, a common annoyance to women both during pregnancy and after childbirth. Much of the calcium from the bones of the pig's trotters, not to mention from the eggshells as well, dissolves during the long period they soak in the vinegar, and it helps to replace the calcium the mother gave to the foetus in her womb for its bone formation. The pig's trotters and the eggs are a source of much needed protein, while last, but not least, the dish as a whole, being deliciously sweet and sour, acts as a tonic to stimulate her appetite, and hence the milk-flow in her breasts needed to sustain and nurture the new babe.

Even if not every part of the pig can claim to have such efficacy, every recipe I have included in this chapter is nevertheless guaranteed to be delicious! *Bon appétit.*

Char Siu

I GREW up eating these scrumptious Cantonese roast pork strips that you can see hanging in the windows of Cantonese restaurants. On reflection, it is also the very first dish I ever learned to cook before coming to England to continue my studies, and, thanks to it, I made many friends who marvelled as much at its succulence as at its intriguingly savoury-honey taste. Since those days, I have experimented with many different techniques and combinations of ingredients and have recently come up with this new version of a marinade which my eldest brother Yan-kin, himself a char siu expert, actually waxes lyrical about!

Although on a large, commercial scale char siu strips are roasted hanging inside a tall, vertical Chinese oven, they can also be cooked most effectively in an ordinary domestic oven, using either gas or electricity. With an electric oven, however, the conventional type rather than the fan oven is more suitable, for the latter tends to make the char siu too dry and fails to caramelise the outside properly. If you wonder at the large amount of sugar in the marinade, it is used for the caramelising effect.

SERVES 6 WITH 3 OTHER DISHES; 4 AS THE MAIN COURSE

1–1.25 kilos (2¼–2½ lb) pork without bone or rind but with the fat, best chump end, neck end and shoulder-blade

about 45 ml (3 tbsp) runny honey, not too thin in consistency

FOR THE MARINADE:
5 ml (1 tsp) salt
120 ml (8 tbsp) sugar
30 ml (2 tbsp) hoisin sauce
30 ml (2 tbsp) ground yellow bean sauce
15 ml (1 tbsp) mashed red bean curd cheese
5 ml (1 tsp) very finely chopped or puréed garlic
60 ml (4 tbsp) thin or light soy sauce
15 ml (1 tbsp) Shaoxing wine or medium dry sherry

Illustrated on Plate 15.

1 Cut the pork into 3 strips. Leave the fat on (or at least half of it) because it is delicately succulent when roasted.

2 Make about 3 diagonal cuts in opposite directions, cutting three-quarters through the width of a strip without cutting it into pieces. This allows for better absorption of the marinade and even heat reception in the oven. It also gives the pork the traditional char siu look.

3 Prepare the marinade. Place in a large bowl the salt, sugar, hoisin sauce, yellow bean sauce, red bean curd cheese, garlic, soy sauce and wine or sherry and stir to mix well. Put in the pieces of pork and coat all over with the marinade. Leave in the bowl for 4–8 hours (no need to leave overnight), turning the pieces over at hourly intervals and spearing with a sharp instrument for better absorption of the marinade.

4 Place the pieces of pork with the fat side on top, leaving a small gap between them, on a wire cake rack (placed on top of the oven rack) in the top third of the oven with a tray of water 1.25 cm (½ in) deep underneath to catch

the drippings. Roast in a preheated oven at 180–190°C (350–375°F) Gas Mark 4–5 for about 25 minutes, at the end of which time the top side will be reddish brown. Remove from the oven, dip each piece into the marinade and return to the rack with the bottom side up. Continue to roast at 180°C (350°F) Gas Mark 4 or less for another 25 minutes. Insert a chopstick or fork into the thickest part of one piece, if no pink juices run out, the pork is cooked. If the fat side does not have the caramelised burned colour, turn the pieces over once more and roast at the highest temperature for about 5 minutes. Take care, however, not to burn them or dry them up.

5 Remove to a wire rack. Immediately brush all over with honey, making sure not to miss the crevices. Let the excess honey, if any, drip through the rack.

6 Pour the remaining marinade into a saucepan and slowly bring it to the boil. Simmer for about 1 minute, then pour into saucers for use as a dipping sauce.

7 Transfer the pork to a serving platter and carve into slices. Serve immediately. The dipping sauce is for optional use, for the char siu is scrumptious without it.

NOTE: As an ingredient char siu is very versatile: sliced and piled on top of boiled rice with some vegetables, such as baak choi or lettuce, it makes a complete and nourishing 'one-plate' meal; chopped and diced, it is used in fried rice and in scrambled eggs, etc. It is also delicious cold and can be reheated in the oven.

Wuxi
Meaty Spareribs

SERVES 6 AS MAIN COURSE

1.5 kilos (3½ lb) sparerib chops or thick end belly pork with the ribs
850 ml (1½ pints/4 cups) cold water
25 g (1 oz) ginger, peeled and bruised

THIS is a very earthy dish bearing the name of a town not far from Shanghai. Two features distinguish these spareribs from other regional ones: their exaggerated sweetness, not always acceptable to non-Wuxi palates, and their relatively large size. I still remember the 'sweet impact' on my own tastebuds when I visited this charming town several years ago and ate them in a small local

Left: Dandan Noodles (p. 244).
Right: Sichuan Steamed Beef Coated with Ground Rices (p. 326).
Top and bottom: Lacquered Cashewnuts (p. 351).

PLATE I I

Top left: Sautéed Bean Curd with Spinach (p. 216).
Middle: Clear-steamed Seasonal Fish (p. 262).
Bottom right: 'Ah, Sweet as Honey' (p. 338).

PLATE 12

restaurant. In cooking the dish myself, I have toned down the sweetness, but retained its other characteristics.

In making this dish, Chinese crystal or rock sugar produces the best results. At a pinch, you could use white or brown sugar.

60 ml (4 tbsp) thick or dark soy sauce
45 ml (3 tbsp) Shaoxing wine or cream sherry
15 ml (1 tbsp) peanut or vegetable oil
50 g (2 oz) rock sugar, ground, about 60 ml (4 tbsp)
2–2.5 ml ((⅓–½ tsp) salt
6.5–7.5 ml (1¼–1½ tsp) Chinkiang (Zhenjiang) vinegar or 5 ml (1 tsp) red wine vinegar

1 Remove the rind from the pork, leaving, however, as much fat on the meat as possible. Discard the rind. Chop the spareribs with the meat into large pieces, say 5 × 7.5 cm (2 × 3 in) or to your own choice. Do not hesitate to ask your butcher to do this job for you.

2 Put the pieces into a large saucepan and add plenty of cold water to cover. Bring to the boil, uncovered, and continue to boil while you skim off the scum that surfaces until the water is relatively clear again. Pour everything into a colander and rinse the pork of any remaining scum. Clean the saucepan, removing the scum attached to the bottom.

3 Return the pieces to the saucepan. Add 850 ml (1½ pints/4 cups) cold water, add also the ginger and the soy sauce. Bring to the boil over a high heat, then add the wine or sherry and let boil for a few more seconds to release the aroma from the alcohol. Reduce the heat, add the lid to the saucepan and simmer.

4 Heat a wok or a small saucepan over a medium heat until just hot. Add the oil and swirl it around. Add the ground rock sugar and let it melt completely. Continue to cook until bubbles are formed on the surface and the sugar has become a coffee-brown colour. Remove from the heat and pour this caramelised sugar over the spareribs, taking care to replace the lid quickly to prevent explosive splashing when the hot sugar meets the liquid. The caramelised sugar enhances the fragrance of the spareribs.

5 Continue to simmer the spareribs for about 1¾ hours or until tender, by which time the liquid will have been reduced by about two-thirds.

6 Add the salt and vinegar and stir for even seasoning. The dish can be prepared up to this point several hours or overnight in advance. When ready to serve, reheat the spareribs in the saucepan, then remove them to a serving dish and keep warm nearby. Reduce the liquid over a high heat until the sauce appears dense and shiny. Remove and discard the ginger, pour the sauce over the spareribs and serve hot.

Braised Pork
Sparerib Chops with Hongzao

900 g (2 lb) pork sparerib chops
30 ml (2 tbsp) peanut or vegetable
  oil
10 ml (2 tsp) finely chopped garlic
10 ml (2 tsp) finely chopped
  ginger
8 giant spring onions, trimmed
  and halved
60 ml (4 tbsp) Shaoxing wine or
  medium dry sherry
90 ml (6 tbsp) hongzao (*see* p. 358)
300 ml (10 fl oz/1¼ cups) stock
285–350 g (10–12 oz) drained
  canned bamboo shoots, cut into
  wedges
5 ml (1 tsp) salt
2.5 ml (½ tsp) sugar

HONGZAO, a Fujian speciality made with red yeast and glutinous rice, is used as a seasoning to give a distinctively fermented, alcoholic and sweet taste to the main ingredients.

1 Do ask your butcher to chop the sparerib chops through the bones into chunks for you.

2 Heat a heavy-bottomed saucepan or casserole over a high heat until very hot. Add the oil and swirl it around to cover the entire bottom. Add the garlic, stir, but before it becomes burned add the ginger and stir several more times. Add the spring onions, stir together about half a dozen more times. Splash in the wine or sherry, let sizzle for a few seconds, then add the hongzao and stir vigorously to blend with the other ingredients. Add the pork, stir so that the sauce will coat. Pour in the stock and bring to the boil. Reduce the heat to the minimum and simmer very gently, with the lid on, for 1 hour. It may be necessary to place a metal heat diffuser underneath the saucepan to prevent excessive evaporation of the sauce.

3 Blanch the bamboo shoots. Meanwhile, bring a pot of water to the boil, add the bamboo shoots and cook for 2–3 minutes. Pour into a colander and rinse under cold running water, then drain. This is to get rid of the unpleasant odour often found in canned bamboo shoots.

4 Season the pork with the salt and sugar, add the bamboo shoots, give the mixture a good stir, then continue to simmer, covered, for another 20–30 minutes. The pork should be very tender by now. The dish can be prepared up to this point hours or even one day in advance.

5 Remove the pork from the saucepan, leaving behind the bamboo shoots, and spoon off excess grease on the surface of the sauce. Turn up the heat and reduce the sauce, uncovered, until it looks thickish and gelatinous. Depending on the amount of liquid, it may take 5–10 minutes. Reduce the heat, return the pork to the saucepan and stir to coat with the sauce. Scoop the mixture into a serving bowl (to give the rustic effect) and serve hot.

Muichoi
Moulded Pork

THE most celebrated Hakka pork dish which calls for the preserved local mustard greens, muichoi, as the main seasoning (*see also* p. 101). The success of this dish depends as much on the technique of loosening the rind of the belly pork, the only cut appropriate for the dish, as in steaming it to make it succulent.

SERVES 8–10 WITH 4–5 OTHER DISHES

225 g (8 oz) muichoi or 'preserved stem mustard', as labelled
2 pieces belly pork with rind, each about 7.5 cm (3 in) wide and 675 g (1½ lb)
30 ml (2 tbsp) thick or dark soy sauce
45 ml (3 tbsp) vegetable oil
5–10 ml (1–2 tsp) tapioca or potato flour dissolved in 15–30 ml (1–2 tbsp) water

FOR CURING MUICHOI
45 ml (3 tbsp) peanut or vegetable oil
10 ml (2 tsp) finely chopped garlic
10–15 ml (2–3 tsp) sugar
15 ml (1 tbsp) Shaoxing wine or medium dry sherry

Illustrated on Plate 8.

1 Rinse off the salt embedded in the stems of the muichoi. Blanch them in a pot of boiling water for about 3 minutes to get rid of some of the excessive saltiness. Drain, then soak them in cold water for about 15 minutes. Drain, then squeeze out excess moisture in the leaves, but leave damp. Cut into strips, then cut crossways at about 1 cm (under ½ in) intervals into small bits.

2 Cure the muichoi. Heat a wok over a high heat until smoke rises. Add the oil and swirl it around to cover a large area. Add the garlic and stir as it sizzles but, before it becomes burned, add the chopped muichoi. With the wok scoop or a metal spatula, toss and turn continuously for about 2 minutes or until fragrant. Add the sugar, continuing to stir for another minute. Splash in the wine or sherry, stirring as it sizzles. Taste the muichoi, which should still be quite salty, as it will season the pork. Scoop on to a dish and keep nearby.

3 Put the 2 pieces of belly pork in a large saucepan and add sufficient cold water to cover with an excess margin of about 2.5 cm (1 in). Bring to the boil, skim off the impurity which foams to the surface until the water is relatively clear. Lower the heat and simmer gently, covered, for about 20 minutes until the pork is just done. Remove from the saucepan and put on a dish, rind side up. The liquid can be saved for the stockpot, if wished.

4 While still hot, pierce the rind with a sharp instrument, making as many needle holes all over as possible. Put 15 ml (1 tbsp) of the soy sauce in a small dish and, using a pastry brush, brush a layer of it over the rind. Repeat the piercing–brushing procedure 2 more times; this will

loosen as well as colour the skin when it is shallow-fried later.

5 Heat a deep sauté pan (or a wok) over a high heat until smoke rises. Add the vegetable oil and swirl it around to cover the entire surface. Add the 2 pieces of pork, rind side down, and immediately cover the pan with a lid to prevent the splashing from getting out of hand. Fry the rind for 4–5 minutes or until russet brown, lowering the heat to medium if the rind becomes burned. Remove the lid and brown the meat sides momentarily. Remove the pork from the pan; discard the oil and grease. (Chinese restaurants execute this step by deep-frying the pork, but most people at home – myself included – would find it difficult; I have therefore devised this shallow-frying, but nonetheless effective, method.)

6 When the pork is cool enough to handle, cut each piece crossways into slices at 1 cm (under ½ in) intervals, leaving the slices in sequence.

7 Line the bottom of a heatproof bowl with sloping edges (a Chinese bowl with a perimeter of 24 cm/9½ in is ideal) with half of the cured muichoi. Arrange the pork slices in 2 rows, in sequence, on top, rind side down. Add the remaining 15 ml (1 tbsp) thick or dark soy sauce on the pork, then cover it with the remaining muichoi. Put the bowl in a steamer and steam over a high heat (*see* p. 355) for 2 hours, at the end of which time the pork is tender enough to eat. But since the flavour of this dish improves overnight, it would be better to leave it until the following day before serving it.

8 Just before serving, cover the bowl with a plate (or tin foil), return it to the steamer and steam for 1–1½ hours. Remove from the steamer.

9 Carefully pour the juices in the bowl that have accumulate from the steaming into a small saucepan. Add the dissolved tapioca or potato flour (5 ml/1 tsp flour to 75 ml/5 tbsp juices)and heat gently, stirring all the time to thicken the sauce slightly.

10 To serve, invert a large serving dish on the bowl; make sure the dish more than covers the perimeter of the bowl. Put your hands, one on top and one underneath the dish/bowl unit, and hold it firmly. Swiftly and decisively reverse your hands, turning the unit upside down. Remove the bowl from the dish, and you will

find that the pork slices are neatly arranged with the russet brown rind on top. Pour the hot sauce over and serve immediately.

Dongpo Pork

EVER since Su Dongpo waxed lyrical about pork in his poem (*see* p. 4), his name has become irrevocably linked with this casserole. Many restaurants in Hangzhou rival with each other in producing the ultimate version. Having eaten several myself, both in China and in Hong Kong, I have since worked out my own interpretation, and have also cooked it by both the easy way and the more lengthy way, both of which are listed below. I have to admit that whilst the easy way makes a delicious enough dish, the lengthy way makes the pork truly scrumptious.

SERVES 4–6 WITH 2–3 OTHER DISHES

about 800 g (1¾ lb) belly pork with rind
90–105 ml (6–7 tbsp) water
30 ml (2 tbsp) sugar
90–105 ml (6–7 tbsp) Shaoxing wine or medium dry sherry
90–105 ml (6–7 tbsp) thick or dark or mushroom soy sauce
8 thick slices ginger, peeled
10 spring onions, trimmed and halved

Illustrated on Plate 13.

1 Tear off and discard the thin layer of caul fat attached to the flesh; leave the rind on the other side intact. Cut the pork into 8 square or rectangular pieces.
2 Blanch the pork. Bring a pot of water to the boil. Add the pork and boil, uncovered, for about 2 minutes to let the scum surface continually. Pour into a colander and rinse the pork with warm water to remove any remaining scum. Drain.
3 Either, the easy way:
   Place the pork, rind side down, in a heavy-bottomed saucepan or casserole. Add 105 ml (7 tbsp) water, 30 ml (2 tbsp) sugar, 105 ml (7 tbsp) wine or sherry and pour 105 ml (7 tbsp) soy sauce evenly over the pork in order to colour it. Add the ginger and spring onion.
   Bring to the boil, then reduce the heat to very low to maintain a gentle simmer, covered, for 1 hour, at the end of which the rind should be dyed ruby red. Turn the pieces over, rind side up, and continue to simmer gently, covered, for 1–1½ more hours. To prevent having to add more water, due to evaporation, it may be necessary to place a heat diffuser underneath the saucepan or casserole.
   Transfer the contents to a bowl, discarding the ginger. Allow to cool and then put into the refrigerator

for a few hours so that the fat on the surface will congeal. Spoon off and discard the fat. The dish can be prepared up to this point 1–2 days in advance.

Or, the lengthy way resulting in more succulent and scrumptious pork:

Place the pork, rind side down, in 1 or 2 clay pots with lids (or with heatproof bowls and plates as lids). Add 90 ml (6 tbsp) water, 30 ml (2 tbsp) sugar, 90 ml (6 tbsp) wine or sherry and pour 90 ml (6 tbsp) soy sauce evenly over the pork in order to colour it. Add the ginger and spring onion. Put on the lid, or lids if 2 pots are used.

Place the lidded pots in a steamer and close-steam (*see* p. 355) over a medium high heat for up to 4 hours. Check the pork for tenderness after 2½ hours. When done, the pork, including the fat, is so succulent and tender that it almost melts in the mouth. There should be no loss of liquid in the pots.

Remove the pots from the steamer; discard the ginger. When cool, refrigerate for a few hours so that the fat will congeal. Spoon off and discard the fat. The dish can be prepared up to this point 1–2 days in advance.

4 When about ready to serve, remove the pork and the spring onions to a dish and keep nearby. Scrape the jellied sauce into a saucepan and boil over a high heat to reduce until it is dense and lightly caramelised. Reduce the heat to low, return the pork mixture to the saucepan and gently reheat until piping hot, spooning the sauce over the pork. Remove to a serving bowl and serve hot.

House of Confucius
Pork Fillet

THIS is an example of the style of cooking of the House of Confucius (*see* p. 86). One of the distinguishing features of this style lies in the ingenious manner in which an ordinary ingredient is treated thereby making it into a sophisticated dish.

1 Marinate the pork. Put the pork into a bowl, add the salt, soy sauce, wine or sherry, Sichuan peppercorns and spring onion rounds and stir to coat thoroughly. Leave to stand for about 15–20 minutes.
2 Gradually add the tapioca or potato flour into the egg white, stirring to mix until smooth and creamy. Pour on to the pork and mix to coat thoroughly.
3 Half fill a wok over a wok-stand with the oil and heat over a high heat until it reaches the temperature of 180°C (350°F). Carefully lower the pork, piece by piece, into the oil and deep-fry for 2 minutes, separating the pieces with chopsticks or tongs. Remove with a perforated disc and drain on kitchen paper. Reheat the oil to 180°C (350°F) and deep-fry the pork a second time for 1 minute to crisp. Remove as before and drain on kitchen paper.
4 Arrange the pork on a serving dish and sprinkle with the green spring onions. Serve hot with the sweet bean dipping sauce.

SERVES 4 WITH 2–3 OTHER DISHES

350 g (12 oz) pork fillet, cut crossways into 6 mm (¼ in) thick pieces
25 g (1 oz/¼ cup) tapioca or potato flour
1 large egg white, lightly beaten
vegetable oil for deep-frying
30 ml (2 tbsp) green spring onion rounds
sweet bean sauce (*see* p. 362) as dipping sauce

FOR THE MARINADE:
2.5 ml (½ tsp) salt
10 ml (2 tsp) thin or light soy sauce
10 ml (2 tsp) Shaoxing wine or medium dry sherry
7.5–10 ml (1½–2 tsp) roasted ground Sichuan peppercorns (*see* p. 359)
15 ml (1 tbsp) white spring onion rounds

The
Yin-Yang Dish

SERVES 8 WITH 4 OTHER DISHES

350 g (12 oz) chicken breast fillets,
cut crossways into slices about
3 mm (⅛ in) thick

350 g (12 oz) pork fillet, cut
crossways into slices about 3 mm
(⅛ in) thick

vegetable oil for deep-frying

60 ml (4 tbsp) peanut or vegetable
oil

8 g (¼ oz) cloud ears,
reconstituted (*see* p. 353) and
broken up

50 g (2 oz) canned bamboo shoots,
cut into thin slices and blanched
(*see* p. 353)

salt

half of 1 long cucumber, cut into
wedges

1 large clove garlic, peeled and
finely chopped

10 ml (2 tsp) finely chopped ginger

8 spring onions, trimmed and cut
into 4 cm (1½ in) sections, white
parts only

15 ml (1 tbsp) Shaoxing wine or
medium dry sherry

175 ml (6 fl oz/¾ cup) chicken
stock

15 ml (1 tbsp) thick or dark soy
sauce

twice 5 ml (1 tsp) tapioca or potato
flour dissolved in 15 ml (1 tbsp)
water, put into 2 separate dishes

MARINADE FOR CHICKEN:
2 ml (⅓ tsp) salt
6 turns white peppermill
10 ml (2 tsp) cornflour
1 egg white, lightly beaten
15 ml (1 tbsp) peanut or vegetable
oil

EVEN though Shanxi province cannot boast of a cuisine like its neighbouring province, Shandong, it nevertheless has produced a dish that is famous all over north China, especially in restaurants. It plays with the yin-yang concept, yin being the chicken and egg white, and yang the pork and egg yolk. The end result is an echo of the same theme, the whitish chicken next to the russet pork. It may look like a long recipe, but it is a fun one to make, particularly if you can enlist some help, for a dinner party.

1 Marinate the chicken. Put the chicken into a bowl. Add the salt, pepper, cornflour and egg white and stir to coat evenly. Leave to stand for about 15 minutes, then blend in the oil.

2 Marinate the pork. Put the pork into a bowl. Add the salt, pepper, soy sauce, wine or sherry and mix well. Sprinkle with the plain flour, add the egg yolk and stir to coat evenly. Leave to stand for about 15 minutes, then blend in the oil.

3 Sit a wok on the wok-stand and half fill it with vegetable oil. Heat over a high heat until it reaches 120°C (250°F) in temperature. Lower the chicken into the oil, separating the pieces with chopsticks, and fry for about 30 seconds until they have turned whitish. Scoop up with a perforated disc, draining the oil back into the wok, and put on to a dish.

4 Reheat the oil to 140°C (275°F) and deep-fry the pork in the same manner for about 30 seconds. Remove with a perforated disc and put on to a dish. Turn off the heat.

5 Heat a second wok (or frying pan) over a high heat until smoke rises. Add 15 ml (1 tbsp) of the peanut or vegetable oil and swirl it around. Add the cloud ears and bamboo shoots and stir for 1 minute over a moderate heat or until very hot. Season with salt to taste, then remove to a dish. Wipe the wok.

6 Reheat the wok as before and stir-fry the cucumber with 15 ml (1 tbsp) oil for 1–2 minutes until very hot, seasoning with salt to taste. Scoop on to another dish. Wipe clean the wok.

7 Reheat the wok over a high heat until smoke rises. Add 15 ml (1 tbsp) oil and swirl it around to cover a large area. Add the garlic, stir a few times, add half of the ginger and half the white spring onions and stir several times to release the aroma. Return the pork to the wok, stir until it is very hot again. Splash in the wine or sherry around the edges of the wok, then, when the sizzling subsides, add 75 ml (3 fl oz/⅓ cup) of the chicken stock and season with the thick soy sauce. Reduce the heat and add half the dissolved tapioca or potato flour, stirring as the sauce thickens. Return the cloud ears and bamboo shoots mixture to the wok, stirring to mix with the pork. Scoop this yang mixture on to one side of a large serving dish. Wash and wipe dry the wok.

8 Reheat the wok over a high heat until smoke rises. Add the remaining 15 ml (1 tbsp) oil and swirl it around. Add the remaining ginger and white spring onions and stir a few times. Reducing the heat, return the chicken to the wok and stir until very hot. Add the remaining stock and the remaining dissolved flour, stirring as the sauce thickens. Return the cucumber to the wok and stir to mix with the chicken. Scoop this yin mixture on to the other side of the serving dish. Serve hot immediately.

MARINADE FOR PORK:

2 ml (⅓ tsp) salt

6 turns black peppermill

10 ml (2 tsp) thick or dark soy sauce

5 ml (1 tsp) Shaoxing wine or medium dry sherry

10 ml (2 tsp) plain flour

1 egg yolk

15 ml (1 tbsp) peanut or vegetable oil

Pork Steamed
in Lotus Leaves

WHILE the Cantonese use lotus leaves to wrap cooked rice, Shanghaiese use them to wrap pork, which they then steam until meltingly tender. The flavour imparted from the leaf works wonders with the pork and the seasoning, making this a truly outstanding dish worthy of all the effort and trouble.

SERVES 8 WITH 4 OTHER DISHES

170 g (6 oz/1 cup) long-grain white rice

5 ml (1 tsp) roasted ground Sichuan peppercorns (*see* p. 359)

2.5–4 ml (½–¾ tsp) five-spice powder

1.5–2.5 ml (¼–½ tsp) salt

800 g (1¾ lb) rindless belly pork (without the spareribs)

5–6 dried lotus leaves, halved, making 10–12

1 Prepare roasted ground rice. Rinse the rice, drain and spread out until almost dry.

Heat a wok over a medium heat until hot but not smoking. Add the rice and the Sichuan peppercorns and fry them, going to the bottom of the wok with the wok

FOR THE MARINADE:

2.5 ml (½ tsp) salt

2.5 ml (½ tsp) sugar

15 ml (1 tbsp) thick or dark soy sauce

15 ml (1 tbsp) Shaoxing wine or medium dry sherry

7.5 ml (1½ tsp) ginger juice (*see* p. 357)

scoop and turning and tossing, for about 10 minutes until the rice is fragrant and brownish. Vary the heat so that the rice does not get burned. Remove and let cool.

Grind the rice in a liquidiser or blender, not to a powder but to a coarse sandy form. Put into a bowl, and stir in the five-spice powder and salt.

2 Cut the pork into rectangular pieces, say 2.5 × 5 cm (1 × 2 in). Cut each piece through the middle horizontally without splitting them into two.

3 Marinate the pork. Add the salt, sugar, soy sauce, wine or sherry and ginger juice to the pork, piercing each piece with a sharp instrument for better absorption. Leave for about 30 minutes; all the marinade should be absorbed.

4 Dip the pork, piece by piece, into the ground rice, coating it generously all over, including the split centre.

5 Either steam (*see* p. 355) the lotus leaves for 5 minutes or soak them in hot water for 10 minutes in order to make them pliable.

6 Place 2 pieces of pork on the inside of 1 piece of lotus leaf. Fold the corners inwards, wrapping the pork well, then turn the parcel over. There is no need to seal. Repeat until all are done.

7 Place the parcels, folds-side down, straight on to the perforated steaming container of a steamer, preferably in one layer, and steam for 1½–2 hours. During this time, much fat from the pork will run out greasing the lotus leaves which, in turn, will impart their fragrance to the pork. If the parcels have to be put in 2 layers, steam for 1 hour, alternate the layers and steam for 1 more hour. The dish can be prepared up to this point hours in advance and reheated (by steaming) until hot.

8 To serve, remove the parcels to a large serving dish. Let individuals take a parcel, unwrap the leaf and eat with chopsticks, or a knife and fork if preferred.

Salted and Fresh
Pork Casserole

A DISH carrying much fame south of the Yangzi River, it features in Shanghai restaurants as well as in homes. Locally, it is made with fresh belly pork and salted leg joints, rendered the more delicious by the use of fresh bamboo shoots during spring-time. Alas, we can only use canned bamboo shoots, although the end result is more than acceptable.

SERVES 6–8 WITH 3–4 OTHER DISHES

675 g (1½ lb) belly pork with rind, cut into pieces about 5 × 2.5 cm (2 × 1 in) in size.
450 g (1 lb) gammon, leg or shoulder, cut into pieces about 5 × 2.5 cm (2 × 1 in) in size.
350 g (12 oz) canned bamboo shoots, cut into wedges
25–45 g (1–1½ oz) ginger, peeled, cut into wedges and bruised
6 large spring onions, trimmed and quartered
30 ml (2 tbsp) Shaoxing wine or medium dry sherry

1 Put the belly pork, the gammon and the bamboo shoots in a heavy-bottomed saucepan or casserole and add sufficient water to cover. Bring to the boil and blanch for about 3 minutes, allowing the scum to surface. Pour into a colander and rinse with cold water to rid the pork and gammon of adhering scum. Wash the saucepan or casserole.

2 Return the pork and gammon only to the pot. Add sufficient water to cover the meat; add also the ginger and spring onions and bring to the boil. Reduce the heat and simmer gently, covered, for about 1½ hours until the meat is tender and succulent. Using a perforated spoon, scoop up the pork and gammon.

3 Reduce the juice in the pot over a high heat to 575–750 ml (20–25 fl oz/2½–3 cups). Test for taste – if the juice has a rich salty taste to it, you have reduced to the right amount.

4 Return the meat to the pot. Add the bamboo shoots, bring to the boil, then add the wine or sherry. Reduce the heat and simmer for another 10–15 minutes. Remove everything to a large, deep bowl and serve hot with the juice.

Shredded Pork
with Fish-fragrant Sauce

SERVES 6 WITH 3 OTHER DISHES

450 g (1 lb) pork fillet or lean
   chump end
15 g (½ oz) cloud ears,
   reconstituted (*see* p. 353)
50–75 g (2–3 oz) canned bamboo
   shoots, blanched (*see* p. 353)
6 water chestnuts, if fresh, peeled,
   if canned, drained
75–90 ml (5–6 tbsp) peanut or
   vegetable oil
10 ml (2 tsp) finely chopped garlic
10 ml (2 tsp) finely chopped
   ginger
4–5 spring onions, trimmed and
   cut into small rounds, white and
   green parts separated
15–30 ml (1–2 tbsp) hot
   broadbean paste
15 ml (1 tbsp) Shaoxing wine or
   medium dry sherry
10–15 ml (2–3 tsp) Chinese rice
   vinegar
7.5 ml (1½ tsp) caster sugar

FOR THE MARINADE:
1.5 ml (¼ tsp) salt
5 ml (1 tsp) tapioca or potato flour
15 ml (1 tbsp) water
15 ml (1 tbsp) sesame oil

FOR THE SAUCE:
4 ml (¾ tsp) tapioca or potato
   flour dissolved in 60 ml (4 tbsp)
   chicken stock or water
22.5 ml (1½ tbsp) thin or light soy
   sauce

SICHUAN is in the western interior of China, with no access to the sea, hence the absence of sea-water fish for local consumption. But the people there, galvanised by their vivid imagination, have invented a flavour they call fish-fragrant – a combination of spicy hot broadbean paste with vinegar and sugar. Meat, such as pork and rabbit, becomes seductively delicious when stir-fried with a sauce of this flavour.

1 Cut the pork into threadlike strips about 5–6 cm (2–2½ in) long and 4 mm (⅕ in) thick. Put into a bowl.
2 Marinate the pork. Add the salt, tapioca or potato flour and water to the meat and stir to coat. Leave to stand for about 20 minutes. Blend in the sesame oil.
3 Cut the drained cloud ears and bamboo shoots into narrow strips; cut the water chestnuts into thin slices.
4 Prepare the sauce. Mix the dissolved tapioca or potato flour with the soy sauce. When ready to cook, add the green spring onion.
5 Heat a wok over a high heat until smoke rises. Add the oil and swirl it around. Add the garlic which will sizzle and take on colour instantly. Add the ginger and white spring onion; stir a few times. Add the broadbean paste, stir, then add the pork, cloud ears, water chestnuts and bamboo shoots. Sliding the wok scoop to the bottom of the wok, flip and toss for 1 minute, separating the pork strips. Splash in the wine or sherry around the sides of the wok, stirring as it sizzles. Add the vinegar and sugar and continue to stir for about 1½–2 more minutes or until the pork, having turned whitish, is cooked. Add the well-stirred sauce, stirring as it thickens.
6 Scoop all the ingredients on to a serving dish and serve immediately.

Yunnan
White-cooked Pork

THE origin of this dish is Manchurian rather than Chinese, even though it has long since become an integral part of the Chinese repertoire, with its regional variations. The Manchus used to make sacrifices to the gods with pigs and, after the ceremony, would serve the pork which was then sliced off by the officers' own swords. A custom gradually developed whereby guests were invited to eat what was called the pork of blessing, or huge pieces of pork plainly steamed or boiled (white-cooked) in water. From this has evolved the northern dish of boiled pork, which is cut into very thin slices and is accompanied by puréed garlic and soy sauce. Migrating from the north to the western interior and southwest, the sauce has taken on a characteristically spicy flavour. The Yunnan sauce is potent indeed, and stimulating.

SERVES 6 WITH 3 OTHER DISHES

1 piece pork, about 550 g (1¼ lb), such as boned fillet chump end (between loin and leg)

FOR THE SAUCE:
15 ml (1 tbsp) very finely chopped garlic
15 ml (1 tbsp) very finely chopped ginger
2.5 ml (½ tsp) red chilli powder
45 ml (3 tbsp) peanut or vegetable oil
45 ml (3 tbsp) thick or dark soy sauce

1 Put the piece of pork in a large saucepan and cover with plenty of water. Bring to the boil, then spoon off the scum that foams to the surface. Pour into a colander and rinse the pork clean of any scum attached to it. Wash the saucepan.

2 Return the pork to the saucepan and add water to cover. Bring to the boil, then immediately reduce the heat to maintain a very gentle simmer to cook the pork, covered, for 30–45 minutes, depending on the thickness. Test by inserting a chopstick or fork into the thickest part; if no pink juices run out, the pork is cooked. If unsure, you can leave it in the saucepan, covered, for another 15 minutes with the heat turned off.

3 Transfer the pork to a colander and rinse under cold water for about 10–15 minutes; this will crisp up the texture. Pat dry and put into the refrigerator, covered, for 3–4 hours or overnight.

4 Prepare the sauce. In a heatproof bowl mix the garlic and ginger thoroughly. Sprinkle on the chilli powder and mix well again. Put the oil in a small saucepan and heat it until smoke rises. Remove from the heat and dribble it over the garlic mixture which will sizzle and

be partially cooked, releasing a heady aroma. Stir to mix. Add the soy sauce and stir again. Pour half of the sauce into another bowl and put both of them on the dining table as a dipping sauce.

5 Put the pork on a carving board and cut into paper-thin pieces of more or less uniform size. Arrange the slices on a serving dish or platter, overlapping each other. Serve cold. Individuals can pick up pieces and either dip them into the sauce or spoon some sauce to put over the pieces.

BEEF
AND
LAMB

IN Liji (Li Chi) or *The Book of Rites*, an ancient record about the regulations governing proper court behaviour during the Zhou dynasty (11th century–221 BC), one of the rites regarding meat consumption is very revealing. Unless it was for a special occasion, feudal lords were not allowed to slaughter an ox, ministers of state were not allowed to slaughter a lamb, scholars were not allowed to slaughter a dog or a pig, and commoners were not allowed to eat meat. It can be inferred from this that the emperor was the only person who was entitled to eat beef whenever it took his fancy; presumably, his consort or concubines, or perhaps some of his children, who were lucky enough to be eating with him, could also taste it.

Animal meat was therefore not just a luxury to be enjoyed only by the upper classes, but it was also graded in this order: beef, lamb, pig and dog. As we have seen from Mencius' discourse with the king (*see* p. 7), the ox was the animal used for making sacrifices. It is not surprising, therefore, that its flesh was considered superior to that of other animals.

Be that as it may, by the 6th century AD, when we can glean information of the northern diet through Jia Sixie's book, *Qimin Yaoshu (see* p. 23), beef and lamb seem to be on a par with each other for those who could afford them. When Jia refers to the methods of cooking meat, whether it be stewing, drying and salting or roasting, he lumps ox and lamb, roebuck and venison as well as pig together. Curiously, in the chapter on steaming and cooking bear, pig, goose, duck and chicken, there is no mention of ox or beef.

That lamb was the predominant meat for north and northwestern China, especially among the nomadic people and the Mongols, is reflected in an important work, *Yinshan Zhengyao* or *Principles of Correct Diet*, written by the Imperial dietician, Hu Sihui or Hoshoi, during the late Yuan dynasty (AD 1279–1368). This contains just a sprinkling of recipes related to ox, such as one using ox trotters, plus a couple using bone marrow, one making baked dry beef cubes and a couple using butter. The recipes dealing with lamb and mutton, however, amount to more than seventy, and use every part of the animal – head, trotters, tail and offals, bone and bone marrow.

Skipping down to the 18th century and over to the eastern region of China, the guiding spirit of the culinary scene, Yuan Mei, also seems to have favoured lamb over beef. In the chapter on beef, lamb and venison in his cookery book (*see* p. 38), he gives only one beef casserole and one ox tongue dish, but eight recipes for lamb. There is one for casserole of lamb's head, one for trotters, one lamb stew, one stir-fried lamb's tripe, one red-braised lamb, one stir-fried shredded lamb, one for roasted lamb on a spit, plus one that concerns the cooking of a whole lamb.

But the southern Chinese have always preferred beef to lamb and mutton which, more often than not, they regard as having a malodorous smell that needs disguising. Many simply will not eat it. There is, however, a folk belief that lamb, unlike beef which is definitely a yang food containing fiery property, is a temperate food with a warming quality beneficial to the stomach. As a child, I remember I used to wonder why my father would, once a year, insist on the whole family eating a mutton casserole during the winter. At the sight of us holding our noses at the table, he would coax: 'Now, now, eat up everything; it will keep you warm throughout the winter.'

Another folk belief about lamb takes the form of a punning prejudice. Southern Chinese refer to epileptic fits as 'lamb's fits'. As a consequence, many mothers still caringly enjoin their pregnant daughters not to eat lamb, lest their children be inflicted with the illness even in the womb.

On the whole, there is, to this day, a divide between the northern and the southern attitude towards lamb. Lamb is consumed more in the north, having a popular appeal at all levels, not just to Chinese Muslims. Cookery books concerned with the Cantonese cuisine will carry but a handful of lamb recipes, while there are many more in those which specialise in the Peking cuisine.

The beef that is sold in China, whether in the south or in the north, is quite green; or, in other words, unlike beef sold in the West, it has not been hung for very long. As a measure to counter the resultant chewiness, Chinese cooks, especially Cantonese ones, are wont to use bicarbonate of soda as a tenderiser when they marinate beef slivers prior to stir-frying them. While it works well in making green beef more tender, I find that when used on well-hung beef, such as that found in Europe and America, it spoils rather than enhances its texture.

Beef in a
Spicy Soup-Sauce

APPARENTLY, this dish originated in the south of Sichuan, where salt wells abounded, and domestic cattle were used to push the carts which brought the water up from the wells. When these cattle became exhausted within six months, they were slaughtered and their meat was used as part payment to the labourers who worked for the salt-producing industry. At first, the labourers could do little more than slice the tough meat as thinly as possible and cook it in water seasoned with plenty of salt, a relatively cheap commodity available to them. As time went by, they found themselves adding local condiments such as Sichuan peppercorns and chillies which, to their delight, not only eliminated what they considered the rank odour of the beef but actually improved its taste, and eating this dish gradually became pleasurable. Eventually, after cooks took it upon themselves to use a good cut of beef and add more condiments to give depth and intensity to the flavours of the dish, it has become a classic, renowned for inducing sweat as you eat it.

水煮牛肉

SERVES 4 WITH 2 OTHER DISHES

450–500 g (1–1 lb 2 oz) rump steak

FOR THE MARINADE:
1 large egg, size 1
20 ml (4 tsp) potato or tapioca flour
5 ml (1 tsp) salt

FOR THE SOUP-SAUCE:
60 ml (4 tbsp) peanut or vegetable oil
4 large dried red chillies, topped
2 large cloves garlic, peeled and cut into slivers
5 ml (1 tsp) finely chopped ginger
15 ml (1 tbsp) hot broadbean or soy bean paste
15 ml (1 tbsp) black beans, rinsed and mashed
2.5 ml (½ tsp) Sichuan peppercorns
4 spring onions, trimmed and cut diagonally at 2.5 cm (1 in) intervals
30 ml (2 tbsp) Shaoxing wine or medium dry sherry
300 ml (10 fl oz/1¼ cups) prime stock (*see* p. 361)
2.5 ml (½ tsp) ground roasted Sichuan peppercorns (*see* p. 359)
1.5 ml (¼ tsp) chilli powder, optional

1 Trim the steak well. There should be about 350 g (12 oz) beef after trimming. Cut across the grain into rectangular pieces about 5 × 4 cm (2 × 1½ in) and 6 mm (¼ in) thick. Put into a bowl.
2 Marinate the beef. Add the egg to the bowl and stir to blend in with the beef. Add the potato or tapioca flour and stir in one direction to mix well. Add the salt and stir to mix. Leave to stand for about 30 minutes.
3 Make the soup-sauce. Heat a wok over a high heat until

smoke rises. Add the oil and swirl it around. Add the chillies, lower the heat to medium, and brown the chillies for a few seconds without burning them. With a perforated spoon remove the chillies, cut them into pieces and reserve nearby.

Add the garlic to the oil, stir, then add the ginger and stir. Add the hot broadbean or soy bean paste and the mashed black beans and stir to blend with the oil. Add the Sichuan peppercorns and the spring onions and stir a few more times. Turn the heat to high and splash in the wine or sherry which will sizzle. As the sizzling subsides, pour in the stock, and gradually bring the stock to the boil.

4 Add the beef and separate the pieces with the wok scoop or a spatula as the stock gradually returns to a simmer. Lower the heat and let the beef simmer for 30–60 seconds or longer, depending on how rare or well done you prefer your beef. Remove the beef with a perforated spoon or disc and put into a serving bowl. Continue to simmer the soup-sauce for another minute or longer. Add the ground roasted Sichuan peppercorns and chilli powder, if used, and stir to mix. Pour the sauce on to the beef and mix. Garnish with the reserved chilli. Serve hot.

Sichuan Steamed Beef Coated with Ground Rices

SERVES 4–6 WITH 2–3 OTHER DISHES

450–550 g (1–1¼ lb) beef, rump or skirt best, trimmed
90 ml (6 tbsp) roasted ground two rices (*see* p. 359)
90 ml (6 tbsp) water
2–3 branches coriander leaves, trimmed and torn up roughly, or 3–4 spring onions, trimmed and cut into small rounds
22.5 ml (1½ tbsp) sesame oil

In the 1980s when I first visited Chengdu, the capital of Sichuan province, I was enchanted by the scene of tall stacks of bamboo steamers staring at me from the front, open kitchen of taverns and food stalls. The whiff of aroma that escaped with the steam and the small size of these baskets – no more than 6.5 cm (2½ in) across – made them the more captivating. I soon discovered that passers-by were buying these baskets and eating the contents right then and there. As I followed suit, I was treated to the Sichuan speciality of beef coated in ground rices. I have since worked out the method and I use larger bamboo baskets in order to feed more people.

1 Cut the beef into rectangular pieces about 5 × 2.5 cm (2 × 1 in) and 6 mm (¼ in) thick. Put into a mixing bowl.

2 Marinate the beef with the spicy marinade: add the ginger juice or puréed ginger, soy sauce, mashed black beans and hot soy bean paste to the beef and stir to coat. Sprinkle with the Sichuan peppercorns and stir again. Leave to stand for about 20 minutes, then stir in the oil.

Marinate the beef with the non-spicy marinade: add the ginger juice or puréed ginger, soy sauce, red bean curd cheese juice and wine or sherry to the beef and stir to coat. Sprinkle with the Sichuan peppercorns and stir again. Leave to stand for 2–3 hours for a better absorption of the 'cheese' flavour. Stir in the oil.

3 When ready to steam the beef, add the ground rices and mix to coat every slice on both sides. Stir in the water which will help to cook the ground rices. Put the beef directly on to the slotted base of either 1 larger or 2 small bamboo steaming baskets. Place the baskets in a steamer and steam (see p. 355) for 15–20 minutes, at the end of which time the rices as well as the beef should be cooked. Replace the lid of the steamer, scatter the coriander leaves or chopped spring onions on to the beef and steam again for 1–2 minutes so that the coriander leaves or spring onions will be partially cooked. Remove the baskets from the steamer and put them on two plates, dribble the sesame oil on the beef and serve immediately.

FOR THE MARINADE:

either spicy:

7.5 ml (1½ tsp) ginger juice or puréed ginger (*see* p. 357)

10 ml (2 tsp) thick or dark soy sauce

30 ml (2 tbsp) fermented black beans mashed with 15 ml (1 tbsp) Shaoxing wine or medium dry sherry

15 ml (1 tbsp) or more hot soy bean paste

2.5 ml (½ tsp) roasted ground Sichuan peppercorns (*see* p. 359)

45 ml (3 tbsp) peanut or vegetable oil

or non-spicy:

7.5 ml (1½ tsp) ginger juice or puréed ginger (*see* p. 357)

15 ml (1 tbsp) thick or dark soy sauce

45 ml (3 tbsp) juice from red bean curd cheese jar (*see* p. 365)

15 ml (1 tbsp) Shaoxing wine or medium dry sherry

2.5 ml (½ tsp) roasted ground Sichuan peppercorns (*see* p. 359)

45 ml (3 tbsp) peanut or vegetable oil

Illustrated on Plate 11.

Numbing and
Fragrant Beef

SERVES 6 WITH 3 OTHER DISHES

350 g (12 oz) fillet or rump or
   flank (skirt) steak, trimmed and
   cut into rectangular pieces about
   2 × 4 cm (¾ × 1½ in) and 8 mm
   (⅓ in) thick
45 ml (3 tbsp) peanut or vegetable
   oil
10 ml (2 tsp) finely chopped garlic
coriander stalks from 8 branches,
   cut into 5 cm (2 in) lengths
15 ml (1 tbsp) Shaoxing wine or
   medium dry sherry

FOR THE MARINADE:
1.5 ml (¼ tsp) salt
10 ml (2 tsp) mushroom soy
   sauce, or thick or dark soy sauce
5 ml (1 tsp) Shaoxing wine or
   medium dry sherry
5–10 ml (1–2 tsp) roasted ground
   Sichuan peppercorns (see p. 359)
1.5 ml (¼ tsp) five-spice powder
5 ml (1 tsp) tapioca or potato flour
15 ml (1 tbsp) water
15 ml (1 tbsp) sesame oil

WITH a title like this, it has got to be a Sichuan dish capitalising on the native Sichuan peppercorns, which leave a tantalisingly numbing effect on the tongue. For those who wish to have a heady dose of the sensation, use the larger amount listed below.

1 Marinate the beef. Put the beef into a bowl, add the salt, soy sauce, wine or sherry, Sichuan peppercorns, five-spice powder and tapioca or potato flour and stir to coat evenly. Add the water and stir vigorously until absorbed. Leave to stand for 15–20 minutes. Blend in the oil.

2 Heat a wok over a high heat until smoke rises. Add the oil and swirl it around several times to cover a large area, heating it at the same time. Add the garlic, stir and let sizzle, but before it becomes burned, add the coriander stalks and stir to release the aroma. Add the beef and, going to the bottom of the wok with the wok scoop, toss and turn, separating the pieces, for about 30 seconds. Splash in the wine or sherry around the edges of the wok, continuing to stir as it sizzles for another 30–60 seconds, depending on how well done you would like your beef. By now the spices, interacting with the seasonings, will have made this stir-fried beef truly fragrant for the nostrils and slightly numbing for the palate. Scoop on to a serving dish and serve hot immediately.

Stir-fried Beef
with Bitter Melon

BITTER MELON has a tangy bitter flavour but at the same time it leaves a cooling aftertaste on the tongue that is quite unique. Not only the Chinese have a penchant for it, but also the Indians and the Caribbeans. Stir-fried with a strong meat, beef, the flavour of which is made the more robust by the black beans and garlic, the overall flavour of the dish is perhaps an acquired taste, but I do recommend it. Once you have acquired the taste, you can't help but sing its praise and recommend it to others.

苦瓜炒牛肉

SERVES 8 WITH 4 OTHER DISHES

675 g (1½ lb) fillet steak, trimmed
675 g (1½ lb) bitter melons, rinsed
salt
120 ml (8 tbsp) peanut or vegetable oil
2 cm (¾ in) Chinese brown sugar in pieces or 5 ml (1 tsp) brown sugar
15 ml (1 tbsp) finely chopped garlic
10 ml (2 tsp) finely chopped ginger
4 spring onions, trimmed and cut into 5 cm (2 in) sections, white and green parts separated
45 ml (3 tbsp) fermented black beans, rinsed and mashed, leaving some whole, if preferred
15 ml (1 tbsp) Shaoxing wine or medium dry sherry

FOR THE MARINADE:
2 ml (⅓ tsp) salt
2 ml (⅓ tsp) sugar
15 ml (1 tbsp) thick or dark soy sauce
10 turns black peppermill
10 ml (2 tsp) Shaoxing wine or medium dry sherry
7.5 ml (1½ tsp) tapioca or potato flour
30 ml (2 tbsp) water
10–15 ml (2–3 tsp) sesame oil

FOR THE SAUCE:
5 ml (1 tsp) tapioca or potato flour
75 ml (5 tbsp) stock or water
10 ml (2 tsp) thin or light soy sauce

1 Cut the beef across the grain into rectangular pieces about 2 cm (¾ in) wide, 4–5 cm (1½–2 in) long and 6 mm (¼ in) thick. Put into a bowl.

2 Marinate the beef. Add the salt, sugar, soy sauce, pepper, wine or sherry and tapioca or potato flour to the beef and stir to coat. To make its texture velvety, add the water, 15 ml (1 tbsp) at first, and stir in the same direction until completely absorbed before adding the rest. Leave to stand for about 20 minutes. Blend in the oil.

3 Halve the bitter melons lengthways. Remove and discard the pulp with the seeds. Cut all the pieces on the diagonal into slices about 6 mm (¼ in) thick. Sprinkle all over with 7.5 ml (1½ tsp) salt and leave for 20–30 minutes. Rinse with cold water, then squeeze out excess moisture. This helps to get rid of some of the bitterness in the melons.

4 Prepare the sauce. Put the tapioca or potato flour in a small bowl. Gradually add the stock or water, stirring to dissolve it. Add the soy sauce.

5 Heat a wok until hot. Add 30 ml (2 tbsp) of the oil and swirl it around. Add the sugar, melt it completely, then add the melons, and stir for 1–2 minutes until piping hot. Remove to a dish and keep nearby.

6 Reheat the wok over a high heat until smoke rises. Add the remaining 90 ml (6 tbsp) oil and swirl it around, heating until smoke rises. Add the garlic, stir, add the ginger, stir, add the white spring onions, stir, and add the black beans and stir to enhance the aroma. Add the

beef and, going to the bottom of the wok with the wok scoop, turn and toss for about 30 seconds until the beef is partially cooked. Splash in the wine or sherry around the sides of the wok, stirring as it sizzles. Return the melons to the wok, pour in the well-stirred sauce and continue to stir as it thickens. Scatter in the green spring onions and scoop everything on to a serving dish. Serve hot immediately.

White-cooked Beef Fillet

SERVES 2 AS MAIN COURSE

285 g (10 oz) trimmed beef fillet
300 ml (10 fl oz/1¼ cups) water
6 thin slices ginger, peeled
8 spring onions, trimmed and cut into 5 cm (2 in) sections, white and green parts separated
15–30 ml (1–2 tbsp) peanut or vegetable oil
1 head lettuce, preferably crisp, like Little Gem, Iceberg or Cos, leaves separated

FOR THE MARINADE:
2.5 ml (½ tsp) salt
1.5 ml (¼ tsp) sugar
10 ml (2 tsp) thin or light soy sauce
5 ml (1 tsp) Shaoxing wine or medium dry sherry
10 turns black peppermill
5 ml (1 tsp) tapioca or potato flour
15 ml (1 tbsp) water
10 ml (2 tsp) peanut or vegetable oil
10 ml (2 tsp) sesame oil

A ONE-COURSE dinner I often make for my son, Hugo, whose favourite foods are simple but delicious dishes accompanied by boiled, rather than fried, rice. With this dish, he gets not only red meat balanced by a green vegetable, but also soup as a side dish so that at the end of the meal not only are his tastebuds satisfied, he feels healthily fed and nourished.

1 Cut the beef across the grain into large slices about 5 mm (⅕ in) thick. Put into a mixing bowl.

2 Marinate the beef. Add the salt, sugar, soy sauce, wine or sherry, pepper, tapioca or potato flour and water to the beef and stir to mix until the water is absorbed. Leave to stand for about 15–20 minutes. Blend in the oils.

3 Pour the water into a fairly large saucepan and bring it to a simmer. Add the ginger and white spring onions and continue to simmer for another minute. Turn the heat to high to bring the water to a bubbling boil. Add the beef, spreading out the pieces and turning over as well. As soon as both sides have turned opaque in colour but are still underdone, remove the saucepan from the heat. Continue to stir and mix for another 10–20 seconds before scooping the beef into a bowl with a perforated disc, leaving the seasoned liquid and ginger and spring onions behind.

4 Reheat the liquid to a boil. Add the 15–30 ml (1–2 tbsp) peanut or vegetable oil. Add the lettuce and green

spring onions and poach for about 1 minute until the pieces are limp but still crunchy. Remove with a perforated disc, leaving all the liquid behind, and line them on a serving dish. Arrange the beef pieces on top and serve immediately.

5 Reheat the liquid in the saucepan, then pour into two small bowls and serve as a soup on the side to accompany rice.

Slippery Egg
with Beef Slivers

AN EVERYDAY Cantonese family dish that makes for a tasty one-plate meal with rice and a few blanched green vegetables. Indeed, Cantonese often serve this to their young or teenage children who need as many vitamins and protein for their growing bodies as flavours for their developing tastebuds.

SERVES 3–4 WITH SOME GREEN VEGETABLES

350 g (12 oz) rump or skirt steak, trimmed and cut into rectangular slivers about 6 mm (¼ in) thick
120 ml (8 tbsp) peanut or vegetable oil
6 large eggs, size 2
2.5 ml (½ tsp) salt or to taste
white or black ground pepper to taste
3–4 spring onions, green parts only, chopped into small rounds
5–10 ml (1–2 tsp) sesame oil

FOR THE MARINADE:
2 ml (⅓ tsp) salt
1.5 ml (¼ tsp) sugar
10 ml (2 tsp) thin or light soy sauce
6–8 turns black peppermill
10 ml (2 tsp) Shaoxing wine or medium dry sherry
5 ml (1 tsp) tapioca or potato flour
15 ml (1 tbsp) water

1 Marinate the beef: put the beef slivers in a bowl and add the salt, sugar, soy sauce, pepper, wine or sherry and the tapioca or potato flour. Stir vigorously to coat. Add the water and stir again until totally absorbed. Leave to stand for about 20 minutes.

2 Heat a wok over a high heat until smoke rises. Add the peanut or vegetable oil and swirl it around to cover a large area. Heat for about 1 minute, then add the beef and stir it in the oil. Lower the heat to medium, continuing to stir until the beef turns opaque, but is still underdone. Scoop on to a dish with a perforated spoon, allowing the oil to drain back into the wok. Let the beef cool off for a few minutes. (If you wish your beef to be well done, stir-fry in the oil for longer.)

3 In a large bowl beat the eggs until homogenised. Add the salt and pepper, and the spring onion, and stir to mix. Add the beef and stir to mix.

4 Reheat the oil in the wok over a medium heat until hot but not smoking. Pour in the egg mixture and, with the wok scoop going to the bottom of the wok, turn and let the liquid egg go to the bottom. Repeat this action until

all the liquid egg has solidified around the beef slivers. Dribble in more oil around the edges if the egg starts sticking to the wok. Transfer to a large serving dish and serve hot. Dribble over the sesame oil.

Braised
Ox Tongue

SERVES 6–8 WITH 3–5 OTHER DISHES

1 large ox tongue (unsalted), about 1.5 kilos (3½ lb)
225 g (8 oz) ham
450 g (1 lb) baby carrots, trimmed
7.5 ml (1½ tsp) salt
52.5 ml (3½ tbsp) vegetable oil
37.5 ml (2½ tbsp) tapioca or potato flour
30 ml (2 tbsp) thin or light soy sauce
15 ml (1 tbsp) sesame oil

FOR THE SPICED LIQUID:
3 whole star anise
10 ml (2 tsp) Sichuan peppercorns
5 ml (1 tsp) black peppercorns
7.5 cm (3 in) cinnamon stick
2 large pieces dried tangerine peel
1 large knob ginger, about 5 cm (2 in), peeled and bruised

Illustrated on Plate 14.

紅
燒
牛
舌

WHEN I went to Taiwan a couple of years ago, I was taken to a famous Peking restaurant which prides itself on serving a dish of ox tongue. Inspired by its taste, I have come up with this recipe which, I'm pleased to say, has won lip-smacking approval from friends who have agreed to be guinea-pig tasters.

1 Place the ox tongue in a large saucepan and cover it with water. Bring to the boil and continue to cook fast for 5 minutes until the scum has gathered on the surface of the water. Pour off the water and rinse the tongue clean with cold water. Wash the saucepan.

2 Replace the tongue in the saucepan and add enough water to cover. Make the spiced liquid by adding the star anise, Sichuan peppercorns, black peppercorns, cinnamon stick, tangerine peel and ginger. Bring to the boil, then reduce the heat to maintain a fast simmer for 1 hour. Remove the tongue and peel off and discard the hard skin covering it. You will find that the pointed end peels off like a glove while the thick end requires the help of a pointed knife.

3 Return the tongue to the spiced liquid and simmer slowly for 2 hours, turning it over once. It should be very tender by now.

4 Remove the tongue and trim off the meaty, muscular parts from the thick end before returning it to the liquid.

5 Add 1 litre (1¾ pints/4½ cups) of the liquid (without any of the spices) to another saucepan, add also the meaty, muscular parts of the ox tongue as well as the ham and simmer for 1–1½ hours to make a tasty stock. Strain and discard the solids. The dish can be prepared up to this point in advance.

6 Blanch the baby carrots for about 3 minutes in half a wokful of water with 5 ml (1 tsp) of the salt and 22.5 ml (1½ tbsp) of the vegetable oil added to it. Drain.

7 Cut the tongue into thin slices and arrange on a large platter. Arrange the baby carrots around them. Keep warm nearby.

8 Prepare the sauce. Put the tapioca or potato flour in a bowl, stir in 30–45 ml (2–3 tbsp) of the stock until dissolved. Pour in 575 ml (1 pint/2½ cups) stock, stirring for smoothness. Add the soy sauce and 2.5 ml (½ tsp) salt.

Heat a wok over a moderate heat until hot. Add the remaining 30 ml (2 tbsp) oil and swirl it around. Gradually pour in the well-stirred stock, stirring in a circular motion as it thickens.

9 Pour the sauce all over the tongue and sprinkle the sesame oil on top. Serve immediately.

White-cooked Veal

AMONG the corps of reader-users of my books, I am gratified to find the young generation of Chinese working in Hong Kong, in Europe and in America. Donna Wong and her husband Desmond Cheung are two of them. Sometimes I try to think what might stimulate the palates of the likes of them after a hard day's work in the financial and legal worlds. Following their motto that dishes should be 'easy and tasty', one evening I prepared a veal dish for them, using the cut known to English butchers as veal medallion, a circular fillet piece from the leg. The preparation met their criterion of 'quick and easy' and the dish, I am pleased to say, was polished off with great gusto by us, washed down with Sancerre.

SERVES 4–6 WITH 2–3 OTHER DISHES

350–450 g (12 oz–1 lb) veal medallion
7.5–10 ml (1½–2 tsp) tapioca or potato flour
22.5 ml (1½ tbsp) peanut or vegetable oil
1.1–1.75 litres (1¾–3 pints/4½–7½ cups) water or chicken stock

continued

1 Cut the medallion of veal crossways into as many paper-thin slices as possible. Freezing the piece for 2–3 hours until quite firm facilitates the slicing. Put into a large bowl.

2 Add the tapioca or potato flour and stir thoroughly to coat. Stir in the oil. The flour will make the veal velvety and the oil will help separate the slices when being cooked.

FOR THE DIPPING SAUCE:

6–8 large spring onions, trimmed
    and cut into 5 cm (2 in) sections,
    then finely shredded
30–37.5 ml (2–2½ tbsp) finely
    shredded ginger
15 ml (1 tbsp) sesame oil
37.5–45 ml (2½–3 tbsp) peanut or
    vegetable oil
2 small dried red chillies, deseeded
    and roughly chopped
15 ml (1 tbsp) hot water
2.5 ml (½ tsp) sugar
45 ml (3 tbsp) thin or light soy
    sauce
ground black pepper to taste

3 Prepare the sauce. Line the bottom of a heatproof serving bowl with the spring onion and the ginger and keep nearby. Put the oils into a small saucepan and heat over a moderate heat until smoke rises. Remove the saucepan from the heat and let cool for about 5 seconds or until the smoke is dissipated. Add the chillies which should sizzle slightly. Immediately pour the hot oil and chillies all over the ginger and spring onion in the heatproof bowl, partially cooking them. Into another small bowl add the water and stir in the sugar until dissolved. Add the soy sauce and ground black pepper to taste. Pour this liquid into the heatproof bowl to complete the sauce. Either put this bowl on the dining table or divide the sauce into small bowls or saucers and put on the table.

4 Add the water or chicken stock to a large saucepan and bring to the boil. Add all the veal and immediately separate the slices with chopsticks or a fork. If the slices are thin enough, they are cooked even before the water or stock is returned to the boil. Scoop up with a perforated disc or slotted spoon on to a serving dish and serve immediately. To eat, dip the slices into the sauce and pick up some ginger and spring onion to accompany them.

Stir-fried Venison

SERVES 6 WITH 3 OTHER DISHES

550 g (1¼ lb) venison steak
    (preferably from the haunch),
    cut into long strips, as in Beef
    Stroganoff
60 ml (4 tbsp) peanut oil
3 large cloves garlic, peeled and
    cut diagonally into slivers
6 stalks coriander and/or Chinese
    celery, rinsed, leaves broken up
    and stalky parts cut into 5 cm
    (2 in) sections

香
荽
鹿
肉
丝

DEER and roebuck have always been in the repertoire of the Chinese cuisine, especially in the colder northern climes. In the West, the venison meat, so well hung and tender, is most suitable to be stir-fried.

1 Marinate the venison. Put the venison in a fairly large bowl. Add the salt, sugar, soy sauce, wine or sherry and the tapioca or potato flour and stir to coat. To make it velvety, add the water, 15 ml (1 tbsp) at a time, and stir vigorously in the same direction until completely absorbed. Leave to stand for about 20 minutes. Blend in the sesame oil.

2 Heat a wok over a high heat until smoke rises. Add the oil and swirl it around to cover a large area. Add the garlic, let it sizzle and take on colour, add the stalky part of the coriander and/or Chinese celery and stir a few times. Add the venison and, going to the bottom of the wok with the wok scoop, turn, toss and stir for about 2 minutes until just done. Add the black peppercorns and salt to taste and stir to mix. Splash in the Cognac or Armagnac along the edges of the wok, stirring as it sizzles, exuding fragrance. Remove the wok from the heat and scoop up the venison mixture on to a serving dish.

3 Add the coriander and/or celery leaves to the wok and stir to incorporate the remaining oil. Remove and put over the venison. Serve immediately.

15 ml (1 tbsp) black peppercorns, pounded in a pestle and mortar
salt to taste
15 ml (1 tbsp) Cognac or Armagnac

FOR THE MARINADE:
1.5 ml (¼ tsp) salt
1.5 ml (¼ tsp) sugar
15 ml (1 tbsp) thick or dark soy sauce
10 ml (2 tsp) Shaoxing wine or medium dry sherry
7.5 ml (1½ tsp) tapioca or potato flour
30 ml (2 tbsp) water
10–15 ml (2–3 tsp) sesame oil

Rinsed Lamb

In Peking, Taiwan and Hong Kong, this dish, which is also known as Lamb Hot Pot, is eaten in restaurants, not at home. Customers cook their own lamb, which is cut into transparently thin slices, in a brass fire pot which is placed in the centre of the table. Fuelled by flaming charcoal in the bottom, the fire pot has a cone shape chimney in the centre to let the smoke escape. When eating this renowned Mongolian-Muslim dish (*see* p. 85) at home, however, a large electric pot is the best and most practical thing to use.

涮
羊
肉

SERVES 4–6 AS A MAIN COURSE

½ leg spring lamb, about 1.2 kilos (2½ lb), boned
115 g (4 oz) cellophane or glass noodles
1 Chinese celery cabbage (Chinese leaves), about 900 g (2 lb)
225 g (8 oz) dried egg or buckwheat noodles

continued

1 Put the lamb into the freezer for about 3 hours or until it becomes firm and hence easier to cut. Trim excess fat and cut into paper-thin slices, each about 10 × 4 cm (4 × 1½ in). Arrange them on serving plates in single layers but overlapping each other. Refrigerate, covered, until ready to eat.

2 Soak the cellophane noodles in plenty of boiling hot water and leave for 30 minutes or longer. Drain. Make 2–3 cuts with scissors to shorten them. Transfer to a serving bowl.

FOR THE DIP:

120 ml (8 tbsp) sesame paste, well stirred in the jar

60 ml (4 tbsp) mashed red bean curd cheese and 30 ml (2 tbsp) own juice from the jar

90 ml (6 tbsp) Shaoxing wine or medium dry sherry

45 ml (3 tbsp) sugar

120 ml (8 tbsp) thin or light soy sauce

45–60 ml (3–4 tbsp) hot chilli oil (*see* p. 357)

60 ml (4 tbsp) sesame oil

60 ml (4 tbsp) fish sauce

100 g (3½ oz) coriander leaves, rinsed and chopped roughly

10–12 large spring onions, trimmed and cut into small rounds

3 Cut the celery cabbage crossways at 2.5 cm (1 in) intervals. Put on to a serving plate.

4 Plunge the noodles into plenty of boiling water, return to the boil, then continue to cook for several minutes until they are *al dente*. Drain and rinse under cold running water. Put on to a serving dish.

5 Prepare the dip. Put the sesame paste into a fairly large serving bowl and gradually add 120 ml (4 fl oz) water, stirring until well blended. Blend the red bean curd cheese with its own juice and 30–45 ml (2–3 tbsp) water to a smooth consistency and then add to the bowl. Add also the wine or sherry, sugar, soy sauce, the oils and fish sauce and stir until well mixed.

6 Place the pot in the centre of the dining table and put all the other ingredient dishes around it. Pour boiling water into the pot to come about halfway up the sides, and bring back to the boil. The rinsed lamb feast is now ready to be enjoyed.

7 To serve, provide each diner with a pair of wooden or bamboo chopsticks, a small wire strainer made specially for this kind of hot pot feast (optional), a bowl and a small side plate.

8 To eat, everyone spoons some sauce into their bowl and adds some coriander leaves and spring onions. They then pick up 1–2 slices of lamb at a time, put them into the strainer (if provided) and immerse them in the boiling water in the pot, removing them after a few seconds when they consider the meat is cooked enough. They then dip them into the sauce before eating.

9 After about half of the lamb has been consumed, and the water in the pot has become a tasty broth, add the cabbage and cellophane noodles to the pot in stages for everyone to share. Again, dip them into the sauce before eating. Whenever necessary, replenish the water level in the pot.

10 After about three-quarters of the lamb has been consumed, put in half or all of the remaining noodles. Dip into the sauce and eat.

11 At the end of the feast, the broth in the pot is shared. Each diner spoons some into their bowl, mixes it with the remaining sauce and then drinks it.

Stir-fried Lamb Kidneys

CHINESE Muslims in Peking are very fond of this dish, which is served both at home and in restaurants. In China it is considered a delicacy, but as lamb kidneys are inexpensive in the West, it makes a tasty everyday dish.

炒
羊
腰

SERVES 6 WITH 3 OTHER DISHES

8 lamb kidneys, about 450 g (1 lb)
250 ml (8 fl oz/1 cup) vegetable oil
50 g (2 oz) canned bamboo
    shoots, thinly sliced and
    blanched (*see* p. 253)
1 large red pepper, trimmed and
    cored, cut into wedges
30 ml (2 tbsp) peanut or vegetable
    oil
15 ml (1 tbsp) finely chopped
    ginger
6 spring onions, trimmed and cut
    into 4 cm (1½ in) sections
8 g (¼ oz) cloud ears,
    reconstituted (*see* p. 353) and
    roughly broken up into pieces
5–10 ml (1–2 tsp) sesame oil

FOR THE MARINADE:
2.5 ml (½ tsp) salt
12 turns black peppermill
5 ml (1 tsp) tapioca or potato flour

FOR THE SAUCE:
5 ml (1 tsp) tapioca or potato flour
    dissolved in 15 ml (1 tbsp) water
15 ml (1 tbsp) thick or dark soy
    sauce
75 ml (5 tbsp) stock or water

1 Remove the membranes encasing the kidneys, if any. Halve each kidney lengthways. Using scissors or a knife, cut off and discard the white, fatty and rank membrane inside. Place each half on a cutting board. With a pointed knife, make shallow, diagonal criss-cross cuts on both sides (or at least on one side) of the kidneys, then cut each half into 3 sections. Put into a bowl.

2 Marinate the kidneys. Add the salt, pepper and tapioca or potato flour to the kidneys and stir to mix well. Leave for about 15–20 minutes.

3 Prepare the sauce. In a small bowl mix together the dissolved tapioca or potato flour, soy sauce and stock or water. Put aside.

4 Heat the vegetable oil in a wok over a high heat for 2–3 minutes or until it reaches 180°C (350°F). Add the kidneys and fry, keeping the pieces separate, for about 1 minute until partially cooked. Scoop up with a perforated disc on to a dish and keep close at hand.

5 Add the bamboo shoots and red pepper to the oil and fry for about 1 minute. Remove with a perforated disc. Discard the oil. Wash and dry the wok.

6 Reheat the wok over a high heat until smoke rises. Add the peanut or vegetable oil and swirl it around. Add the ginger and spring onion and stir for a few seconds to release the aroma. Return the lamb kidneys, bamboo shoots and pepper to the wok, adding also the cloud ears. Add the well-stirred sauce, lower the heat and cook for 1–2 minutes to let the kidneys absorb the sauce. Scoop on to a serving dish, sprinkle on the sesame oil and serve hot.

'Ah, Sweet as Honey'

SERVES 6

450 g (1 lb) well-trimmed fillet of
lamb from the leg
300 ml (10 fl oz/1¼ cups)
vegetable oil
30 ml (2 tbsp) sesame oil

FOR THE MARINADE:
30 ml (2 tbsp) sweet bean sauce
(*see* p. 362)
10 ml (2 tsp) tapioca or potato
flour
15 ml (1 tbsp) peanut or vegetable
oil

FOR THE SAUCE:
5 ml (1 tsp) tapioca or potato flour
30 ml (2 tbsp) sugar
15 ml (1 tbsp) thick or dark soy
sauce
15 ml (1 tbsp) Shaoxing wine or
medium dry sherry
9 ml (1¾ tsp) ginger juice (*see*
p. 357)
10 ml (2 tsp) Chinese rice vinegar

Illustrated on Plate 12.

THE Empress Dowager Cixi (Tz'u-hsi) virtually
ruled China during the second half of the 19th
century, even though the reigning monarchs were
first Emperor Tongzhi, her son, and then Emperor
Guangxu, her nephew. From information gleaned
from private diaries at court, her wielding of political power was matched only by her love for food.
The Western Imperial Kitchen, which catered
exclusively for her every culinary whim, was manned by
chefs hand-picked by her. Unlike some of her more virtuous royal ancestors, it is said that she used to keep a table
of more than 100 dishes every day. Her chefs, whose
repertoire of dishes ran into several thousand and of
dimsum more than 100, never slackened in stretching their
skills to make new dishes to please her. They knew well
that if the 'Old Buddha', the flattering honorific title with
which she liked to be addressed, was especially delighted
with a dish, she might ask her eunuchs to reward them on
the spot with a silver tael or two. One day, a dish of lamb,
the slices shining ebony-red and exuding a mouth-
watering fragrance, was served to the Empress Dowager.
'What is the name of this dish?' she asked, having savoured
the morsels and found them sweet and succulent. As the
attending eunuchs did not know, the chef who cooked it
was summoned. Kowtowing to her whilst shaking at both
knees, the chef said, 'Imperial Old Buddha, as yet this dish
has not got a name. Since you like it so much, I beg you to
bestow it with an Imperial name.' Cixi thought for a while
then blurted out, 'Ah, sweet as honey'. One and all
applauded and echoed the name in a chorus. The chef was
rewarded with a couple of silver taels, and the dish has
ever since been known by its Imperial name.

1 Cut the lamb fillet across the grain into slices about
3 mm (⅛ in) thick and 2.5 × 5 cm (1 × 2 in) in size. Put
into a mixing bowl.
2 Marinate the lamb. Add the bean sauce and tapioca or
potato flour to the lamb and stir to mix well. Leave to
stand for 15–20 minutes. Stir in 15 ml (1 tbsp) oil to
make the pieces less sticky.
3 Prepare the sauce. In a small bowl combine the flour,

sugar, soy sauce, wine or sherry, ginger juice and vinegar and stir to mix well. Put aside.

4 Sit a wok on the wok-stand and add the vegetable oil to it. Heat until warm, reaching 150–160°C (300–325°F). Add the lamb and spread out the pieces with chopsticks or a wooden spoon. Fry for about 30–60 seconds until partially opaque yet still pink. Scoop out with a per-forated disc, letting as much oil drip back to the wok as possible. Pour the oil into a container for further use, wash and dry the wok.

5 Reheat the wok over a moderate heat until smoke rises. Add the sesame oil and swirl it around. Lower the heat and pour in the well-stirred sauce. Stir continuously to incorporate the oil as the sugar melts and the sauce thickens, becoming caramelised.

6 Return the lamb to the wok and coat the pieces thoroughly with the sauce. The pieces will glisten, appearing dark copper brown in colour. Remove the wok from the heat. Scoop the lamb on to a serving dish and serve immediately.

Stir-fried Lamb
with Coriander Leaves

SERVES 4 WITH 2 OTHER DISHES

either 2 lamb shoulder fillets
  about 450 g (1 lb) or 285 g
  (10 oz) leg fillet, well trimmed
  and cut into matchstick-sized
  strands
45 ml (3 tbsp) sesame oil
1–2 large cloves garlic, peeled and
  cut into thin slivers
4 large spring onions, trimmed,
  halved lengthways, then cut into
  5 cm (2 in) sections, white and
  green parts separated
4 branches coriander leaves,
  trimmed, leaf and stalk parts
  separated, stalks cut into
  5–7.5 cm (2–3 in) sections
22.5 ml (1½ tbsp) Shaoxing wine
  or medium dry sherry

FOR THE MARINADE:
2.5 ml (½ tsp) salt
7.5 ml (1½ tsp) ginger juice (see
  p. 357)
5 ml (1 tsp) cornflour
15 ml (1 tbsp) egg white, lightly
  beaten
15 ml (1 tbsp) sesame oil

FOR northern Chinese and Chinese Muslims who like lamb in any case, the coriander leaves, with their special scent, will enhance its flavour, while for many southern Chinese who rightly or wrongly dislike what they think of as the malodorous smell of lamb, the leaves will help to counter it, making the dish palatable.

1 Marinate the lamb. Put the lamb in a bowl, add the salt, ginger juice, cornflour and egg white and stir vigorously to coat. Leave to stand for 15–20 minutes. Blend in the oil.

2 Heat a wok over a high heat until smoke rises. Add the sesame oil and swirl it around. Add the garlic, let it sizzle, but before it burns, add the white spring onions and coriander stalks. Stir for a few seconds to release their aroma. Add the lamb and, going to the bottom of the wok with the wok scoop, turn and toss for about 1 minute when the lamb will become opaque. Splash in the wine or sherry along the edges of the wok, continuing to stir until the lamb is just done. Add 15 ml (1 tbsp) water if the wok becomes sticky. Scatter in the green spring onions.

Remove the wok from the heat. Add half of the coriander leaves, stir a few times to mix. Scoop everything on to a serving dish and garnish with the remaining coriander leaves.

Top right: Mustard Greens with Salt-cured Egg Soup (p. 160).
Middle: Dongpo Pork (p. 313).
Bottom left: Fujianese Fried Rice (p. 241).

PLATE 13

Left: Braised Ox Tongue (p. 332).
Top right: Stir-fried Oyster Mushrooms (p. 200).
Bottom right: Stir-fried Chicken with Cashewnuts (p. 290).

PLATE 14

SWEET
DISHES

THE format of a Chinese meal, which consists of rice and savoury dishes of a variable number, does not traditionally end with a sweet dish, or dessert. Instead, seasonal fruits are served as the last course, followed by Chinese tea. This custom has a long history, going back two thousand years to the Han times, or even earlier. If you peruse a Chinese restaurant menu, which often runs to several hundred dishes of vegetables, poultry, meat, fish and shellfish, you will see that the dessert section, even if it exists, is conspicuously spartan, featuring a few items such as commercially made ice creams, canned litchi and perhaps the Peking speciality, 'toffee' apple or banana, which seems to have the most popular appeal to Western palates. This is not to say, however, that in the vast Chinese repertoire of dishes there is not a plethora of sweet ones. On the contrary, there are many Chinese cakes and other sweet delicacies which the Chinese seem to eat at random moments of the day or in between meals, rather than at a set time.

The sweet things Chinese eat in the evening, usually as a snack some while after dinner rather than as dessert at the end of dinner, tend to come in a liquid form, which is sometimes, albeit misleadingly, referred to by Westerners as sweet soup. The most common ingredients used are nuts and root vegetables, the latter of which may seem very strange to Westerners. Among the nuts, almonds and walnuts are popular in both the north and the south, as are sesame seeds, both the black and white kinds, and they are made into a warm paste, known as woo in Cantonese and hu in Mandarin, which is something like an English fool. To make woo, the nuts are ground into a liquid form with water and a small amount of rice, which is drained – preferably twice for the best result – then cooked and sweetened with sugar. Among the root vegetables, cubed sweet potato and taro cooked in water and sweetened with sugar are very popular in the south, if only as a way of taking more liquid to counter the oppressive heat in the summer. Another similar sweet dish is made with azuki or mung beans, respectively red and green beans as the Chinese call them. These will be served warm or cold, to individual taste, and the current trend is also to serve them with single or double cream, or condensed milk.

Another type of Chinese sweet things is based on glutinous rice, made either with the grains or the flour. In northern China, there is the celebrated glutinous rice pudding made with cooked rice which, possibly due to the oppressive sub-tropical heat, has never become very popular in the south. What are popular on a national scale are the Chinese New Year Pudding and round dumplings, both of which are made with glutinous rice flour and are imbued with symbolism (*see* p. 48).

Accepting that Chinese sweet dishes do not have the same kind of universal appeal as do Chinese savoury dishes, I am including only a sprinkling of them in this chapter, intent on giving just a taste of what I myself think is delicious.

Chinese
New Year Pudding

SERVES 10–12

10 pieces or 350 g (12 oz) Chinese
  brown sugar (labelled brown
  sugar in pieces)
750 ml (1¼ pints/3 cups) cold
  water
115 g (4 oz/¾ cup) cornflour
450 g (1 lb/3¼ cups) glutinous
  rice flour (labelled powder)
1 pinch salt
30 ml (2 tbsp) peanut or vegetable
  oil
1 red date, pitted

Illustrated on Plate 10.

CALLED nian gao in Mandarin and nin go in Cantonese, this sticky pudding is eaten all over China during the Chinese New Year because of the punning symbolism around the sound gao or go, which means both pudding and to grow. The consumption of this food is thus an act beckoning the physical growth of one's children, or the growth of one's business, if not more explicitly, of one's pile of banknotes! Symbolism aside, I love the viscous texture half sticking to my teeth.

1 Put the pieces of sugar into a saucepan and add 300 ml (10 fl oz/1¼ cups) of the cold water. Slowly bring to a simmer, then continue to cook letting the sugar dissolve completely. Remove from the heat. Add the remaining water and leave the liquid to cool.

2 In a large mixing bowl add the cornflour to the glutinous rice flour and mix well. Add a pinch of salt. With a large wooden spoon, make a well in the centre of the

mixture, gradually pour in the sugar liquid and draw in the flour to mix until thoroughly homogenised. The mixture becomes quite runny in consistency. Stir in 15 ml (1 tbsp) of the oil.

3 Brush a round cake tin or enamel dish about 24 cm (9½ in) in diameter and 4 cm (1½ in) high with the remaining oil – no need to use all of it. Place a close wire sieve over it and strain the rice flour mixture through the sieve to ensure there are no lumps in the mixture.

4 Place the tin or dish in a steamer and steam (*see* p. 355) for 3 hours until the pudding is done. After 2½ hours, you can start checking by piercing the pudding with a sharp instrument. If it comes out smooth and clean, the pudding is ready. Insert the red date in the centre of the pudding, half burying it. Remove the tin or dish from the steamer and let cool.

5 Cut the pudding into slices and serve warm. It is sticky in consistency, so bear this in mind when you cut it.

Fried Ningo

MORE often than not, ningo is not served straight-away after it is steamed but served sautéed later. Fried ningo is partially crisp on the outside and stickily chewy inside, the texture and consistency of which, likened to chewing toffee by some European friends of mine, is what the Chinese adore. Keep the ningo in the refrigerator to firm up its consistency until ready to serve. Cut up slices, allowing 2 or 3 per person, then put the remainder back into the refrigerator. Most people like to dip the pieces in lightly beaten egg before frying them so as to prevent the pieces from sticking together. The egg also adds some fragrance and crispness.

SERVES 4–6

1 large egg
16 slices ningo, each about 8 mm (⅓ in) thick and 5 cm (2 in) long
30 ml (2 tbsp) peanut or vegetable oil

1 Lightly beat the egg in a fairly large bowl. Dip 4 slices of ningo in the egg at a time and coat both sides.

2 Heat a large flat frying pan over a high heat until very hot. Add the oil and swirl it around to cover the entire surface. Pour half of the oil back into a small bowl. Reduce the heat to low.

3 1 piece at a time, add the 4 slices of ningo to the frying pan, leaving a small gap between the pieces to prevent sticking. Fry them slowly for about 2 minutes or until the bottom is partially brown and crisp. In the meantime, dip another 4 slices in the egg and add to the frying pan. Turn them over, one by one, and drip in drops of oil from the small bowl. Fry the other side for another 2 minutes or until partially brown and crisp. Whenever 1 piece is ready remove it from the frying pan and put on to a serving dish. Add the remaining oil and repeat the procedure until all are done. Serve warm.

Ginger Custard

SERVES 2

30–45 ml (2–3 tbsp) sugar
100–175 ml (4–6 fl oz/½–¾ cup) hot water
2 eggs, size 2
175 ml (6 fl oz/¾ cup) homogenised milk
10 ml (2 tsp) ginger juice (*see* p. 357)

WHEN the people of one culture borrow an ingredient or a recipe from another culture, they more often than not adapt it to suit their own tastes and in the course of doing so use their own methods to achieve the desired effect. In making egg custard with milk, the Chinese prefer a less dense consistency than that Westerners are accustomed to, and they prefer to eat it hot, just as a snack food, usually in the evening a couple of hours after dinner. The Chinese usually make this in their regular-sized rice bowls, each capable of holding about 300 ml (10 fl oz/1¼ cups) liquid.

1 Use 2 Chinese rice bowls or comparable heatproof bowls. Add half the sugar to each bowl and pour in half of the hot water to dissolve the sugar. Leave to cool.

2 Lightly beat the eggs separately, then add half of the milk to each egg. Beat a few more times to blend. Pour the mixture into the sugar liquid through a tea strainer to get rid of foam. Add half of the ginger juice to each bowl and stir a couple of times to blend.

3 Either cover the bowls with Chinese flax tissue paper dampened with water or with a plate and place them on the steaming container of a steamer and steam (*see* p. 355) for 10 minutes if Chinese flax tissue paper is used, or 15 minutes if a plate is used, at the end of which time the custard should be set. (Covering the bowls will prevent water condensed from steam from falling into the custard.) Remove from the steamer and serve hot, having of course removed the flax tissue paper or plate.

Deep-fried
'Lamb's Tail'

THIS recipe is based on a northern Chinese Muslim dish made originally, as the title suggests, with a lamb's tail deep-fried in oil. So ethnic and so strong in taste, it only found favour with a minority of people. Gradually, chefs came up with a look-alike recipe. Using egg white to envelope red bean paste, they transformed the lamb's tail into this now celebrated sweet dish retaining, however, the original name. Chefs of Peking restaurants in Hong Kong have gone one step further: they use one stuffing within another to hold the shape and they changed the name to 'High energy red bean paste puffs', descriptive of the highly beaten egg white. You can, however, use only one stuffing and arrive at just as satisfying a result (see note below).

SERVES 4; MAKES 12–13

25–40 g (1–1½ oz) sweetened canned red bean paste
about 3 not overripe bananas, peeled
egg white from 4 large eggs, size 2, about 150–175 ml (5–6 fl oz/ ⅔–¾ cup)
20 ml (4 tsp) self-raising flour
vegetable oil for deep-frying
about 30 ml (2 tbsp) icing sugar

Illustrated on Plate 16.

1 If the red bean paste on the surface of the can is too runny, spoon it off. Refrigerate the amount of paste required for 1–2 hours in order to firm it. Divide it into 12–14 portions and roll into lumps. Put on to a plate.

2 Cut the bananas crossways into 2 cm (¾ in) sections, trimming to make the ends even. Core the centre of each section.

3 Stuff 1 section of banana with 1 lump of red bean paste, trimming to make it fit in. Don't worry if the stuffing causes the edge of the banana to break open as long as it holds the stuffing.

4 Beat the egg white in a bowl until very stiff – standing even when you turn the bowl upside down. Add the self-raising flour and beat again. Leave for about 10–15 minutes.

5 Sit a wok over the wok-stand and half fill it with oil. Heat over a high heat until it reaches 200°C (400°F).

Beat the egg white again. Using an ice-cream scoop with a spring releaser, fill 1 scoopful of egg white from the bowl at a time, scraping off excess with a small knife. Insert 1 stuffed banana section in the centre and cover the top with some egg white. Release the scoopful into the hot oil and deep-fry one side, which will puff up and expand slightly, for about 30 seconds until pale golden, then roll it over with a wooden spoon or chopsticks to deep-fry the other side for another 30 seconds, remove with a perforated spoon or chopsticks and put on kitchen paper to absorb excess oil. Repeat this procedure until the egg white is used up, taking care to adjust the heat if the oil gets too hot or is not hot enough. In the latter case, the egg white will absorb a lot of oil and the puffs will be very greasy. Instead of using an ice-cream scoop, you can submerge 1 section of banana in the egg white at a time and scoop it up with a tablespoon, making sure the egg white envelops the stuffing.

4 Put the puffs on to a serving plate. Dust on the icing sugar and serve immediately.

NOTE: If you find the 'one-stuffing-within-another' technique too complicated, you can do away with the red bean paste and just use whole sections of bananas as stuffing. I assure you the end result is just as good.

Tangyuan

SERVES 4; MAKES 18

170 g (6 oz/1¼ cup) glutinous rice flour (labelled powder)
about 150 ml (5 fl oz/⅔ cup) tepid water
18 marble-sized pieces black sesame stuffing (see p. 348)

Illustrated on Plate 15.

THIS is the symbolic food for the Lantern Festival which concludes the celebration of the Chinese new year festival (see p. 50). But, because it is easy to make, it is also eaten at any time of the year.

1 Put the glutinous rice flour in a bowl and make a well in the centre. Gradually pour in the water and draw in the flour to make into a dough. Unlike wheat flour, rice flour is not liable to become lumpy. There is no need to knead at all, but the dough should be soft.

2 Remove the dough from the bowl and halve it. Roll

each piece into a sausage and divide each into 9 pieces, rounding them off.

3 Make the tangyuan. Hold 1 piece of dough between the index finger and thumb of one hand and, with the thumb of the other hand, press down to make a deep indentation. Put in 1 'marble' of stuffing. Gently pressing the stuffing down with the thumb, push up the dough by turning it with the fingers to enclose the stuffing until completely covered. Make sure the 'marble' has an even covering of the dough, lest it burst when being cooked. Roll this tangyuan between your palm to make it round. Repeat until all 18 are made.

4 Bring a large saucepan of water to the boil. Gently add the tangyuan, one by one, into the water and return to the boil. Continue to boil them, uncovered, for about 3 minutes. Add about 100 ml (4 fl oz/½ cup) cold water to the saucepan and bring to the boil again, then continue to cook for another minute. Repeat this procedure once more. The cold water cools down the temperature, hence preventing the tangyuan from bursting. By now they should be cooked and will float to the surface. Remove the saucepan from the heat.

5 To serve, put the tangyuan and some of the boiling water into bowls. The water is not for drinking but is meant to keep the tangyuan warm. Eat with chopsticks and a spoon. Habitually, the Chinese would take a bite of a tangyuan rather than have it whole in one go.

Tangyuan Stuffing

MAKES ABOUT 70–80 MARBLE-
SIZED PIECES

225 g (8 oz) black sesame seeds
225 g (8 oz/1 cup) icing sugar
75 ml (5 tbsp) melted lard
15 ml (1 tbsp) sesame oil

THERE is a range of stuffings for Tangyuan (*see* recipe on p. 347), from a small lump of Chinese brown sugar to red bean paste, but none can top the black-sesame-seed stuffing in fragrance and in popularity. People in Peking and Shanghai adore this stuffing. Dr William Fong, originally from Peking, showed me how to make his version of it using electric gadgets, including a coffee grinder. We had great fun making it.

1 Roast the seeds. Heat a wok over a moderate heat until hot. Add the sesame seeds and stir constantly for about 20 minutes. Taste a few to test from time to time; when they are ready, they will be crisp, dry and fragrant. Take care not to burn them as this will result in a bitter taste. Remove to a dish and leave to cool.

2 Grind the seeds, 2–3 spoonfuls at a time, in a coffee grinder (or a fine herb mill), until they are reduced to a powder form. For the best result, do the grinding twice; before the second grinding, give the already ground seeds inside a good stir first. Transfer to a large and deep bowl.

3 Using an electric egg beater in slow motion, mix in the icing sugar until well blended. To prevent dust caused by the icing sugar, partially cover the bowl with a cloth or plastic bag.

4 Still in slow motion, gradually drip in the lard and the sesame oil to blend until the mixture becomes a dense paste. Remove from the bowl.

   At this point the stuffing is made. But to make working with it easier, it is advisable to put it into a freezer bag and freeze for about 1 hour or longer to make its texture firmer.

5 Remove the lump of stuffing from the bag and cut it up into pieces, each about 5 ml (1 tsp) in volume. Shape and roll each piece between your palms into a marble. Count the number of marbles you need, 1 marble for 1 tangyuan. Before the marbles become too soft, put the rest into a freezer bag and store in the freezer for future use. They will not stick together.

Taro 'Soup'

CANTONESE people are very fond of making a liquid sweet dish – sweet soup by Western standards – with beans, such as the red azuki or the green mung beans, or with root vegetables, such as sweet potato or taro, which they eat warm.

芋汁西米露

SERVES 6

450 g (1 lb) well-peeled taro, cut into rough cubes
55 g (2 oz) tapioca, rinsed in cold water
170 g (6 oz/¾ cup) sugar
1 small can coconut milk, about 175 ml (6 fl oz/¾ cup), or fresh single cream

1 Put the taro into a large saucepan and add 1.3–1.5 litres (2¼–2½ pints/5½–6 cups) water. Bring to the boil and continue to cook, covered, over a medium heat for about 30 minutes or until the taro disintegrates and the liquid is reduced to about 1–1.2 litres (1¾–2 pints/4–5 cups). (Some taro takes much longer to cook.) Remove from the heat and mash the taro in the cooking liquid and stir to blend, but by all means leave some little lumps if you prefer to have some bites of taro.

2 In a smaller saucepan bring 575 ml (1 pint/2½ cups) of water to a rolling boil. Add the tapioca and stir with a wooden spoon until the water returns to a rolling boil. Add the lid to the saucepan and immediately remove from the heat. Leave for about 5 minutes during which time the tapioca will expand in the hot water.

3 Pour into a colander and rinse under cold running water. This helps to get rid of some of the slimy texture of the tapioca and separate the grains.

4 Add the sugar to the taro and heat over a low heat until it has dissolved. Add the tapioca, stir to blend. The tapioca will both thicken the consistency and provide that viscous texture loved by the Cantonese. Transfer to a serving bowl. Serve hot or warm. Let individuals add coconut milk or cream to taste. This 'soup' can also be served cold.

Taro Mud
with Ginkgo Nuts

SERVES 4–6

115 g (4 oz) drained canned
   ginkgo nuts (or cooked fresh
   ginkgo nuts)
75 ml (5 tbsp) sugar
325–350 g (11–12 oz) peeled taro
75–90 ml (5–6 tbsp) peanut or
   corn oil
2–3 spring onions, trimmed and
   cut into small rounds

白
菜
芋
泥

ALTHOUGH taro and ginkgo nuts may seem unlikely ingredients for a sweet recipe, this is a celebrated Chaozhou pudding. Lard is traditionally used to make the dense consistency of the mashed taro – mud – richer and more fragrant, but I have been assured by many Chaozhou natives that for the sake of cutting down on cholesterol, they use peanut or corn oil which has had spring onion fried in it in order to enhance the fragrance and make up for the flavour lost by not using lard. By all means use rendered lard to achieve the real McCoy, if you wish.

1 Put the ginkgo nuts on a dish and sprinkle on 30 ml (2 tbsp) of the sugar and mix thoroughly. Leave for about 2 hours or longer; you may leave them overnight, if you wish.

2 Cut the taro into about 8 pieces and place directly on to a steaming container or bamboo basket and steam over a high heat (*see* p. 355) for about 40 minutes until tender.

3 In the meantime, prepare the oil. Heat a wok over a high heat until smoke rises. Add the oil and swirl it around. Add the spring onion and stir a few times. Reduce the heat to medium and continue to fry the spring onion until brown so as to enhance the fragrance of the oil. Strain the oil through a small wire sieve; discard the spring onion which will have soaked up some oil.

4 While the taro pieces are still hot, mash them. Add the remaining 45 ml (3 tbsp) sugar, add also 45 ml (3 tbsp) of the oil and blend well. This can be done effectively in a food processor. If the consistency is too dense, add about 15 ml (1 tbsp) water. Transfer this mixture to a heatproof bowl, lightly oiled. Preparation can be done up to this point several hours or even a day in advance.

5 Place the bowl in a steamer and steam (*see* p. 355) over a high heat for 15–20 minutes until very hot. The steam that circulates inside the steamer will make the consistency of the taro mud less dense.

6 In the meantime, prepare the ginkgo nuts. Heat a wok over a moderate heat until hot. Add 15 ml (1 tbsp) oil

and swirl it around. Add the ginkgo nuts and scrape in
all the sugar which will melt, foaming around the nuts.
Fry the nuts for about 8 minutes when the sugar will
become slightly thicker, coating the nuts. Remove the
wok from the heat before the sugar turns brown,
becoming caramelised. Using a slotted spoon, remove
the nuts and put on to a small serving dish.

7 Transfer the taro mud to a serving dish and serve hot.
Let your guests help themselves to the ginkgo nuts
which should be eaten with the taro mud.

Lacquered Cashewnuts

THESE nuts are very welcome titbits when served
with Chinese tea after dinner and, as they are not
cloyingly sweet, they go equally well with drinks
before dinner. Caramelising nuts, then deep-frying
them, is perhaps the most complex of Chinese
cookery techniques. To ensure success, it is therefore best to use ready-made golden syrup, rather
than caramelising sugar from scratch. I am indebted
to Michael Leung, executive chef of Now and Zen in
Covent Garden, for the success of this recipe.

焦
糖
腰
果

SERVES 20

500 g (1 lb 2 oz) unroasted large
   cashewnuts
85 g (3 oz/⅓ cup) sugar
about 250 g (8½ oz) or 150 ml
   (5 fl oz/⅔ cup) golden syrup
vegetable oil for deep-frying
15–30 ml (1–2 tbsp) roasted white
   sesame seeds (*see* p. 359)

Illustrated on Plate 11.

1 Boil the cashewnuts over a high heat in about 1.75 litres
(3 pints/7½ cups) water in a wok or a saucepan for
about 5–6 minutes, spooning off any impurities that
surface. Pour into a colander and drain. Return the
cashewnuts to the wok or saucepan and add about 1.5
litres (2½ pints/6 cups) boiling water. Add the sugar
and boil again over a high heat for another 6 minutes,
stirring once or twice. Pour into a colander and drain.
Wash and dry the wok or saucepan.

2 Heat the wok or saucepan over a low heat until hot.
Remove from the heat. Add the still hot cashewnuts to
the wok or saucepan. Pour in the golden syrup and stir
to mix well. Make sure that the syrup glazes every nut,
as this is crucial to the eventual success of the recipe. If
the syrup has been diluted too much by the residual
moisture in the nuts, put the wok or saucepan over

medium to high heat, and stir the nuts in it for 20–30 seconds. Pour everything into a colander and let the excess syrup drain off.

3 Sit a wok over its stand and half fill it with the oil. Heat over a high heat until the oil reaches 180°C (350°F), Carefully pour all the nuts into the oil, which will foam. Using a large wooden spoon or a metal spatula, gently stir the nuts so that they do not stick to the bottom and get burned. Deep-fry for about 7–8 minutes or until the moisture in the nuts has been drawn out and the syrup glazing the nuts has turned golden. Turn off the heat. Using a large wire hand strainer, scoop up the nuts and let the oil drain back into the wok. Put on to a clean, cool surface and immediately sprinkle with the sesame seeds. Separate the nuts straightaway and leave to cool completely, during which time the glazing should harden and the nuts become very crisp. Put the nuts on baking paper to absorb the excess grease before storing them in a jar. They should keep crisp for about 1 week.

PREPARATORY TECHNIQUES

*Blanching canned
bamboo shoots*

Cut the bamboo shoots as directed in the recipe. Add to boiling water and blanch for 1–2 minutes in order to refresh them. Drain thoroughly.

*De-veining
shelled prawns*

Stand a shelled prawn on a surface and hold it between two fingers. With the pointed end of a small knife, slit along the centre of the back, then remove the black vein, if any, and discard it.

*Reconstituting
dried ingredients*

Rinse the dried ingredients, such as dried Chinese black mushrooms, cloud ears, wood ears and golden needles, and put into a bowl. Unless otherwise stated, pour over enough warm or hot water to cover by about 5 cm (2 in) and cover the bowl. Leave to soak for 30–60 minutes or longer, during which time the ingredient will expand, becoming pliable again. Clip the stalks of mushrooms before or after the soaking and save them for the stockpot; the soaking liquid can also be used. For the other fungi and golden needles, use the soaking liquid to wash them, rubbing with your fingers to rid them of impurities, and pluck off the hard knobs and tops. Drain and wash again with water until clean.

Refreshing
bean curd

Chinese bean curd cakes are sold in lidded plastic boxes (usually 2 to 4 cakes per box), containing water inside. To refresh the bean curd, drain off the water, rinse the bean curd with cold water, then steep it in warm or hot water for 15–30 minutes. Drain thoroughly.

STEAMERS
AND
STEAMING

To cook food by steaming is an ancient Chinese cookery technique (*see* p. 75), which is achieved using a steamer constructed in one of the following ways:

Using a wok set and a stand: sit a wok on its stand on top of the burner. Put a stand (a metal trivet or a bamboo basket, etc.) in the centre of the wok. Put the food to be steamed in a shallow heatproof dish, so that the juices are retained in the dish when the food is cooked, thus preserving its goodness and taste. Place the dish on the stand. Now fill the wok with boiling water to within about 2.5 cm (1 in) of the base of the dish in order to prevent the bubbling water from getting into the dish and spoiling the food. Cover the wok with its lid, turn up the heat and maintain it at the same intensity to ensure that plenty of steam rises from the boiling water and circulates inside the covered wok to cook the food. If the food is to be steamed for a long time, be sure to replenish the water from time to time. Refrain from lifting the wok cover unnecessarily, however, for every time you do so steam escapes and you will need to steam the food for a longer period in order to make sure it is cooked.

Using a wok set and bamboo containers: sit a wok on its stand on top of a burner. Place a large slotted bamboo steaming basket on the sloping sides of the wok. Fill the wok with boiling water to within about 2.5 cm (1 in) of the base of the basket. Put the food to be steamed either directly in the basket or in a shallow heatproof dish and put the dish in the basket. Add the fitted bamboo lid, turn up the heat and continue as above.

Using a metal steamer: this is usually made of aluminium or stainless steel or enamel, round or oval in shape and consisting of a base container and two perforated steaming containers. Place the base container on top of the burner and half fill with boiling water. Place the food to be steamed either directly in one steaming container or in a heatproof dish and put the dish into the container. Put on the lid, turn up the heat and continue as above. If both steaming containers are used, change the top one to the bottom (and vice versa) halfway through the steaming time.

Top: Three-coloured Vegetables (p. 205).
Middle: Char Siu (p. 307).
Bottom right: Tangyuan (p. 346).

PLATE 15

Top left: Deep-fried 'Lamb's Tail' (p. 345).
Middle: Five-willow Fish (p. 270).
Bottom right: Hand-torn Chicken (p. 297).

PLATE 16

BASIC INGREDIENTS

Chilli Hot Oil

1 Put the chopped chilli into a heatproof glass jar. Heat the oil in a saucepan just until it smokes. Remove from the heat and let cool for 3–4 minutes. Pour into the jar, where the chilli flakes will rise to the surface but will eventually sink to the bottom again. The oil becomes spicy hot almost instantly, but leaving the chilli to steep in it makes it even more spicy.

12 long dried red chillies, or 24 small ones, deseeded and roughly chopped
250 ml (8 fl oz/1 cup) peanut or vegetable oil

Ginger Juice

GINGER juice is the juice pressed from ginger. Many Chinese home cooks keep a small jar of it in the kitchen so that it is easily to hand whenever it is called for. To preserve it, they add to it a very small amount of cooking wine.

YIELDS ABOUT 30 ML (2 TBSP) GINGER JUICE

50 g (2 oz) ginger, peeled
2.5 ml (½ tsp) Shaoxing wine or medium dry sherry

1 Either chop the ginger very finely by hand or mince it in an electric herb mill or grate it with a ginger grater.
2 Using a garlic presser, press out, 1 presserful at a time, the juice from the ginger, which will include some puréed ginger. Discard the pulp.
3 If the juice is not to be used straightaway, add the wine or sherry and keep in a small jar in the refrigerator.

Hongzao
or Red Sediment

1.2 kilos (2½ lb) white glutinous
  rice, rinsed
750 ml (1¼ pints/3 cups) cold
  water
3 wine yeast balls
55 g (2 oz) red rice (yeast)
1 bottle rice wine

HONGZAO (hungjo in Cantonese) is a favourite ingredient
of the Fujianese, who use it as a seasoning sauce for
chicken, duck and pork and for making soups. Sweet and
alcoholic, it adds a rich and distinctive quality to the main
ingredients that is all its own. In Fujian, Taiwan and Hong
Kong, one buys this basic ingredient from a shop, but as it
is not easily available in Chinese shops abroad, we have to
make our own.

1 Soak the white glutinous rice in sufficient cold water to
   cover by about 2.5 cm (1 in) for 3–4 hours. Drain.
2 Put this rice in a heatproof dish with raised edges and
   put into a steamer. Add the water, then steam the rice
   over a high heat (see p. 355) for 30 minutes until
   thoroughly cooked. Allow to cool for about 30 minutes
   until the rice is warm, but not totally cold.
3 In the meantime, pulverise the wine yeast and red rice
   together in a food processor or using a pestle and
   mortar.
4 Assemble the dish in a large earthenware pot or jar with
   a fitted lid. Starting with 1 layer of red rice mixture at
   the bottom, add alternate layers of glutinous rice and
   finish at the top with 1 layer of red rice mixture. Cover
   the top of the pot or jar with a cloth before adding the
   lid. Cover the whole pot or jar with blankets, then leave
   in a very warm place for 3 days, during which time the
   ingredients will start to ferment. It is important therefore that the pot or jar is no more than about 70 per cent
   full.
5 Remove the lid and give the gluey and fermenting mixture inside a thorough stirring. Add the wine and stir to
   mix well. Add the lid and wrap with blankets again.
   Leave in a warm place for 10 days, at the end of which
   give the mixture another thorough stirring. Repeat this
   procedure 2 more times. After 30 days, the red sediment, in pasty and gluey form, should be ready.

Roasted Ground Sichuan Peppercorns

1 Heat a wok or a frying pan until hot. Add the Sichuan peppercorns and stir continuously over a medium heat for 2–4 minutes or until the peppercorns become very aromatic. Transfer to a dish and let cool.
2 Pulverise the peppercorns either in a food processor or with a pestle and mortar. Transfer to a fine wire sieve and sift to obtain the ground Sichuan pepper. Discard the coarse husk left in the sieve.

55–115 g (2–4 oz) Sichuan peppercorns

Roasted Ground Two Rices

1 Spread out the two rices together and leave them until they are almost dry again.
2 Heat a wok until very hot. Add the rices and, going to the bottom of the wok with the wok scoop, turn and toss over a medium heat for about 20 minutes or until the rices are dry and have taken on some colour and exuded an aroma. Transfer to a dish and let cool.
3 Use a food processor to pulverise the rices until they resemble grains of sand but are not reduced to powder form. Transfer to a lidded jar and store in a cool place.

85 g (3 oz/½ cup) glutinous white rice, rinsed and drained
225 g (8 oz/1¼ cups) long-grain white rice, rinsed and drained

Roasted Sesame Seeds

1 Heat a wok or a frying pan until hot. Add the sesame seeds and stir continuously over a medium heat for about 8 minutes or until the seeds have turned pale golden in colour. Transfer to a dish and let cool completely. Keep in an airtight jar.

115 g (4 oz) white sesame seeds

Salt-cured
Duck Eggs

450 g (1 lb) sea salt
1.75 litres (3 pints/7½ cups)
  boiling water
24 duck eggs, about 1.8 kilos
  (4 lb)

THE Chinese hard-boil salt-cured eggs, then serve them as a side dish to go with rice or congee. They also use them as a seasoning in soups. Even though they are usually bought in a Chinese supermarket, they are also fun, and easy, to make.

1 Put the salt in a clean container. Pour in the boiling water to dissolve the salt, giving it a big stir. Leave to cool completely.
2 Wash the eggs, brushing with a fine brush so that the pores are open for better absorption of the brine later. Wipe dry.
3 Put the eggs into an earthenware pot or a large glass jar. Make sure there are no cracks in any of the eggs; otherwise the whole lot may be spoiled. Add the cold brine. Some eggs will float to the surface. Put a plate or saucer on top of the eggs to help to submerge them. Cover the pot with the lid or screw the top on the jar. Leave in a cold place for a minimum of 28 days at the end of which take one out to try. When cracked, the egg white should be cloudy and the yolk coagulated. When hard-boiled, the egg white should be very salty, and the egg yolk golden and oily. If they are not ready, leave them for 1 to 2 more weeks, moving those close to the surface to the bottom. Use a long wooden spoon or other implement to do so, take care not to contaminate the brine.

Spiced Salt

60 ml (4 tbsp) salt
5 ml (1 tsp) ground white or black
  peppercorns
5 ml (1 tsp) roasted ground
  Sichuan peppercorns (see p. 359)

1 Heat a wok over a medium heat until hot. Add the salt and stir for about 4–5 minutes until the salt is very hot and turning slightly greyish in colour. Transfer to a container and let cool.
2 Add the ground peppercorns and Sichuan peppercorns and mix well.

STOCKS

UNTIL the 20th century when monosodium glutamate (MSG) travelled from the Japanese kitchen to the Chinese kitchen, the Chinese used stock, in conjunction with other condiments, to enrich the flavour of their food. The first yield from the ingredients is known as prime stock, and the second yield is known simply as stock, or secondary stock. The best stock is made with chicken, pork and ham, as well as some flavours from the sea, such as pieces of dried abalone or conch, in order to enhance the intensity of the taste. Time was when ordering a banquet in a restaurant, the price would depend on what kind of stock was required. Making stock may be time-consuming, but it is the unbeatable way to achieving unadulterated taste, and is therefore worth the time and trouble.

However, for simplicity I have specified a particular type of stock only when its use is essential for the success of a recipe. On all other occasions I have suggested chicken stock.

Prime Stock

MAKES ABOUT 2 LITRES (3½ PINTS/8 CUPS)

1 large knob ginger, about 25 g (1 oz), peeled and bruised
900 g (2 lb) chicken pieces, drumsticks, thighs, neck and wings
675 g (1½ lb) lean pork without rind or lean spareribs
675 g (1½ lb) ham or mild gammon, without rind
50 g (2 oz) dried abalone pieces (if available), rinsed
25 g (1 oz) stalks from dried Chinese black mushrooms (if available), rinsed
4 litres (7 pints/16 cups) water

1 Put the ginger, chicken pieces, pork, ham or gammon, abalone and mushroom stalks into a large stockpot and add the water. Bring to the boil over a high heat and skim off the scum and foam which surfaces for several minutes or until the water is relatively clear.
2 Reduce the heat to maintain a gentle simmer and continue to cook, uncovered, if you wish the stock to be clear, for 3–4 hours.
3 Transfer the liquid through a sieve into a storage container. This liquid is the prime stock. It will keep in the refrigerator for 3–4 days; to keep it longer after this period, bring it to the boil again.

Stock

MAKES ABOUT 1.5 LITRES
(2½ PINTS/6 CUPS)

left-over ingredients from prime
   stock (see p. 361)
2.25 litres (4 pints/9 cups) water

1 Refill the stockpot containing the left-over ingredients from the prime stock with the water and bring to the boil. Reduce the heat to maintain a fast simmer and cook, uncovered, for 1–1½ hours, reducing the liquid to about 1.5 litres (2½ pints/6 cups). This is the ordinary, sometimes also called the secondary, stock.

'Milk' Stock

MAKES ABOUT 1 LITRE
(1¾ PINTS/4 CUPS)

1 large knob ginger, about 25 g
   (1 oz), peeled and bruised
about 900 g (2 lb) pork spareribs,
   pork bones and 1 pig's trotter
about 675 g (1½ lb) chicken
   thighs, drumsticks, carcass ,
   neck and wings
3 litres (5 pints/12 cups) water

1 Put the ginger, pork and chicken pieces into a large and deep stockpot and add the water. Bring to the boil over a high heat and skim off the scum and foam which surfaces until the water is relatively clear. Continue to boil, covered, over a slightly reduced but still high heat for 1–1½ hours until the stock appears milky in colour and is reduced to about a quarter. Drain this milk stock through a sieve into a container. Return the ingredients into the stockpot, add about half the original amount of water and boil, covered, for another 45–60 minutes. Drain, adding to the first lot of milk stock.

NOTE: Some cooks, at a pinch, will add a small amount of fresh cow's milk to the stock in order to achieve a more pronounced effect.

Sweet
Bean Sauce

15 ml (1 tbsp) water
150 ml (10 tbsp) ground yellow
   bean sauce
150 ml (10 tbsp) caster sugar
15 ml (1 tbsp) peanut or vegetable
   oil

RESTAURANTS in Peking serve Peking ducks with sweet flour sauce made with fermented wheat flour while many Chinese restaurants abroad use hoisin sauce bought in a jar or bottle. Ever since I started making Peking duck at home some twelve years ago, I have devised this simple sauce which, of course, I commend to you.

1 Put the water in a wok or saucepan. Add the yellow bean sauce and sugar. Heat over a low heat for about 4 minutes or until the sugar has completely dissolved, stirring all the time to mix into a smooth sauce. Stir in the oil.

2 Leave to cool and serve at room temperature. The sauce, if transferred to a jar, can keep for 2–3 months in the refrigerator.

GLOSSARY

Bamboo fungus, dried (*Dictyophora indusiata*)

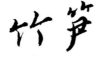

Often misrepresented as the pith of bamboo, this is in fact a fungus which grows on the ground of bamboo groves in Yunnan and other provinces in western China. About 7.5–15 cm (3–6 in) long and 2.5 cm (1 in) wide, the dried fungi, beigey in colour, have hollow tubes with tapering closed ends. Some of them carry a 'fish-net parasol' at the top end. When reconstituted in water, they look rather like condoms, while the fish-net parasols give a rather spectacular appearance. Spongy and crisp in texture, they are regarded by the Chinese as one of the most delicate and delicious fungi.

Bamboo shoots

The young shoots of many species of bamboo are cultivated for the table in China, winter shoots being available from November to January, spring shoots from January to April and summer shoots from April to July. They are canned in chunks, in tips and in slices for both the Chinese and foreign markets. On the whole, the canned product – our mainstay in the West – retains much of the crisp texture that is characteristic of bamboo shoots, which are used to give a good contrast of texture to other ingredients in a dish. For best results, they should be blanched briefly before use, especially if they come sliced in the can.

Bean curd, doufu (Mandarin), dowfu (Cantonese), tofu (Japanese)

Ivory-white curd made from ground soy beans varying in size, but usually 6–6.5 cm (1¼–1½ in) square and 2.5–3 cm (1–1¼ in) thick. There is a Western version of bean curd sold in health food shops and supermarkets under the Japanese name tofu. It differs from Chinese bean curd on two counts: it is much denser in consistency, and the natural flavour of soy beans, which is attractive to the Chinese palate but presumably unattractive to the Western, is removed from it. Unless otherwise stated, the bean curd used in this book is Chinese bean curd.

BEAN CURD 'CHEESE', RED FERMENTED

Also known as southern 'cheese', this is bean curd fermented with salt, red rice and rice wine, with the result that it is brick-red in colour and very strong and cheesy in flavour. It is usually sold in cans or earthenware pots in 2.5–5 cm (1–2 in) square cakes and is used for flavouring pork, poultry and vegetarian dishes. The accompanying juices are also used.

BEAN CURD 'CHEESE', WHITE FERMENTED

Ivory in colour, sold usually in a glass jar in 2.5 cm (1 in) cakes, it comes in two kinds: the plain and the chilli hot. It is used to flavour certain vegetables, or is served as a side dish with rice or congee.

BEAN CURD PUFFS

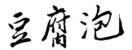

Fresh bean curd cubes, deep-fried until golden in colour and airy inside; usually sold in polythene bags.

BEAN CURD SKIN

Literally the skin formed on the surface of the simmering milky liquid of ground soy beans. For details, *see* p. 140.

BEAN SPROUTS (*Phaseolus aureus*)

High in protein, these tender sprouts from small green mung beans are now available in many Western supermarkets.

BITTER MELON (*Momordica charantia*), BITTER GOURD, KARELLA (INDIAN)

Pale or dark green in colour, this melon is distinguished by the warty lumps all over the skin and a bitter flavour, apparently due to the presence of quinine. It is a favourite of southern Chinese, who stuff it with pork or stir-fry it with beef and fermented black beans.

BLACK BEANS, FERMENTED

Whole soy beans fermented and preserved in salt and ginger, they are tangy and slightly bitter, but when combined with garlic and oil they become the famous black bean sauce used in a whole range of dishes. Some black beans are canned in brine but the dried ones, in polythene bags or cardboard containers, are by far the best.

BROADBEAN PASTE OR SOY BEAN PASTE, SPICY HOT

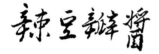

An important ingredient for making Sichuan dishes, it is a very spicy paste of broadbeans or soy beans crushed with chilli, salt and sugar. Usually sold in jars.

CELLOPHANE OR GLASS NOODLES, TRANSPARENT VERMICELLI OR BEAN THREADS

Made from mung beans, these are sold in a bundle tied by thin threads. Wiry and hard in their dry state, they have to be soaked in plenty of cold or warm water and drained before use. They provide a slippery texture but require robust seasonings.

CHILLI HOT OIL

Sold in small bottles under the names of hot oil, chilli oil and hot chilli oil, this is peanut or vegetable oil in which red chilli flakes have been steeped. The oil has a faint reddish colour.

CHINESE BLACK MUSHROOMS, DRIED
(*Lentinus edodes*)

The Chinese refer to them as fragrant mushrooms and the Japanese call them *shiitake*. Almost black in colour, they vary in size and thickness according to their quality and price. Generally speaking, three grades are marketed: the best have floral patterns on the surface of the caps, which curl under (called *fa gu* in Cantonese and *huagu* in Mandarin), the second best are those with thick caps, which also curl slightly inwards, and the ordinary ones have thin and flat caps. What is usually available in Chinese stores are packets of mixed quality and size. When reconstituted (*see* p. 353), they both impart flavours to other ingredients and absorb flavours from them. Among Chinese fungi, they are the most popularly and widely used.

CHINESE BROCCOLI (*Brassica oleracea var alboglabra*), CHINESE KALE, GAI LAN

The leaves have a bluish-green sheen and the flowers in the middle of the plant are white. The stalk is like that of broccoli but the taste is more reminiscent of asparagus. Its popularity with southern Chinese is only second to *choi sum*.

CHINESE BROWN SUGAR IN PIECES

True to the label, these brown pieces of sugar, sold in cardboard boxes, are about 12.5 cm (5 in) long, 2.5 cm (1 in) wide and 5 mm (¼ in) thick.

CHINESE CABBAGE (*Brassica chinensis*), BAAK CHOI (CANTONESE), BAICAI (MANDARIN)

This cabbage, which is about 30 cm (1 ft) long, has thick, white stalks extending to dark green leaves. But one species, called Shanghai 'small' cabbage, which is about half the normal size, or less, has a more succulent taste when cooked.

CHINESE CELERY CABBAGE (*Brassica pekinensis*), TIANJIN BAICAI, CHINESE LEAVES, WONG NGA BAAK

 A tight head of cylindrical white stalks extending into yellowish-white crinkled leaves. This cabbage has become ubiquitous in Western supermarkets.

CHINESE CHIVES (*Allium tuberosum*)

 Although similar to chives in appearance, they are darker green in colour, more fibrous in texture, stronger in flavour and have flat rather than tubular leaves. The blanched chives, which are tender yellow in colour and much more subtle in taste, are valued as a delicacy by the Chinese.

CHINESE PADI-STRAW OR GRASS MUSHROOMS (*Volvaria esculenta*)

 Cultivated on rice-straw in the south of China, in Taiwan, the Philippines and Malaya, they are available only in cans outside of these areas, and they provide a slippery texture to other ingredients.

CHINESE RED VINEGAR

 Red in colour, this vinegar is mild in flavour. It is often used as a dip to go with noodles or steamed crabs.

CHINESE RICE VINEGAR

Clear in colour and used in cooking or pickling vegetables, this vinegar is neither as pungent nor as sharp as malt vinegar and is milder than white wine vinegar. But it is not as sweet as Japanese rice vinegar.

CHINESE ROCK OR CRYSTAL SUGAR

Labelled rock sugar, this crystallised, pale topaz-coloured cane sugar comes in lumps of different sizes and has a 'pure' taste by Chinese standards.

CHINESE WOLFBERRIES, DRIED (*Lycium chinense*)

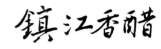

These are dark orangey-red berries, ovoid in shape and slightly sweet in flavour. Used mainly in soups, the Chinese believe that they reinforce the liver and the kidney and, above all, that they improve eyesight.

CHINKIANG VINEGAR

Reminiscent of Italian balsamic vinegar both in colour and flavour – only much cheaper – this thick, dark brown vinegar has a special fragrance and is used in cooking or as a dip.

CHOI SUM (*Brassica parachinensis*), CHINESE FLOWERING CABBAGE

The favourite vegetable of the Cantonese, it is distinguished by its yellow flowers and long stems of about 15–20 cm (6–8 in), and is generally known by its Cantonese name, *choi sum*.

CHRYSANTHEMUM GREENS, (*Chrysanthemum coronarium*)

The edible chrysanthemum greens resemble the florist ones not only in size and colour but also in smell. The Chinese love their distinctive flavour and eat them blanched or stir-fried.

CLOUD EARS, DRIED (*Auricularia auricula*)

Edible tree fungi grown in large quantities in the western provinces of Sichuan and Yunnan. Sold dried, they are dark brown in colour, thin and brittle to the touch, and need to be soaked before use. They are used as an absorber of tastes while lending a slimy yet crunchy texture to other ingredients.

CORDYCEPS, DRIED (*Cordyceps sinensis*)

Called descriptively winter-worm-summer-grass in Chinese, they are caterpillar fungi which abound in Sichuan province. Sold dried, and tied into small bunches of 6–7, they are yellowish-brown in colour, and 4–5 cm (1¾–2 in) long. The Chinese use them as a temperate tonic to benefit the lungs and the kidney, to arrest bleeding and dispel phlegm, and believe in their efficacy for impotence and seminal emissions. Slightly bitter on their own, they are usually cooked with meat to make a tonic soup.

CORIANDER (*Coriandrum sativum*), CHINESE PARSLEY, CILANTRO

Fresh, green herbs with a long stalk branching into flat, serrated leaves, the Chinese call them 'fragrant vegetable' because they are at once pungent and aromatic. They are used both as a garnish and an accompaniment to main ingredients.

EGG NOODLES, FRESH OR DRIED

Made of wheat flour, egg and water, either threadlike or ribbonlike, these are the all-purpose Chinese noodles, often plaited into 'cakes'. Noodles from other countries can be used as a substitute; the only difference is that Chinese noodles are more elastic in texture.

EDIBLE JELLYFISH (*Rhopilema esculenta*)

Beige in colour and rubbery to the touch, dried jellyfish is sold either in folded sheets or cut up into strips, packaged in plastic bags. It is enjoyed solely for its crunchy texture.

FISH SAUCE

A thin sauce made from fermented fish and salt, it has a distinctive flavour all of its own. Used as a dipping sauce or in marinades, it is part and parcel of Thai and Vietnamese cuisines, and is sold in bottles labelled nam pla or nuoc mam. The Chinese use it occasionally in their food.

FISH MAW, DRIED

It is the swim-bladder from large fish and large eels. Sold dried and cured in shops, it is a delicacy for the Chinese who adore its slippery and viscous texture.

FIVE-SPICE POWDER

A finely ground golden-brown powder made up of five or six spices, including star anise, cassia or cinnamon, fennel seeds, cloves and Sichuan peppercorns. It is used in marinades.

GALANGAL

Of the ginger family and known to the Chinese as southern ginger because one type, the lesser galangal, is native to southern China. Even though knobbly in appearance, like ginger, it is not spicy hot but is aromatic in flavour, and is often used in stews.

GINGER (*Zingiber officinale*)

The spicy hot, knobbly, yellowish underground rhizomes or stems of the plant are used both to provide flavour and to counter rank odour, especially fishiness. Like garlic and spring onion, it is an essential ingredient in Chinese cookery dating back to the Han times.

GINGER POWDER

Beigey in colour, ginger powder has a heady aroma which hits the nostril, and a faintly bitter aftertaste. Sold in packets, it is used with salt and oil to enhance the aroma of sauces.

GINKGO NUTS (*Ginkgo biloba*), SILVER APRICOT

The ginkgo tree was originally a sacred Chinese tree but it now grows in Japan and other parts of the world. The nuts, the seeds of the ginkgo fruit, have to be cracked and peeled. Unfortunately, the flesh inside the beige shell seems to dry up easily, with the result that exported nuts are often rotten and hard inside. Albeit reluctantly, I therefore recommend the use of canned ginkgo nuts. Mild and tender, they are a favourite of vegetarians, providing a viscous texture to a dish.

GOLDEN NEEDLES OR TIGER-LILY BUDS
(*Hemerocallis fulva*)

 Dried buds of the tiger-lily flowers which grow in abundance in northern China. Usually about 7.5 cm (3 in) long, they are called golden needles because of their shape and colour. They absorb the flavours of other ingredients that they are cooked with and also provide a subtle lightness of texture.

GREEN DUCK EGGS, PRESERVED

 Duck eggs preserved in potassium carbonate obtained from burned charcoal ashes which is mixed with lime, husks of grain, salt and water. Even though nicknamed 'thousand-year-old' eggs, the preserving course takes only about one month for the eggs to be ready for consumption, the egg white having become jellylike and brownish in colour and the yolk greenish and creamy in consistency. The eggs are ready to eat with no further cooking. The Cantonese love to serve them in slices with pickled ginger as an *amuse-gueule*.

GROUND (CRUSHED) YELLOW BEAN SAUCE

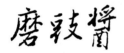 A brown purée of fermented yellow soy beans, wheat flour, salt and water, it is usually sold in cans and used in marinades.

HAIR MOSS

 An algae, greenish-black in colour and hairlike in appearance, it grows in shallow streams and is much valued as a delicacy by the Chinese. Produced in the northwestern provinces of Shaanxi, Gansu, Ningxia, Qinghai and Inner Mongolia, it is sold in a dried form and must be reconstituted by soaking. Totally tasteless on its own, it provides a slippery-bouncy texture to the dish whilst it absorbs other flavours.

HOISIN SAUCE

Meaning fresh fragrance of the sea and looking lusciously dark brown, the sauce has a savoury-sweet and tangy taste. It is made of salt, sugar, soy beans, wheat flour, vinegar, garlic, chilli and sesame oil and is sold in cans and bottles.

HONGZAO OR RED SEDIMENT

A favourite condiment of the Fujianese used to give sweet, alcoholic flavour to the sauce. For details, *see* p. 358.

LAIFEN OR RICE STICKS

Tubular rice noodles which are sold both dried and fresh in Chinese stores. *See also* p. 236.

LOTUS LEAVES, DRIED

Beige-brown in colour, dried lotus leaves have to be soaked in warm water or steamed for a short time to become pliable again. Used to wrap rice, poultry or pork, they lend a special lotus fragrance to them.

LOTUS ROOTS (*Nelumbo nucifera*), FRESH AND DRIED

The young perforated rhizomes of an Asian aquatic plant which has waxy green leaves and white flowers floating on the water. Crisp to the bite, they have a characteristic flavour and are eaten as a vegetable. When the root is cut crossways, silken fibrous threads are pulled between the pieces. Beige-pink dried slices are sold in packets, and they are mainly used for soups.

MANGE-TOUT (*Pisum sativum*), SNOW PEAS, PODDED PEAS, HELANDOU

These tender green peapods containing flat, barely formed peas are originally Mediterranean rather than Chinese, though the Chinese name for them, *helandou*, means Dutch peas.

MEI KUEI LU WINE

Made from Chinese sorghum and the petals of a species of rose, this is a strong liqueur with a unique aroma. It is used more for cooking than for drinking.

MUSTARD GREENS (*Brassica juncea*), MUSTARD CABBAGE, GAI CHOI

There are many varieties, but the most commonly available in the West are the leaf mustards whose green stalks extend into single, large oval, ribbed leaves. They have a pleasantly pungent flavour.

OYSTER SAUCE

A special southern Chinese sauce made from extracts of oysters. It looks brown because of the caramel and is usually sold in bottles but sometimes also in cans. Its value lies in the savoury-sweet and 'meaty' taste it lends to other ingredients, whether meat, vegetables, rice or noodles. It is much more expensive than soy sauce. It can be used as a dipping sauce or as a finishing touch to a dish.

PICKLED LIMES

The Chinese call limes 'green lemons'; perhaps this explains why the label on a jar of limes preserved in brine reads 'pickled lemons'.

RED BEAN PASTE

Sold in cans, it is thick, reddish-brown paste made from puréed, sweetened red beans or azuki beans. If there is too much liquid in the can, drain before use.

RED CHILLI OR CHILLI PEPPERS, DRIED (*Capsicum frutescens*)

Crimson-red, they come in different lengths, ranging from 2.5 cm (1 in) to 7.5 cm (3 in) or longer. They provide the fiery spiciness in Sichuan and Hunan dishes.

RED-IN-SNOW (*Brassica juncea var. multiceps*)

Called *xuelihong* in Chinese, this is a mustard plant grown in eastern China which, being resistant to cold, can be seen sprouting up through the spring snows, hence the name. Cut up and preserved in salt, it is sold in cans with a misleading label of 'pickled cabbage'.

RICE, LONG-GRAIN AND SHORT-GRAIN

The ideal daily staple for the Chinese, it is usually boiled and eaten with dishes. For more details, *see* p. 223.

RICE, WHITE GLUTINOUS

Also called sticky rice because the grains stick when cooked, it is eaten by the Chinese both as a savoury and as a sweet dish.

RICE FLOUR

Labelled rice powder and sold in packets in Chinese stores, it is made from non-glutinous rice and is much finer than ground rice. It is used for making savoury puddings.

RICE FLOUR, GLUTINOUS

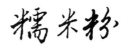

Labelled rice powder (glutinous), it is made from glutinous rice and is used for making sweet puddings.

SALT-CURED DUCK EGGS

Fresh duck eggs which have been immersed in brine for about 1 month. When cracked open, the yolk is coagulated while the white is cloudy. *See also* p. 360.

SCALLOPS, DRIED

Golden and round, with the large ones weighing 10–15 g (⅓–½ oz) each, these are white scallops which have been dried. Inherently sweet, they are used to add a savoury-sweet flavour to other ingredients, but they are also used as main ingredients on their own.

SESAME OIL

Thick, aromatic and light brown in colour, this oil is pressed from roasted white sesame seeds. It is quite different from the cold-pressed Middle Eastern sesame oil, which should not be used as a substitute.

SESAME PASTE OR SAUCE

Thick, aromatic paste of pulverised roasted sesame seeds sold in jars. The paste has to be thoroughly stirred to incorporate the oil covering it before use. Tahini paste should not be used as a substitute.

SESAME SEEDS, BLACK AND WHITE

Tiny, flat black and white seeds from the sesame plant.

SHANGHAI RICE PUDDING

The basic ingredient to make the dish of the same name. *See also* p. 230.

SHAOXING (SHAOHSING) WINE

Named after the town Shaoxing, this amber-coloured wine is fermented from glutinous rice and is used both for drinking and cooking. To drink, it tastes much better warmed; for cooking, a medium dry sherry can be used as a very satisfactory substitute.

SHRIMP PASTE OR SAUCE

Made from ground shrimps fermented in brine, it is sold in a purée form in a jar. It is used to enhance the taste of bland ingredients, such as squid and hollow spinach.

SHRIMPS, DRIED

Peeled shrimps of various sizes, salted and dried, they are used as a seasoning for bean curd, vegetables and meat, and are very often used in stuffings.

SICHUAN PEPPERCORNS OR FAGARA
(*Zanthoxylum armatum*)

These are the reddish-brown dried berries of a plant native
of Sichuan and western China. Not as burning hot as black
peppercorns, they produce a slight numbing and cooling
effect and have an enticing aroma.

SICHUAN PRESERVED VEGETABLE

Called *zhacai* in Mandarin and *ja choi* in Cantonese, it is the
stems of a species of mustard green grown in Sichuan
province which have been preserved in brine then pickled
in fine red chilli powder. It is advisable to rinse off the
chilli before use. Spicy-hot and salty, it gives both a crisp
texture and a unique flavour to other ingredients. Sold in
cans, it is often used in soups and in stuffings.

SILVER EARS, DRIED (*Tremella fucifomis*)

Like cloud ears, these are dried wood fungi, but they are
white in colour, and each is a cluster of crinkly folds. After
soaking in water, they are used as an absorber of flavours
as well as a provider of texture.

SOY BEAN PASTE, HOT

See Broadbean paste.

SOY SAUCE

Made from fermented, protein-rich soy beans, this is the
indispensable seasoning of the Chinese cuisine. There are
two main kinds, the thick or dark and the thin or light.
Thick soy sauce is darker in colour, thicker in consistency
and less salty in taste than thin soy sauce. They are often
used together in conjunction with salt, but since thick soy
sauce gives a reddish-brown hue to food, do not use it to
marinate or season ingredients when a light appearance is
called for. A third kind is called mushroom soy sauce,
which is thicker and richer than thick soy sauce and has a
mushroom flavour. Soy sauces are usually sold in bottles,
but they also come in cans.

Spring roll wrappers

Transparent like rice paper, 20–25 cm (8–10 in) square in size, they are usually sold frozen in packets but are easily pulled apart when defrosted.

Star anise (*Illicium verum*)

The fruit of an evergreen tree native to southern China, it is an eight-segmented, reddish-brown hard spice with a liquorice taste. It is used to flavour braised dishes.

Tangerine peels, dried

Dark brown, hard and brittle peel of tangerines, often used in conjunction with star anise and Sichuan peppercorns. They should be soaked in cold water to make them pliable again, and the slightly bitter pith on the inside should also be scraped off.

Taro (*Colocasia antiquorum*)

A root vegetable which, whether small, like potatoes, or long and fat, like yams, has a dark brown skin, often with earth-encrusted root hairs, and a grey or purple flesh. When cooked, it is slightly slimy and it is often cooked with duck or fatty pork.

Thickening agents

Cornflour, potato flour and tapioca flour are the most commonly used thickeners in Chinese cooking. As potato and tapioca flours are more gelatinous than cornflour and will therefore hold a sauce together better, they are preferable to cornflour. But because they are gelatinous, regard must be paid to the quantity, lest the sauce becomes abhorrently gluey. Arrowroot, lotus root flour, water chestnut flour and mung bean flour are also used, though less commonly, for specific dishes.

TIANJIN (TIENTSIN) PRESERVED VEGETABLE

Tianjin cabbages (Chinese leaves), preserved in salt and garlic and cut up into small pieces, are sold in earthenware jars sealed with flax tissue paper. Salty, yet with a savoury-sweet taste, they are used as a seasoning to enhance the taste of other ingredients.

WATER CHESTNUTS (*Eleocharis dulcis*)

Fresh water chestnuts are the walnut-sized corms of a sedge cultivated in swampy paddy fields or in muddy ponds. Washed and peeled, they are crisp, subtly sweet and are eaten raw. Canned water chestnuts, although less crisp and sweet, will provide a crunchy texture to vegetables and meat dishes.

WHEAT FLOUR VERMICELLI

Cotton-threadlike noodles from Amoy, Fujian province, *see* p. 245.

WHEAT STARCH

Snow-white in colour and sold in plastic bags, it is the starch from wheat flour after gluten has been extracted. As it has a very light texture, it is used to make the shells of certain dimsum.

WIND-DRIED PORK

As it is belly pork that is wind-dried, it must be cooked before eating. It is usually steamed, then sliced and served as a side dish or used as a flavouring in stuffings.

WIND-DRIED SAUSAGES

There are two kinds, both of which are about 15 cm (6 in) long; pinkish pork sausages with white pork fat showing through the casing, and pork and duck liver sausages which are dark brown. Sold in pairs, they must be cooked before eating. They are steamed for about 8 minutes, then sliced and served as a side dish with rice. They can also be used as a flavouring in stuffings.

WINTER MELON (*Benincasa hispida*), WINTER GOURD, WAX GOURD

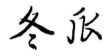 As the weight of this green melon or gourd with a white pulp varies enormously, it is often cut up and sold in wedges. It is generally used in soup or braised.

MAIN REFERENCES

Anderson, E. N., *The Food of China*, Yale University Press, New Haven and London, 1988.

Blofeld, John, *The Chinese Art of Tea*, George Allen & Unwin, London, 1985.

Bredon, Juliet, and Mitrophanow, Igor, *The Moon Year*, Paragon Books, New York, 1927, reprinted 1966.

Burkhardt, V. R., *Chinese Creeds and Customs*, South China Morning Post, Hong Kong, 1982.

Chang, Kwang-chih, *Food in Chinese Culture*, Yale University Press, New Haven and London, 1977.

Christie, Anthony, *Chinese Mythology*, Newnes Books, Middlesex, 1983.

Davidson, Alan, and Knox, Charlotte, *Seafood*, Mitchell Beazley, London, 1988.

Feng, Chengjun, ed., *Yingya Shenglan Jiaozhu*, Zhonghua Shuju, Beijing, 1955.

Gernet, Jacques, *Daily Life in China on the Eve of the Mongol Invasion 1250–1276*, George Allen & Unwin, London, 1962.

Graham, A. C., trans., *Chuang-tzu: The Inner Chapters*, George Allen & Unwin, London, 1981.

Griffiths, D. A., *Hong Kong Fungi*, Government Printer, Hong Kong, 1977.

Han, Yi, ed., *Yiya Yiyi*, in Zhongguo Pengren Guji Congkan, Zhongguo Shangye Chuban She, Beijing, 1984.

Hansheng Jiyi Congshu, *Zhongguo Mishi*, Echo Publishing, Taipei, 1983.

Harper, Donald, 'Gastronomy in Ancient China', *Parabola*, vol. 9, no. 4. California, 1984.

Herklots, G. A. C., *Vegetables in South-East Asia*, George Allen & Unwin, London, 1972.

Hu, Sihui, *Yinshan Zhengyao*, in Zhongguo Pengren Guji Congkan, Zhongguo Shangye Chuban She, Beijing, 1988.

Jia, Sixie, *Qimin Yaoshu*, in Zhongguo Pengren Guji Congkan, Zhongguo Shangye Chuban She, Beijing, 1984.

Keys, John D., *Chinese Herbs*, Charles E. Tuttle, Tokyo, 1976.

Kong Chen, Pearl, 'Sheji Yijiu', 2 parts, *Yinshi Shijie*, vols. 50, 51, Hong Kong.

Larkcom, Joy, *Oriental Vegetables*, John Murray, London, 1991.

Lau, D. C., trans, *Confucius, The Analects*, Penguin Books, London, 1979.

—. *Mencius*, Penguin Books, London, 1970.

Le Gros Clark, Cyril Drummond, *Su Tung-P'o*, Jonathan Cape, London, 1931.

Li, Yu, *Xianqing Ouji*, in Zhongguo Pengren Guji Congkan, Zhongguo Shangye Chuban She, Beijing, 1984.

Lin, Haiyin, ed., *Zhongguo Doufu*, Chunwenxue Chuban She, Taipei, 1971.

Lin, Hong, *Shanxia Qinggong*, in Zhongguo Pengren Guji Congkan, Zhongguo Shangye Chuban She, Beijing, 1985.

Lin, Yu-tang, *The Gay Genius: The Life and Times of Su Tung-P'o*, William Heinemann, London, 1948.

Liu, Huakang, *Zhongguoren Chide Lishi*, Changchunshu Shufang, Taipei.

Liu, Pinhua, trans., *Dalu Mingjiu Yibai Xuan*, Xingguang Chuban She, Taipei, 1990.

Lu, Buwei, *Lushi Chunqiu Benweipian*, in

Zhongguo Pengren Guji Congkan, Zhongguo
    Shangye Chuban She, Beijing, 1983.
McGee, Harold, *On Food and Cooking*, Charles
    Scribner's Sons, New York, 1984.
Ni, Zan, *Yunlin Tang Yinshi Zhidu Ji*, in
    Zhongguo Pengren Guji Congkan, Zhongguo
    Shangye Chuban She, Beijing, 1984.
Qiu, Pangtong, Yu Yiwen, *Gudai Mingcaidian
    Daguan*, Jiangsu Kexue Jishu Chuban She,
    Jiangsu, 1984.
Shangyebu Yinshi Fuwuye Guanliju, ed.,
    10 vols., *Zhongguo Mingcai Pu*, Zhongguo
    Caizheng Jingji Chuban She, Beijing, 1962.
Shih, Sheng-han, *A Preliminary Survey of the Book
    Ch'i Min Yao Shu*, Science Press, Beijing,
    1982.
So, Yan-kit, *Yan-kit's Classic Chinese Cookbook*,
    Dorling Kindersley, London, 1984.
So, Yan-kit, *Wok Cookbook*, Judy Piatkus,
    London, 1985.
So, Yan-kit, *Yan-kit So's Chinese Cookery*, Walker
    Books, London, 1988.
So, Yan-kit and Bloomfield, Paul, *Party Eats*,
    Judy Piatkus, London, 1988.
Tao, Gu, *Qingyi Lu*, in Zhongguo Pengren Guji
    Congkan, Zhongguo Shangye Chuban She,
    Beijing, 1985.
Tao, Wentai, *Zhongguo Pengren Shilue*,
    Jiangsu Kexue Jishu Chuban She, Jiangsu,
    1983.
Tao, Zhengang, Zhang, Lianming, *Zhongguo
    Pengren Wenxian Tiyao*, Zhongguo Shangye
    Chuban She, Beijing, 1986.

Tun Li-ch'en, trans. Bodde, Derk, *Annual
    Customs and Festivals in Peking*, Hong Kong
    University Press, Hong Kong, 1965.
Waley, Arthur, *Yuan Mei*, George Allen &
    Unwin, London, 1956.
Wang, Mingde, Wang, Zihui, *Zhongguo Gudai
    Yinshi*, Shaanxi Renmin Chuban She, Shaanxi.
Wang, Renxing, *Zhongguo Yinshi Tangu*,
    Qinggongye Chuban She, Beijing, 1985.
Werner, E. T. Chalmers, *Myths and Legends of
    China*, George G. Harrap, London, 1922.
Wu, Zhengge, *Manzu Shisu Yu Qinggong Yushan*,
    Liaoning Kexue Jishu Chuban She, Shenyang,
    1986.
Wu, Zhihe, ed., *Zhongguo Chayi Luncong*, Dali
    Chuban She, Taipei, 1985.
Wu, Zimu, *Mengliang Lu*, in Zhongguo Pengren
    Guji Congkan, Zhongguo Shangye Chuban
    She, Beijing, 1982.
Xie, Baochen, *Sushi Shuolue*, in Zhongguo
    Pengren Guji Congkan, Zhongguo Shangye
    Chuban She, Beijing, 1984.
Yuan, Mei, *Suiyuan Shidan*, in Zhongguo
    Pengren Guji Congkan, Zhongguo Shangye
    Chuban She, Beijing, 1984.
Zeng Yi, *Zhonggui Lu*, in Zhongguo Pengren
    Guji Congkan, Zhongguo Shangye Chuban
    She, Beijing, 1984.
Zhang, Lianming, *Kongfu Mingzhuan*, Shandong
    Kexue Jishu Chuban She, Jinan, 1985.
Zhongguo Mingcai Jijin Bianji Weiyuanhui, ed,
    Zhongguo Mingcai Jijin, 9 vols, Ke'ai Chuban
    She, Taipei, 1982.

INDEX